Rethinking Latin American
Social Movements

Latin American Perspectives in the Classroom
Series Editor: Ronald H. Chilcote

Rethinking Latin American Social Movements

Radical Action from Below

Edited by Richard Stahler-Sholk,
Harry E. Vanden, and Marc Becker

ROWMAN & LITTLEFIELD
Lanham • Boulder • New York • London

Published by Rowman & Littlefield
A wholly owned subsidiary of The Rowman & Littlefield Publishing Group, Inc.
4501 Forbes Boulevard, Suite 200, Lanham, Maryland 20706
www.rowman.com

Unit A, Whitacre Mews, 26-34 Stannery Street, London SE11 4AB, United Kingdom

British Library Cataloguing in Publication Information Available

Library of Congress Cataloging-in-Publication Data
Rethinking Latin American social movements : radical action from below / edited by Richard
Stahler-Sholk, Harry E. Vanden, and Marc Becker.
pages cm. — (Latin American perspectives in the classroom)
Includes bibliographical references and index.
ISBN 978-1-4422-3567-0 (cloth : alk. paper) — ISBN 978-1-4422-3568-7 (pbk. : alk. paper) —
ISBN 978-1-4422-3569-4 (electronic)
1. Social movements—Latin America. I. Stahler-Sholk, Richard. II. Vanden, Harry E. III. Becker,
Marc (Professor of history)
HN110.5.A8R476 2014
303.48098—dc23
2014030142

♾ ™ The paper used in this publication meets the minimum requirements of American
National Standard for Information Sciences Permanence of Paper for Printed Library
Materials, ANSI/NISO Z39.48-1992.

Printed in the United States of America

Contents

List of Acronyms

ADES	Economic and Social Development Association (Asociación de Desarrollo Económico y Social)
ALBA	Bolivarian Alliance for the Americas (Alianza Bolivariana para los Pueblos de Nuestra América)
AMOS	Mexican Alliance of Social Organizations (Alianza Mexicana de Organizaciones Sociales)
ANAP	National Association of Small Farmers (Asociación Nacional de Agricultores Pequeños)
ANIPA	Plural National Indigenous Assembly for Autonomy (Asamblea Nacional Indígena Plural por la Autonomía)
AP	Country Alliance (Alianza País)
APPO	Popular Assembly of the Peoples of Oaxaca (Asamblea Popular de los Pueblos de Oaxaca)
APUVIMEH	Association for a Better Life, Honduras (Asociación para una Vida Mejor en Honduras)
ARENA	Nationalist Republican Alliance (Alianza Republicana Nacionalista)
ASIC	Friends of San Isidro Cabañas Association (Asociación de Amigos de San Isidro Cabañas)
ASP	Assembly for the Sovereignty of the People (Asamblea de los Pueblos)
ATC	Association of Rural Workers (Asociación de Trabajadores del Campo)

BRIC	Brazil, Russia, India, and China
CAC	Cabañas Environmental Committee (Comité Ambiental de Cabañas)
CAFTA	Central American Free Trade Agreement
CASOTA	Autonomous Oaxacan Solidarity House for Self-Managed Work (Casa Autónoma Solidaria Oaxaqueña de Trabajo Autogestivo)
CCR	Chalatenango Association of Communities for Development (Asociación de Comunidades para el Desarrollo de Chalatenango)
CDM	Center for Women's Rights (Centro de Derechos de Mujeres)
CEMH	Center for Women's Studies (Centro de Estudios de la Mujer)
CESMECA	Centro de Estudios Superiores de México y Centroamérica
CESOL	Social Libertarian Center (Centro Social Libertario)
CIECOM	Investment and Trade Research Center (Centro de Investigación sobre Inversión y Comercio)
CIEL	Center for International Environmental Law
CIPRODEH	Center for Research and Promotion of Human Rights (Centro de Investigación y Promoción de Derechos Humanos)
CISPES	Committee in Solidarity with the People of El Salvador
CLADEM	Latin American and Caribbean Committee for the Defense of Women's Rights (Comité de América Latina y el Caribe para la Defensa de los Derechos de la Mujer)
CLOC/VC	Latin American Coordination of Peasant Organizations-Vía Campesina (Coordinadora Latinoamericana de Organizaciones del Campo-Via Campesina)
CNI	National Indigenous Congress (Congreso Nacional Indígena)
CNTE	National Education Workers Coordinating Committee (Coordinadora Nacional de Trabajadores de la Educación)

COB	Bolivian Workers Central (Central Obrera Boliviana)
COCEI	Coalition of Workers, Peasants, and Students of the Isthmus (Coalición Obrera, Campesina, Estudiantil del Istmo)
COFADEH	Committee of Relatives of the Disappeared in Honduras (Comité de Familiares de Detenidos Desaparecidos en Honduras)
CONAIE	Confederation of Indigenous Nationalities of Ecuador (Confederación de Nacionalidades Indígenas del Ecuador)
CONAMUP	National Coordinator of the Urban Popular Movement (Coordinador Nacional del Movimiento Popular Urban)
CONIC	National Coordination of Indigenous Peoples and Campesinos (Coordinadora Nacional Indígena y Campesina)
CONTAG	National Confederation of Agricultural Workers (Confederação Nacional dos Trabalhadores na Agricultura)
COPINH	Civic Council of Popular and Indigenous Organizations (Consejo Cívico de Organizaciones Populares e Indígenas de Honduras)
CPT	Pastoral Land Commission (Comissão Pastoral da Terra)
CRIPDES	Rural Communities Association for Salvadoran Development (Asociación de Comunidades Rurales para el Desarrollo de El Salvador)
CSUTCB	United Union Confederation of Peasant Workers of Bolivia (Confederación Sindical Única de Trabajadores Campesinos de Bolivia)
CTU	Urban Land Committee (Comité de Tierra Urbana)
CUT	United Workers' Federation (Confederação Unificada dos Trabalhadores)
DEA	U.S. Drug Enforcement Administration
DS	*diálogo de saberes*
EGTK	Tupac Katari Guerrilla Army (Ejército Guerillero Tupac Katari)

ERP	People's Revolutionary Army (Ejército Revolucionario del Pueblo)
EZLN	Zapatista Army of National Liberation (Ejército Zapatista de Liberación Nacional)
FDN	National Democratic Front (Frente Democrático Nacional)
FENCOMIN	National Federation of Mining Cooperatives (Federación Nacional de Cooperativas Mineras)
FENOCIN	National Confederation of Peasant, Indigenous, and Negro Organizations (Confederación Nacional de Organizaciones Campesinas, Indígenas y Negras)
FESPAD	Foundation for the Study of the Application of Law (Fundación de Estudios para la Aplicación del Derecho)
FIFA	International Federation of Association Football (Fédération Internationale de Football Associacion)
FLACSO	Latin American Faculty of Social Sciences (Facultad Latinoamericana de Ciencias Sociales)
FMLN	Farabundo Martí National Liberation Front (Frente Farabundo Martí para la Liberación Nacional)
FNMCB-BS	Bartolina Sisa National Federation of Bolivian Peasant Women (Federación Nacional de Mujeres Campesinas Bartolina Sisa)
FNRP	National Popular Resistance Front (Frente Nacional de Resistencia Popular)
FPFV	Francisco Villa Popular Front (Frente Popular Francisco Villa)
FPFVI	Independent Francisco Villa Popular Front (Frente Popular Francisco Villa Independiente)
FPL	Farabundo Martí Popular Liberation People's Forces (Fuerzas Populares de Liberación Farabundo Martí)
FSLN	Sandinista National Liberation Front (Frente Sandinista de Liberación Nacional)
FTAA	Free Trade Area of the Americas
FUTH	Unitary Federation of Honduran Workers (Federación Unitaria de Trabajadores de Honduras)

GANA	Grand Alliance for National Unity (Gran Alianza por la Unidad Nacional)
GMO	genetically modified organism
HIJOS	Daughters and Sons for Identity and Justice against Forgetting and Silence (Hijos por la Identidad y Justicia Contro el Olvido y Silencio)
IALA	Latin American Institute of Agroecology Paulo Freire (Instituto Universitario Latinoamericano de Agroecología Paulo Freire)
ICSID	International Centre for Settlement of Investment Disputes
IDB	Inter-American Development Bank
IMF	International Monetary Fund
INGO	international nongovernmental organization
INMECAFE	Mexican Coffee Institute (Instituto Mexicano del Café)
INVI	Federal District Housing Institute (Instituto de Vivienda del Distrito Federal)
IPSP	Political Instrument for the Sovereignty of the Peoples (Instrumento Político por la Soberanía de los Pueblos)
IWW	Industrial Workers of the World
JBG	Good Governance Council (Juntas de Buen Gobierno)
LGBTQ	lesbian, gay, bisexual, transgendered, questioning
LGBTTI	lesbian, gay, bisexual, transsexual, transgender, and intersex
LIBRE	Liberty and Refoundation (Libertad y Refundación) Party
LVC	The Campesino Way (La Via Campesina)
MADJ	At-Large Movement for Dignity and Justice (Movimiento Amplio por la Dignidad y Justicia)
MAREZ	Zapatista Autonomous Rebel Municipalities (Autodenominados Municipios Autónomos Rebeldes Zapatistas)
MAS	Movement Toward Socialism (Movimiento al Socialismo)

MBR-200	Bolivarian Revolutionary Movement (Movimiento Bolivariano Revolucionario)
MDR	Movement of Diversity in Resistance (Movimiento de Diversidad en Resistencia)
MIM	Independent Women's Movement (Movimiento Independiente de Mujeres)
MMTR	Rural Women Workers' Movement (Movimento de Mulheres Trabalhadoras Rurais)
MNR	National Revolutionary Movement (Movimiento Nacional Revolucionario)
MNU	Unified Black Movement (Movimento Negro Unificado)
MPL	Free Passage Movement (Movimento Passe Livre)
MST	Landless Rural Workers' Movement (Movimiento dos Trabalhadores Rurais Sem Terra)
MTD	Unemployed Workers Movement (Movimiento de Trabajadores Desocupados)
MUCA	Unified Farmworker Movement from the Aguán Valley (Movimiento Unificado de Campesinos del Aguán)
MUPP	United Plurinational Pachakutik Movement (Movimiento Unidad Plurinacional Pachakutik)
NAFTA	North American Free Trade Agreement
NGO	nongovernmental organization
OCMAL	Latin American Mining Conflicts Watch (Observatorio de Conflictos Mineros de América Latina)
OFRANEH	Black Fraternal Organization of Honduras (Organización Fraternal Negra de Honduras)
OIR-LM	Leftist Revolutionary Organization—Mass Line (Organización de Izquierda Revolucionaria—Línea de Masas)
PCV	Communist Party of Venezuela (Partido Comunista de Venezuela)
PEMEX	Mexican Petroleum (Petróleos Mexicanos)
PFP	Federal Preventive Police
PM	Mesoamerica Project (Proyecto Mesoamérica)

PPP	Plan Puebla-Panamá
PRD	Party of the Democratic Revolution (Partido de la Revolución Democrática)
PRI	Institutional Revolutionary Party (Partido Revolucionario Institucional)
PRV	Party of the Venezuelan Revolution (Partido Revolucionario Venezolano)
PSP	Patriotic Society Party (Partido Sociedad Patriótica)
PT	Workers' Party (Partido dos Trabalhadores)
REDLACTRANS	Latin-American and Caribbean Network of Transgender (Red de Personas Trans de Latinoamérica y el Caribe)
RMALC	Red Mexicana de Acción frente al Libre Comercio
RN	National Resistance (Resistencia Nacional)
SAP	structural adjustment program
SEMAPA	Cochabamba Municipal Water Services (Servicio Municipal de Agua Potable de Cochabamba)
SHARE	Salvadoran Humanitarian Aid, Research and Education Foundation
SNTE	National Education Workers' Union (Sindicato Nacional de Trabajadores de la Educacion)
SOF	Always Alive Feminist Organization (SempreViva Organização Feminista)
TIPNIS	Isiboro Sécure National Park and Indigenous Territory (Territorio Indígenas y Parque Nacional Isiboro Sécure)
UABJO	Benito Juárez Autonomous University of Oaxaca (Universidad Autónoma "Benito Juárez" de Oaxaca)
UCISV-L	Union of Settlers, Tenants, and Housing Applicants—Libertad (Unión de Colonos, Inquilinos y Solicitantes de Vivienda—Libertad)
UMOPAR	Mobile Police Unit for Rural Areas (Unidad Móvil Policial para Áreas Rurales)
UNAM	Universidad Nacional Autónoma de México
UNES	Salvadoran Ecological Unity (Unidad Ecológica Salvadoreña)

UNESCO	United Nations Educational, Scientific, and Cultural Organization
UNHCR	United Nations High Commissioner for Refugees
UNICACH	University of Science and Arts of Chiapas (Universidad de Ciencias y Artes de Chiapas)
UNOPII	National Union of Popular Organizations of the Independent Left (Unidad Nacional de Organizaciones Populares de la Izquierda Independiente)
UNORCA	National Union of Autonomous Regional Peasant Organizations (Unión Nacional de Organizaciones Regionales Campesinas Autónomas)
UPREZ	Emiliano Zapata Popular Revolutionary Union (Unión Popular Revolucionaria Emiliano Zapata)
VOCAL	Oaxacan Voices Constructing Autonomy and Liberty (Voces Oaxaqueñas Construyendo Autonomía y Libertad)
WTO	World Trade Organization

Chapter One

Introduction

New Directions in Latin American Social Movements

Richard Stahler-Sholk, Harry E. Vanden,
and Marc Becker

The traditional mold is being broken. Events in Latin America are challenging elitist rule, pacted democracy, and party politics. Much of the radical action that is sweeping through the region comes from below. Social movements force governments out of power, advocating in favor of policies that benefit them, and bring ever more pressure and power to bear in the decision-making process. This work explores many of these new radical social movements, their internal practices and horizontal nature, and how they have developed. From small communities to the streets of São Paulo, radical horizontal politics from below are changing the way the political game is played, if not the way power itself is defined.

Popular resistance to exclusionary governance has been a feature of Latin American societies since the colonial era, but different historical periods have seen upsurges in grassroots mobilization, with distinct social movement dynamics and characteristics in each context. This book examines the importance of the movement away from vertical to more horizontal forms of social (movement) organization. It does so against the background of significant changes in the context affecting twenty-first century grassroots struggles in Latin America.

Horizontal organizing, or horizontalism (*horizontalidad*), is one of the central features of a new wave of social movements. In Latin America these social movements emerged out of the resistance to neoliberal globalization of the 1990s and 2000s and the eventual exhaustion of the neoliberal model, as well as frustration with traditional elitist party politics and with the shortcomings of conventional political institutions. The essays in this volume explore the deeper meanings, practices, and outcomes of the evolving social movements and the increasing horizontalism and other "new ways of doing politics" that are cropping up in a wide range of geographic and thematic case studies. It also features essays that theoretically position horizontalism within the historical development of Latin American social movements, and other essays that illustrate a range of important topics for understanding contemporary social movements.

This volume explores several questions surrounding the changing context of social movements in the region. **First**, we explore the significance of the hegemonic breakdown of the Washington Consensus (neoliberal economic paradigm) for Latin America's social movements. **Second**, we examine how the internal dynamics and strategies of Latin America's social movements have been transformed since the publication of our first volume in 2008 (Stahler-Sholk, Vanden, and Kuecker 2008). Here we explore the possibilities and dilemmas involved in movements modeling new social relations rather than directly tackling the more traditional structures of political power. How have the dynamics of resistance and repression shaped the development of social movement strategies, and how are the movements interacting with the recent "pink tide" of left-of-center governments in the region? **Third**, given the longevity of several of Latin America's social movements—such as the Zapatistas in Mexico and the Landless Rural Workers' Movement (MST) in Brazil—how can we assess movement outcomes and future directions? In the emerging post-neoliberal era, how have transnational networks of resistance and solidarity changed, and are they as relevant? On balance, what are the continuities in the social movement dynamics we explored in the first volume, and what are the important new tendencies in the context of current changes affecting the region? This volume advances a series of core themes about Latin American social movements that illustrate the continuities in social movements from Latin America's neoliberal period, but also show the new formation of resistance in the post-neoliberal period.

NEOLIBERALISM AND ITS AFTERMATH

An important part of the background for understanding the contemporary cycle of protest in Latin America has been the impact of neoliberal globalization that swept the region in the 1980s, and the decline and ongoing reformulation of neoliberal policies in the succeeding decades. Under the influence of monetarist economists at the University of Chicago (dubbed the "Chicago boys") who used Chile after the 1973 military coup as their laboratory for ultra–free market policies, U.S. government and international financial institutions zealously enforced a standard package of economic policies across

Latin America, particularly in the wake of the 1982 Third World debt crisis. Economist John Williamson (1990) famously summarized and labeled the formulaic prescriptions—fiscal and monetary austerity, price liberalization, and privatization—as the "Washington Consensus."

There is now general consensus that the negative impact of the standard neoliberal program, which fell disproportionately on the poor, was a significant factor in the moral outrage that fueled the resurgence of social movements in Latin America beginning in the 1980s (Eckstein and Wickham-Crowley 2002). The connection between the harsh impact of these policies and direct protest action generated the term "IMF riots," referring to conflagrations such as those following the imposition of International Monetary Fund structural adjustment programs (SAPs) in the Dominican Republic in 1984, and the Venezuelan *Caracazo* in 1989. The neoliberal downsizing of the state, and reframing of the citizen pact between state and civil society, also allowed for the reassertion of diverse identities as emerging social subjectivities disputed the spaces once considered the commons, a trend that Alvarez, Dagnino, and Escobar (1998) analyzed as "cultures of politics, politics of culture."

In our previous volume on Latin American social movements, we highlighted the impact of neoliberal globalization in galvanizing resistance, as well as the conjunctural overlap of these policies in the 1980s with the general political opening and transition to electoral regimes in the region during this period. The combination helped explain both motive and opportunity for the upsurge in mobilization. At the same time, the return of conventional political parties and institutions (which mainstream political scientists characterized as part of a wave of "transitions to democracy") sat uneasily with the empowering experience of grassroots participation and unconventional direct action (Dangl 2010), even if liberal representative democracy of a low-intensity variety ("polyarchy") could be molded to fit the neoliberal agenda (Robinson 1996).

Revisiting the region's movements in the 2010s, a major shift in context is the declining hegemony of the Washington Consensus. Alongside the widespread discrediting of several decades of neoliberal policies, the twenty-first century has seen a shift toward the electoral left in much of the region, a trend labeled the "pink tide," bringing to office governments that ride the wave of grassroots social mobilization. The full implications of that trend for social movements are complex and still evolving, but one of them is the diversification of economic policies now being promoted by Latin American governments.

The decline of neoliberal hegemony (Hershberg and Rosen 2007), however, does not by any means imply that the forces promoting the neoliberal agenda have surrendered, or that there is a consensual new development paradigm for the region. Indeed, there is considerable disagreement among practitioners and academics about what "post-neoliberalism" might look like (Rovira Kaltwasser 2011), and about whether progressive change can be directed by the state (Prevost, Oliva Campos, and Vanden 2012).

Some see the return of more state-centered development models as a revival of the structuralist thinking promoted in the pre-neoliberal era by the United Nations Economic Commission for Latin America, and by Latin American critical thinkers, including those working in the dependency theory tradition. This interpretation has produced a divide between those who take a favorable view of the prospects for a reformist, social democratic future for the region (Levitsky and Roberts 2011; Grugel and Riggirozzi 2012), and those who argue that fundamental change cannot come from what is still essentially the capitalist state, even if self-defined leftists like Lula in Brazil are elected into government (Leiva 2008).

Others see the state-directed projects initiated by presidents Hugo Chávez in Venezuela, Evo Morales in Bolivia, and Rafael Correa in Ecuador as blazing a path toward a new kind of "twenty-first century socialism" (Burbach, Fox, and Fuentes 2013). Mainstream critics of these projects argue that they are little more than an unsustainable new variant of populism, fueled by commodity bubbles and run by charismatic authoritarians (Weyland 2013). On the other hand, some left critics see some of these projects as reformist at best, using the discourse of socialism and the organizational base of social movements for electoral agendas that largely coincide with the interests of global capital.[1]

An offshoot of these debates that a number of Indigenous[2] groups, which have been a major component of the current wave of Latin American social movements (Quijano 2005), have placed on the agenda is the idea that we need to move beyond the goals of conventionally defined "development." These groups call for refounding the state (Santos 2010b) based on decolonizing our thinking and recognizing a plurality of ways of knowing (*otros saberes*), including various Indigenous concepts of *buen vivir*, or a framework of non-market values of living well collectively in society and in harmony with nature (Gudynas 2011). Some of the "pink tide" governments brought to power with the help of Indigenous mobilizations, for example in Bolivia and Ecuador, have argued that this can be accomplished through "neo-extractivism," in which left governments nationalized extractive industries such as mining and petroleum in order to redistribute the resources in a more equitable and participatory fashion. Yet the record so far has been decidedly mixed, and some critics argue that neo-extractivism is not really post-neoliberalism but merely a more palatable repackaging of the agenda of global capital (Veltmeyer and Petras 2014).

Despite the unresolved debates about the possible directions of post-neoliberalism, what is clear is that the declining hegemony of the neoliberal paradigm, and the experimentation with more state-directed development models under pink tide governments, have altered the context for social movement organizing in the region (Webber and Carr 2012; Goodale and Postero 2013; Motta 2013a; Ellner 2014). Movements forged in resistance to neoliberalism that had creatively occupied new social spaces (Zibechi 2012; Katsiaficas and Rénique 2012) and innovated new ways of doing politics through more horizontal social relations based on flattening out hierarchies and broadening participation (Sitrin 2012) now faced a different set of dilemmas in dealing with the post-neoliberal state.

A central concern in this second volume on social movements is coming to an understanding of the relationship between horizontal social movements and state regimes that gain power through their opposition to neoliberalism. These new state actors, we contend, present a unique challenge to social movements, especially those movements born during the neoliberal period and constituted through the logic of autonomy (Hellman 1992). The progressive and often radical agendas of these new governments mean that they represent powerful potential allies for the grassroots. Yet, these regimes also present the dangers of hierarchy and its associated inequities and inequalities in the relations of power. In this context, horizontal movements may appear to some as reactionary movements, obstacles to progressive or radical state projects, or even threats to the authority and legitimacy of social change from above. For others, truly radical transformation is that which comes from below and is internalized through participatory practices. The relationship between the new progressive governments and horizontal movements is one of the more significant landscapes of social change in the post-neoliberal period.

FRAMEWORKS FOR UNDERSTANDING TODAY'S MOVEMENTS

Latin America saw an upswing in the cycle of contentious politics (McAdam, Tarrow, and Tilly 2001) in the 1980s and 1990s, and a first generation of scholarship sought to explain the trend in terms of the context of the times: a growing awareness of culture and identity (Slater 1985; Alvarez, Dagnino, and Escobar 1998), social protest against neoliberal austerity (Eckstein and Wickham-Crowley 2002), and the confluence of democratic opening with the contradictory forces of globalization (Johnston and Almeida 2006). Scholars sought to delineate both the changes and the continuities in grassroots organizing (Hellman 1995). In our previous social movement volume, we examined the interaction between these structural factors and the evolving dynamics and strategies of popular struggle.

In the seven years since our previous book compilation appeared in print, a second generation of scholarship has examined several significant new trends affecting social movements in the region. One such trend is the delegitimation of, and retreat from, the neoliberal framework that defined the old Washington Consensus of economic policies for the region (Hershberg and Rosen 2007). A new post-neoliberal paradigm has yet to fully take shape (Goodale and Postero 2013), but a pink tide of progressive and left governments swept into office promising alternatives, often riding the wave of grassroots social mobilization.

On the world stage, the Arab Spring and Occupy-era protest movements in Greece, Spain, Turkey, and the United States have suggested just how contagious are the ideas of social mobilization through social movements that first spread through Latin America. Works like Manuel Castells's *Networks of Outrage and Hope: Social Movements in the Internet Age* have charted their growth and analyzed the new means of electronic communication that have stimulated and fostered these movements and so rapidly helped to make them transnational phenomena (Castells 2012; Mason 2012).

In this new post-neoliberal period, Indigenous groups in particular—from the Zapatista movement in Mexico (Harvey 1998) to Pachakutik in Ecuador (Becker 2012) and the mobilizations that made Evo Morales the first Indigenous president of Bolivia (Webber 2012)—challenged old liberal formulations of citizenship with new claims of group rights (Quijano 2005; Yashar 2005; Postero 2006). Indigenous concepts such as *buen vivir* have begun to find their way into the refounding of the state, while the pink tide governments—and particularly the more radical Bolivarian variants, such as in Venezuela and Bolivia—have proposed controversial development strategies of neo-extractivism, based on nationalization of natural resources and social programs to redistribute the earnings.

New tensions between elected left-of-center and radical governments and the social movements that supported them are a central feature of the Latin American landscape today (Prevost, Oliva Campos, and Vanden 2012; Webber and Carr 2012). Movements in the region have made strikingly different choices regarding their interaction with political parties and governments, ranging from the Zapatista model of autonomy in Mexico that rejects all government programs and electoral politics, to the Brazilian landless workers' uneasy relationship with the Workers' Party, to the Venezuelan movement's embrace of state institutions as vehicles for change. Understanding the shifting relations between states and social movements (Dangl 2010; Johnston 2011; Reyes 2012) is a key challenge for activists and academics today.

An aspect of this evolving relationship that points toward a third generation of scholarship is the way social movements are occupying, physically and metaphorically, new social spaces (Zibechi 2012). Rather than seeing Latin American social movements as reacting only to the specificities of neoliberal policies in the region, they now have to be considered in the broader comparative perspective of global economic, ecological, and other intertwined crises (Hall and Kuecker 2011) and the corresponding delegitimation of the state (Katsiaficas and Rénique 2012). As part of a broader "alter-globalization" wave, social movements in Latin America today are sidestepping the state in ways that carve out and occupy new spaces (Hesketh 2013). In those spaces, they are practicing new forms of what some have called prefigurative politics (Maeckelbergh 2009), modeling radical participatory-democratic, horizontal practices (Edelman 2001; Santos 2007; Motta 2009; Motta 2013a). A new look at Latin American social movements in the midst of the current global cycle of protest will sharpen our theoretical understanding of the dynamics of how movements operate in social spaces, including transnational spaces, outside the state.

Scholarship on the region's social movements is only beginning to drill down into the micropolitics of these new practices while exploring their potential for fundamental change at the macro level (Sitrin 2012; Zibechi 2012), recognizing the complex interplay between the global and the local in "glocal" struggles. Careful work is needed to link case studies to social movement theory in order to consider the polemical question posed by John Holloway (2002) about whether it is possible to "change the world without taking power," that is, whether or how new practices of horizontalism in social mobilization can bring about larger systemic change. The advantages and pitfalls of focusing horizontally on social relations rather than on state power echo, in some ways, classic debates on the left between anarchists and communists. Is vanguard leadership or mass grassroots mobilization more important in achieving profound and lasting changes? While many will recognize that as a false quandary, examining interactions between different visions for how to organize social movements remains a useful exercise for understanding social change in Latin America. These strategic dilemmas will be of keen interest to comparativists seeking theoretical frameworks for understanding the region, as well as activists seeking to apply their analysis to struggles for social change (Hale 2008). The evolving power configurations may herald new ways of doing politics in Latin America and beyond, and may radically affect global political culture and a myriad of political institutions throughout the world.

CENTRAL QUESTIONS AND THEMES

This new formation of resistance has several defining features. To begin, it is characterized by organizing "from below," where varying degrees of autonomy from conventional political institutions define the disarticulation of the grassroots that is historically rooted in Latin America, and more specifically in the ways the neoliberal period separated the state from society. Among these points of disarticulation, we count the distance and disconnect between the grassroots and the apparatus of the state, traditional political parties that contest for state power, old-line labor unions that the state recognizes, and nongovernmental organizations (NGOs). These entities constitute the "formal" institutions of society that serve to organize divergent groups and interests of society into a regulated, regimented, and hierarchical system within the power constellation of the modern nation-state. Processes of creating community and new subjectivities from below—what Hardt and Negri (2001) call "constituent power" (as opposed to constituted power)—shape identities in reclaimed social spaces that characterize the new social movements of the post-neoliberal period. This process places them outside modern mechanisms of regulation, regimentation, and hierarchy. It makes ample use of informal means of communication through social interactions and through the (decentralized, horizontally based) electronic media and social media in particular (Castells 2012).

The nonvertical, nonelitist, popular, horizontal essence of Latin America's contemporary social movements is a core theme of this book. Horizontalism here connotes the flattening out of relations of power that promote equity and equality within society and the social movements. It is, to varying degrees, a rejection of the modern revolutionary strategy of vanguardism, where an elite leadership is deemed necessary for creating the conditions of social change, leading revolutionary participants through the destruction of the ancien régime, and governing once the revolution has seized state power. It is also a means of contesting the power that national and international financial elites and the corporations to which they are linked have accumulated. The horizontal approach to social change further rejects the strategy of taking state power as the primary goal of radical change. Instead, these contemporary social movements seek to create change without taking state power (Holloway 2002).

A central premise of horizontalism is the rejection of hierarchical relations of power that are created and reproduced through vanguardism, political and economic elitism, and the goal of seizing rather than transforming state power. Feminist and postcolonial theories have made a major contribution to rethinking the concept of power, which can be understood not simply in conventional hierarchical terms as power-over but instead power-to, or empowerment from below. Horizontalism seeks to eliminate the inequities and inequalities of leadership and decision making, and explores forms of radical/participatory democracy as alternatives to both Leninist and liberal representative models. Yet social movements still face challenges in dealing with the sometimes latent power structures within organizations, in national societies and states, and in transnational networks.

In advocating for an understanding of contemporary social movements from the horizontal lens, we are concerned with issues of continuity and change. Horizontal approaches, for example, have deep roots in radical thought, reaching back to the great debates between Lenin and Luxemburg at the start of the twentieth century. Our concern, however, is for contemporary articulations, especially how recent forms of horizontalism were born from the particular social, political, economic, and cultural contingencies that neoliberal globalization has created in Latin America, which was a major focus of our efforts in our first volume. In this context, we see a continuity from the struggles against neoliberal reforms, where people began to form highly autonomous methods of organizing and resisting in the spaces that the neoliberal reconfiguration of state-society relations created. We see these evolving social relations, their practices, and their mentalities as a key continuity in current social movements.

We understand that neoliberal globalization continues throughout Latin America and the world. However, it is clear that in Latin America the hegemony of the Washington Consensus is over, a reality that has fundamentally shifted the landscape of political economy that defines the relationship between state and society. From this perspective, we see an important rupture within Latin America's political economy. This rupture creates new historical contingencies for the region's social movements that highlight horizontalism as a key social movement formation in the post-neoliberal period.

The theme of continuity and change points to the ways social movements have evolved since the neoliberal period began. This volume explores how grassroots movements have matured in recent decades, especially through the school-yard of resistance where better forms of communication, internal processes of conflict, contestation, and developing the practice (praxis) and meaning of being autonomous have deepened the process of social change, both within the movements and in the relationship between movements and society. We see the internal processes of continuity and change, the "revolutions within the revolutions" (Reyes 2012), as fundamental to understanding social movements in the post-neoliberal period, but "structurelessness" (Freeman 1973) can create its own challenges and hidden hierarchies.

We also find great importance in understanding how the internal processes interact with the external, especially the vexing problem of how horizontal movements relate to the external world. We find two important themes in the external articulation. The first concerns how horizontal movements link with allies through social networks, many of them forged during the neoliberal period. Here, we consider the importance of how particular social movements interact with other domestic grassroots movements, and how these connections hold the promise of larger societal transformation. Likewise, we find importance in the topic of transnational social movements and transnational communication, especially how the grassroots connect with transnational networks of organizations, activists, and solidarity seekers. In this context, an important question is how horizontal movements work with nongovernmental organizations that are their allies. Forming transnational movement networks may be strategically necessary in an era of globalization, but it remains to be seen whether this scale shift undermines the empowerment and identity of local communities. Second, we consider how horizontal movements face their enemies, especially more hierarchically constituted structures of authority where the mechanisms of power actively threaten horizontalism with tactics of co-optation, appropriation of discourse, deceitful negotiation, or direct forms of repression. We see a dialectical process of internal and external influences, where each is constitutive of the other, and we see this dialectic as important to understanding the process of continuity and change within the landscape of post-neoliberal social movements.

Given the thesis that horizontal practices of social movements expanded during the neoliberal period, one core theme we explore is the issue of transformation. Revolutionary movements in the past were defined by the challenge of consolidation, a process that comes about after the initial period of energy, enthusiasm, and optimism that follows a victorious seizing of state power. Consolidation confronted revolutions with the problem of creeping inequalities and inequities, the reemergence of prerevolutionary problems and stratification, and the ossification of practices and mentalities that limited the innovative and transformative power of revolutionary change. Horizontalism confronts similar issues of consolidation, which threatens to undermine their very ability to be horizontal movements. This point is especially relevant for the discussion of internal processes, but it also concerns the topic of how horizontal movements confront external enemies, including hostile states and the forces of global capital. We explore how horizontal movements keep themselves fresh, relevant, and innovative.

While contemporary Latin America can be interpreted as a post-neoliberal period, in some parts of Latin America neoliberalism is very much present. What has changed, however, is the understanding that neoliberalism is weakened. It has lost its hegemonic grasp. In this context, we examine how horizontal movements persist in resistance to neoliberal forms of capitalism and the ways it organizes politics and society. Likewise, we consider the importance of the hybrid states, those that have progressive elements contrary to the extreme forms of neoliberalism that dominated during the period of the Washington Consensus. From a comparative perspective we see a landscape of horizontal movements struggling to craft strategies to confront an arc of states that range in their positioning relative to neoliberalism: those that reject it, those that embrace certain aspects, and those that are full supporters of the neoliberal project. This volume highlights the fact that this arc of regimes marks today's social movements as distinct from those in our first volume.

A notable feature of Latin America's social movements during the neoliberal period was the importance of identity politics as the quality distinguishing many of these movements from their antecedents. Issues of gender, race, ethnicity, sexual identity, *campesino* and other class positions, as well as causes such as the environment, housing, health care, or education tended to define how movements came into formation and their agendas into play. This volume retains a focus on issues of identity and the ways in which "the culture of politics and the politics of cultures" (Alvarez, Dagnino, and Escobar 1998) are core dynamics that nurture and sustain social movements. On this theme we bring focus to the challenges that identity politics present, especially the predicaments that emerge with bringing change to society at large. As neoliberal, progressive, and radical states have gained experience with deploying multiculturalism in their arsenal of power, horizontal movements defined by identity find complicated landscapes of resistance and perseverance.

A final theme that this second volume explores is the relationship between resistance and repression. In the first volume we identified a dialectical pattern between resistance and repression that found escalation between them to be a defining feature of how social movements of the neoliberal period were constituted. In this volume we continue with this theme, but add the variable of different regime types to the mix. We also explore the more nuanced and sophisticated ways that state oppression operates, as well as the strategies that capitalist interests deploy in confronting the challenges that horizontalism presents. We examine how social movements respond to these new forms of repression, and how that response has an important influence on internal dynamics within social movements striving to practice new social relations and new ways of doing politics.

ORGANIZATION OF THE VOLUME

This book is a follow-up to our previous edited volume, *Latin American Social Movements in the Twenty-first Century: Resistance, Power, and Democracy*. This new volume includes revised essays from a special edition of the journal *Latin American Perspectives* ("A Second Look at Latin American Social Movements," January 2011), as well as solicited new essays that include discussions of the importance of the movement away from vertical to more horizontal forms of organization.

Part I of this volume provides a theoretical framework for understanding the changing political contexts that require new responses for social movements. Sara Motta's chapter analyzes the theory and practice of what she calls "reinventing revolution" in Latin America today, highlighting "the emergence of subjects historically rejected and ignored by capitalist colonial modernity." She uses decolonial theory to reveal the ways in which subaltern actors and their "other" forms of knowledge are invisibilized, and to focus on the experiential dimension of popular struggles, including the feminization of resistance. This chapter frames the study of contemporary movements in terms of "prefigurative epistemologies" in which social subjects themselves, through their everyday practices (including horizontalism), challenge the dominant discourses of inevitability and put forward an alternative methodology to the existing academic and political representations of their struggles.

In part II, authors examine the new dynamics, strategies, and identities that social movements are putting forward. Raúl Zibechi takes a case of urban popular organizing in Mexico City after the 1985 earthquake as a point of departure to analyze the political culture of community building through the everyday practices and dynamics within the Frente Popular Francisco Villa Independiente (FPFVI). Building on his earlier work on "territories in resistance" (Zibechi 2012), he shows how carving out autonomous community spaces and experiences (based on nonhierarchical, reciprocal, and solidarity relationships) can empower new collective subjects in antisystemic struggles.

Maurice Magaña's study of the legacy of the 2006 Oaxacan uprising highlights the role of youth in the creation of alternative political cultures of protest. He argues that youth, including graffiti artists and the punk movement, set a vital example in creatively defying Mexico's prevailing "authoritarian clientelism." Magaña applies a "meshwork" analysis to the complicated interaction between horizontal and vertical organizing styles, in examining the movement's ultimate inability to hold occupied spaces. Yet he concludes that the experience on the barricades changed the consciousness of participants in a way that persisted even after massive state repression dislodged protesters from the city's physical spaces.

Daniela Issa examines the motivating *mística* of Brazil's Landless Rural Workers' Movement (MST) as it developed from Latin American liberation theology and rural practice. She finds that the term is generally interpreted as love for a cause, solidarity experienced in collectivity, and belief in change, and that it helped to buttress the horizontal nature of the movement. It not only has an emotional element, but also a praxis of pedagogy and culture, developed by the movement to construct its collective identity and preserve its cultural roots against the homogenizing impact of globalization. Activists use art and symbolism in practices that not only educate, but also empower by example and reflect the collective memory of the landless. The movement incorporates these practices into its struggles, keeping the inspiration alive without institutionalizing the *mística*.

Alicia Swords examines the transnational organizing practices of civil society networks that emerged in opposition to the Plan Puebla-Panamá (PPP), a development proposal to integrate more fully the Mesoamerican region from southern Mexico to Panama into the global market. Swords surveys how grassroots activists and NGOs that were opposed to the PPP's vision of development created local, regional, and transnational networks to oppose the plan and propose development alternatives. While these organizing strategies were successful in terms of halting PPP plans and forcing a change in strategy by investors and government leaders, Swords also points to potential risks involved with transnational organizing. She highlights the need to study moving targets, vulnerabilities, and contradictions of regional development plans.

Suyapa Portillo Villeda's analysis of the National Popular Resistance Front (FNRP) that coalesced after the 2009 coup d'état in Honduras documents the exuberance of an extraordinarily diverse constellation of social forces. Particularly noteworthy is the central role of the lesbian, gay, bisexual, transsexual, transgender, and intersex (LGBTTI) community, which effectively marshaled transnational alliances around a human rights discourse to frame their struggle in the wake of massive repression. While breaking down many of the divisions that hampered unity of the old left, new lines of fracture within the LGBTTI and feminist communities and differences over whether to back the electoral option of the Libertad y Refundación (LIBRE) party in 2013 left the movement in a state of flux.

In her chapter on popular feminism in contemporary Brazil, Nathalie Lebon notes that the generally shared narrative about the origins of Brazilian women's movements revolves around the confluence in the 1970s of middle-class feminist groups with roots in left-wing opposition parties, and organized women in urban popular movements during the dictatorship. She argues that organized women in other settings, in particular "popular feminisms" rooted in urban and rural trade unions, have often been overlooked in general accounts of early mobilization. With time, while some brought feminism "into the fold," other women from the working-class and working-poor sectors started organizing autonomously and later claimed a feminist identity. Lebon finds that popular feminisms are partly a response to the challenges encountered by mainstream feminisms in working toward horizontalism.

In his chapter on the Black cultural politics in Salvador da Bahia, Kwame Dixon examines Afro-Brazilian social movements and the rise of civil society in Brazil from the middle of the 1970s until the present. He analyzes the burgeoning rise of *blocos afros* (carnival blocks or clubs) as horizontal Black social movements that burst onto the scene in Brazil, and specifically Salvador, in the 1970s and 1980s. Many of these movements were deemed "cultural" as they emphasized Afro-diasporic music, religion, identity, and Black consciousness. At the same time, similar but more politicized Black movements arose in Rio de Janeiro, São Paulo, and Salvador, with a discourse explicitly framed around questions of racial equality, social discrimination, and citizenship. These various formations—*blocos afros*, Black social movements, and the rise of Black electoral politics—have their early foundations in the emergence of Brazilian civil society during the transition to democracy in the mid- to late 1980s. They were central not only to expanding concepts of citizenship, but also to developing new means of participation that were more horizontal than vertical in nature. In this context the *blocos* in the early days (1970s to 1980s) represented grassroots, horizontal structures organized alongside already existing structures of Brazilian politics and civil society. Dixon argues that Afro-civil society in Brazil and more specifically in Salvador emerges as a specific response to a broad set of complex issues and conditions deeply embedded in Brazil's unequal vertical social relations, political institutions, and cultural formations.

A key issue that Latin American social movements are currently facing is how to confront the new challenges that pink tide governments present to grassroots activists. In Part III, authors examine how social movements have responded to these new state structures. Two decades after the uprising in Chiapas, Mexico, the Zapatista challenge to an electoral authoritarian regime still resonates across Latin America as a model expression of organizational demands for autonomy. In his chapter, Richard Stahler-Sholk explains how Zapatista distancing from electoral politics and formal government institutions opened space for horizontal forms of organization. Rather than negotiate with the government, Zapatista communities empower themselves by practicing de facto autonomy in their everyday lives. A result is a social movement that is less hierarchical and less institutionalized than many others, and one that is resistant to co-optation by outside forces or domination by a small cadre of leaders.

Marina Sitrin roots her discussion of horizontalism in a discussion of autonomous social movements that emerged in Argentina in the aftermath of economic crisis and the collapse of neoliberal governing structures in 2001. Sitrin explains what it means for activists to reject traditional forms of political power, and to create alternative autonomous models of people power (including worker takeovers of factories and innovative civil disobedience of the *piquetero* movement) in its place. In Argentina, these debates have been particularly intense as the Kirchner governments attempted to rebuild a political consensus based on progressive notions of social justice. Most importantly, Sitrin builds a social movement critique of cultural hegemony as activists negotiate maintenance of their own autonomous political agenda.

Harry Vanden analyzes how social movements in Brazil attempted to gain the attention of the government and the Worker's Party leadership to change the neoliberal economic model that concentrated wealth in the hands of the better off while leaving the marginalized rural and urban masses behind. Vanden critiques the government for squandering scarce government resources on stadiums and megaprojects while neglecting schools, health care, and employment for the newly trained sons and daughters of workers. This message dramatically emerged into the national consciousness after massive June 2013 street demonstrations.

The Bolivarian Revolution is the best example of the state-centered political changes currently sweeping across Latin America as part of the rising tide of leftist governments, but as George Ciccariello-Maher explains, this is only part of the story in contemporary Venezuela. "Chavismo," a political ideology associated with the late President Hugo Chávez Frías, does not represent the entirety of the revolutionary movement, and the movement is not simply one aimed at seizing state power. Rather, the political changes that emerged in Venezuela over the last several decades represent a negotiation between grassroots movements and centralized governmental structures. As Ciccariello-Maher argues, the success of the Bolivarian Revolution is built on walking a fine line between horizontalism and government structures that allows for political changes to surge forward through pressure from below.

Marc Becker's chapter on Indigenous movements and the writing of a new progressive constitution in Ecuador in 2008 examines the document and what it meant for the country and the movements. Indigenous leaders questioned whether the new constitution would benefit social movements or strengthen the hand of President Rafael Correa, who appeared to be occupying political spaces that they had previously held. The chapter shows that Correa's relations with Indigenous movements point to the complications, limitations, and deep tensions inherent in pursuing revolutionary changes within a constitutional framework. Although the Indigenous movements, as well as most social movements, shared Correa's stated desire to curtail neoliberal policies and implement social and economic strategies that would benefit the majority of the country's people, they increasingly clashed over how to realize those objectives. The political outcome of the new constitution depended not on the actions of the constituent assembly, but rather on whether organized civil society could force the government to implement the ideals that the assembly had drafted.

In the chapter on Bolivia's MAS (Movement Toward Socialism) and its relation to the movements that brought it to power, Leonidas Oikonomakis and Fran Espinoza note that when Evo Morales and his MAS party took power in 2005, the national and international left cheered. The formation of the first government cabinet of 2006, with strong participation by union and Indigenous leaders, made clear that the MAS was bringing to the political frontline the movements that helped it grasp state power. Vice President García Linera famously argued that "the MAS represents a new form of government, one which is run by and for Bolivia's social movements," which "are now in control of the state apparatus." The chapter examines what has happened to this "government of movements" eight years later. The authors argue that, within the cabinets of the Morales administrations, participation by people with grassroots or social sector backgrounds has dropped steadily over eight years. Additionally, the party's structure has imposed top-down control over the very groups that conceived it as a political tool—the *cocale-*

ros of Chapare—and in this way exposed the limitations of the "state-power road" to social change.

In the final part of the volume, we turn to transnational organizing efforts. Rose Spalding's examination of the antimining movement in El Salvador shines a critical spotlight on the neo-extractivist development policies being pursued by left-of-center as well as neoliberal governments throughout the region. She highlights the circumstances that led a horizontalist grassroots movement to engage with the state and to expand its network of domestic and international linkages, focusing on the ways in which external actors can undermine democratic decision making at home. This interplay between the "scale shifting" that can boost movement impact in the era of globalization, and the struggle to maintain community control, holds important lessons for today's Latin American social movements.

María Elena Martínez-Torres and Peter M. Rosset analyze a transnational social movement, the Latin American Coordination of Peasant Organizations-Vía Campesina (CLOC/VC). They show how, in light of the breadth of the coalition, horizontal processes of decision making and consensus building foster a "*diálogo de saberes,*" a dialogue among diverse political cultures that valued local knowledge about concepts such as agroecology. They argue that this approach, stemming from a critique of the hegemonic colonial cosmovision, offers a promising model for flexibly resolving internal movement differences that will inevitably arise in confronting global capitalism.

Taken together, the cases and themes examined here offer a cross-section of a vibrant and diverse wave of grassroots mobilization sweeping Latin America. Focusing on social movements—loosely structured agglomerations of groups and individuals taking collective action for social change, outside the framework of conventional institutions and forms of participation—is a good way to take the pulse of social and economic change, as well as to highlight by contrast the shortcomings of existing political institutions. This volume is intended to provide accessible and provocative contributions to reflections and debates among scholars, students, and activists. The authors' arguments will be of interest to anyone concerned with the comparative politics, political economy, sociology, and anthropology of Latin America, and to all those struggling to envision and bring about a better world.

NOTES

1. See for example on Bolivia, the critique of the Evo Morales government in Webber 2012, and the polemic between Jeffery Webber and Federico Fuentes in the journals *International Socialist Review* (http://isreview.org/issue/73/rebellion-reform and http://isreview.org/issue/76/government-social-movements-and-revolution-bolivia-today) and *International Socialism* (http://www.isj.org.uk/index.php4?id=856; all accessed 26 April 2014).

2. The *Chicago Manual of Style* (15th edition, 2003, section 8.41) indicates that names of ethnic and national groups are to be capitalized, including adjectives associated with these

names. Because "Indigenous" and "Black" refer to such groups, the editors have decided to capitalize these terms in this book.

Activists carry the rainbow *wiphala* flag through the streets of Quito, Ecuador during a June 2010 protest march. (Marc Becker)

I

Changing Contexts,
Changing Responses

Chapter Two

Latin America

Reinventing Revolutions, an "Other" Politics in Practice and Theory

Sara C. Motta

. . . that doesn't offend or hurt anyone. That is truly a dignified life.

What Are You Waiting For?

I was born a woman in times of breast cancer,
when sexism killed many sisters,
when lesbians were hunted as witches,
among secret abortions, aids and sex slavery.
I am one among so many, and the few . . .

who like me have suffered the failures.
Always so similar, and yet, very different from each other.
We are the majority . . . only, when it comes to statistics.

What are you waiting for to tell your truth?
Life itself is becoming extinct amidst the darkness.
What are you waiting for, to stop waiting?
Do it for yourself, for all women. Take a step forward!

We have been denied our history.
We have been and continue to be used.
Our voices have been appropriated by other mouths.

We want to fly but our wings are broken.
We were born free, but live on our knees.

We hide our injuries with shades of pink make-up
no respect or dignity, in our lives. This is why our fight is not over.
What are you waiting for to tell your truth?

Life itself is becoming extinct amidst the darkness.
What are you waiting for, to stop waiting?
Do it for yourself, for all women.
Take a step forward!

Just like you, I found out about violence,
and what respect is worth.
But I decided to change all this bullshit.
And now I simply ask, What are you waiting for?
I don't want to wait for my self nor for other sisters.
And be one more who is dominated.
Today I raise my voice, against this lie.
And I invite you women to raise your fist.

What are you waiting for to tell your truth?
Life itself is becoming extinct amidst the darkness.
What are you waiting for, to stop waiting?
Do it for yourself, for all women. Take a step forward!

—Mare Advertencia Lirika, Oaxacan rap artist and MC [1]

Indigenous women of color like Mare are subject to multiple oppressions, including political and epistemological invisibilization in which their perspective on community and life liberation is very rarely heard. If it is heard, it is as Lugones (2006, 78) describes, represented "as insane or deviant, as inferior, or as threatening." They, like many of those on the margins, are the "nonsubjects" of contemporary capitalist coloniality, invisibilized and denied within the antipopular neoliberal script of politics.

Yet arguably subjects such as Mare articulate a voice from the margins, from the space of disposability that is constitutive of today's capitalism, which attempts to reduce the peoples of Latin America to a life barely liveable. Her voice and the multiple other voices of the oppressed being articulated across the region speak the unspeakable. They are at the heart of a reinvention of an "other" politics;[2] of a popular revolutionary politics, with a small r; of a politics that transgresses traditional left conceptualizations of popular political subjectivities and the nature of political and social change.

In order to be able to hear, see, and speak with/as the disposable nonsubjects of contemporary capitalism, one must "exceed its logic." For critical scholars committed to such excess, this means stepping beyond the comfort and privilege found in clinging to long-held conceptual, methodological, and epistemological practices. It also means willingness to embrace, as Lugones (2010, 746) describes, "a praxical task . . . [to] critique the racialized, colonial, and capitalist heterosexualist gender oppression as a lived transformation of the social. As such it places the theorist in the midst of the people in a historical, peopled, subjective/intersubjective understanding of the oppressing-resisting relation at the intersection of the complex systems of oppression."

This chapter aims to contribute to this praxical task through an exploration of Walter Mignolo's (2009, 4) call to "change the terms of the conversation" by politicizing the traditional division of labor between the knower and the known, and committing to experiment with and explore methodologies and pedagogies that reflect the postrepresentative politics[3] that many of these movements are forging (see also Motta, 2013a). I specifically focus on the challenges this reinvention presents to twentieth-century political categories and conceptualizations of left alternatives, thematize and conceptualize key elements of these revolutionary practices, and offer some ways in which critical scholars might imagine an epistemological and methodological praxis—through the concept of prefigurative epistemologies (see Motta 2011a for an extended discussion of this concept) and the figure of the storyteller—that exceeds the logic of capitalist coloniality.

THE ABOLITION OF POLITICS AND THE EMERGENCE OF AN "OTHER" POLITICS

As Mendieta (2008, xii) argues, the ideological prophets and political architects of neoliberalism represent our current era as one of the "abolition of politics"; without memory of a peopled and contested past and without possibility of a different future, as if "the global capitalist colonial system is in every way successful in its destruction of people's knowledges, relations and economies" (Lugones 2010, 748). This was and is a fiction. Mare's visceral and embodied articulation of indignation, dignity, and affirmation is symbolically representative that the oppressed subject is "neither simply imagined nor constructed by the colonizer and coloniality" (Lugones 2010, 748). Rather these subjects declare and demonstrate that "other worlds are possible."

The "nonsubjects" from the margins that are reinventing revolutions in Latin America can be found in social-movement, community, and cultural struggles—the recovered-factories movement in Argentina; the Movimento dos Trabalhadores Rurais Sem Terra (MST, Landless Rural Workers Movement) in Brazil; the water movements in Uruguay; the Indigenous movements in Ecuador and Bolivia; the urban land committees in Venezuela; feminist political organizing in Colombia; and socially committed dance, theater, and music collectives in Mexico, to name but a few. I focus political and epistemological attention on these political subjects and their everyday forms of resistance and transformation because, as Ana Ceceña (2012, 118) points out, "places of dislocation and epistemological invention . . . are created on a daily basis. It is from such spaces that the new world springs."

Transgressing traditional left conceptualizations of popular political subjectivities and the nature of political and social change, this revolutionary reinvention from below presents a challenge to the dominant androcentric social-cultural matrix of the twentieth-century left, in which organized labor was often viewed as the key agent of popular struggle and the state as the key political tool of social transformation. This was combined with particular forms of political organization—the party and the union, for example—and expressed in a laborist moral economy and political culture, in which the key site of political struggle was often the workplace as opposed to the home or the community (see Leiva 2012 for an analysis of this in the case of the Chilean labor movement). In the realm of knowledge the role of the theorists/intellectuals was conceptualized as guides of the political activities of movements, and a *uniform* utopia and strategy were proposed in which true knowledge was to be found in the realm of rational thought (Motta 2012, 394–95). Thus, theory was assumed to take the form of conceptual and theoretical knowledges, invisibilizing other forms of knowledge. Theory was conceptualized as a practice occurring through a process of abstraction perfected by individual thinkers who analyzed the nature of power and of resistance, inevitably speaking for the oppressed.

Such a paradigm of theoretical production reproduced a representational politics of knowledge in which there was a division of labor between thinkers and doers, intellectual labor and practical labor, and an invisibilization and delegitimization of "other" forms of knowing and creating knowledge (Motta 2012, 394–95). The logics of the political became a performance of the knower who sought to disprove and eradicate his political opponents and convince others of the rationality and truth of his arguments and analysis. Such a politics of knowledge and resultant political practices mirrored and reproduced the separations between mind/body, intellect/emotion, and practice/theory embedded in the politics of knowledge of capitalist coloniality (Mignolo 2009, 15–19). Yet these new movements and practices transgress the political, ontological, cultural, and epistemological assumptions and practices dominant in twentieth-century revolutionary theorizing. According to Enrique Dussel (2008, xvi), they "represent signs of hope, in the face of which we must begin to create a new theory. This new theory cannot merely respond to the presuppositions of the last five hundred years of capitalist and colonialist modernity."

Rather, it must first, as Ceceña (2012, 118) explains, develop knowledge for and by those excluded from and on the margins of political power and theory production. Second, it must speak from the placed body or the particular (Gutiérrez 2012, 61) and thus from the experience of oppression. Third, it must foster the emergence of subjects historically rejected and ignored by capitalist colonial modernity (Mignolo 2009). In Ceceña's words (2012, 118), "Speaking about and from these knowledges involves putting them, from the beginning, on a different plane from the practices of power that have condemned popular learning. . . . It is necessary to dislocate the planes, moving from a Euclidean plane to another (or to others) with multiple perspectives that break up and expand the dimensions of understanding, opening them to the penetration of other cosmologies."

The development of new concepts and theories is thus embedded in a commitment to a politics of knowledge that begins from the ground up and builds from the realities of popular politics in community struggles, movement organizing, and everyday life. Embracing a practice of knowledge such as this foregrounds the multiplicity that is at the heart of this reinvention and the necessity to speak and theorize in the plural. In speaking with, through, and about new forms of popular politics, what is suggested is that what is being experienced and built in Latin America is not a model that can be transported from one place to another but emerges from concrete places, bodies, traditions, cosmologies, spatialities of power,[4] forms of capital and the state, epistemologies, and histories of struggle.[5]

The urgency of comparative engagement with this revolutionary reinvention from below is not only empirical and political but historiographical and ethical. The communities, subjects, and movements that are the lifeblood of this reinvention are commonly "spoken over" by discourses that misname and misrepresent their struggles. These misrepresentations are enacted not only through bourgeois accounts but also through the conceptual framings of much twentieth-century-left–inspired thought and practice.

As Diniz and Gilbert (2013, 22) discuss in relation to the Movimento Sem Terra of Brazil, such discourse colored the MST's initial development, in which the leadership criticized the *camponeses* (peasants/rural workers) for "an isolationist attitude with respect to union organizing" that was "structurally incompatible . . . with the development of character and social participation." This was a misreading of *camponês* culture in that it missed the complex interplay of tradition, culture, and meaning in the sociabilities, moral economies, and forms of anticapitalist labor relations that developed in MST settlements.

As Diana Rodríguez Quevedo (2013) demonstrates in the case of Vallenato music produced by displaced Afro-Colombian communities from Chocó, Colombia, dominant representations (of both left and right) represent it as merely a commodified form of cultural escapism that reproduces hegemonic subjectivities and understandings of the world. Yet, as she argues, Vallenato is an embodied popular culture in which the contradictions and tensions in the lived realities of the subjects on the margins are articulated. In this song, music and dance can play a role in giving testimony to those lives lived in a way that demonstrates and facilitates their dignity, agency, and wisdom.

These cultural traditions and popular histories concretely demonstrate how, despite misrepresentations of the popular that invisibilize, pathologize, or patronize subaltern subjects, something always escapes. Twentieth-century-left conceptual and political categories often blind us to the complexities, nuances, and intricacies of that which escapes. There is therefore an urgent ethical and political need to stretch our understanding of the content, form, and nature of left politics and political subjectivities. This involves the concrete practice of facilitating an "other" historicity in which those invisibilized and silenced tell their story—both of pain, trauma, and denial; and of dignity, survival, and resistance.

To enact the creation of an "other" historicity involves a commitment to a methodology that begins from the specificity of the place of the community and movement experience. It also means embrace of an ethics and politics of knowledge that politicizes not only the content but also the process of knowledge production—that builds upon communities' lived realities and embodied experiences of oppression to develop theories and strategies capable of transforming those conditions. As Mignolo (2009, 4) argues, this implies "changing the terms of the conversation":

> Changing the terms of the conversation implies going beyond disciplinary or interdisciplinary controversies and the conflict of interpretations. As far as controversies and interpretations remain within the same rules of the game (terms of the conversation) the control of knowledge is not called into question. And in order to call into question the modern/colonial foundations of the control of knowledge it is necessary to focus on the knower rather than the known.

Changing the terms of the conversation is to commit to politicizing the traditional division of labor between the thinker/analyst/knower and the known and replacing it with methodologies and pedagogies that reflect the democratic and participatory practices that many of these movements are forging (see, e.g., Chukaitis 2009; Colectivo Situaciones 2003; Mignolo 2009; Motta 2011a).

Through a dialogue between my participatory research with the MST in Ceará, Brazil; the Comité de Tierra Urbana (CTU), Caracas, Venezuela; the Escuela Política de Mujeres Pazíficas (Escuela), Cali, Colombia; and the Movimiento de Trabajadores Desocupados de Solano (MTD Solano), Argentina; and engagement with the work of critical scholars Sandra Gadelha, Ernandi Mendes, Bruce Gilbert and Aldiva Diniz (MST), Norma Bermúdez (Escuela), Jennifer Martinez and Andres Antillano (CTU), and Marina Sitrin (Argentinean movements)—who enact in differing ways such an ethics and practice of research—I move to a conceptual mapping of the reinvention of Latin American revolutions from below.

COUNTERSPATIALITIES

Many of the popular movements and community struggles constitutive of this revolutionary reinvention are involved in occupations of physical space. Yet, as Diniz and Gilbert (2013, 25) argue (quoting Almeida) in relation to the MST, the fulfilment of their goals "requires not merely the occupation of land" but "the whole conjuncture of actions carried out to this end." It is this "conjuncture of actions" that enables ontological shifts in ways of life and practices of self. Such shifts and transformations can be understood as "reoccupations of self" in which rural communities that have experienced expulsion from the land and reduction of their humanity into a commodity transform such dehumanizing conditions of existence. As Sandra Gadelha (2006, 66) describes,

> The arrival [of families] to the settlement is represented [by the community] as liberation from this subjectification, as a reintegration of the subjectivity that is desired. In other words, the process of constructing a settlement involves the reconstruction of sociability.

In the process of negotiating the organization of a settlement, communities build on extant knowledge of cultivating, planting, building, constructing, and movement organizing. These differentiated experiences can enable an enriching dialogue of knowledges in which individuals and families learn new form of relating premised on, as Sandra Gadelha[6] describes, "dialogue, respect of others and recognition of difference." In this process rural communities learn to live with different experiences and conceptualization of the world, to negotiate with the state and its institutions, and to collectively organize production and social reproduction. As Neves conceptualizes (1997, 21), this produces a "process of unrooting and re-rooting as part of the re-elaboration and reorganization of the social conditions of life" against and beyond capitalist coloniality.

Thus, as the example of the MST illustrates, what is at issue is not just the physical occupation of land but a challenge to the colonization of space by neoliberal capitalist logics through the creation of counterspatialities. This challenge occurs along multiple axes—political, social, economic, cultural, epistemological, embodied, affective, and cosmological—and reinvents the political.

REINVENTING THE POLITICAL: SOCIAL REPRODUCTION AND FEMINIZED RESISTANCES

A key place of the reinvention of the political is the community. Community struggles over health care, education, land ownership and use, housing, and community and family life have emerged. Here social reproduction is politicized, enabling new social relationships and ways of community life to emerge.

In the case of the CTUs—which were created in 2002 from a presidential decree regarding the legalization of individual land titles to shantytown dwellers—many achieved this legal recognition relatively quickly. Yet it became clear that this did not solve the broader problems of exclusion, including overcrowding, social violence, and lack of sanitation, public space, education, and employment. Through collective debate and deliberation, CTUs extended their strategy to develop a notion of "city democratization" in which access to decent living conditions, democratic participation in the organization of community relations, and a dignified life and decent infrastructure within communities were seen as integral to the questions of housing and environment (CTU 2003). The methodology that informs their political organizing is based on the precepts of popular educators such as Paulo Freire (2000) and movement educators' experiences (see Martinez 2013 for further details), in which the creation of movement strategy and identity is guided by the experiences and needs of communities in their struggle for emancipation.

For the Escuela, their practices developed from within the Colombian context, marked by conflict in which politics is seen as a continuation of war and vice versa. The Escuela shifts the site, practice, and conceptualization of the political away from its representational and patriarchal assumptions, and therefore brings the private and the subject into the center of their popular educational practices. Additionally, the organization embeds its practice in a commitment to multiplicity, care, life, and tenderness. As Norma Bermúdez (2013, 4–5) describes:

> We knew that the debate and dialogue that we had opened would have major consequences for us and for moving beyond the old formulas of politics. We were facing something deeper: to question the meaning of politics, of its objectives and of its means, to question the sense of power, that power is enacted not only in parliaments and battlefields, but also in social relations, on the streets, in the square, at home and in the bedroom.

Further, because women are at the heart of the community, many of these experiences are marked by a feminization of resistance (see Motta 2013b for discussion of this in the case of the CTUs). Women play key roles in the reconstruction of the possibilities of family and community social reproduction and the development of new forms of collective organization of health care, education, and land. Their resistance counters frameworks that victimize them by suggesting that they need external guidance or intervention or focus on their poverty (on the feminization of poverty see, e.g., Chant 2008; González de la Rocha, 2001; Olivera 2006). It contests the individualization, isolation, and competition that mark feminized labor in neoliberal capitalism and transforms them into solidarity, dignity, and collectivity.

This reinvention of revolutions from below involves a shift in focus in the political to the everyday, the private, and the informalized world of work. Their practices thus foreground the urgent need to direct traditional left conceptualizations of politics and the site of political struggle away from a narrow focus on the point of production and the public script of politics to be found in political parties, unions, and the state.

THE REFUSAL AND REIMAGINING OF CAPITALIST LABOR

Many movements practice a refusal and reimagining of capitalist labor. The new practices are often embedded in a commitment to collective need, community dignity, and the creation of solidarities of mutuality and equality. The Argentine MTD Solano movement of the unemployed developed production units in their community, as they did not desire participation in the labor market, which was viewed as a place of exploitation and domination. Instead they sought other forms and relationships of production not centered on exploitation or the need for profits. As Neka Jara (Argentina Indymedia 2002) explains:

> In the productive units we discuss the type of relationships we wish to develop, in this way a form of organisation develops from the collective . . . the way we move ahead is based on agreements; before doing anything we work out together what we want to produce, for where and how we wish to achieve this. Only after all of us are clear we begin to work. We then reflect, in weekly meetings, whether we are achieving our objectives.

These processes of refusal and reimagining of capitalist labor also result in significant subjective and affective transformations that dislodge from the hearts and minds of workers their experiences of alienation and dehumanization. An MST member told Diniz and Gilbert (2013, 25), "Before, we worked for the boss, but today we work for ourselves. . . . For me everything is better because I am no longer a prisoner. . . . To be a prisoner is to live the way the bosses want." Emerging from the concrete struggle to defend their jobs or ensure their survival are complex and multilayered alternatives to capitalist labor relations that involve much more than control of the means of production (see Ceceña 2012, 120–21; for historical analysis built upon oral histories of the role of the reimagining of labor in developing a deeply democratic socialism and forming solidarity and consciousness in the reorganization of work in the Chilean case, see Winn 1989).

In these open, creative, and unpredictable struggles, the workers, movements, and communities are building relationships of solidarity, horizontal ways of organizing, and affective politics (see Sitrin 2012 and Motta 2011b; on the revolutionary potential of cooperative forms of production, see Lebovitz 2006). Reflecting upon such moments and experiences of struggle, Holloway (2005, 42) argues:

> The event [co-operative] is a brick thrown through a metaphorical window, but the brick does not just make a hole, the hole has fingers or cracks that reach out, cracks that are extended by the determined and unspectacular work of those who dedicate their lives . . . to the creation of a different world, the creation of different social relations, the struggle for dignity.

These processes thus have the potential to transform commodified social relationships into noncapitalist structures of feeling,[7] moral economies,[8] subjectivities, and ways of life.

"OTHER" COSMOLOGIES AND EVERYDAY RELIGIOSITIES

Movements build upon (and also forge) alternative cosmologies and everyday forms of spirituality and religiosity (for an exploration of the role of cosmologies in movement identity, strategy, and practice in the case of La Vía Campesina, see Martínez-Torres and Rosset 2014). These often act as foundational frameworks that shape the worldviews, embodied commitments, and affective landscapes of their popular political practices. Diniz and Gilbert's (2013) and my work with the CTUs (Motta 2009b, 2011a, 2011b) and MTD Solano (Motta 2009a) show how everyday religiosity shapes the building of moral economies and political commitments, at the interface of liberation theology with disillusionment over a politics of traditional elites and traditional left forces in which peasants and shantytown dwellers were patronized or ignored.

At other times, as Norma Bermúdez discussed with me[9] in relation to the emergence and practice of the Escuela in Cali, the rebuilding of feminist subjectivity, voice, and agency involves the creation of hybrid and multiple political cultures. This can combine Indigenous philosophies and cosmologies with religious beliefs and practices that, while forced on communities under colonialism, have become part of their religious practice. As Ceceña (2012, 119) argues, the development of popular political horizons and cosmologies involves "people unlearn[ing] their community customs and the memories of time that reaffirm them, recreat[ing] them, and invent[ing] others, maintaining the length of the roots but multiplying the complexities, mestizajes, and variations."

This makes clear that the subjectivities, moral economies, and world-views that shape movements confound any analysis that seeks to treat their beliefs and practices as backward or as false consciousness. Rather, they suggest the complexities of subaltern subjectivities, the methodological imperative of learning to listen, and the necessity of building conceptual, epistemological, and political categories that engage in solidarity, recognition, and humility with popular moral economies and cultural practices.

NEW POPULAR REVOLUTIONARY SUBJECTIVITIES

It is not political parties, institutions, or charismatic leaders that have been pivotal in the building of a new popular politics, but largely invisible labor-intensive community organizing: projects involving art, music, photography, and theater as tools of critical understanding; bible study groups that link the reading of the New Testament with the struggle for social justice and paradise on earth; and communal meals in the street to bring people together to talk and break down the individualization that often afflicts poor communities. As Elizabeth recounted in relation to this process in the La Vega shantytown of Caracas:

> Francisco Wuytack, the "Padre de la Vega,"[10] was key in organizing the community in the late 1960s. He and other comrades began a series of bible readings and then social projects that motivated the community to have faith in their capacities. (interview, La Vega, Caracas, August 9, 2006)

These everyday processes of construction, often exhausting and often lonely, rarely result in visible political events, but it is only through this kind of creative, unpredictable, and painstaking work that the foundations for the reconstruction of structures of feeling, narratives of understanding, relationships of solidarity, and cultures of resistance can be built. As Elizabeth continued, this enabled the community "[to have faith] in our capacity to lead and make decisions, to organize without leaders and without the manipulation of the "politicos." We began to fight for water rights and for recognition."

At the heart of these processes are new popular political subjects—the shantytown dweller, the precarious and unemployed worker, the Black single mother, the illiterate peasant, the Indigenous. Often presented as passive victims of poverty and exclusion, uneducated, lacking consciousness, and only secondary agents in the struggle for social and political change, they are taking center stage in the struggle for revolutionary alternatives. Their assumption of this position suggests the need to challenge conceptual and political frameworks that mask the processes of political construction from which they emerge. It also suggests a decentering of the assumption of the masculinized subjectivities of worker, voter, and parliamentarian as the key subjects of the political.

IN, AGAINST, AND BEYOND REPRESENTATION

The political practices and institutional logics that crisscross these movements and experiences are marked by differing commitments to participation, voice, mutuality, and self-government, or what Marina Sitrin (2012) calls "horizontalism." Mistrust of liberal party systems, the liberal state, and representative politics is widespread among Latin America's popular classes and is a result of political experience, struggle, and reflection. For many, the experience of liberal democracy (historically and during the democratic transitions of the 1980s) was one of political, social, and economic exclusion in the context of a party system and a representative democratic state. It is because of this experience (and how this was mirrored in the practices of the traditional left) that mistrust of political parties and representative politics emerged. As María Teresa, an activist in La Vega (Caracas), put it, "We don't want to be 'politicos' in the old sense but to re-create politics from our practices and experiences, in a way that will overcome corruption and the misuse of power. We don't want political leaders or parties; we want to create our own popular power from below" (interview, La Vega, Caracas, August 20, 2006).

The development of forms of participatory and direct democracy also emerged out of popular struggles throughout the 1980s and 1990s. For movements such as the MST, the CTUs, and the MTD Solano, their commitments and practices were influenced by liberation theology—a radical and popular Catholic tradition characterized by an ethical commitment to the body of suffering poor people, faith realized through action for the oppressed, the Bible reread collectively, a focus on direct access to the word of God, and a commitment to self-actualization of the oppressed through their own liberation (Boff and Boff 1987, 1–9). As Boff and Boff (9) describe it, it is a biblical frame of reference in which "knowing implies loving, letting oneself become involved body and soul, communing wholly—being committed." In the collective practices and moral economies inflected by this tradition, all had the right to speak and to play a part in realizing their faith and self-liberation.

In the Escuela, the combination of Indigenous cosmologies with elements of Catholicism has produced popular beliefs, ways of life, and new forms of politics that stretch from the street to the bedroom. These tend to be organized around the common good and created through relationships of respect for each other and the land, with all living things being viewed as possessing divine energy. These hybrid spiritual practices and cultures have contributed to the creation of structures of feeling, moral economies, and participatory forms of politics and community life. These traditions of popular organizing have created fertile terrain for the development of postrepresentative logics of the political and political organizing.

The existence of horizontal political practices and cultures does not mean that representative forms of politics are absent from movement practice; the two forms coexist. However, the new forms of popular left politics are stretching traditional conceptions of the political beyond their representative foundations. In the process they challenge the separation between private and public and everyday life and politics upon which they were often premised, the division between leaders and led that they reinforced, and the separation between thinkers and doers that they fostered (see Holloway 2002; Motta 2011a; Santos 2007; Sitrin 2012).

ON THE PEDAGOGICAL TURN

The politics of knowledge of this revolutionary reinvention brings the pedagogical to center stage (see Motta and Cole 2014), with "pedagogical" used broadly to refer to an articulation of educational aims and processes in social, ethical, spiritual, and affective as well as cognitive relationships. Pedagogical practices help to constitute the processes of unlearning dominant subjectivities, social relationships, and ways of constituting the world and learning new ones. They are at the heart of the production of subjects and communities differently (see Gibson-Graham 2006, for a conceptualization of producing ourselves differently; see also Motta 2013c, for a discussion of the role of the pedagogical in social and political transformation in Latin America).

Thus many movements develop pedagogies embedded in popular education traditions which have a focus on dialogue, the horizontal, collective, and political nature of knowledge production; an understanding of everyday life as the substance of critical theoretical reflection; and the overcoming of the distinction between thinkers and doers in movement strategizing and research.[11]

The CTU's methodology builds on reflections upon the everyday practice of struggle and experience of oppression, based on a methodology of democratic practice that involves five steps: 1) the accumulation of information (*la echada de cuentos*) to develop generative questions; 2) the coding of information (*codificación*); 3) analysis of each them (debate) in small groups; 4) the synthesizing of the debate into an agreed upon assessment of practices and proposals for moving forward (*síntesis*); and 5) evaluation (see Martínez

2013). This aims to enable communities to transform the material conditions of their habitat (housing, health, sanitation, infrastructure, education) at the local scale, but also more broadly.

The MST develops critical readings of the world that involve building learning spaces in which the totality of participants' experiences are engaged with (Gadelha de Carvalho and Mendes 2011). This means taking the spiritual and cultural traditions of communities seriously, and as fonts of wisdom and knowledge; thus the movement has developed *mística* as a means of constructing the conditions for integral liberation (see Issa chapter in this volume). A *mística* is an artistic/cultural practice that opens and closes MST events, including workshops, meetings, occupations, and marches. It can take the form of poetry, a reenacting of popular struggle and history, dance, and song, and it often ends with all participants touching each other by holding hands or through a collective embrace. Thus the use of *mística* involves pedagogies of the body in which new intimacies and levels of trust are developed between participants in their embodied enactment of their histories of struggle and experiences (see Motta 2013c).

The politics of knowledge of the Escuela presents an affirmative challenge to the epistemologies of colonial patriarchal capitalism by embracing and nurturing a dialogue of knowledges—from the women's everyday lives, activist practice, feminist philosophers, and legal experts—that weaves a rich tapestry of understanding and agency. The emancipatory practices of the Escuela are multiple as movement conceptualizes the workings of power as manifested through the construction of docile gendered bodies, subjectivities, and social relationships (Bermúdez 2013). Social and political transformation therefore involves the reoccupation and remaking of the space of public politics, but also of their everyday lives and brutalized bodies.

The pedagogical practices of the Escuela are therefore also multiple. The practices seek to overcome the separations between mind and body and emotions that characterize the militarized patriarchal capitalism of Colombia, and more globally the body becomes both a site of transformation but also the font of embodied pedagogies. Pedagogies that include ritual, dance, theater, sacred touch, and embrace enable the unlocking of the embodied traumas experienced by subaltern women. This opens the door to a deepened consciousness of their possibilities and agency. These pedagogical practices create the possibilities of individual and collective voice and joy, which as Norma Bermúdez[12] describes "reenchants the world and awakens the powers of the periphery."

The politics of knowledge and the pedagogies that result do not simply engage with intellectual and theoretical production as disembodied processes. Rather, they seek to overcome the separations between intellect and emotion, mind and body, and thought and action that characterize "one-dimensional man" and many twentieth-century-left alternatives, and to create what

Boff and Boff (1987) call "integral liberation." Thus affective and embodied pedagogies foreground different ways of being and relating to each other and the earth. They enable marginalized and oppressed communities to become embodied political subjects. They bring popular subjects in all their complexity to the heart of the reinvention of revolution from below.

INTO THE BORDERLANDS . . .

The knowledges, philosophies, cosmologies, institutions, and practices developed suggest that as critical scholars, in addition to learning to listen we must, as previously suggested, "change the terms of the conversation." Andrés Antillano, one of the founders of the first urban land committees in La Vega, said that besides learning to listen, we need to unlearn many of the taken-for-granteds of twentieth-century-left political categories. This is a call not to forget but to enter the borderlands, where "to step across the threshold is to be stripped of the illusion of safety because it moves us into unfamiliar territory and does not grant safe passage" (Anzaldúa and Keating 2002, 3). Embracing the discomfort that arises when our assumptions about left politics, subjects, categories, and strategies are decentered is an act of decolonization[13] of our selves as critically engaged scholars, committed to enacting alternatives to neoliberal capitalism with others and in our everyday lives.

How might we decolonize the subjectivity of the knower without rein-scribing the power over relationships and practices of ontological and epistemological denial constitutive of capitalist coloniality? How might we imagine a practice of (social) political science that fosters the creation of ourselves and our worlds differently to these logics of denial? There are multiple contingent answers to these questions, and their development is itself a praxical and open task. However, the thinking through of the condition and possibilities of such an affirmative decolonizing epistemological practice is an urgent political and ethical responsibility for those of us concerned with the development of an emancipatory politics of knowledge. Thus in the final section, I sketch out some ideas in relation to this praxical task around the figure of the storyteller and the notion of prefigurative epistemologies (Motta 2011a). I hope that this will be of use to critical scholars who seek to engage with this popular revolutionary reinvention in ways that transcend the logics of capitalist coloniality in thought and practice.

DECOLONIZING KNOWING AND THE KNOWER: THE STORYTELLERS AND PREFIGURATIVE EPISTEMOLOGIES

Stoler (cited in Agathangelou and Ling 2004, 41) suggests that to transform colonial capitalism requires recalling ''other kinds of memories . . . and stories to tell.'' This involves dwelling in the margins, embracing multiple literacies and tongues; song, dance, theater, text, and image; and entering the borderlands to produce ourselves and our communities anew with prefigurative epistemologies. The figure of the storyteller offers us ways to conceptualize what such practices of epistemological decolonization in thought, practice, and being might involve.

The storyteller dwells out of necessity and choice on the margins.[14] She dwells out of necessity in the margins, for she emerges out of her lived contradictions between the subjectification and oppression, and processes of active resistant agency. As Lugones (1992, 32) describes for the Chicana experience, but which is eminently relevant here:

> Anzaldúa describes two states of the self being oppressed: the state of intimate terrorism and the Coatlicue state. These states are two sides of the experience of being oppressed . . . the self as multiple . . . If the self is being oppressed, then she can feel its limits, its capacity for response, pushed in, constrained, denied. But she can also push back. This is not a fantastic or metaphysical leap out of the reality of oppressed. Rather Anzaldúa knows the weight of oppressed worlds and the hard, risky work of resistance.

The storyteller dwells out of choice in the margins when, as a self that is oppressed, she makes a choice at the crossroads of these two states and ethically commits to politicize this in-betweenness through an epistemology of border thinking which deepens, generalizes, and facilitates ontological and epistemological multiplicity and nonhierarchical difference.

The storyteller thus does not seek aesthetic, epistemological, and cultural separation from, or control over, the popular. The storyteller imbues the embodied experiences of oppressions with epistemic power, and from the sharing of stories and bearing witness to multiple oppressions co-constructs critical readings (as thought and practice) of the world and ourselves. She commits to practices that decenter dominant literacies by reclaiming, recovering, and reinventing the knowledges of the body, heart, and land. She disrupts the coloniality of knowledge through fostering a rerooting of communities in other sociabilities and ways of relating to each other and the world.

The multidimensional storyteller is thus intensely embodied in the present and processes of (their) bodies and attentive to the concrete and rootedness of community in history, spatiality, cosmology, culture, and social relations. This involves transgressing the one-dimensional masculinized subject constituted through splitting, in which the knowing self as rational mind is separated from, and/or gains control over, the heart and the body of the self and other. The research practice of the storyteller thus turns the conversation that has structured modernity's critique on its head, focusing our attention not on the known but on the knower and their imbrication in processes constitutive of capitalist coloniality.

This involves transgressing a practice of knowing as mastery through creating practices of self- (other) knowledge. Thus the storyteller enters the process of collective co-construction of emancipatory knowledges as a means to also unlearn herself and reweave herself through and with others: "The meaning and worth of my [work] is measured by how much I put myself on the line and how much nakedness is achieved" (Anzaldúa, cited in Keating 2009, 1). Thus individually and collectively bearing witness through rooting critical scholarship in the embodied experiences of oppression comes to the heart of the storyteller's practice.

It is of no surprise that decolonizing epistemological practices come from those who inhabit the epistemological margins. They emerge out of the struggle and practice against ontological and epistemological denial as "outsiders within"[15] in formal education and in the multiple informal spaces of everyday life and community organizing against processes of subjectification of coloniality. These processes of subjectification are, as Lugones (2010, 748) describes, "met in the flesh over and over by oppositional responses grounded in a long history of oppositional responses and lived as sensical in alternative, resistant socialities." It is also of no surprise that there is so little written about decolonizing work for activist-researchers, for as Gil et al. argue (2012, 11), "[there] is limited representation of these peoples in the academy."

Thus the storyteller does not emerge from the epistemological center, bound as it is to the logics of knowledge of coloniality. The storyteller makes an active choice of and from the margins as a "location of radical openness and possibility." The storyteller comes to this space through her experiences of suffering and of dwelling in and from her wounds. She does not herald their message as a truth to be followed but creates spaces from which we can bear witness and remember to create "a new location from which to articulate our sense of the world" (hooks 1990, 153).

The storyteller as always resisting the dominant logics of subjectification of coloniality is a border-thinker who bridges communities and sociabilities on the margins. As Lugones (1992, 33) describes in relation to Gloria Anzaldúa's conceptualization of border thinking, this is to commit to enter a Coatlicue state of creation[16] in which, "the against-the-grain storyteller pushes against the limits of oppression . . . it is a state of separation from harmful sense."

The storyteller thus actively commits to "separation from harmful sense" through decentering academic privilege and disrupting the subjectivity of the subject-knower of modernity, for she realizes that this subjectivity reproduces dehumanizing logics against all others, including herself. Through fostering dialogue between and within the multiple moments and places on the margins the storyteller becomes part of a new epistemological terrain "toward a newness of be-ing . . . retaining creative ways of thinking, behaving, and relating that are antithetical to the logic of capital . . . incarnating a weave from the fractured locus that constitutes a creative, peopled re-creation" (Lugones 2010, 754).

Anzaldúa explains that the storyteller takes us into alternative borderlands of affirmative coauthoring of ourselves and the world. In her practice, the storyteller disrupts and attempts to dissolve the dualisms, divisions, and hierarchies reinscribed by the subject-intellectual of modernity. As Lugones (2010, 752) explains, "Our possibilities lie in communality rather than subordination; they do not lie in parity with your superiors in the hierarchy that constitutes this coloniality. That construction of the human is vitiated through and through by its intimate relation with violence." Thus her capacity for affirmative intellectual practice cannot, as Lorde reminds us, be forged with the master's tools, for "these tools will never dismantle the master's house" (cited in hooks 1990, 19). Rather, we need to reimagine this practice away from its embedding in the epistemological logics of coloniality, which universalize one form of knowing, knowledge, and knower toward an embrace of multiple epistemologies, multiple subjects of knowing, and multiple practices of creating knowledge.

Prefigurative Epistemologies

The storyteller enters in her integrity and wholeness in this process of epistemological reinvention. She does not enter as an external liberated knower to educate and speak for the unfree masses. She does not reproduce a victim representation of the oppressed in her practice, but rather begins from a commitment to weaving together subjects, practices, and stories of agency, dignity, and survival. She becomes part of the creation of prefigurative epistemologies premised upon the collective construction of multiple readings of the world in which we speak in multiple tongues, rethinking and creating what it means to speak, to write, to theorize. As Anzaldúa (2007, 81) describes in relation to her experience—eminently applicable here—"I will no longer be made to feel ashamed of existing; I will have my voice. . . . I will have my serpent's tongue—my woman's voice."

Prefigurative epistemologies (Motta 2011a) are inherently pedagogical in that they involve the development of methodologies that have relevance to our lived lives in a way that enables transformation of conditions of oppression. Critical to decolonizing pedagogies such as these is an overcoming in practice of the dualism between mind and body, theory and practice, and education and life. Key to this is a politics of dialogue as opposed to monologue in which all become co-constructors of knowledge, our social worlds, and our selves. As Paulo Freire (cited in Ghiso Cotos 2013, 112) describes:

Dialogue is an existential demand and enables a form of meeting which fosters reflection and action . . . Dialogue is the terrain which grants meaning to desires, aspirations, dreams, hopes and makes possible an exchange of ideas and critical conversations that emerge from reality . . . To exist humanly is to speak the world. . . . Dialogue is the meeting of people mediated by the world, which enables such a speaking of the world.

Dialogical construction breaks the domination of monological thought, practice, and being as it opens up the space for multiplicity, for doubts, questions, and discontent with the world as it is (both internal and external).

Thus dialogue isn't just about deepening understanding, but enabling transformation embedded in praxis. Praxis involves the steps of application, evaluation, reflection, theorization, and then a return to practice. Decolonizing epistemological practice is the product of praxis at the collective level situated at the level of lived experience. This, as Mignolo and Walsh argue (2002, 19), enables a disruption of coloniality's illusion "that knowledge is disembodied and de-localized and that it is necessary in all parts of the planet to follow modernity's epistemology."

Through decentering the logics of knowledge of coloniality, those on the margins become resisting subjects rather than objects of enquiry. Through this process they choose the borderlands as a place of becoming, and deepen their transgression of the coloniality of being toward a new be-ing and autonomous dwelling in the world. As subjects with mastery over their own learning, they become actively engaged in the creation of knowledge and in their own destinies, finding our voices through renaming the world (Freire 2000).

This suggests that the decolonizing epistemological practice of the storyteller fosters the creation of spaces of dialogical cocreation, in which a multiplicity of knowledges and ways of creating knowledge flourish. This inevitably involves a decentering of dominant literacies, in which the word is separated from the world and the embodied, affective, spiritual, and place-based knowledges of communities are denied and devalued. Part of this process is the cocreation of dialogues of knowledges including the textual, oral, historical, spiritual, and affective, which decenter the universalizing claims of neutrality and objectivity of coloniality.

Key in this process, as Anzaldúa (2007) and Lugones (2006) insist, is the creation of another historicity to that of the stories of coloniality that reproduce the silencing, devaluing, and destruction of other knowledges, ways of life, and histories of resistance.[17] This can, for example as in the work of the Escuela, build on cultural traditions of storytelling, enabling a retelling of stories of trauma as a means to transform these stories creatively with a pedagogy that facilitates a distancing from the most painful experiences. Collective processes of storytelling create links of solidarity and enable an overcoming of the monologue of isolation into dialogues of understanding, voice, and pleasure. As Pilar Restrepo[18] explains, "Telling stories is a way of reconstructing reality, and sometimes, it also enables the healing of deep wounds."

Through storytelling we enter the borderlands of the Coatlicue (see Selbin 2010 for a comparative analysis of the power of story in popular politics). The storyteller commits to exploring, experimenting, and learning how to facilitate decolonizing prefigurative epistemologies such as these as a means to decenter the politics of knowing and being of coloniality and embrace different and multiple epistemological grounds of becoming that exceed the logic of coloniality in theory and practice.

AN "OTHER" POLITICS IN PRACTICE AND THEORY

This exploration of the reinvention of revolutions from below in Latin America dispels neoliberal capitalism's fantasy that it could eradicate popular politics, political imaginaries, and ways of life. Rather it is the "nonsubjects" of contemporary capitalism who are developing new languages, practices, and subjects of the political, which resist and transgress capitalist coloniality.

I have thus sought to demonstrate the complexities, nuances, and multiplicity in this revolutionary reinvention, highlighting the creation of counter-spatialities, politicization of social reproduction, feminization of resistance, the refusal and reimagining of capitalist labor, the emergence of a multiplicity of new popular subjectivities, and the intertwining of popular cosmologies, everyday spirituality, and cultural beliefs.

Importantly, underlying all the movements and communities explored is a politics of knowledge that questions conceptual frameworks and political categories embedded in representative understandings of the political, developing practices and experiments in post-representative, participatory, and horizontal forms of organizing community life and resistance. Here the pedagogical takes center stage as it enables the unlearning of dominant subjectivities, social relationships, and ways of life, and the learning of new ones.

These new forms of popular revolutionary left politics are thus also epistemological struggles, and as such, as Rosalba Icaza and Rolando Vázquez (2013, 684) argue, they open "an invitation not so much to study them as objects, but rather to recognize the questions that they pose to forms of understanding." These questions pose a profound challenge to conceptual, methodological, and epistemological assumptions that underlie dominant twentieth-century traditions of left intellectuality and revolutionary theorizing, for these were often embedded in representational assumptions that reproduced the logic of coloniality in thought and practice.

In response to these challenges, I have sought to sketch some ways we might imagine a practice of critical scholarship that moves beyond this logic.

Through the figure of the storyteller I have conceptualized a methodology of everyday life through which to unlearn the subjectivity of the knowing-subject of coloniality. The storyteller dwells of necessity and choice in the margins. This enables her to embrace a scholarly practice that decenters dominant regimes and rationalities of knowledge through prefigurative epistemologies in order to foster multiple grounds of epistemological becoming, in which we create the world and ourselves anew.

NOTES

1. See Mare Advertencia Lirika y Son Altepee, "Y Tú Qué Esperas?" http://vimeo.com/43781147 (accessed March 11, 2014).

2. For discussion and conceptualization of an "other" politics, see the special issue "Autonomy and Emancipation in Latin America," edited by Álvaro Reyes, *South Atlantic Quarterly* 111 (1): Winter 2012.

3. I employ the term "postrepresentative politics" to capture dynamics of organizing power, authority, and decision making that contest and at times violate the paradigm of representation (through delegation of power) dominant in twentieth-century politics. It includes both experiments in participatory governance that work to deepen representative democracy and those with a focus on self-government that seek to transcend this paradigm. It suggests a conceptual and empirical focus on the practices, political subjectivities, and institutions that emerge from this political imaginary.

4. David Harvey (1997) and Henri Lefebvre (1991) have argued that capitalist development has a spatial dynamic that creates the conditions for uneven and combined forms of economic, political, and social power across space (urban/rural, core/periphery, industrial/postindustrial) that are actively reproduced, contested, and/or transgressed by popular-class political agency.

5. See Hale and Stephen's (2013) collection that explores eight projects that are part of the *Otros Saberes* (Other Knowledges) project, which is a fascinating and important example of such a politics of knowledge in practice.

6. Author interview with Sandra Gadelha, Paris, France, February 13, 2013.

7. Originally identified by the British socialist Raymond Williams, structures of feeling are emotions and intuitions—however buried, undefined, and fragile—of unease with and difference from the values and practices of the oppressor. As Wainwright (2011) suggests, "'Structures of feeling' can help us to understand the renewed unease at the social consequences of the rampant free market system on daily life, and provide insight to the lived experiences of co-operative, solidaristic values and open, anti-authoritarian organisational logics that are in a process of formation." They can also help us understand the processes that underpin the emergence of oppositional moral economies, subjectivities, and institutions.

8. The informal system of norms and values that regulates economic and social interaction in poor and marginal communities, often autonomous from formal legal structures or dominant liberal norms of economic behavior. First developed in the work of E. P. Thompson (1971) and James C. Scott (1976) to refer to precapitalist peasant forms of resistance to the advance of capitalist social relations.

9. Author discussions with Norma Bermúdez, April 2012.

10. The former priest, who was expelled for subversive activities in 1972, had arrived in Venezuela in 1966 to start a worker-priest mission, which was banned by the pope. While living in La Vega, he helped to organize communities and took part in a famous strike at the local cement factory (for further details on Wuytack's experiences in Venezuela and La Vega, see Angulo Ruiz 2006).

11. See Freire 2000 for an introduction to popular education; see Martínez-Torres and Rosset 2014 for a mapping and analysis of how such processes work across multiple move-

ments and spatial scales through the concept and methodology of *diálogo de saberes* (dialogue of knowledges) in La Vía Campesina.

12. Author interview with Norma Bermúdez, April 10, 2012, Nottingham, UK.

13. The idea of decolonization builds on the philosophical work of postcolonial and Latin American subalternist thinkers who suggest that the politics of coloniality often structure the practices and theories developed by critical scholars engaging with popular politics. It suggests a deconstruction of colonial frameworks and the affirmative production of ourselves in a way that transgresses their logics (Mignolo 2009; Motta 2011a, 2012).

14. As Lugones (2006, 79) describes in relation to Anzaldúa's conceptualization of the margins, "[it] is inhabited by all of those who cross over the confines of the normal 'atravesados/as.'"

15. Lugones (1987, 3) names the outsider within a world-traveller who "has necessarily acquired flexibility in shifting from the mainstream construction of life where she is constructed as an outsider to other constructions of life where she is more or less 'at home.' This flexibility is necessary for the outsides but it can also be wilfully exercised by the outsider . . . what I call world-travelling." She continues, "I affirm this practice as a skilful, creative, enriching and, given certain circumstances, as a loving way of being and living. I recognise that much of our travelling is done unwillfullly to hostile White/Anglo worlds."

16. As Lugones (1992, 32) explains, "The Coatlicue state is a state of creation. The self being oppressed, the self-in-between. . . . Caught in between two harmful worlds of sense that deny her ability to respond, the self-in-between fashions herself in a quiet state. Anzaldúa recognizes here that the possibility of resistance depends on this creation of a new identity, a new world of sense, in the borders. The Coatlicue state is one of stasis because it is a state of making new sense. It is a state of isolation, separation from harmful sense." Coatlicue, or "Serpent Skirt," was the Aztec earth goddess.

17. See also Farthing and Kohl (2013) for a discussion of the role of another historicity and collective memory in the formation and sustainability of Bolivia's Indigenous social movements.

18. Author interview with Pilar Restrepo, participant and cofounder of La Máscara Theater, Santiago de Cali, Colombia, 14 December 2010.

Congreso Nacional Indígena-Istmo de Tehuantepec, Gui'xhi'ro'—Álvaro Obregón, Oaxaca, Mexico, 29 March 2014. (Richard Stahler-Sholk)

II

Movement Dynamics, Strategies, and Identities

Caminante, no hay camino,
se hace camino al andar.
[Traveler, there is no path,
one makes the path by walking.]
—poem by Antonio Machado, set to music by Joan Manuel Serrat

In contrast to more dogmatic movements of the old left and the heyday of armed struggle for state power, many of today's social movements in Latin America see the path to radical change as an open-ended and participatory process, in which subjective consciousness and patterns of social relations are transformed through the lived experience of organized struggle. That process of creating new social subjects does not assume that identities and interests flow mechanically from class positions, but recognizes the pluriverse of overlapping identities (intersectionality) that include experiences filtered through the lenses of race, class, gender, sexual orientation, generation, religious/spiritual outlook, and cosmovision. The assertion of various combinations of identities can reshape landscapes of struggle, generating new movement dynamics, alliances, and strategies.

As the "time-space compression" of globalization has blurred the old significance of geography, the role of states in the international capitalist system has changed, and the boundaries of social organization have also become more fluid. The 1992 mobilizations marking five hundred years of Indigenous, Black, and popular resistance in Latin America highlighted a growing awareness of identities and commonalities that colonialism and neo-colonialism had suppressed. Movement activists are increasingly focusing on horizontal relations within society rather than on the colonial constructions of the nation-state, remembering and resignifying symbols and identity markers of popular resistance through creative new strategies.

The authors in this section explore the relationship between shifting identities of social subjects and the strategies and dynamics of social movement organizing. Raúl Zibechi and Maurice Magaña each look at moments of urban popular organizing in Mexico. For Zibechi, a key factor in the expanding mobilization of poor barrios in Mexico City in the 1980s was the set of horizontal and participatory practices (neighborhood assemblies, "people's schools," alternative spaces such as workshops and sports fields, and a myriad of locally run centers and projects), all of which were fundamental in building community and collective identity. This new political culture staked out what he calls "territories in resistance." Yet Zibechi also examines the dilemmas of engaging with the state to secure resources, the contradictions of building community in an alienating urban space, and the challenges of interfacing with other strategies of autonomy such as the Zapatistas' "Other Campaign." Magaña's study of the 2006 Oaxaca uprising and aftermath notes simultaneously the spontaneous energy brought to the movement, especially by countercultural youth (including punks and graffiti artists), but also the long organizing roots that made it possible. This combination created some tension between older, more institutionalized/vertical forms of organizing and newer horizontal dynamics, which Magaña analyzes using the concept of "meshworks." He paints a vivid picture of the identities and alliances that emerged through shared experiences on the urban barricades, arguing that the collective memory of those intense moments created elements of a new political culture—carried forward by the youth—that outlasted the heavy-handed state repression. Together these two chapters raise important issues about the challenges of horizontalism in urban organizing, and strategies for confronting the state. They also suggest that a focus on collective identity and community building sheds new light on movement outcomes and legacies.

Daniela Issa's chapter on the Brazilian Landless Rural Workers' Movement (MST), Alicia Swords on Mesoamerican organizing against the Plan Puebla-Panamá (PPP), and Suyapa Portillo on the popular movement of resistance after the 2009 coup in Honduras, all offer valuable insight into movement cultures and strategies. Issa underscores the importance of liberation theology as a unifying frame for rural land occupiers in Brazil, and specifically the practice known as *mística*, consisting of role plays and other group exercises that reinforced collective identity, commitment, and empowerment within the movement. Her chapter illustrates a strategy for creating consciousness that was fundamental for rural workers in constituting themselves as social subjects and resisting the forces that would construct them as faceless labor power. Alicia Swords applies frame analysis to examine how activists understood their identities as they organized against PPP, a mega-development scheme of global capital unveiled in 2000 and repackaged in 2008 as the Proyecto Mesoamérica. The study highlights the challenges of forging collective identities, effective networking strategies, and counternarratives to confront the slipperiness of globally mobile capital. Suyapa Portillo examines the unusually broad "movement of movements" that forged the National Popular Resistance Front (FNRP) in post-coup Honduras. In the face of intense state repression against lesbian, gay, bisexual, transsexual, transgender, and intersex (LGBTTI), *campesino*, and other segments of the movement, activists faced dilemmas that challenged the unity of their diverse coalition, such as whether to join forces with the electoral campaign of the wife of the ousted former president. Portillo's chapter highlights the complex interface between transnational networks and the effort to maintain horizontalism in domestic organizing, illustrated by the highly visible role of LBGTTI organizers in framing resistance in terms of an international human rights discourse.

The chapters by Nathalie Lebon and Kwame Dixon focus on gender, class, and racial identities as mobilizing forces in Brazil. Lebon's study of Brazilian women's activism emphasizes the complex intersectionality of identities, in which popular sector and urban middle-class feminists and white and Afro-Brazilian women experienced gender-based organizing differently. She emphasizes the often overlooked role of popular feminism, Afro-Brazilian women's activism, and lesbian and transgender mobilization in promoting horizontal strategies of organizing that contribute to the diversity and vitality of the movements. Kwame Dixon's study of Black social movements in Brazil, focusing on Salvador da Bahia, shows how Black cultural politics took shape in response to the country's highly vertical and exclusionary social relations and political institutions. He examines how the movement redefined power relations in new spaces such as the *blocos afros* since the 1970s, rooting grassroots in these new horizontal cultural spaces that were critical to the construction of counterhegemonic power. Yet the contradictions and pitfalls of identity politics are seen in the folklorization and commercialization of popular culture, as well as the continued exclusion of Afro-Brazilians from local institutions of formal political power.

Chapter Three

Mexico

Challenges and Difficulties of Urban Territories in Resistance

Raúl Zibechi

Autonomy is the political form that communities in resistance have adopted in order to change the world. To illustrate these hypotheses I propose to reconstruct a small segment of the vast urban popular movement in Mexico since 1968, with the understanding that autonomy is a never-ending process: one of comings and goings that are visible not in declarations or programs, but in the traces left by daily life.

The Comunidad Habitacional Acapatzingo is one of the most important urban autonomous experiences in Latin America, for the depth of its construction of community,[1] for its duration,[2] for its vocation of transforming the whole of society,[3] and for its fierce resistance[4] to state power at all levels. I will highlight some aspects that contribute to an understanding of this singular experience—how it came to be what it is, and the paths taken and not taken. In short, I will examine the exhausting uphill climb involved in any autonomous process that seeks to avoid subordination by existing institutions.

Secondly, I offer a brief reconstruction of what the community is and what it does, the daily lives of the families that compose it, their internal and external links, and their modes of organization. Every human collective has its own style and ways of proceeding that distinguish it from others, and while the Acapatzingo community has similarities with other Latin American movements (or, more accurately, it contains features of other movements both rural and urban), some of its style and customs are original, and these constitute its most distinctive features.

Thirdly, I propose to reflect on some general characteristics of "autonomies from below," based on the experience of the Frente Popular Francisco Villa Independiente (FPFVI), with which the Acapatzingo community is affiliated. The main question is how to deepen the construction of autonomy in an era in which state and capital demonstrate a renewed ability to bury autonomous communities through a combination of repression and social programs.

FROM THE OLD TO THE NEW CACIQUISMO

[handwritten annotation: "the rule of local chiefs or bosses, political structure"]

After the student revolt of 1968, popular sectors in Mexico managed to gain a foothold against the domination of the party-state. The acceleration of urban population growth forced the popular sectors to occupy lands on the peripheries of Mexico City and other large cities. In 1952 the capital's metropolitan area had 2.3 million people, of whom 14 percent lived in self-constructed housing. By 1970 the figures were 7.3 million and 47 percent respectively, and by 1990 the area contained 15.7 million people of whom 60 percent, or 9.5 million, lived in self-constructed housing settlements (Gisbert 1997, 104). The Mexico City region grew at a rate that overwhelmed its legal framework and led its inhabitants to create, in effect, a new city: the Distrito Federal, joining the existing capital to adjacent cities whose annual growth rate topped 10 percent in the 1950s (Alonso 1980, 44).

An early characteristic of Mexico City's mid-century urbanization was the appearance of numerous invasions, as in Ajusco in 1948 when migrants decided via an assembly to occupy vacant lands, which were legally granted to them two decades later after further rounds of invasion and conflict (Alonso 1980, 306). In some cases, as in Monterrey in the 1970s, up to 100,000 settlers grouped into twenty-four communities and joined together in the Frente Popular Tierra y Libertad to occupy lands (Castells 1986, 277). The scale of the invasions was a result of massive rural-urban migration and a growing urban housing deficit.

According to Castells (1986), two factors contributed to the new urban movements: the reformism of the Luis Echeverría government (1970–1976), which "came to recognize, to a point, the right to protest at the margins of established channels," and above all the political radicalism of post-1968 students, who "supplied a base upon which to build a new form of autonomous political organization" (275). The first claim is debatable, as the author recognizes, while the second claim needs to be developed. The Echeverría regime's relative permissiveness was based in large part on the Institutional Revolutionary Party's (PRI) past experience of delegating local political leaders (caciques) to control community organizations by offering them the support and recognition of the authorities; therefore, "illegal land invasions were not in themselves a challenge to the social order" (Castells 1986, 275). Caciquismo was functional for the party-state, legitimating it even in the face of mobilizations. This is one of the central characteristics of the regime, based on the popular and revolutionary roots of the PRI, which could more or less do as it pleased by channeling popular mobilization.

The new revolutionary left arose precisely to contest this elite-directed way of operating, and the first cracks in the political culture were apparent in 1968. Castells (1986, 275) mentions that many students and professionals who supported the October 2 settlement (*campamento*) in Ixtacalco, inhabited by 4,000 people, did not just support them from the outside but came to live among the inhabitants and joined them in a January 1976 confrontation with the police that left many people injured and much of the settlement in flames. This joining of university militants and settlers helps to explain the autonomy that the families claimed against government attempts at co-optation.

This attitude was not just because of the support of the student movement. From the late 1960s onward, "ex-activists of the student movement of 1968, promoters of Christian Base Communities, and militants of the non-party Left" played a key role in fomenting and politicizing the movement (Ramirez 2003, 6). These currents permitted the organization and mobilization of the urban popular sectors, but they were also able to promote local leaders and militants through active training processes as occurred in other Latin American movements (Zibechi 2013a). It is worth noting that this confluence of leftist Christian militancy was also present many years later in the origins of the Zapatista movement.

After a decade of intense mobilization, in which the still-new urban popular movement carried out countless land invasions, demonstrations, and other actions seen as "combative, radical, anti-government and anti-party" (Ramírez 2003, 7), a new era began. Around 1980 several "mass organizations" were created, including the Unión de Colonias Populares del Valle de México, which worked to "coordinate at the regional level" (Moctezuma 1984, 72). These in turn gave rise to national meetings, out of which developed the Coordinador Nacional del Movimiento Popular Urban (CONAMUP) in 1981. This entity, composed of more than 100 organizations from across the country, carried out ambitious national actions such as the National Day Against the Cost of Living in September 1982 and a march of 60,000 people to the Zócalo in Mexico City, as well as forums and political and cultural events, all designed to "forge the unity of the mass movement from below" (Moctezuma 1984, 80). In May 1983 the fourth national meeting laid down the bases for a unity process between the popular movement and the rest of the left, with the goal of promoting a "national day of struggle" in June and a general strike in October.

A political culture with strongly centralist tendencies, dedicated to the construction of the most solidly structured organization possible, coexisted within the movement alongside what Moctezuma (1984, 72) calls an "alternative culture" expressed through bulletins, pamphlets, songs, murals, political caricatures (*calaveras*), and street theater. Meanwhile, women's groups within the organization at all levels emphasized the need to modify social relations through criticism, ideological struggle, collective work, study circles, and festivities.

Several important characteristics of today's urban popular movement were already visible in the early 1980s, even before the 1985 Mexico City earthquake and the 1987 Neighborhoods Assembly. We can see this through the example of one of the most important organizations of the era, the Unión de Colonos, Inquilinos y Solicitantes de Vivienda-Libertad (UCISV-L), associated with the Unión Popular Revolucionaria Emiliano Zapata (UPREZ). This organization, founded in 1987, was linked to the Organización de Izquierda Revolucionaria-Línea de Masas (OIR-LM), one of the most influential currents in the urban popular movement and in CONAMUP. The UPREZ itself contained several neighborhood organizations (Barragán 2010, 95).

The UCISV-L is one of the four organizations whose members settled on the El Molino parcel, which eventually brought together between 3,000 and 5,000 people seeking housing. They were organized into brigades of twenty-five families each, with several brigades forming a group with an elected coordinator (Sánchez 2003, 29). During the first phase they held weekly meetings and assemblies, and staged takeovers of government offices with the active participation of university professors and cadres of the OIR-LM. The brigades were active in the "self-construction" (*autoconstrucción*) of housing, building a total of 1,086 units based on a master plan that the residents, with the guidance of advisers chosen in an open competition, had developed. The integral character of the plan was noteworthy, including a plaza or community space every four blocks "to promote the communication and community life among residents," and kitchens located in the front of each house "so that mothers could see their children playing outside" (Sánchez 2003, 31). The residents took an active role in all aspects of design and planning, in the administration of the construction process, in generating popular enterprises to create employment, and in job training through a "people's school." The UCISV-L developed a fully fledged alternative urban project, based upon environmental sensitivity (including a plastics recycling workshop and drainage works), education (including preschool, adult education, and a library), a strong civic culture component to promote communal harmony and strengthen community traditions, health care (including both conventional and alternative medical centers), small business (for example, producing construction materials for neighborhood housing and clothing design), a cooperative store and a marketplace, and soccer fields and basketball courts (Ariza and Ramírez 2005, 344–45).

In the late 1990s the UCISV-L began to weaken, although the origins of this process can be found a decade earlier in the crisis of the PRI on a national level and the development of a convergence among the electoral left, led by Cuauhtémoc Cárdenas and the Frente Democrático Nacional in a four-party alliance, along with splinter groups from the PRI and independents who came together to participate in the 1988 election. As Barragán (2010, 78) observes, by the time of the 1988 federal elections a popular movement that had already spent ten or more years in nonelectoral struggle, arguably without much to show for it, faced a difficult and contentious decision. By 1990, according to Barragán (2010, 79), "we are left with a movement whose struggle would take place alongside political parties," namely the four member parties of the FDN. In her analysis, this quickly led to "the disappearance of the ideas and practices of people power," based on assemblies and land invasions, in favor of the pursuit of housing within the idiom of political and citizenship rights, "based on negotiations between a leader and state institutions via a political party" (Barragán 2010, 83). Hierarchies returned, and opportunities for ordinary people to exercise power within the movement were closed off. In short, the old political culture of subordination to the PRI returned, this time as subordination to the parties of the National Democratic Front (FDN); the letters changed, but the essence was largely the same.

The movement of so many people into positions in the state bureaucracy or to elective posts deprived the movement of its leadership (Ariza and Ramírez 2005, 347). This institutional insertion took place in a context of antagonistic party currents within the UCISV-L, all of which "wanted to keep their ties to politicians and officials in order to obtain resources for their group, without regard for the others" (Ramírez 2003, 37). As immediate and factional interests took precedence over longer-term collective interests, the organization fragmented and the community disintegrated. The loss of organization built up through long processes of struggle and resistance, and the rise of a political culture of corruption and individualism, became irreversible tendencies.

In 1989, as most of the urban popular movement was being integrated (with fatal consequences) into party and government institutions, the Frente Popular Francisco Villa (FPFV) was founded through a long process of land invasions, violent expulsions, and extensive debates in Ajusco, the southern-most and highest zone of Mexico City. It was born in the university through the Frente Estudiantil Revolucionario y Popular, and from the militants of the Cooperativo Allepetlalli in El Molino (a 1985 land invasion), which was itself a confluence of various experiences ranging from anthropology and political science students of the Universidad Nacional Autónoma de México (UNAM) to leaders and members of CONAMUP-affiliated housing cooperatives and residents of irregular settlements and popular *colonias*, coming from diverse left traditions. Within a few years FPFV became the largest urban popular organization in the capital. In 1996 its congress defined the FPFV as a "broad organization of the masses" focused on land and housing, but also on "the organization of production and consumption" in its territories (FPFV 1996). The group defended a "proletarian morality" based on principles of collectivism and mutual aid between comrades, labor, and study discipline, and "ideological, political, and organic independence with respect to the State and its parties."

The FPFV had strong support from as many as 10,000 taxi drivers (Los Panteras), street and other informal merchants, and operators of market stalls (Sánchez, 2003). But at the fourth congress in 1997, a motion was presented to support Cárdenas as governor of the capital district in the first popular election for that post in Mexican history. The majority voted to set aside their policy of abstaining from elections in favor of a "strategic and conjunctural political alliance" with the candidate's PRD (Sánchez, 2003), while the dissident minority withdrew and took the name of "Independent" (FPFVI, Frente Popular Francisco Villa Independiente).

THE SLOW CONSTRUCTION OF A NEW POLITICAL CULTURE

The 1997 election season followed the same script as in 1988: everything built up over years of hard struggle at the base level was squandered on a candidate and his slogans. I would suggest that the urban popular movement is facing a challenge that can only be overcome by a new political culture that can displace the hegemonic institutional one. (Although it is not the topic of this chapter, it is worth considering the Zapatista rejection of the 2006 presidential campaign of Andrés Manuel López Obrador—an attitude judged "intransigent" by many leftists—in the light of these two negative experiences.) The schism in the FPFV was brought about by militants who after years of struggle saw the electoral option offering "the possibility to grow and widen the social base of the FPFV . . . without losing sight of its strategic objectives, its identity as an organization, and its struggle to defend popular causes" (Sánchez, 2003).

Mexican political culture has proved more resistant to change than the protesters of 1968 imagined, especially those who survived the Tlatelolco massacre and subsequent despair to continue their efforts to change the world.

> Mexico's urban popular sectors have always been well organized at the community level, and this organization has served two important functions: it has permitted them to exercise pressure in favor of their demands to remain on the lands they have occupied and to obtain basic services, and it has represented a

fundamental channel of political participation subordinated to the PRI. Both aspects have been, in the end, complementary, and local leaders [caciques] have been agents of this process. (Castells 1986, 275)

The greatest challenge to this political culture is the Zapatista Army of National Liberation (EZLN) and its over 1,000 Zapatista communities. In the urban setting the FPFVI, with its 596 families and 8 settlements, is working to overcome the old culture through the creation of autonomous "communities in resistance" on the periphery of one of the world's largest cities. The members are the inheritors of a tradition of urban struggle described above, enriched by the experience of the EZLN as well as by popular organizations in other countries (Lao and Flavia 2009).

The land on which the Acapatzingo-La Polvorilla community was built, in Iztapalapa to the east of Mexico City, was progressively occupied in 1994 by expelling the intermediaries who profited through land speculation. The settlers bought the land in 1998 with a credit from the Instituto de Vivienda del Distrito Federal (INVI) and began to build houses in 2000 (Lao and Flavia 2009; Zibechi 2009). The group was composed of families who arrived from other land invasions like El Molino, or from failed attempts like Puente Blanco. They first built temporary housing for the homeless, and once these were completed they built permanent single-family units that were distributed to families.

The houses of members of a brigade (the base-level unit) are contiguous and are all painted the same color. Temporary housing is maintained to house other families who are in the process of occupying land and building communities elsewhere. In this sense Acapatzingo is a school for the movement as a whole. In mid-2013 the community had two seedling nurseries growing food crops, a community radio station run by teenagers, recreational spaces including a skating rink and bicycling area for children and the elderly, two basketball courts, and an open-air theater. A health clinic and schools (preschool, primary, and secondary) are under construction. A vigilance commission, staffed on a rotating basis by all of the residents, regulates entry to the community and police may not enter except by permission of the community, and must be unarmed.

The construction of the community was a long process in which cultural and subjective factors played a more important role than physical constraints—a barren landscape was radically transformed into a beautiful neighborhood and community. The inhabitants describe the process this way:

We came together bit by bit, like raindrops forming a river; we walked together in struggle and solidarity, we faced and overcame our fears to take on the bureaucracy, official negligence, the State. . . . We developed our arms, mobilization was fundamental in reaching our objectives, while at the same time we developed our own culture, and we continue to build it, a community culture, one of life and not death, and we strengthen it with our patrolling, our work details, with our radio station and with our cultural project. (FPFVI-UNOPII 2009c)

Through this brief description, highlighting the two central ideas of community and culture, I want to reconstruct what I consider to be decisive aspects in the formation of this *autonomous community in resistance*: the change in subjectivities, the internal organization, and the understandings that made possible the community life (*convivencia*) of the families making up the community. I assume that these three aspects are intimately linked, and I separate them only so they can be analyzed in greater depth. My goal is to understand *how* community can be created out of the sum of a large number of individuals.

Subjectivities were modified over a long process of internal and external interactions, particularly those critical moments of repression and division that showed participants who they (collectively) were, what they did and did not want to be, and with whom they could and should work. A beautiful semi-internal document details this process, emphasizing the "arrests of our leaders, [and] the rupture with those who were previously our comrades but who betrayed the principles of our organization by becoming elected officials, and those who decided to go with them because it would get them out of working" (FPFVI-UNOPII 2009b).

Repression and betrayals generated "disenchantment" but also isolation and impotence, as those left behind had to carry on in worse conditions. They speak of their pain at those who died in the struggle, but also of "broken marriages, children who have left," and the enormous collective effort of working ten-hour days in badly paid and precarious jobs to earn a living. This shared pain is one of the bases of community creation: as Antonio Negri (2003, 161) has written, "all great collective subjects are formed through pain."

The members of FPFVI and the Acapatzingo community note that the pain of separation, of repression, and of hard work "purified us, leaving behind the best, the most combative, the real comrades" (FPFVI-UNOPII, 2009b). Without this purification there could be no internal growth, and without the betrayals and deaths they would not have reached their current stage. It should be recalled that over 100,000 families took part in the Mexico City urban popular movement in the 1970s, and that the 1988 front brought together 10,000 families, while the FPFVI consists of only a thousand families. The rest were lost along the way—they were dispersed, or they joined the system and lost their autonomy. This is part of the learning process, the lesson being that under the current Mexican political system, "only pain constitutes consciousness" (Negri 2003, 184).

A change in subjectivity is produced when people begin to be able to overcome "their own fears, fight the traumas imbued in us from childhood, and break with egoism and apathy" (FPFVI-UNOPII 2008b). This interior project is "individual in collective," in other words neither one nor the other; it breaks the individual/collective polarity, conserving the concepts but dissolving their opposition. This is evident in land occupations and in the meetings converted into open-air schools, where "assemblies, marches, patrols, and work details become a collectivity, an expression of concern for one another" (FPFVI-UNOPII 2006). In short, *I am to the extent that I share with others. I do not exist in isolation, and it is only through others that my individuality can grow and be affirmed.*

As Eric Hobsbawm (1995, 308) noted about early twentieth-century workers, the fundamental element of their lives was "the collectivity, the dominance of 'we' over 'I,'" because they understood that people like themselves could only improve their situation through collective rather than individual action, to the point where "life was, in its most pleasant aspects, a collective experience." This explains why individual escapes are described as "treason," a broad term applied within the FPFVI to those who collaborate with the police, abandon the community in favor of an individual path, join wider elected institutions, or seek the patronage of outside politicians. Any of these steps typically bring a more comfortable life, similar to the lives of outright enemies of the communities in resistance.

This noteworthy change in the subjectivity observed in members of the urban movement has roots in the "natural" communitarian nature of Mexican *colonias*. The FPFVI has rescued this orientation from the risks of the market, the political parties, and the patriarchy. The subject of the changes already exists, which is the community culture itself; the task is "merely" to safeguard it, expand it, and liberate it from "prejudices and traumas" such as racism and domestic violence, which "can be defeated by prevention and by community care" (FPFVI-UNOPII, 2006).

The organization of the front itself is oriented toward the tasks of rescuing and strengthening community. The base is always the same: the brigades of twenty-five families each, whether at established sites like Acapatzingo or at the most recent occupations and settlements. Each brigade determines the leadership of its "commissions," which are typically press, culture, vigilance, and maintenance. Acapatzingo has twenty-eight brigades, while other settlements have different numbers according to the number of families. The commissions in turn name representatives to the general council of the settlements, where the brigades are brought together.

Enrique Reynoso explains that the idea behind the brigades is to create centers "where people can generate a link, while the commissions are two-way transmission paths between the organization and the families," so as to improve the work of everyone (Zibechi 2009). At the brigade level there is both the time and the interpersonal confidence required to deepen discussions, for instance about whether to ally with the Zapatista Otra Campaña, and the results of these brigade-level discussions are brought to a general assembly of the whole settlement (monthly for Acapatzingo, weekly in some others) as the highest decision-making body.

It is important to look more closely at what happens at the brigade level, which is not only the basic unit of the organization but also of the community. Each family has one vote at brigade meetings, where the overall rules of the settlement are debated and revised until all brigades are in agreement. The brigade also handles conflicts, including domestic ones, and if the conflict is severe it can ask for intervention by the settlement's vigilance commission or general council. Each brigade takes charge of the settlement's security for one day per month, but the notion of security or vigilance is not the traditional one of control but rather of community self-protection, with a strong educational aspect. "The vigilance commission can't be the settlement's police force," explains Reynoso, "because we would just be repeating the power of the state" (Zibechi 2009).

The vigilance commission also has the assignment of marking off the borders, and determining who can and cannot enter. This is perhaps the most important aspect of community autonomy, which implies a physical and political differentiation between inside and outside. This is how living organisms function, by creating a perimeter within which interactions occur that permit many to function as one (Maturana and Varela 1995). This is the same "closure" that operates in Zapatista communities, permitting social links to develop differently within the perimeter to give the community its distinctive characteristics. But it is not a closed system—it has multiple links to the outside. The Acapatzingo community works intensively with its surrounding neighborhoods, training them in the creation of base-level committees and community security; they also provide advice about how to respond to evictions, which the recipients repay in food. They have made presentations in surrounding schools about student safety, and neighboring merchants even advertise on the community radio station. "We are seeking a utopia that is not an island, but rather an open space that can have a contagious effect on society," explains Reynoso (Zibechi 2009). Other settlements, almost all in the Pantitlán area, work with surrounding neighborhoods in planning Carnival and other festivities that transcend community borders.

Since their participation in the Zapatista Otra Campaña, the FPFVI's members have been spearheading the organization of minibus operators displaced by the expansion of Mexico City's Metro, but also of the informal venders who work within the Metro trains and stations. They have organized ten alternative transportation routes and three vendor organizations with 3,000 members each, as well as artisans and shoe-shiners, all joined in the Alianza Mexicana de Organizaciones Sociales (AMOS), based in the eastern part of the city with some 15,000 members. FPFVI members also participate in the Red de Resistencias Autónomas Anticapitalistas along with a dozen other organizations from throughout Mexico.

One of the central tasks of this organization, perhaps the most central, is to include education and training as part of an overall alternative cultural project. Through its twenty years of history the FPFVI has enjoyed the support of university students and professionals who have led its cultural work. In the early stages of the El Molino community, the Huasipungo cooperative proposed a "pedagogical center" to train preschool teachers with the agreement of the teachers' union, since there were few schools in the area and children from the community faced discrimination. Along with movie screenings, block printing workshops, and the encouragement of sports, these initiatives were the precursor of what would later become a "cultural project."

In 1999, two years after the division that gave rise to the "independent" FPFVI, the organization established a relationship with striking students at the Psychology and Exact Sciences faculties of the National University, with professors and students of the Pedagogical University and with musical and cultural groups during the construction of the La Polvorilla community. Acapatzingo's culture commission channeled these links into initiatives such as the book club, a center for early education, and literacy campaigns (FPFVI-UNOPII, 2008b).

At its third congress the FPFVI resolved that "one of the priorities of the organization is to develop a cultural project . . . in order to generate the conditions for change and transformation in society" (FPFVI-UNOPII 2008b, 4). In its first stage the center for early education worked with single mothers, the Centro Pedagógico para el Desarrollo Integral de las Inteligencias provided study help, university students created "Saturday sessions" to develop the creativity of children, and a community loudspeaker "radio" was started, in addition to a movie club and adult literacy classes.

During the second stage the work was reoriented along three axes: science, culture, and political training. The goal was to "work for the construction of our own educational system, all the way from preschool through high school, . . . that would affirm the organization as a way of life and as the only way to face the system of exploitation" (FPFVI-UNOPII 2008b, 5–6). Several initiatives arose in parallel: a space for young people, initially called "youth assemblies"; events about sexuality, drug addiction, gangs, domestic violence, and other topics: as well as workshops on producing clothing, videos, and musical instruments. A group of psychologists was created to work with cooperative members to build a less alienating lifestyle. According to the psychologists, their work with the community has taught us, and has developed within us, a very different notion of society than what we practice in other settings. It is a psychology that does not try to adapt the person to society as it is, but rather strengthens and supports the person to develop the ability to transform society into the society we need. (FPFVI-UNOPII 2008b, 7)

In subsequent years they established relationships with more collectives, such as Jóvenes en Resistencia Alternativa and Brigada Callejera, which enriched their cultural and political work. In October 2012 they held the first "meeting of commissions" with the theme of "Capitalism, Autonomy, Socialism" in Acapatzingo. In general, all of the initiatives work on the basis of methods and criteria spread by popular education: collective self-training with facilitators, roundtables to encourage participation, flip charts to record points of agreement and discussion, discussions based on daily experiences, the awakening of the critical spirit, and understanding reality in order to transform it, among others.

Another important question has been the overall community rules (*reglamento*). By way of example we will examine the *reglamento* of the Centauro del Norte settlement, which was established on land occupied in 2007 in the Pantitlán area. There are around fifty families in temporary housing in rows with a central path, differentiated by color as they are all part of a single brigade. The houses are rudimentary but solid, with permanent walls and roofs, and concrete floors. The settlement is characterized by cleanliness and order, with an overall climate of dignity and spatial organization, including a children's play area. There are several emergency alarms, and designated assembly points in case the alarms sound.

The general *reglamento*, which is very similar to that of other settlements, is twelve pages long and was approved by all residents. The community, according to the text, seeks to provide a housing alternative for families who lack it, and who "agree to break with individualist habits and practices" to construct a collective project toward "the construction of Popular Power" (FPFVI-UNOPII 2009a, 2). Attendance at assemblies is mandatory, and repeated absence can be cause for expulsion from the settlement. The assembly created four commissions: maintenance (in charge of collective work), vigilance, culture, and health. The final commission works on preventive mental and physical health, attention to the chronically ill, and nutrition and vaccination campaigns.

The *reglamento* strictly governs matters of *convivencia* or community life: it prohibits physical or psychological abuse and the playing of loud music, and it calls for conflict between neighbors to be solved through dialogue while providing that the vigilance commission can intervene in grave cases. When there is an act of physical violence, "the aggressor must cover the costs for care and recovery of the victim," and is also subject to temporary or permanent removal. Robbery or theft leads to removal regardless of the amount stolen, and the culprit's entire family may be removed as well (FPFVI-UNOPII 2009a, 6–7). On the nonpunitive side, the *reglamento* provides for play areas and the creation of children's assemblies and commissions with adult support. Common areas must be kept clean and free of drugs and alcohol. The calendar and timing of patrols is strictly regulated, and collective workdays are obligatory when decided by the assembly or commissions.

In the Centauro del Norte settlement one observes that the most active residents are women, who show off the community to visitors with pride, including the health centers and library, and who explain the work of the commissions in detail. Children, starting at age ten, are willing to participate in collective activities. Each settlement has a space for assemblies that often functions as a dining hall. In all of the settlements I visited, I asked what they did about domestic violence, and they all said the same thing: the aggressor has to leave the community for whatever duration the victim requests, from weeks up to three months, "to think about it." He can only return when the victim accepts him, and the community provides emotional support to the family.

In some settlements there are prominent billboards with the names of persons not permitted to enter. In Acapatzingo the residents say that when there is any domestic violence the children come out into the streets with their whistles, the practice used by the community in the event of emergency. The overall peacefulness is such that even in the most populated settlements like Acapatzingo, with 3,000 residents, it is common to see children playing alone with total confidence, in a safe space protected by the community.

AUTONOMY AND COMMUNITY: THE NEW WORLD

The experience of the Acapatzingo community and those of the FPFVI show us that urban communities can be created even in the face of enormous difficulties and the "structural obstacle" represented by their members' dependence upon precarious employment (Pineda 2013, 58). It also shows us that the world does not change thanks to large-scale demonstrations on the major boulevards, but rather on a small scale and at the margins of the system: "The great transformations do not start from above, or with epic and monumental acts, but rather from small movements that appear irrelevant to the politician and pundit up above" (Subcomandante Insurgente Marcos 2007).

Societies change from daily local practice, in defined autonomous spaces, because autonomy is the perimeter that protects counterhegemonic practices. Autonomy is the means by which other worlds can exist, worlds that need protection by virtue of being different. When and how these practices and ways of life might expand is impossible to predict, much less determine and direct. Militants can push the world toward a certain state of affairs in a certain space, but they cannot—and should not—try to design "from on high" a new reality.

In order to survive, subalterns (*los de abajo*) need to strengthen their ties to others like them, strong ties that can demonstrate resistance and resilience. Along the way they create diverse forms of community that generally are made up of groups of families with some stability and permanence. They see themselves and are seen by others as communities, in the widest sense of the word. They live in a defined physical space, their territory, typically on urban peripheries but sometimes not. Regardless, they are always in marginal spaces from the perspective of capital accumulation, spaces that have been subjected to environmental or physical degradation.

By "community" we mean practices, ways of working and living, of producing and reproducing, that take place in spaces, modes, and times for decision making and with the mechanisms to make sure those decisions are respected. In other words, the community is also a form of power, unique in that it is neither state nor hierarchical. Among the practices that make community are *reciprocity*, which differs from solidarity in that it is based not on a subject-object relationship but rather on the plurality of subjects; and *siblinghood* (*hermandad*), which is based on an integral material and spiritual bond that is one of the horizontal forms of community.

The practices that make community are based upon the assembly, which takes decisions and determines the order and rotation of tasks and the control of assigned tasks by the members, through the seven principles of "servant leadership" as synthesized by the Zapatistas: serving others rather than oneself, representing rather than superseding, constructing and not destroying, obeying and not dictating, proposing and not imposing, convincing and not vanquishing, and self-abasement rather than putting on airs (*bajar y no subir*). This series of practices indicates that the community is not an institution or an organization, but rather a way of working, based on collective work and agreement.

Collective work is a key piece, even the heart, of the community, and as the Zapatistas note, it is the motor of the community's autonomy. Community is not just collective property—it must be sustained by permanent and constant activity that modifies the habits and inertia of individualism and egocentrism. In those societies that were based on collective or state ownership of the means of production but not based on collectively organized work projects, the result was the reproduction of the values and culture of the capitalist system.

The Western view of community is based on collective property, even in Marx. In his correspondence with the Russian populist Vera Zasulich about the rural commune, Marx wrote that its fundamental characteristic was "the common ownership of land," and therefore of the product (Marx 1980, 40). Collective property certainly plays an important role in the existence of community, but to grant it sole importance is an economistic oversimplification. Seeing the community as practices—of production, of health, of education, and so forth—opens up the concept rather than closes it off as merely a type of property.

One of the central aspects of these practices is collective labor dedicated to producing, empowering, and protecting the common goods of the community. We have previously noted the vigilance patrols as one form of collective work in Acapatzingo, but there are others, including public works (streets and storm drains). These projects are the result of long debates in the assemblies, which take all the time necessary to reach agreement by consensus rather than by majority vote. Agreement carries with it the recognition that the community has the power to carry out its decisions, but this coercion is unlike the state's coercion because it is not exercised by a specialized body that stands apart from the community (bureaucracy), but by the community itself. The *reglamento* plays a double role: it represents both agreement and the mechanisms of implementation.

Communities, with their territorial basis, are necessarily under siege by the system, by the state and capital, which need to impose their order on all spaces and to impose their laws on all persons. Faced with this, communities can choose to submit to the state-capital order, or seek to resist outside that order. If they choose the latter, they become communities and territories in resistance. To affirm their characteristics and to defend themselves against attempts to subjugate them, they must affirm themselves as autonomous, that is to say self-governing, spaces.

Can we speak of autonomy, concretely in the case of Acapatzingo, when the land was purchased with a thirty-year loan from a government agency that also financed the design of the settlement and the construction of the houses? In political and academic circles there is one understanding of autonomy that precludes any contact with the state, but I wish to outline several reasons why a nonsubordinate relationship to the state (including loans, or donations of construction materials) need not undermine autonomy.

First, in cases like this, the state is responding to social and collective pressure from the movements themselves. The movements demand and the state concedes, to use the state's own language, loans or materials or technical assistance. Second, the construction of Acapatzingo was the product of years of negotiation and pressure that permitted construction on twice the area originally approved by the state, thanks to family and community labor. Something similar took place with the construction of water and sewer lines, for which the community provided labor and the state provided materials.

This was, then, a relationship between two powers, neither of which was subjugated by the other.

Third, the Acapatzingo community was able to discuss its own project with the state's technicians, proposing solutions to break bureaucratic impasses set by the government's policies and practices. This debate and exchange with the technicians is a key point, since in many experiences of cooperative housing construction in Latin America the technical and "professional" issues are left outside the control of communities (Programa Regional de Vivienda y Hábitat, 2012). Lastly, it is important to note that although community is not synonymous with autonomy, the existence of solid, active organizations, with rotation of tasks and spaces of a communal character, typically strengthens and empowers the autonomous action of collective subjects. In this sense, community life is itself a skill that can improve the life of its members by giving them knowledge and capacity that they previously did not have.

To be sure, as in all human organizations, in the communities there is oppression. In communities in resistance, whether rural like the Zapatistas or urban like Acapatzingo, oppression is not hidden: it is out in the open, and can be addressed, particularly in the case of generational and gender oppression that impacts young people and women. In many activities in which I participated, I could see that women spoke up in discussions three or four times more than men, something that distinguishes Acapatzingo even from other urban communities in resistance, where men usually are the ones who speak even when the majority of inhabitants are female.

While there is a strong gender division of labor in the community, many jobs that in capitalist society are solely female are part of the collective work set out in the *reglamento*, so while women may be in the majority, they are not the sole participants. This is the case, for example, for cleaning and maintenance, for gardens, and for health and education. These activities are not considered inferior to salaried or "productive" work. The community has some ability to regulate and intervene in family matters and in situations of domestic violence. Reproductive work is not devalued or made invisible.

Urban communities have their limits and problems. They are framed by urban life, the nucleus of the power of the dominant classes, of the repressive apparatus of the state, of the mafias, and of consumer culture. They cannot secure their subsistence without joining the outside labor market, since they lack sufficient land for self-sufficiency in food. On the other hand, they can more readily establish alliances with health and education professionals, as the FPFVI communities have done.

The most significant critique comes from those who downplay local experiences as insufficient to resolve the problems of humanity. David Harvey (2012, 184), for instance, recently launched a harsh attack on radical democracy and horizontality as concepts that "can function well in small groups but which cannot be applied at the scale of a metropolitan area, not to mention the seven billion people who currently inhabit the planet." In my view, this position has two major problems, one regarding the construction of the subject, and the second regarding the kind of transition that is imagined and promoted.

Academics typically refer to subjects, or to antisystem movements, in very general terms, without taking into account that these actors can only take shape in concrete spaces and in concrete relations, in other words, in spatial and temporal settings relatively controlled by subalterns. In other eras these settings were, at least in cities, the factory, the tavern, the neighborhood, the church, or the university. The system has sought to destroy these settings, whether by repression or by commodification. In the current reality of capitalism, people who would participate in movements must create settings in which to relate and rediscover (starting with themselves), to exchange experiences, and to construct a collective subject through community radio stations, cultural and interest groups, even the community gardens that Harvey (2013) mocks—in short, in any space that is born in opposition to the dominant culture. Militants are not formed by reading classic or even current authors—although that reading can be useful at a later stage—but by doing and sharing.

The second question is about how the transition to a different world should occur. If we imagine a transition that can take charge of common goods on a global scale, we are thinking of a state-directed transition that changes things from the top. This has never happened and it is not a plausible future; in any event, it is just more "Enlightenment" Eurocentric thinking. It seems necessary to reflect on other transitions, such as the movement from feudalism to capitalism, a transition that took many centuries and was not directed but rather chaotic, not linear but progressive, and full of uprisings, insurrections, and revolutions.

We are going through the final phase of the world system, and of U.S. domination, and all the evidence—including environmental—suggests that it will be a disordered transition, one that will take the form of disintegration. This will be painful, but it can create the conditions for reconstruction on new foundations (Wallerstein 1998). In this reconstruction, urban and rural communities in resistance will play a relevant role, and can serve as a decisive point of reference for the society of the future. Something like this has happened several times before in history. To get to this new world, we should work to deepen, improve, and expand the handful of truly autonomous communities.

NOTE

The chapter was translated by Richard Stoller.

Chapter Four

Mexico

*Political Cultures, Youth Activism, and the Legacy of the
Oaxacan Social Movement of 2006*

Maurice Rafael Magaña

For six months in 2006, a broad-based social movement exercised grassroots control over the capital city of the southern Mexican state of Oaxaca.[1] Originally formed in response to government repression of a strike by the local wing of the National Education Worker's Union, the movement came to include over 300 existing social movements and organizations, as well as individuals without such affiliations or previous organizing experience. The movement, which has been called the first insurrection of the twenty-first century, brought together an incredibly diverse set of actors with different experiences, norms, political agendas, and visions of social change.[2] This included those activists who had been politically formed through their militancy in vertical organizations such as leftist opposition groups and labor unions, as well as libertarian,[3] anarchist, and autonomist youth who vehemently rejected any form of hierarchical organizing. In this chapter, I will offer an ethnographic account of how these vertical and horizontal organizing forms and norms operated simultaneously in the context of the social movement of 2006.

The movement lost control of the city in late 2006 following a sustained and violent campaign of paramilitary and police repression. Attempts to hold the movement together post-2006 proved difficult, as internal fractures were deepened by the government's dual strategy of repression and co-optation. These pressures, coupled with the loss of territory, caused currents within the movement to move in different, sometimes complementary and at other times contradictory directions. Importantly, however, the history of the Oax-

67

acan social movement does not end in 2006. I argue that the horizontalism experimented with during the grassroots takeover continues to be honed through subsequent youth political and cultural projects that are part of the movement's legacy. Youth participated in various capacities during the social movement, including erecting and managing a citywide network of barricades, creating protest art, participating in movement-run radio stations, video documenting and disseminating, and forming the frontlines in self-defense and defense of territory against attacks by police and paramilitary forces. Youth translated these experiences into the formation of political and cultural collectives rooted in the horizontal organizing logics and ideals that were part of the experiential knowledge they gained during the grassroots takeover.

Horizontalidad, translated as horizontalism or horizontality, is both the goal and tool for social movements that attempt to construct the horizontal (flattening out of) social relations they seek in the present. Horizontalism "involves—or at least intentionally strives towards—non-hierarchical and anti-authoritarian creation rather than reaction. It is a break with vertical ways of organizing and relating" (Sitrin 2006, 3). Importantly, horizontalism is a dynamic process and not a static outcome to be achieved, celebrated, and then abandoned. In this chapter, I argue that the social movement of 2006 served as a self-organizing incubator for a culture and practice of horizontalism that activists continue to experiment with years later. Youth activists who came of political age through their varied participation in this social movement have been important in carrying on the horizontal politics of the movement beyond 2006. In this chapter, I will focus on the vital role that youth played in expanding the horizontal dimensions of the movement during the six months of grassroots control in 2006. The production of social movement spaces that were organized around antiauthoritarian and participatory decision making was a crucial aspect of the expansion of horizontalism within the movement.

AUTHORITARIANISM AND GRASSROOTS ORGANIZING IN OAXACA

Oaxaca is a mostly rural state in southern Mexico, rich in natural resources and ethnic diversity. It is home to sixteen Indigenous groups, each with its own language and culture, making it both the most diverse state in Mexico and home to the most Indigenous language speakers in the country. Similarly, the state has the highest percentage of communally owned land in the country, and the Indigenous communal assembly is officially recognized as the decision-making structure in 418 of the 571 municipalities in the state, meaning that governance through political parties and electoral politics takes place in a minority of municipalities (Esteva 2010, 982).

Although the state remains mostly rural, the neoliberal abandonment of the countryside (i.e., massive cuts in subsidies and price supports for small- to medium-scale farmers) over the past two decades or so has led to massive migration to urban centers and large-scale agriculture centers throughout Mexico and the United States.[4] Over that same time, Oaxaca has seen a proliferation of grassroots, Indigenous, women's, peasant, urban, youth, student, and labor organizing movements. Notable among these have been struggles to democratize labor unions (Cook 1996; Zafra, Hernández-Díaz, and Zepeda 2002), the right to Indigenous self-determination and control over local development (Campbell 1994; Howe 2011; Rubin 1997), access to education (Rénique 2007; Zafra, Hernández-Díaz, and Zepeda 2002) as well as the development of community and alternative media (Stephen 2013; Zires 2009). These organizing efforts by civil society have been met by increasingly authoritarian state and national regimes that enforce unpopular policies and repress dissenting voices. Especially important when considering the social movement of 2006 is the fact that political violence and political arrests in Oaxaca were widespread under then governor Ulises Ruiz, and his predecessor, José Múrat (Martínez Vásquez 2007).[5]

Most political struggles in Oaxaca, at one point or another, manifest themselves in urban public space. Even though local politics have long been brokered through local caciques (political bosses), the official institutions of the state have been housed in the historic center of Oaxaca City since colonial times. For this reason, political conflicts throughout the state often result in marches, roadblocks, and/or encampments in the center of Oaxaca City, with the *zócalo* (main square) being the most regular target. Part of this is because the Palacio de Gobierno (state capitol building) has been housed in the *zócalo* for centuries. This changed, however, when Governor Ulises Ruiz took office in 2004. One of his first acts was to relocate the executive branch from the *zócalo* of the capital city to Tlalistac de Cabrera, a town outside of the city where the new Ciudad Administrativa (Administrative City) currently sits behind large metal fences and armed guards. His reasoning for doing so was clear, yet ultimately unsuccessful—to avoid encampments in the *zócalo* (Díaz Montes 2009). The investment in public space, by both protesters and government, highlights the centrality of public space as a significant terrain for politics and the exercise, negotiation, and contestation of power.

One of the most powerful organizing forces in Oaxaca has been Sección 22 (Local 22)—the local dissident wing of the National Education Workers' Union (SNTE). The SNTE is the largest and arguably most powerful labor union in Latin America with 1.2 million members, although the administration of President Enrique Peña Nieto threatens to weaken the union with neoliberal educational reforms and the February 2013 imprisonment of longtime leader Elba Esther Gordillo (Hérnandez Navarro 2013).[6] Originally formed in 1943 under the corporatist system of the postrevolutionary Mexican state, the teachers' union was granted a monopoly on representing all of the nation's educational workers in primary and secondary schools, and like other "favored" unions their membership was converted into vast electoral reserves to be tapped during election cycles (Monroy 1997). Gordillo continued this legacy of corporatism during her tenure as the head of the SNTE, where she was largely seen as a corrupt leader who served the Institutional Revolutionary Party (PRI) and their interests above that of rank-and-file teachers or students. Teachers in Oaxaca, however, have been part of a national struggle to democratize the union, a struggle that has lasted over forty years and has cost over one hundred teachers their lives in Oaxaca alone (Bacon 2006; Cook 1996). Political scientist Jonathan Fox refers to this strategy of fostering, co-opting, and repressing unions in Mexico as part of the Mexican government's system of "authoritarian clientelism" (1994). In 1979, the struggle to democratize the union led to the formation of the democratic caucus within the SNTE, the National Education Workers Coordinating Committee (CNTE).

Local 22 of the CNTE, Oaxaca's dissident wing of the teachers' union, has mobilized its membership of over 70,000 teachers on an annual basis for the past three decades in order to pressure the state to renegotiate their contracts. On May 1, 2006, Local 22 continued this tradition and mobilized in Oaxaca City, presenting the government with a list of demands for a new round of contract negotiations. The list contained seventeen demands including the restructuring of wages, classrooms/schoolhouses for rural communities where teachers were forced to teach outdoors, scholarships, and uniforms and shoes for low-income students (Martínez Vásquez 2007, 60). That year, however, Governor Ulises Ruiz refused to enter into meaningful negotiations with the union. He entered office with a hard-line stance against protests, declaring an end to sit-ins and marches. Instead of negotiating, Ruiz launched a media campaign aimed at turning public opinion against the teachers. Union officials also accused the secretary general of the state of fomenting internal divisions within the union. Most notably, union leader Enrique Rueda Pacheco was widely believed to have accepted bribes from the government.

On May 22, 2006, Local 22 set up an encampment in the *zócalo*, and on May 31 the members mobilized and blocked access to gas stations and main roads in the historic downtown area of the capital. At this point public opinion was divided, as many people seemed to be as tired of the frequent protests by the teachers as they were skeptical of the governor, who entered office amid widespread allegations of fraud. On a national level, attention was largely focused on the highly contested presidential elections to be held on July 2. Felipe Calderón was declared president-elect, although he entered the presidency on very weak political footing amid widespread popular protest and allegations of electoral fraud. Parallel to the elections, the Zapatistas spearheaded La Otra Campaña, a project meant to strengthen connections between communities, groups, and social movements in Mexico as an alternative to the process of political party campaigns. Also in May of that year San Salvador Atenco, a town near Mexico City, was besieged by state and federal police after residents set up roadblocks in support of flower vendors who were attacked by police. The government responded to this act of solidarity by sending in police, who, according to a 2008 human rights report, killed two youths, arrested over 200 people and sexually assaulted and tortured forty-seven female detainees (Comisión Civil Internacional de Observación por los Derechos Humanos 2008, 15). The swiftness and brutality with which the state responded can be partially explained by the fact that Atenco was already a beacon of hope for social movements and communities in resistance. In 2002 residents of Atenco formed the People's Front in Defense of the Land (Frente del Pueblo en Defensa de la Tierra) and successfully resisted the federal government's attempt to displace them in order to construct a new airport on their land (Arellano Chávez 2010; Gibler 2009). The siege of Atenco in 2006, the contested presidential elections, and the momentum surrounding La Otra Campaña are all significant background for understanding the importance of the social movement that emerged that summer in Oaxaca and the brutal response by local, state, and federal government.

THE OAXACAN SOCIAL MOVEMENT OF 2006

It is in this context of ongoing struggle that the 2006 social movement emerged, giving surprising coherence to the grievances of a highly diverse segment of Oaxacan society. The final action that triggered the formation of this social movement occurred during the very early morning hours of June 14, 2006, when police forces numbering anywhere from 870 to 3,000 officers (Osorno 2007; Martínez Vásquez 2007) violently removed sleeping teachers and their families from the encampment in the *zócalo*. Police used batons, dogs, guns, and tear gas launched from privately owned helicopters on the sleeping teachers. The indiscriminate bombing of the area with tear gas left hundreds of people seeking refuge and medical assistance—including many nonteachers who lived, worked, or had other business in the busy downtown area that morning. The police repression resulted in 113 people registering at local hospitals with injuries ranging from gunshot wounds to miscarriages and perforated lungs (Martínez Vásquez 2007, 66).

In addition to the encampment, the union had a radio station called Radio Plantón, which served as a parallel public space to that of the encampment.

According to Margarita Zires, a professor of communications and politics, once the union set up its encampment in the *zócalo* on May 22 "this radio began to convert itself into an important voice of the Movement, a alternative media public space . . . it formed part of the milieu of the encampment in the *zócalo*" (2009, 164). In fact, the radio warned of the possibility of a police action directed at clearing the encampment in the days leading up to June 14. When the time came and the police attacked the encampment, they also attacked the teachers' union headquarters and the radio tower, taking the station off the air.

The governor's decision to repress the teachers immediately backfired, however. Many people who were not otherwise sympathetic to the teachers union joined them and their supporters in the streets, and by midday they retook the *zócalo* (Sotelo Marbén 2008). The coalition that formed that day included a wide range of people and organizations with varied agendas and motivations for participating. For example, a retired nurse I spoke with named Doña Inés[7] lent her medical services to those in need on June 14 at an impromptu medical clinic set up at a nearby church. She made a point of emphasizing that she had always been "apolitical" and not necessarily in agreement with Local 22's tactics, although she respected the rank-and-file teachers and had family members who were active in the union. Her support that day and in the following months was borne out of the outrage she shared with many *Oaxaqueños* when they learned of the indiscriminate and unprovoked use of force ordered by the governor. On the other end of the spectrum, many of those who came to the defense of the teachers following their eviction from the *zócalo* were youth. Some helped repel the police and retake the *zócalo* because they had family members who were teachers; others lived nearby and were affected by the indiscriminate tear-gassing that morning; yet others participated in large part because of an antagonistic relationship with police that predated the movement.

The participation of graffiti artists and punks, for example, has particular antecedents as many of them were already accustomed to being profiled, arrested, and mistreated by police. The criminalization of their lifestyles and of their very bodies has marked many of them deeply, as has their social marginalization. Several *graffiteros* and punks mentioned their relationships with police prior to 2006 as part of the reason they were ready and willing to be at the frontlines of battles with police on June 14 and in the months and years that followed. A young man who has been a part of the "punk movement" since he was a teenager in the early 2000s explained his participation on June 14 to me in an interview several years later—he asked to be cited as *Mentes Liberadas* (Liberated Minds):

> Before that [repression of June 14] we were already coming down to the
> *zócalo*, to the teachers' encampment. There, we would run into people from

other collectives and from our own collective, CESOL [Social Libertarian Center]. We were already on the lookout because there were always the rumors that they were going to be evicted from their encampment and all of that. When the repression started on June 14 . . . a friend called me, it must have been 5:30 or 6:00 in the morning and he asked me if I was ready because the repression had begun. By that time we were already living here [a popular neighborhood in the Northwest outskirts of the city], so I got on my bicycle and rode towards downtown. Once I arrived, I ditched the bike and joined the teachers. When I arrived, I saw several friends and thought "Holy shit this is really it!" It was cool, you know. It lasted several hours; I think it was around 11:00 a.m. that we were able to recover the *zócalo*. In my opinion what motivated the *banda*[8] to go and support the teachers [was that] we were sick and tired of so much repression. That was the moment for all of us to show them that we were fed up with so much injustice by all pouncing at the same time against the police. They were the ones who were always fucking with us. This way we would show the government that it wasn't cool to keep doing what they were doing anymore.

Overwhelmed by the sheer numbers of people who mobilized against them, the police returned to their barracks and refused to take further action against protesters. Teachers reestablished their encampment in the city's *zócalo* but were now joined by other formal organizations and youth collectives who also set up encampments. Simultaneously, university students at the Benito Juárez Autonomous University of Oaxaca (UABJO) organized the takeover of their university's radio station, Radio Universidad. This radio station proved to be as crucial for the emerging movement as Radio Plantón had been for the teachers, helping organize actions and mobilizations. Two days after the police attacks, hundreds of thousands of Oaxacans participated in a massive march demanding the governor's removal.

On June 17, the teachers union convened a public assembly, inviting over 300 organizations and movements who were active in Oaxaca to discuss how best to capitalize on the momentum generated over the past days. The teachers proposed extending the structure of their union's assembly-style decision-making body, the State Assembly of Local 22 Delegates, to the larger Oaxacan civil society (Martínez Vásquez 2007). They called the new organizing structure the Asamblea Popular de los Pueblos de Oaxaca (Popular Assembly of the Peoples of Oaxaca, or APPO).[9] The assembly is far from a union invention; it has a long and dynamic history in Oaxaca as the main decision-making structure in a majority of the state's municipalities where Indigenous communities are governed by *usos y costumbres* (Indigenous customary law and tradition). While the APPO assembly was far more inclusive than the existing political institutions of the state, it was largely dominated by organizations that brought preexisting, often vertical, political practices and agendas to the movement. It should also be mentioned that youth, women, and unmarried men are often barred from participating in community assemblies, and while such exclusions were not explicit, many of the social forces behind them were replicated in the APPO assembly. For example, with one notable exception youth were largely excluded from participating, and the assembly was dominated by an aggressive masculine style of debate that alienated many people who had not been formed in such political cultures.

After the first meeting, the assembly agreed on the resignation of Ruiz as their principal demand, though it would be a mistake to limit the grievances of the APPO to this single goal (Osorno 2007). The APPO also pushed for a new state constitution that represented the pluralism of the state and demanded an end to the repression of political dissent. The APPO was the main organizing structure and "civic space" of the movement, made up of large numbers of civic organizations, nonprofits, and political associations and organizations, all with diverse agendas (Esteva 2010). It is important, however, to acknowledge that many individuals and collectives who participated in the movement did not necessarily identify as *appistas* (APPO members). For this reason it is important not to conflate the broader social movement of 2006 with the APPO. This is an especially pertinent distinction when considering participation of youth who identified as libertarian or anarchist, and others who participated in the more horizontal spaces of the movement but rejected the more formal spaces that tended to privilege established organizations, activists, and political styles.

Ultimately, through both horizontal and vertical organizing, the movement was able to control the capital city of Oaxaca from June to November of 2006. During those six months of popular control, the movement held cultural events, massive mobilizations, and executed state functions such as policing, trash collection, and governance, and also the transmitted original grassroots radio and television programming throughout the state, and internationally via the Internet. These channels became widely accessible after a group of several hundred women marched to the main public radio and television station and requested airtime. When they were denied airtime, they decided to take over the public station. A teacher named Maribel[10] explained the situation leading up to the takeover:

> Unfortunately, the media always says that nothing is happening in Oaxaca—this is because they are all bribed by the government. This is why we women took *Canal 9.* We had to tell our side of the story. We had to show that yes, there is something happening in Oaxaca and it is not what the bad government or its media say. We Oaxacan women had to take the TV and radio to show that in our state *el pueblo* stood up and said, "Enough, we have had enough of this corruption, of this violence, of these bad politicians."

With support from fellow activists in the movement, women maintained control of the station for several weeks. Eventually, however, paramilitary forces succeeded in destroying the transmission towers. The movement responded by taking over the remaining thirteen radio stations in Oaxaca. Movement-run radio and television stations were essential for internal and external communication, but they were also central mediums for grassroots participation in the movement and for public visibility for women, youth, Indigenous language speakers, and other marginalized groups who otherwise lacked access to such forums. In addition to the radio and television stations, youth denounced government repression and advertised popular resistance in Oaxaca through political street art, which covered the city and was highly visible for local, national, and global audiences.[11] Through these actions, the popular movement reclaimed, reconfigured, and redefined public spaces and severely challenged the government's ability to govern.

YOUTH AND SPACES OF HORIZONTALITY

Movements like the Oaxacan social movement of 2006 offer valuable lessons for those interested in the study and practice of social movements, especially in relation to the potential of horizontalism in social movement organizing, as well as the challenges involved in such emergent organizing forms. Elsewhere (Magaña 2010), I analyze the simultaneity of vertical and horizontal organizing logics in the Oaxacan social movement of 2006 through the framework of what Arturo Escobar (2008) and Manuel De Landa (1997) call meshworks. The meshwork lens allows us to follow the parallel power structures operating within the Oaxacan social movement in order to appreciate how they act to yield a total effect. Here, I focus on the important role that youth played in developing and advancing horizontalism within the social movement and within Oaxacan popular politics more generally. In the paragraphs that follow, I offer examples of how youth participation in a citywide network of barricades in 2006 prefigured an emergent horizontalism.

An essential element that allowed the social movement to maintain control of Oaxaca City for six months was a citywide network of barricades. Numbering some 1,500, the barricades were originally raised as part of a grassroots strategy of self-defense and protection for the antennas of the radio and television stations that women from the movement had taken over. They were erected between 8:00 and 11:00 p.m. every night, and most were removed every morning at 6:00 a.m. to allow traffic to circulate, although some were more permanent, especially after the mass deployment of the Federal Preventive Police (PFP) in late October who were sent by the federal government to retake the city and disarticulate the movement. Neighbors gathered rocks, tires, downed trees, cars, commandeered buses, and semi-trailers, or whatever objects they could acquire to build the barricades.

The dense network of horizontally organized barricades provided the physical space for many young people and others with little or no previous organizing experience to foster a sense of ownership in the movement. If you lived in an urban or peri-urban neighborhood you could participate in the growing movement without even leaving your neighborhood. This was especially important for those for whom the political rhetoric or aggressive style of established opposition groups that dominated the more formal spaces of the movement did not resonate. This was the case for many young activists who were not accustomed to this style of politics, and as Lynn Stephen (2013, 249) documents, the "sometimes nasty debate discouraged people who came from rural and Indigenous communities" as well. In many of the barricades, however, it was families, neighborhoods, anarchist youth collectives, and graffiti crews, *not* opposition parties, unions, or NGOs, that served as the main organizing forces.

For many, the barricades served as an entrée into the movement. Silvia, a young woman who was active in the social movement, explained her involvement to me in 2010:

> Many of us met for the first time in the barricades in 2006 . . . . the barricades became part of my daily life but they were also part of a greater strategy. That was how we protected ourselves and the radio, but also how we showed, through our civil disobedience, that the government could not govern the city. [12]

Silvia migrated to the city from a town in the *Costa* (coastal) region of the state, and was studying sociology at the public state university in 2006. Her involvement with the movement began as a researcher, but one of the most important barricades in the city, Cinco Señores, blocked the entrance to her neighborhood so she passed through it every day. As she began spending more time there with her neighbors, her participation soon changed from researcher to *barricadera* (participant in the barricades). In the above quote, Silvia makes the important point that beyond the practical strategy of self-defense and defense of territory, the barricades were a symbol to the government, media, and local residents that signaled popular control of the city. Moreover, the barricades acted as hubs for local, grassroots control of territory. In the barricades, people were not subject to the political will of external forces but rather made decisions among themselves in response to their needs, desires, and principles.

The barricades quickly became community spaces where neighbors who may have never spoken before would spend all night drinking coffee, eating, dancing, and talking while reclaiming the streets, their neighborhoods, the historic city center, and their right to be free from violence. As the street is a basic unit of public life, an everyday public space where people are brought together to interact (Tonkiss 2005), it is not surprising that the reclaiming and reconfiguring of Oaxaca's streets in 2006 proved to be a transformative

experience for the countless people who participated. The raising and guard-
ing of barricades turned strangers into comrades, and turned neighborhood
residents into active participants in radical direct-democracy, a dynamic that
Dace Dzenovska and Iván Arenas describe as "barricade sociality" (2012,
646).

The social space created by the barricades provided a laboratory for experimenting with the alternative, nonhierarchical social relations that are
integral to practices of horizontality. These spaces were extended in subsequent youth projects, which Silvia alludes to above when she states that
"many of us met for the first time in the barricades." She is referring to the
fact that she and other youth who met through their participation in the
barricades formed what proved to be one of the most prominent (youth)
collectives to emerge from the movement, VOCAL (Oaxacan Voices Constructing Autonomy and Liberty) in 2007. VOCAL provides an organizing
space where young activists continue to hone the praxis of horizontalism that
emerged in the barricades.

Graffiti artists also played an important role in the movement, partially
through their artwork in the barricades, which served to demarcate territory
and disseminate news. When I asked members of local street art crews Arte
Jaguar and AK Crew about their participation in the barricades in a group
interview in 2010, several mentioned being asked by their neighbors to contribute pieces to their barricades. One of the artists who belongs to both
crews, and lives in the colonia of Pueblo Nuevo, remembers painting a piece
at his neighborhood barricade:

> I was at the barricade the first day of the *desmadre* [PFP repression]. I painted
> a semi-trailer for the people of my barrio because they asked me, since they
> knew that I painted, "Why don't you paint something over here, in the barrio?"
> I said "Of course!" [It read] *¡Viva Pueblo Nuevo! Oaxaca, Mexico* . . . I
> remember vividly, it had a woman with her fist raised, and the damn phrase
> took up the whole trailer.

Arte Jaguar was one of the more prolific and respected street art crews in
Oaxaca at the time the social movement emerged. Members came mostly
from *colonias* throughout the city, although some were migrants to the city
from Indigenous villages. As a collective, members were weary of being
labeled as "political artists" or of having their work pigeonholed to 2006.
Like many graffiti artists, however, they were active in the social movement
as artists, barricader@s[13] and in confrontations with the police. In fact, the
barricades became rich sites for the production and display of graffiti and
other public visual art, as well as grievances and words of protest scrawled
on any available surface. Testimonies like the one quoted above remind us
that the cultural and social space of the barricade, where community elders
validated youth participation, was vital in fostering a sense of youth owner-

ship in the movement, their neighborhoods, and the city. This collective experience and sense of belonging for otherwise marginalized youth proved to be transformative, not only for youth but also for the expansion of the social movement beyond the more formal spaces of the teachers' union and the APPO.

In addition to being an entrée into the struggle for many, the network of barricades, along with a series of occupied radio and television stations taken over by women in the movement, were crucial in deepening the grassroots power of the movement, which encompassed broad sectors of Oaxacan society cutting across vast differences and geographies. Oaxaca-based intellectual Gustavo Esteva supports this view of the barricades:

> The sudden presence in the movement of groups from the popular neighborhoods . . . was unexpected. It was not known to what extent the communal social fabric also existed in those neighborhoods. The barricades arose spontaneously as a popular response to the governor's attacks on the APPO encampments, and rapidly took on a life of their own, to the extent of becoming autonomous focal points for social and political organization. Long sleepless nights provided the opportunity for extensive political discussion, which awakened in many young people a hitherto nonexistent or inchoate social consciousness. (2010, 985)

Esteva highlights the importance of the barricades in fostering the participation of Oaxaca's popular neighborhood residents and youth in particular. While I am cautious about overstating the "nonexistent or inchoate social consciousness" of young people pre-2006, young people in Mexico are among the most vulnerable to the impacts of the recent global economic crisis and the neoliberal assault on social programs and public education. In fact, the current generation of youth in Mexico carries with them the stigma of being referred to as the generation of "*Ninis—ni estudian, ni trabajan*" (they don't study, they don't work). The implication is that the marginalization of Mexican youth is a result of their own laziness and complacency, not the effect of global economic restructuring and neoliberal policies. For poor and working-class youth in Oaxaca there were (and continue to be) very few spaces open to them where they could feel their participation was legitimized by larger Oaxacan society. It was in this social milieu that youth with diverse levels of political training and organizing experience found a space for meaningful participation in the barricades.

The way that barricader@s organize today is greatly influenced by their experiences in the barricades. Instead of replicating age, race, gender, class, and other existing social hierarchies, the more radical barricades were social movement spaces where everyday Oaxacans were able to construct new social relations and identities based on principles of inclusiveness and equity. People began to identify as being from Barricade X or Barricade Y, and among youth we see the emergence of an identity as "barricader@s," or participants in the barricades, which continues to carry significant social capital. A young activist named Monika, for example, remembered the horizontal power produced in the barricades as one of the more important legacies of the social movement:

> I think that all of us that are in the movement, that are still in the movement, were and are barricader@s. That is where we come from. That is where we learned so many things . . . things that I had never done before nor could have imagined doing. That is where the people came together and when it was time to act, and if we all felt it was correct, we would do it. Even if, for example, [Local 22 leader Enrique] Rueda Pacheco tried to stop us.

The grassroots power produced in these moments, when the barricader@s chose actions that challenged the leadership class of organizations, strengthened horizontal relations created in the barricades. These kinds of alternative, counterhegemonic relations are much more difficult to produce from within established organizations and movements where existing social inequalities tend to become entrenched and reproduced, despite the most sincere of revolutionary intentions. In 2010, I asked a VOCAL activist named Daniel, who participated in the barricades, what is was like to mobilize and organize alongside individuals and organizations that were used to having a leadership class, and he responded:

> That would be the organic or structural part of the Popular Assembly of the Peoples of Oaxaca. That [space] was mostly formed by people who were already organized by organizations that have been around for many years. Many of them already had the vices that were taking shape here in Oaxaca. It's a way of interacting that is very complicated, in part because it was such a wide spectrum of organizations that were found within the organizing structure within the APPO . . . what we tried to do and what we keep trying to do, is to stay faithful to the principles of the movement: no negotiating with the government; no participating in political parties; and seeking profound change. These are things that do not agree with the agendas of the more visible members of the organizations. It has been a give-and-take within the assembly but ultimately the consensus has been to stay faithful to the principles of the movement.

When Daniel speaks of the "vices" entrenched in more established organizations within the APPO, he is referring to the complicated history of authoritarian clientelism, whereby the Mexican government fosters or co-opts those organized sectors that it finds politically useful and represses those that are not (Fox 1994). This strategy has given rise to a particular political culture where groups with enough political capital know that if they mobilize their membership, the government will likely offer them economic and/or political concessions. Depending on the organization, the concessions may or may not be distributed among the bases. Through collectives like VOCAL, young activists attempt to decenter the state by focusing their organizing energy and power toward the creation of horizontal relations between various sectors of society (locally, nationally and internationally). In doing so, collectives like VOCAL are extending the horizontal, participatory political culture that emerged from the barricades in 2006.

Importantly, some activists who contributed to the development of horizontalism in the barricades had previous experience organizing in leaderless movements. Mentes Liberadas, the young man from the punk movement who I cited early, shared his history of activism with me as follows:

> We are from the punk movement . . . in the punk movement is where I actually found what I was looking for, which is an autonomous movement, a libertarian movement where there are no leaders, where I can contribute. Where I could build a fanzine, a flyer and distribute it, build a pamphlet and make it move. Where I could express myself against something without the necessity of having to report my actions to anyone or having a leader who would tell me what to do and where to go. It's not like that [in the punk movement]. What I enjoyed about it was collective participation, getting together with various people, exchanging points of view about the things that actually mattered to us. And in doing so, none of us who were involved at the time were after power or profit where if we do this then the government will sit us down to negotiate and they will say to us "Here's the deal, I will give you this amount of money, now go relax." These were the things we didn't want. Before 2006 we already had a participation, [we have been active] since about 2000 . . . I was 16 or 17 years old.

Mentes Liberadas began his testimony speaking about collectivity and belonging. He makes clear that the punk movement is not just about a particular aesthetic or music but that it is about social and political participation. He stressed this point frequently, using the word *participación* (participation) and the phrase *tener una participación* (to have a participation) repeatedly during our two-and-a-half-hour interview. He spent a lot of time talking about his early involvement in the punk movement and various collectives such as Centro Social Libertario[14] (Social Libertarian Center or CESOL) pre-2006. He was making clear that his political participation did not begin in 2006 and that the space opened by the punk movement for youth like himself to participate on their own terms, without an imposed agenda or leadership, were key aspects of what attracted him to the movement.

While the punk movement was an important antecedent for leaderless horizontal organizing among young people before 2006, the barricades provided an important space for horizontalism within the 2006 social movement. In a published interview, David Venegas, one of the few members of the APPO Council who was a youth activist and who was a founding member of

VOCAL, described the impact that the barricades had in decentering the formal spaces of the movement and expanding the more horizontal spaces:

> That's when my participation, along with the participation of hundreds of thousands of others, began to make a more substantial difference. . . . We eventually started discussing agreements and decisions made by the APPO Council and the teachers' union. There were a number of occasions when the barricade chose actions that went against those agreements, which in my view only strengthened our capacity for organized resistance. In this way, the barricades reestablished and modified the social fabric of the neighborhoods. (quoted in Denham et al. 2008, 290–91).

Here, David contrasts the horizontal decision making at the barricades to the top-down practice of the "APPO Council and the teachers' union," which speaks to some of the tensions within the movement that led youth to form their own spaces built on more horizontal models experimented with in the barricades. David's analysis echoes Monika's and Gustavo Esteva's in terms of the role that the barricades played in expanding the horizontal power of the movement. David grounds the long-term impacts of the barricades in the city's *colonias* vis-á-vis novel and strengthened social relations. Subsequent organizing efforts by movement youth, such as VOCAL, seek to extend these social relations to greater Oaxacan society and political organizing.

During a discussion in February 2010 at a youth-run cultural and political center named CASOTA (Autonomous Oaxacan Solidarity House for Self-Managed Work), David again referred to the tensions between the horizontal and vertical structures within the APPO. He described an occasion when the APPO Council entered into negotiations with the government and offered to remove the barricades, even though the government had yet to address any of the movement's demands. David explained:

> People who claimed to speak on behalf of the assembly told us [at the Brenamiel barricade] to let the ADO [private bus company] through because they had come to an agreement with them. *Ni madres* (fuck that) we told them! We took control of this street and they are not going through here. If you want them to go through, let them through the streets that you have taken.

In November of 2006, following one of the more violent battles with federal police, the barricade in Silvia's neighborhood (Cinco Señores) produced a flyer addressing the issue of ongoing negotiations with the state. In it, the authors criticize the APPO Council for offering to remove the barricades without consulting the barricades as collective actors. The authors go on to acknowledge the need to engage the state, particularly in order to end the repression, but denounce the fact that the council acted unilaterally without consulting the barricades. This was just one of several moments when the competing logics of vertical and horizontal organizing within the movement proved to be contradictory. These were important moments, however, where the horizontalism practiced in later projects such as VOCAL and CASOTA was honed in action and in contrast to the vertical models exhibited in other movement spaces. These examples, both of what youth activists want and don't want, continue to serve as important reference points as they continue the difficult project of enacting social relations that break with the dominant relations in society that perpetuate hierarchy and privilege.

YOUTH AND SOCIAL MOVEMENT LEGACIES

The social movement that emerged in Oaxaca in 2006 underwent many fractures, mutations, and revivals in the years following the grassroots takeover of the capital city. A combination of brutal repression, co-optation, and internal divisions has left participants with very different understandings of the movement's impact and legacy. Some participants remain disillusioned that key figures and organizations sold out the movement for personal gain, and feel that the opportunity to create real change was lost when they lost physical control of city. Others are convinced that the movement never died, that it is alive in the collective conscience of all who were touched by the extraordinary events of 2006, and that when the time is right, people will again take to the streets to continue what they started. I argue that focusing on the projects of youth activists that emerged out of the social movement provides a window into the movement's legacy.

Many of the youth who helped erect and maintain the citywide network of barricades continued organizing after the Mexican federal police crushed the barricades in late 2006. VOCAL, for example, was formed in 2007 and brought together dozens of youth from various barricades, and provided them with an organizing space through which they could continue forging and strengthening a sociality and politics based on horizontalism and grassroots power. The physical and social spaces produced though reappropriated public space was essential for the incubation of an emergent horizontalism in 2006, but collectives such as VOCAL provided laboratories for the process to continue once occupying that space became unsustainable. It is through the horizontalism that youth and other participants in the social movement continue to expand and reshape, that the legacy of the Oaxacan movement lives on.

NOTES

1. I was afforded the time, space, and intellectual support for the writing of this chapter thanks to an Institute of American Cultures Postdoctoral Fellowship through the Chicano Studies Research Center at the University of California, Los Angeles, as well as support from a

Ford Foundation Dissertation Fellowship and the Visiting Scholars Program at the Center for U.S.-Mexican Studies at the University of California, San Diego. The Wenner-Gren Foundation and the Tokyo Foundation funded the fieldwork on which this chapter is based. I would also like to thank Lynn Stephen, Maylei Blackwell, Sandra Morgen, Lamia Karim, Daniel Martinez HoSang, Juan Herrera, the editors of this volume and the anonymous reviewers for their feedback on different versions of this work.

2. See Osorno (2007) for claims of the Oaxacan social movement being the first insurrection of the twenty-first century.

3. In this study, libertarian reflects my translation of activists' own identification as being *libertario/a*; this does not coincide with the libertarianism found in the Libertarian Party or certain sectors of the Tea Party Movement in the United States, which emphasize the rights of the individual and fiscal conservatism. Rather, libertarians in this study are more in line with a libertarian-socialism and in some cases use the labels "libertarian/ism" and "anarchist/ism" interchangeably.

4. See Cohen (2004), Kearney (1996), and Stephen (2007) for more on Oaxacan migration.

5. See also Comisión Civil Internacional de Observación por los Derechos Humanos (2008) and Latin American Studies Association (2007).

6. The education reforms are part of larger neoliberal reforms aimed at weakening labor unions and the power of public workers in general. Elba Esther Gordillo remained in power despite being widely unpopular due to her loyalty and utility for Peña Nieto's Institutional Revolutionary Party (PRI). Her loyalty had come into question, and her imprisonment can be seen as a calculated political "sacrifice" by the PRI to give the impression of a "new PRI" that was entering the presidential office by cracking down on the corruption of the "old PRI" that exercised single-party rule over postrevolutionary Mexican politics until 2000.

7. I gave everyone who participated in this research the option of using pseudonyms to protect their identity. Some, including "Doña Inés," opted to use a pseudonym, while others chose to have only their first name used for security reasons.

8. *Banda* is a word used repeatedly by many of the youth in my study. This word is sometimes translated as gang but that is not the usage here. In this context, *banda* tends to refer to youth from popular neighborhoods or specifically to the speaker's group of friends. I chose to retain the original *banda* in my translations of interviews because of the messiness of translation.

9. Originally the *Pueblos* (Peoples) in APPO was singular, the *Pueblo* (People), but was soon changed to reflect the plurality of Oaxaca's people and of the movement.

10. Pseudonym.

11. See Freidberg (2007) for captivating video documentation of these moments.

12. Interview conducted by author and Lynn Stephen, August 9, 2010.

13. The use of the "@" is meant to challenge the de facto masculine designation of the "o" ending by including the feminine "a." It is a political statement that many youth are making throughout Latin American and the United States. I include this usage here since it is the usage that the majority of youth activists and collectives use. Other alternatives are to replace the "@" with an "x" or with an "A" inside an "O," which is also the common symbol for anarchy.

14. CESOL is one of the libertarian groups that has been more active in Oaxaca over the past decade and is composed largely of punks. They have been active in publishing fanzines, organizing punk concerts, and mobilizing in support of political prisoners, among other work.

Chapter Five

Brazil

Praxis of Empowerment: Mística and Mobilization in Brazil's Landless Rural Workers' Movement (MST)

Daniela Issa

On Utopia—
Only the future will tell us which
aspiration was or was not "unattainable."
—Michael Löwy

In their fight for land reform over the past thirty years, the Landless Rural Workers' Movement (MST, Movimento dos Trabalhadores Rurais Sem Terra) in Brazil has been advocating an alternative way of life. It is a struggle that goes beyond land redistribution. The Sem Terra (landless) resist the homogenization imposed by globalized capitalism, which aims at reducing them to wage laborers, to the detriment of their culture and their most basic rights. They resist, first and foremost, through the belief in change—*mística*—and by proposing a livelihood based on subsistence farming, food sovereignty, agroecology, adequate health care, and housing. In reaffirming their right to exist as family farmers, they have brought about transformation and internationalized their struggle, refusing to be spectators of the system. They are agents of change.

While a subjective feeling experienced individually and/or collectively, mística is also a critical manifestation of the MST's antiestablishment outlook. It is utopian and emancipatory in its belief in transformation and eminently critical in its nonacceptance of the facticity of the capitalist system and is, therefore, profoundly romantic. Mística helps create the objective conditions that foster change, through the conscious realization of their role as subjects of history. It is empowering. The Sem Terra are able to resist reification (*coisificação*), that is, selling their labor power in the market (the only commodity they possess, yet which is inseparable from the human person), to survive and reproduce themselves as workers, as Lukács theorized. By resisting wage labor, they also resist reification in its most extreme form, which in rural (and urban) Brazil sometimes means falling prey to slavery (*trabalho escravo*): commodities producing commodities. As is argued in this chapter, the mística of the MST, as praxis of empowerment, is an integral component of organization. By carrying out místicas through the use of symbols and art, the Sem Terra pedagogically convey concepts and revive the collective memory of the Brazilian peasantry, all of which promote their culture and construct identity.

The MST's mística is rooted in the religious ethics of liberation theology—preferential option for the poor—which can be best explained by Weber's concept of elective affinity. It is a process by which two cultural forms (social classes and religious orders) converge in a relationship of attraction and mutual choice under specific historical and social conditions (Löwy 2004, 8). In this sense, the elective affinity between a particular world vision and the class interests of the rural poor provided the basis for the emergence of the MST, which since its inception was mobilized and empowered through the transmission of religious and political knowledge of this progressive theology's pedagogical base work.

On April 17, 2006, the MST and its supporters gathered in São Paulo's Praça da Sé to remember the tenth anniversary of the Eldorado de Carajás massacre by the military police in the Amazonian state of Pará, Brazil, a massacre that started as a peaceful protest by the MST and ended with the annihilation of nineteen members and the wounding of sixty-nine others. The Carajás massacre was the largest massacre committed against the MST since its founding in 1984. In contrast to the massacre committed in Corumbiara, in the state of Rondônia, a year earlier, which had outraged public opinion and forced Brazilians and the international community to face the reality of rural violence in Brazil, this massacre had national and international coverage. Five years later, in June 2001, only two defendants were sentenced to life in prison despite the presence of over 150 military policemen at the massacre. The MST had organized the demonstration not only to honor the dead and wounded, but also to remind the community, which all too often suffers compassion fatigue, of the disposability of the lives of the poor and the lack of urgency and justice on the part of the state. Under drizzling rain, politicians, union leaders, and representatives of the MST delivered their speeches as a sign of support for the movement and indignation over the violence perpetrated against the Sem Terra. As the demonstration ended, night had fallen, and nineteen members of the MST wrapped in the movement's flag were solemnly carried away from the square with a song from the folk singer Chico Buarque[1] accompanying the procession in the background:

Essa cova em que estás com palmos medida,
é a conta menor que tiraste em vida
é de bom tamanho, nem largo nem fundo
é a parte que te cabe deste latifúndio

Observers silently watched the bodies disappear in the darkness, and the song was replaced by occasional drumbeats as they were symbolically transported to the scene of the funeral of the massacred members. Some had tears in their eyes.

This last is an example of what is referred to in the Brazilian social science literature as a *mística*—the representation through words, art, symbolism, and music of the struggles and reality of this social movement—and is a distinctive characteristic of the landless movement. *Mística* is also used to refer to the more abstract, emotional element, strengthened in collectivity, which can be described as the feeling of empowerment, love, and solidarity that serves as a mobilizing force by inspiring self-sacrifice, humility, and courage. This element is clearly not unique to the MST. Its origins are found in the spiritual mysticism of liberation theology, which sees the poor as the object of love. Although most scholars agree on the meaning of the term *mística*, its translation into English varies, and it is used in different ways. This study examines the role of *mística* as a mobilizing element by tracing its roots and characteristics, discussing it as praxis (in its pedagogical and cultural application), and analyzing its contribution to the uniqueness and effectiveness of Latin America's largest social movement. *Mística* not only inspires but also serves as pedagogy of empowerment. This pedagogy relies on symbolism to convey concepts and values to a class characterized by low levels of formal education and/or literacy, and therefore is not limited to producing knowledge; it narrates history and experience, reviving the collective memory of the Brazilian peasantry, and ultimately contributing to the formation of a collective Sem Terra identity. The cultural contribution of *mística* as praxis is resisting the homogenization of globalization; it is the Gramscian counterhegemonic alternative. Therefore in addition to its inspirational element, *mística* empowers members by creating their collective identity and reviving their culture, contributing to the movement's organization.

Though *mística* is the object of this study, other factors such as the role of organization, leadership, ideology, strategy, and historical structures must be taken into consideration for a more comprehensive understanding of how the MST has been effectively mobilizing for three decades. The political "opening" of dictatorial Brazil to democracy with the transition to electoral regimes on the continent since the 1980s has made the organization of social movements possible by providing the political structure for freer collective action. Yet this liberalized political framework has failed to confer citizenship rights—the right to have rights—on the subaltern members of society (Alvarez, Dagnino, and Escobar 1998). Moreover, the masses in Latin America have been adversely affected by free-market globalization, witnessing a continuously increasing gap in the distribution of income and an export-led orientation of their economies. Rural social movements such as the MST and the Zapatistas in Mexico have mobilized to retain or gain access to land that will ensure their subsistence and preserve their culture. The agrarian social order of Brazil is one of the most conservative in Latin America when it comes to the inequality of land distribution, slave labor, human trafficking, and landlessness (see Sutton 1994; Comissão Pastoral da Terra 1998; Adriance 1996; Branford and Glock 1985; Wright and Wolford 2003). Brazil is a country that has never had a revolutionary or institutionalized break with a colonial legacy of *latifúndios*, nor has there been the will on the part of the state, much less the landed oligarchy, to carry out land reform.

ORIGIN OF THE MST'S MÍSTICA

The term mística, when used in analysis of the MST, has been translated into English as "mysticism" (Wright and Wolford 2003),[2] élan (Veltmeyer and Petras 2002), "millenarianism" (Löwy 2001), and "mystique," also used alternatively by these writers and others (Almeida and Sanchez 2000; Harnecker, 2003). *Mística* in social movements is a subjective experience in collectivity, and, insofar as one is referring to the feeling and not the praxis of mística (the art, music, and symbolism used to express the "feeling" and in constructing identity and culture), the above terms can be used interchangeably in the analysis of various social movements. In the context of the MST in particular, there is no English equivalent that truly reflects what mística signifies in Portuguese: one can speak of "*a força da mística*" (the power of mística) and one can say, "*Eles fizeram uma mística linda*" (They did a beautiful mística). The terms "mystique," "mysticism," "mystical component," and so forth, are not applicable to the second of these uses; it would make no sense to say "I observed three 'mystiques' today." Mística in this sense is understood as a symbolic political representation and social movement frame (Johnston 1995; Johnston and Klandermans 1995) for the interpretation and articulation of a counterhegemonic alternative by MST participants; it is cognitive praxis (Fernandes 1996, 232).

The MST's mística has its roots in liberation theology, which emerged in the 1960s as a result of the Second Vatican Council and the Conference of Latin America Bishops in Colombia, in order to address the human suffering, political oppression, and material deprivation of the Majority World. This new theology adopted a preferential option for the poor and sought to liberate the oppressed through *conscientização* (conscientization; see Freire 1967), or the process of "gaining consciousness," and participation through ecclesiastical base communities, which worked with the masses at a grassroots level by encouraging lay people to interpret Bible readings in terms of their reality. Ecclesiastical base communities played an important historical role in dictatorial Latin America by providing the space for discussion, education, and consequently mobilization of the poor when political organization was illegal. The MST was a social movement that emerged from the support of this progressive theology, particularly the Comissão Pastoral da Terra (Pastoral Land Commission—CPT), an organization created in 1975 to serve the interests of the rural poor in Brazil. The CPT was directly involved in the formation of the MST as a national organization, assisting with conscientization, providing logistical support for meetings throughout the country, and adopting an ecumenical approach that avoided sectarianism (Stedile and Fernandes 2000; Fernandes 2000; 1996).[3] The MST's adaptation of liberation theology ideals and Christian mística allowed it to build on its version of mística even after liberation theology itself went into decline in the late 1980s.

The etymology of mística is traced to "mystery" and "mysticism," which the religions of the world interpret as occult to the ordinary person but revealed to a select few. The mística derived from liberation theology is precisely the opposite: it is not a doctrine, an ideology, a mystification of reality, or a secretive/selective way of looking at things, but a communal religious experience (Boff 1994a; Betto 2001a). In contrast to the traditional Judeo-Christian view of the Kingdom of God as a reward in the afterlife for the sufferings of this one, it calls for idealizing and materializing the utopia of the Kingdom of God in the here and now. As Frei Betto (2001a, 62) explains, calling on people to be the agents of their liberation, "the Kingdom of God is not up there but in front of you." The poor are central to mística, because, as the theologian Leonardo Boff explains, Christians see the passion for the poor as the passion of Jesus that continues to agonize in the incarnation of his brothers and sisters, and a parallel is drawn between the martyrdom of Jesus and the massacre of the people (1993, 16):

> Christian mística, because it is historic, is oriented toward following Jesus. This implies a commitment of solidarity with the poor, since Jesus was one of them and personally opted for the marginalized of the streets, countryside, and squares of the cities. It implies a commitment of personal and social transformation, present in the utopia preached by Jesus of the Kingdom of God that is realized in justice for the poor and, from that, [justice] for all and for all creation.

Frei Sergio Görgen (1997, 290) sees the cross as not only representing Jesus's faith, resistance, and presence among the people, but also helping construct a "mística of resistance" to the suffering of life in the encampments as an analogy to that of Jesus's persecution. Liberationists recognize that the desire to transform society is not exclusively a Christian or a religious aspiration, and that an attitude of mística—self-sacrifice for the collective good—is "accessible to all, without exception, as long as one is human and sensitive" (Boff 1993, 13). The practice of humility is an integral legacy of religious mística for the MST. Boff (1994a, 13) argues that to nourish the mística one must show an openness to learning from various sources and cultural traditions, a "venerating humility toward reality." As Stedile explains, liberationists' example of humility helped create a movement open to "all truths, not a single truth," one that learns from the experience of past struggles and heroes and recognizes its "limitations" and the "temporary nature of its participation" in the history of popular struggles as a link to future ones—features that differentiate the MST from the traditional leftist orthodoxy (Stedile and Fernandes 2000, 58–59). Humility is the difference between a *militante* and a *militonto/a*, the latter being an egotistic activist who adopts a "know-it-all" attitude in leadership positions, thus losing touch with the community (Betto 2001b). In the words of one MST member (Adão, interview, April 19, 2006), "The true militant should always put the interest of others before his, should be the last one in line to eat and the first to volunteer for a difficult or dangerous task."

Catholic ritualism has been identified as another attribute of liberation theology in the mística of the MST (Löwy 2001; Lara Junior 2005a). While there is consensus on the ritualistic nature of mística practices in the MST as a Catholic legacy, there is a scarcity of research that accounts for the contributions of Indigenous and African religiosity to mística, considering how integral they are to Brazilian culture. Boff (1994b, 94) and Betto (1994, 44) discuss the influence of non-Western, non-Christian místicas found in Indigenous and Afro-Brazilian religion, such as Umbanda, as based on a relationship with God through nature. As Betto explains, the spirituality of the poor is not institutional but animistic, incorporating belief in the sacredness of nature. Despite the ritualistic nature of Catholic mística, the "ritual" (if one can call it that) employed by the MST is not the same as that of institutionalized religion in that it lacks formal rules that *must* be followed. Místicas follow generic recommendations such as providing participants with the lyrics of a song when music is presented, but they do not have to start with any particular set of practices (poem, singing, theater) or incorporate the use of any particular set of objects (candles, machetes, seeds) in the representation of the message every time they are practiced. Místicas can be conducted as ritual, depending upon the circumstances, but this is not always the case; they are spontaneous manifestations marking time and culture. Because death is very much a part of Brazilian peasant culture, many místicas are conducted with the solemnity of a funeral; this solemnity and the Catholic religious tradition have influenced the tone and general practice of other místicas, which consequently can be interpreted as ritualistic in character. Taylor and Whittier (1995, 176–77) identify marches, rallies, riots, and rebellions as rituals of mobilized groups and argue that they are central to the study of collective actions because they represent the emotions that drive protest. To qualify místicas as ritualistic in the general sense of the word can be construed as reductionist (see Stedile and Fernandes 2000, 130–31). Like mass protests, they are ritualistic in a broader sociological context but, above all, praxis.

CHARACTERISTICS AND INTERPRETATIONS

It is tempting to see mística in everything, given its interrelatedness with many aspects of the Landless Movement, such as ideology, strategy, and participation. In addition to empowering subjects to continue mobilizing for the cause of land reform, mística as praxis serves a pedagogical and cultural function. The following are some general characteristics of the MST's mística: It involves the use of symbols. It is strengthened by collectivity and has a strong emotional component, but is not the absence of reason. It is creative and artistic. While part of the movement, it is not institutionalized. It may be ritualistic but is not religious or denominational. Its themes center on social causes as they pertain to the MST's reality. It is experienced in the movement but also derives inspiration from outside. It fosters identity and *pertença* (belonging), which is the creation of identity by association with a group, in this case a class-based, peasant identity—the membership, partnership, and inclusion of otherwise excluded subjects lacking citizenship rights.

In *O vigor da mística* (2002), published by the MST, Bogo argues that mística has been the key element animating the MST's struggle. It is the powerful force in the fight for social causes, the "fire" based on solidarity, generosity, ethics, and morality that is embodied in the symbols of the movement: "Anytime something moves toward making a human being more humane, that is when mística manifests itself" (Bogo 1999, 126–27). Peloso (1994, 2), who has worked with the MST through the years as a lecturer and educator, describes it as the decisive force that inspires people when they are discouraged or deceived, the "food" that reinvigorates the masses when oppression creates the perception that efforts to overcome it are pointless. Stedile, one of the founders and a national leader and spokesperson for the MST, defines mística as a "feeling directed toward an ideal" and the "social practice that makes people feel good about participating in the struggle" (Stedile and Fernandes 2000, 129–30). The MST sees mística as important to the construction of its identity. Applying a psychosocial framework of analysis to the movement, Lara Junior (2005a) found that mística contributes to the consolidation of the MST's collective identity through its religious, cultural, and political elements. While Caldart's (2000) definition of mística is very similar to that of these writers, she is unique in arguing that it necessarily occurs in collectivity. In addition to identity construction, she points out, mística is an experience that produces culture. Fernandes (1996, 232–33) sees mística as a practice that enhances the MST's organization; he defines it as "a combination of practices developed in all of the spatial dimensions of political socialization." It is the interactive space for communication, which is fundamental for the construction of knowledge and the development of relations and alliances. Consequently, this space becomes the nonmaterial territory of the movement (Bernardo Mançano Fernandes, interview, San José, Puerto Rico, 2006).

MST members describe mística as follows:

 It's not easy to explain, it's easier to live it. . . . It's a source from which we feed and continue fighting, the representations of our life and what the struggle means to us. . . . [Mística] comes from those who worked with the church, that's the origin. It was combining the dream with the political. Others in the left criticized us because it [mística] was viewed as idealism, ritualistic, and also because it came from the church. It was as if it had no foundation. . . . Without mística we cannot be militants. We get nourished from this, and if you can't feel emotion with the *lonas pretas*,[4] the children in school, the MST's flag, then why continue? How do you face fear and stay away from your family? One of the legacies of the movement is militancy based on mística, love for the cause. (Clarice, interview, April 20, 1996)

Mística moves us, it's everything, dedication. We're not in the MST for a salary or promotion. As a militant, there's an increase in responsibility, not in salary, so it's the mística that moves us to become a militant. It moves us to cry, to joke around. The militant does not live without mística. It comes from within, your hope of a dream, of constructing. . . . the objective and the cause are one; follow Che's example. (Messias, interview, April 19, 2006)

The militants construct mística with the awareness that there is a need to change. [Mística is] when I come to the realization that I want land, food, and life for others, not just for me. That's the meaning of the militant's mística. (Gorete, interview, April 18, 2006)

To me it's this secretive thing that motivates us, it gives us impulse. It's something that you don't explain, you feel it. There's symbolism and a church legacy. . . . Mística is present in our daily lives as militants, just working at the base is a moment of mística, of *pertença*. [Mística] is created in our collective way of life. We inherited a lot from theory, but in the MST it is enriched in collectivity. Why is it that these people who live under *lona preta* live smiling, singing, and happy? It's because of mística. In school we create mística, a necessity to study more. . . . Mística is a way of making the struggle happen. There's the mística of acting out the mystical act, where we remember martyrs through poetry or in the marches—and there's the mística that you live day-to-day. This mística is carried to professors, intellectuals, students, the outsiders, who also feel it. It moves you and makes you question, it's not just feeling. (Regilma, interview, April 19, 2006).

If mística didn't exist, the movement wouldn't be what it is. Every moment is difficult, and it's the mística that lifts you. When it comes time to learn, mística helps you. The MST wouldn't be what it is if it didn't have mística. It would exist, but not as it is. There are times when [mística] is uplifting, sad, or makes you think. It's not only uplifting, it teaches you, and you feel indignation. (Miltinho, interview, April 20, 2006).

The general sense of authenticity of mística is due to the fact that it has not been institutionalized; as Stedile states, "We realized that if you allow mística to become formal, it dies out. No one receives orders to be emotional; you get emotional because you are motivated as a result of something" (Stedile and Fernandes 2000, 130). Tasks are performed in the MST through the formation of working groups or committees. If a march is organized, for example, there are committees to attend to such concerns as the participants' health, food, representation in the media, and mística. Mística committees form for organizational purposes, not to formalize the practice. Those who serve on them cannot volunteer at all times for the task; there must be rotation of participants. There is minimal documentation on guidelines for consideration in the practice of mística, and místicas are generally not documented or recorded, except when they mark important events or when outsiders are studying them. As one militant notes,

[Mística] is extremely creative and free, and it's that liberty which makes it mystical. Sometimes we're asked: Why don't you write down the místicas? They are so beautiful! And we don't do it because it's creative; it's created in the moment. The murderers of Carajás, who [enjoy] impunity, cause us indignation, and so we represent that. Mística is not a theatrical representation with a script, it's more [a creation] in the moment, despite preparation. (Regilma, interview, April 20, 2006)

In a letter to Bogo, Peloso created an outline to help orient those participating in místicas. His purpose in putting his reflections on paper was to clarify what he understood as an erroneous conception of místicas as being created to dramatize for entertainment purposes, to convey mystery, or to shock. When they acquire any of the above characteristics, místicas are no longer authentic and would fall into the category of mysticism. The following considerations have been discussed in the MST, but not institutionalized (Peloso, personal communication, May 2006).[5]

The celebration is beautiful when it is practiced with brevity, a certain solemnity, and simplicity. It is good to use symbols, gestures, cultural expressions, personal testimonies, but one must avoid having it become a merely theatrical representation.

A mística should not be expressed for entertainment purposes—no surprises or sensationalism. People should be involved in the process of preparing it. If a poem is used, a copy of the text should be provided so that people will have access to what is being read, and the same for music.

It is important to avoid the use of mística to adorn a meeting ("Now that the mística is over, let's get down to business"). It should not become the task of "specialists," even though some are more creative and sensitive than others. It should not occupy one's entire focus ("I couldn't attend the course, because I had to prepare the mística"). It must not turn into a competition ("Their mística was better than yours"). Something that worked in the Northeast of Brazil would be out of context and inauthentic in the South. Preparation is necessary to avoid improvisation, but should not become a torment to those who are coordinating the celebration.

Místicas can be conducted at the beginning of a meeting to help get everyone's attention and recall the spirit that unites the group, but a song, poetry reading, silence, or "word of order" (encouraging expression) can be presented at any appropriate moment.

Navarro (2002, 11) argues that the MST's mobilization has not emancipated MST members and that its national leadership has become more radical and centralized over the years. This leadership has control over the intermediary militants, who display "an almost religious devotion" to the movement but are not strong enough to control it, and this is why "indoctrinating mechanisms" such as education and mística are necessary. Navarro does not explain how mística is used for indoctrination, and while it is not central to his argument, the question may be raised whether this is the case. There is no question that the practice of místicas is centered on social themes relating to land reform, rural violence, and the cultivation of peasant identity, and in this sense they are limited in scope, as they are a reflection of the reality of the Sem Terra. Yet within such scope, the themes vary greatly in subject and from region to region, because they are interpreted subjectively and created spontaneously. The preparation of a mística can take anywhere from a few minutes to a few hours, except when it marks an important event or requires rehearsal (for mime, dance, or theatrical representation). Místicas are participatory and decentralized cultural practices; they are in virtually every activity undertaken by the movement, some of them created on the spur of the moment, and it would be difficult to control their creation or execution most or all of the time. In addition, místicas are often used for encouragement, where a social cause is the underlying theme, but the primary purpose is building morale, so characterizing them as merely a reflection of ideology is reductionist and incomplete. For top-down indoctrination to occur as Navarro seems to suggest, místicas would have to be institutionalized or bureaucratized and members would have to be sanctioned when they deviated from the rules dictated from above. Despite the consensus that the MST has become institutionalized as a social movement over time because of its organization (see Martins 1997; Stedile and Fernandes 2000; Welch 2006), no such institutionalization or bureaucratization has occurred. Were one to argue that místicas are indoctrinating because they reflect the ideology of the movement, then practically everything in society could be considered similarly indoctrinating: the media, the schools, the universities, the corporations, and the other institutions of the established order.

MÍSTICA AS PRAXIS: PEDAGOGY AND CULTURE

Pedagogy

Associated with Freire's (1967) work and general Marxist theory, praxis is the application of theory to practice. Learned concepts acquire meaning as theory is applied to one's experience. The purpose of mística as praxis is communicating concepts and messages through symbolism that serve to educate largely unlettered people on a variety of subjects—political, cultural, and historical—while asserting their identity in the process. The pedagogical outcome of mística is therefore not only knowledge, but the creation and reassertion of values and the construction of a class- and culture-based identity that leads to empowerment. Empowerment through mística takes various forms, not just inspiration to mobilize politically, as is the general perception. For example, a group may want to conduct a mística to convey the values of self-sacrifice and courage. To do so, it may choose to represent Che Guevara as a primary example of those values or recall the courage of Oziel, one of the fallen in the Carajás massacre, whom many members knew personally. While for some Che is remembered with almost saintly devotion, remembering *companheiros/as* in their struggles also contributes to value reinforcement and to identity construction and reformation.

On April 18, 2006, students of the Florestan Fernandes National School conducted a mística to encourage one another to finish the course through the second phase of the curriculum. Although these students were educated, highly articulate, and politicized members, they carried out a mística to relay the importance of continuing to study, because a few students in their class had dropped out weeks before. The classroom was adorned with the flag of the MST, a basket lying on top of it, seeds, and a number of red folders and badges with the students' names on them. Each of the folders contained course material, a notebook, and a pen. The mística started with a samba dedicated to the importance of education in Brazil. When the music finished, two students read a poem and a third passed a red folder and a badge to the person whose name was on the badge, offering that person a word of encouragement to continue studying. This person did the same to the next person, and so on, until everyone had received a folder and a word. Then they all pronounced the word of order and sang the MST's anthem. The act of passing on the folders symbolized the militants' wish to pass on to colleagues their personal desire to continue studying. The underlying theme of this mística was the importance of education, but the purpose was to encourage students to get through the course.

Use of Symbols

Místicas rely on symbolism and art to convey feelings, stories, messages, concepts, and values (see Bogo 2002, 109–34). Given that the peasant culture has been largely based on the oral tradition, the use of symbols in the practice of mística has great value. Symbols materialize the abstract, and acquire various meanings and connotations. The cross has been a particularly strong symbol from the beginning, marking historic occupations such as that of Encruzilhada Natalino, but today it is giving way to the MST's flag (Caldart 2000, 135). The flag is red with a map of Brazil and two rural laborers, a man and a woman, representing the family. The black plastic tarps (*lonas pretas*) used in the initial stage of an occupation have become another symbol associated with the MST as occupation became the method of struggle and access to land, the means by which agrarian reform will be brought about in Brazil (Fernandes 2000; 2001). To many in the MST the sight of *lonas pretas* provokes mística.

Seeds have very strong symbolism, representing, among other things, family farming, subsistence, and hope. In recent years, they have also symbolized the MST's position against the use of transgenic seeds. Many *camponesas* habitually set aside seeds for future generations. The use of seeds as a symbol in místicas has also been noted in Lara Junior (2005a) as forward-looking representation of hope, dreams, and utopia. Additional symbols include tools, the monthly *Jornal Sem Terra*, and others that reflect a much more local culture and subjective impressions (Stedile and Fernandes 2000, 132). Symbols are used not only in the mística itself but also to adorn the meeting place as part of creating the atmosphere for the delivery of the message. Lastly, there are human symbols, those whose legacy influences the movement and become frames of reference, such as Che and Oziel (see Stedile and Fernandes 2000, 59–62). Symbols have been used to communicate from time immemorial, but the MST has employed them as an artistic reflection of the deeply creative nature of the Brazilian popular classes. Communicating and evoking feelings through symbols is itself an art, and in that sense the movement has operationalized symbolism as a form of speech. Lara Junior (2005b, 8) argues that artistic manifestations in general have not been recognized as a political and revolutionary force throughout history, despite being present since the emergence of the MST, at first through religious songs: "I was still in the settlement, but we had already started to mix this Christian and religious thing with other mística methods, like, for example, we started to express the mystical moment by singing, in reality songs of the struggle, of *companheiros* that wrote and spoke of the struggle, and we continued to carry the cross and all the other main symbols as well." He points to the importance of music, in particular, in inspiring members with courage to face the difficulties of their reality and místíca as the stage for "spontaneous artistic manifestations and creation of the symbolic universe" of the MST. Music has acquired a "super dimension" as a part of the peasant nature and an authentic expression of the "soul of the masses" (Bogo 2002, 149).

Collective Memory

The construction of movement identity occurs by rescuing the collective memory of past peasant struggles, reviving the contributions of proponents and martyrs of land reform and those who fought for the rights of the oppressed and repressed. It recovers a past that contradicts the myth of Brazilian passivity. In essence, it is the story that must be told to a largely unlettered class, and the use of representation, celebration, and ritual is not only a creative method, but a highly effective one. The collective memory of the Brazilian peasantry is constructed from recollections of *quilombos* like Palmares, messianic movements like Canudos and Contestado, rural social movements like the Peasant Leagues of the 1950s—heroic moments of popular resistance to structural inequality of land distribution in Brazil. [6] The MST sees itself as a continuation of these historic movements, especially the Peasant Leagues, while also incorporating the lessons and contributions of other Latin American peasant movements, revolutions, and organizations (Stedile and Fernandes, 2000, 39). This legacy of resistance is a part of the Sem Terra identity, as was their resistance to the military dictatorship's (1964–1985) modernization policies of the 1970s. The government's desire to exploit the Amazon and provide land in the region encouraged migration from all over the country. Its failure to back up its colonization plans with adequate infrastructure and to control the spread of *grilagem* (appropriation of land through fraudulent titles), in great part carried out by investors, companies, and powerful individuals, made the Amazon an unsafe and inhospitable place for the landless (Branford and Glock, 1985). [7] The MST was born out of southern migrants' resistance to being uprooted to the Amazon (north) to satisfy the military's quick fix for landlessness (Stedile and Fernandes 2000; Fernandes 1996).

Pertença (Belonging)

The importance of místíca as praxis in elitist and hierarchical Brazil is evidenced by the empowerment it brings to those who are deemed inferior subjects, stripped of identity, rights, and *pertença*. Dagnino (1998, 47–48) characterizes Latin America's elitism as a form of *social authoritarianism*, which produces a social classification by class, race, and gender that establishes distinct "places" in society; these *social places* distinguish those whose equal rights are guaranteed by the nation-state from those perceived to be inferior and therefore unworthy of being bearers of rights (as seen in the delay to bring justice in the cases of the Eldorado de Carajás and Corumbiara massacres). At the same time, members of the elite and ruling class are deemed beyond the reach of the law. It is what Baierle (1998, 121) calls *social apartheid*, arguing that the masses in Brazil do not perceive public spaces as public at all; in fact, the formal spaces of politics and government are viewed as private spaces of the educated and privileged.

In exercising collective memory, the Sem Terra remind themselves that there is an abundance of agricultural land in Brazil and, while they have historically been denied access to part of it, they will only gain access through organization. They understand that their struggle should not be simply for access to land, and that as long as there are landless in Brazil they will continue mobilizing. Theirs is an identity based on a belief in change and the possibility of a better future.

Mística influences the identity of the Sem Terrinhas (children of the Sem Terra), who have been born into the collaborative and communal culture of the settlements, with the sacrifices and difficulties inherent in land occupations. According to educator Deise Arenhart (2003), their identity, based on the rural context, the working class, and the movement, is distinctive because of the collective nature of their lives. She demonstrates that a key element in creating that identity is mística as it is used in the representation of history and in passing on the memory of their parents' struggles. Arenhart reports that children see mística as a source of learning and a form of expression: "When children feel the power of an occupation, a word of order, a song that talks about them, it seems that they learn their origin, history, reasons, strength, and the value of the Sem Terra people" (2003, 6). She has also observed, however, that when children conduct místicas, they focus not so much on the content of the message as on the pleasure of representing. In one particular mística, the children represented an occupation, the violence of the police and landowners, and the care of the nurses for the wounded. At the end they invited everyone to a party and asked all the participants (landowners, police, and Sem Terras) not to fight anymore. Everyone agreed, and the mística concluded with a message of peace. This example illustrates the fact that children conduct místicas with the authenticity and naivety characteristic of their age, once again displaying the freedom to create and interpret that is seen in the movement.

CONCLUSION

Democratization has provided the structural context for the MST's mobilization, but mística, in conjunction with organization, strategy, and leadership, has transformed an otherwise amorphous and alienated mass through identity formation, from passive to active agents as an organized social movement. This emotional component, characterized as the love for a cause, is also the praxis of pedagogy and culture that creates identity through *pertença* and revives the collective memory of the MST. Conscious of the extraordinary power of místicas, the MST has used them to educate members and rescue their culture, by promoting solidarity, self-sacrifice for the common good, and the family while insisting that the equitable distribution and proper use of land are the solution to most of Brazil's social ills. Through this praxis of empowerment, which utilizes art and symbolism, the MST reinforces the class politics that the forces of neoliberalism have fractured.

The lives of the Sem Terra are marked by great sacrifices, and the continued struggle and organization of the MST can be in part explained by mística. Without hope and the belief that the movement can effect significant change in Brazil, the struggle would be far more challenging. The praxis of mística in constructing the MST's collective identity and preserving its culture is the articulation of a counterhegemonic alternative to globalization. Paraphrasing a poet, Salete, a student at the Florestan Fernandes School said, "To dream is detrimental to the established order, and organization is what the dominant class fears, because what they fear isn't weapons, but these two elements."

NOTES

1. Buarque's song is dedicated to the Carajás massacre; the lyrics are an excerpt from the poetry found in João Cabral de Melo Neto's (2006) *Morte e Vida Severina*. The translation of the verse is as follows: "This grave where you find yourself, measured in palms, is the smallest concern you took from life. It is the right size, neither wide nor deep, it's your share of this latifundio."

2. Wright and Wolford (2003, 310–11) use the terms mística and "mysticism" interchangeably.

3. Stedile also notes the contribution of the Lutheran Church in the South in assisting with the MST's formation (Stedile and Fernandes 2000, 19).

4. *Lonas pretas* are the black plastic tarps used as tents in the initial phase of land occupation.

5. This information is derived through personal communication. According to Peloso, these are simply general considerations used for theorizing and discussing mística; there are no "rule books" or written directives on místicas.

6. Martins (1997) explains that through the Land Law of 1850, the Brazilian landed aristocracy created a legal mechanism, in anticipation of the abolition of slavery (1888), to ensure that former slaves and the rural poor would not be able to occupy and work on the land in a country that even today has the greatest amount of agricultural land in the world. Additionally, it was a means to ensure that landowners would have a massive workforce at their disposal after

slavery (Martins 1997, 16–17). The Land Law essentially determined that land could be acquired only by those who paid for it (see also Fernandes 2000, 29).

7. The military's modernization plan exacerbated the problem of agrarian inequality and violence in the region as landlessness, *grilagem*, and slavery in the Amazon increased and went largely unchecked by the government. At the root of these problems was the award of massive land grants and fiscal incentives to Brazilian and foreign private investors and corporations to exploit the Amazon on a grand scale. These policies mark the beginning of intense deforestation (see Branford and Glock 1985).

Chapter Six

Central America/Mexico

*Network Politics in the Movement against
the Plan Puebla-Panamá*

Alicia Swords

The Plan Puebla-Panamá (PPP) was proposed to facilitate capital expansion in Mesoamerica. Revealed in 2000, it was a vision by investors, international financial institutions, and governments to integrate the region from southern Mexico to Panama into the global market. Even as the Latin American "pink tide" disrupted the hegemony of neoliberalism in Latin America (Goodale and Postero 2013), global capital advanced via the PPP, exemplifying ongoing "accumulation by dispossession" (Harvey 2003). As people in the region learned about the plan, many were troubled by its lack of public consultation and its vision of development. The PPP's welcome to transnational extractive industries, biological and agricultural technologies, and tourism was perceived as a threat to local livelihoods and Indigenous rights (Harvey 2004). Some critics saw it as integral to the government counterinsurgency plan against the Zapatistas (Fazio 2001; López y Rivas 2003). Yet as the plan evolved, opposing this moving target required new strategies. Marching to a state capital or making demands of a single government would not suffice. Instead, grassroots activists and representatives of nongovernmental organizations (NGOs) in Mesoamerica built on existing networks to activate a substantial transnational campaign, based in practices of horizontalism (see the introduction to this volume). At its strongest between 2001 and 2003, the anti-PPP campaign contributed to a temporary paralysis of the PPP in southern Mexico in 2003. By 2008, however, the plan was reborn and expanded as the Proyecto Mesoamérica (PM), which represents new challenges for social and ecological justice and human rights in the region.

In applying Antonio Gramsci's concepts to the epoch of globalization, Robinson (2008) suggests that the struggle for hegemony, or social domination, is not a dispute among nation-states, but rather among transnational social groups.[1] An emergent transnational capitalist class, the owners and managers of transnational corporations, private transnational financial institutions, and other capitalists represent a potentially hegemonic globalist historical bloc or global social order. In this context, the PPP exemplifies efforts by transnational capital to remold the national economies in Mesoamerica to facilitate ongoing accumulation by transnational capital.

This chapter chronicles the birth, death, and rebirth of the PPP as a guiding development concept, drawing on scholarship on transnational social movements, the Zapatista uprising, and the PPP. Based on ethnographic observations at network activities and interviews with activists between 2000 and 2003 and additional interviews ten years later,[2] this project examines the construction of networks to oppose the PPP in southern Mexico. With other contemporary struggles, the anti-PPP networks share an approach of horizontalism, defined as an orientation based on contesting financial elites and corporate power, not through taking state power but through experiences of participatory democracy and efforts to create social relations based on equality (see introduction). To characterize and give nuance to our understandings of horizontalism in practice, this chapter describes the anti-PPP networks focusing on participants' experiences with four dimensions of network politics: organization, education, leadership, and counternarratives. Unlike some manifestations of horizontalism, network politics does not reject all forms of power differences, but acknowledges the importance of developing an agreed-upon division of labor among people in a shared struggle. Network politics also does not reject leadership but creates modes of leadership that embody "rule by obeying." The limits of the anti-PPP network highlight the need to study moving targets, vulnerabilities, and contradictions of regional development plans.

THE BIRTH OF THE PLAN

Mexican president-elect Vicente Fox announced the PPP in September 2000. The Inter-American Development Bank (IDB) began promoting the PPP to integrate the economies of Mesoamerica with the global market. The plan may be interpreted as a temporary consensus between a number of governments, investors, and international institutions, a relatively rare moment in which hegemonic forces aligned and revealed a shared vision. Yet from the beginning, official proposals for the PPP, by the IDB and the Office of the President of Mexico, were inconsistent in terms of their scope and the projects they included.[3] From 2001 to 2003, the official PPP website included plans for three major highway corridors, railroads, ports, airports, and an electrical grid, along with unspecified projects for "social and ethnic development." Other reports included dams and secondary highways and roads (McElhinny and Nickinson 2004). It is difficult to obtain public information that clarifies which proposals have been approved or funded (See Call 2002; McElhinny and Nickinson 2004).

Among the eight initiatives of the PPP,[4] the Mexican government's 2002 budget for the PPP ($697.4 million) dedicated 82 percent of its funding to transportation, but only 2.9 percent for health and social development (Call 2002). Preliminary budget information suggested that 90 percent of the funding for the PPP would go toward transportation and energy interconnection (Call 2002). The remaining initiatives received a limited proportion of the budget and advanced much less in their execution.

Within a couple of months of its announcement, a transnational network of organizations had emerged to challenge the plan. Inspired by the Zapatista movement, a loose network emerged, combining organizing traditions from liberation theology, *campesino* organizing, women's issues and feminism, and Indigenous struggles. In 2002, the PPP was frequently mentioned at the top of their lists of concerns.

Civil society organizations' readings of the official proposals did not always match the conclusions of the IDB and presidential plans. NGOs and grassroots groups pointed to connections between the PPP and multinational corporations' pressures on the government to privatize and commodify genetic, biological, and mineral resources; to open the area to free trade; and to allow accumulation via dispossessing local communities. In conferences, workshops, interviews, and in educational materials, members of NGOs, Indigenous, and human rights groups noted that the PPP included controversial hydroelectric dams, gas and oil pipelines, the biosphere reserves of the Mesoamerica Biological Corridor, and free trade assembly zones. According to the IDB, the PPP did not contain any dam projects, but did include a regional electric grid that would require expanding hydroelectric production (Call 2003a).

State government officials held a range of views about the PPP. According to Harvey's research in 2002, rural development bureaucrats, whose responsibility was to negotiate with local leaders about the PPP's projects, expressed concerns about how their local projects would continue to be important. State economists, who were in charge of attracting foreign investment and promoting local businesses' engagement in global markets, saw other challenges, including that of creating a new business culture (Harvey 2004).

GREATLY EXAGGERATED REPORTS OF
THE DEATH OF THE PPP

By 2004, the *Economist* had declared that "there was no trace of the PPP in southern Mexico" and that the PPP "flopped" ("Plan Qué?" 2004, 28). Though it would not die completely, a number of factors temporarily frustrated efforts to implement the PPP in southern Mexico. By 2004, the plan's proponents had to reformulate their strategy (Pickard 2004; Harvey 2004). The anti-PPP campaign was one factor. In addition, for several reasons the PPP didn't obtain the financing its proponents had hoped for. The global and Mexican economies fell after September 11, 2001; the IDB refused preferential rates for financing; and private financing did not appear as expected (Pickard 2004). Key government ministers who favored the PPP backed down, and President Fox lost the political cachet to advance the plan (McElhinny and Nickinson 2004).

By my observation, and as documented by Pickard (2004), official IDB and Mexican government websites about the PPP were disabled around this time. There was a moratorium on publicity for the plan from June 2002 to November 2003, because publicizing any project of the PPP "was equivalent to mobilizing the civil society against it and risking its obstruction, delay or cancelation, as occurred, in fact, in various points of its geography" (Pickard 2004). Grassroots efforts contributed, among other factors, to the temporary paralysis, public disappearance, and disintegration of the PPP in Mexico.

THE SECRET LIFE OF THE PPP

From 2003 to 2008, as the Mexican government and the IDB worked to restructure the PPP,

> The IDB reacted to the effective mobilization against the PPP by creating two scripts, a public one, and a private one, each accompanied by its projects, consultations and public relations. The private script was designed for its principal audience, private-sector investors, reassuring them that the [PPP] was progressing. The public script was created in essence to hide the private one, seeking to give the PPP a human face. (McElhinny and Nickinson 2004, iii)

Critics documented that the PPP's projects were continuing under other names, and urged continuing resistance (Wilson 2008; Pickard 2006; Unión de Comunidades Indígenas de la Zona Norte del Istmo 2006). According to analyst Miguel Pickard (interview, 2013), in the face of resistance, a tactic of the PPP's proponents has been to "disappear" the large projects, but continue them with less publicity.

South of Mexico, grassroots criticism forced proponents to implement a well-researched public relations campaign to sustain the plan, based on public consultations and careful efforts to gain support of Indigenous organizations (see Call 2003b; McElhinny and Nickinson 2004). In 2003 the IDB hired the U.S. public relations firm Fleishman-Hillard International to bolster its image (Call 2003b). In Mexico, grassroots organizing prevented the IDB from using "participatory consultations" to co-opt opposition (McElhinny and Nickinson 2004).

When Felipe Calderón took the presidency in 2006, he announced that he would relaunch the PPP after reworking it. At the Campeche Summit in 2007, heads of state from Mexico and Central America acknowledged that the PPP did not have an adequate public relations strategy, and recommended improvements (Facultad Latinoamericana de Ciencias Sociales 2007). The IDB published an evaluation of the PPP in 2008, acknowledging factors that jeopardized its effectiveness, including a decision-making process that did not including countries' finance ministers, its lack of measurable baseline objectives, and problems in financing the project. Further, it admitted very low civil society participation in the initiative (Linhares Pires 2008). The evaluation concluded, "Although PPP included a broad range of interventions, transportation and energy surpass the other initiatives by a large measure in both terms of the amount of financing (87% of US$8,076 million) and the number of loans (74% of 39 loans)" (Linhares Pires 2008, 4). Yet this negative evaluation did not signal the definitive demise of the PPP.

THE PPP REBORN

In June 2008, the PPP was reborn with a new name and public image. The Proyecto Mesoamérica (Mesoamerica Project, PM) explicitly continues and expands upon the PPP (see www.proyectomesoamerica.org). Many of the PPP's development initiatives are still included, including the highway network, telecommunications, energy, and electrical integration. It extends the plan to Colombia and adds regional security measures to combat drug trafficking, terrorism, and undocumented migration, along with programs in health, education, biofuels, and housing (Zunino 2010), and territorial restructuring through agroindustry plantations, tourist theme parks, and "rural cities" aimed to concentrate dispersed rural residents (Wilson 2008).[5]

Resistance dispersed after the PPP's projects were taken on by the PM. The Mesoamerican forums lost sight of the need to oppose both free-trade agreements and the PPP, and of the need to unite legislative work with struggle on the streets (Pickard 2006). According to Pickard and Marco Antonio Velázquez Navarrete, former technical secretary of Red Mexicana de Acción frente al Libre Comercio (RMALC), forums specifically opposing the PM lost momentum due to internal dynamics that require attention, as in the experience of organizations in post-coup Honduras; costs for travel to attend forums; and disunity between Mexico and Central America due to differences in history, strategy, and organizing. The forums' breakdown means that a coordinated regional strategy for stopping the PM has not yet emerged; the lack of a strategy also makes it difficult to coordinate forums. Regional forums on specific topics, such as dams, water, and mining continue to be held (Pickard, email message to the author, March 15, 2014). In addition, organizations continue to resist specific projects, including La Parota Dam in Guerrero, wind-powered electric generation in the Isthmus of Tehuantepec, megaprojects and the state oil company (PEMEX) in the isthmus, El Tigre Dam on the Honduras-El Salvador border, and others (Pickard 2006), but it remains to be seen if transnational resistance will resume strength to challenge the PM.

Francisco Gallardo of the NGO Trans-forma Chiapas explained in a 2013 interview that the PPP's projects are at varying stages of completion. He compared incomplete projects to vampires and zombies. They are akin to zombies, Gallardo explained, because though they do not fulfill their proposed regional development goals, they never really die. Since construction companies and financiers must still be paid, the projects suck, vampire-like, from the public purse. Gallardo noted that while the Tuxtla-San Cristóbal highway was successfully completed, airports in Comitán and San Cristóbal were built but subsequently closed and never used; the Chiapas marine port is not in operation; and the railway through the Isthmus was never built. He stated, "Construction is the business." Gallardo inferred that higher profits are derived from financing and construction, so project completion was not necessary.

The remainder of this chapter builds on Harvey's (2004) inquiry into state bureaucrats' attitudes toward the PPP with an interpretive approach that critically examines the meanings of these policies for its grassroots opponents in Chiapas, Mexico.

TRANSNATIONAL NETWORKS: FROM ZAPATISMO TO ANTI-PPP

This study of meanings about the PPP builds on the inquiry of social movement scholars who have focused on how movements create and interpret meaning by aligning, expanding, bridging, and transforming frames, especially related to actors' identities, efficacy, or understandings of a social problem (see Snow et al. 1986). As global integration increases, scholars have documented growth of transnational social movements (see Smith, Chatfield, and Pagnucco 1997). In conceptualizing activism across borders in

Mesoamerica, recent scholars do not assume that cross-border activism necessarily constitutes a transnational social movement. Spalding (2008) and Zugman Dellacioppa (2011) use Keck and Sikkink's (1998) concept of "transnational advocacy network." This conceptualization acknowledges that transnational grievances do not alone lead to coordinated collective action (Tarrow 2005). It also recognizes that it is difficult to sustain and coordinate transnational actions, and that the prevailing economic model does not change easily (Spalding 2008). While earlier work on transnational activism emphasized the "boomerang effect," in which activists in the global South pressure NGOs in the global North to achieve changes within their home states, newer works describe coordination among activists in the global South, and diffusion from South to North, particularly highlighting the transnational influence of zapatismo (Oleson 2005; Khasnabish 2008; Andrews 2011; Spalding 2008).

The 1994 Zapatista uprising and the networked activities it generated set the stage for the anti-PPP campaign. As the Zapatistas worked to build participatory democracy (Starr, Martínez-Torres, and Rossett 2011) and community-based autonomy, they sponsored participatory forums or *consultas* to connect their struggles more broadly in civil society (Stahler-Sholk 2008). Their international gatherings or *encuentros* and Internet-based communications strategy (Cleaver 1998) created a model for transnational networks that would influence the emerging anti-PPP campaign.

Since the early 2000s, grassroots organizations, NGOs, activists, academics, and journalists have described and analyzed the PPP and the anti-PPP campaign.[6] Call (2002) describes four main strategies of the campaign: 1) to insist on being included in the planning and implementation process, and refuse to accept the plan otherwise; 2) to gather and disseminate information on PPP projects; 3) to challenge the plan with direct action, media advocacy, government pressure, and other strategies; and 4) to document and promote alternative development strategies being planned and implemented locally.

Critical examinations of the trajectory of the PPP have studied the policy negotiation process, popular resistance, and official responses to the resistance.[7] According to McElhinny and Nickinson (2004, 50), "When certain projects become lightning rods for opposition (Usumacinta dams, the Salvador Atenco airport, the Mexico Millennium Project and the San Salvador Anillo Periférico) they are conveniently excised from PPP portfolio." A key strategy in analyzing the PPP has been to show its contradictions. Harvey (2004) showed the contradictions between the Indigenous law, *Ley Cocopa*, and the PPP. Later, Harvey (2006b) examined the phases of the PPP, arguing that the forums pointed out the contradictions between infrastructure projects and sustainable development, and between the PPP's weak mechanisms for participation and the limited constitutional reforms on constitutional rights.

This chapter builds on and contributes to existing ethnographic description and analysis of the anti-PPP network forums. Kalny's (2010) study of the anti-PPP organizing in El Petén, Guatemala, showed that local actors make their own, locally appropriate interpretations of powerful institutions. Spalding (2008) chronicled the Foro Mesoamericano's growth to as many as 1,747 people in attendance at the San Salvador forum in 2004, acknowledging the network's function as an "integrating mechanism" to align values and link organizations with shared meanings. She found that the Foro challenged the PPP and Central American Free Trade Agreement (CAFTA), but results were elusive in the face of new government strategies including decentralizing project administration, repackaging programs, and public relations campaigns. Spalding (2014) contextualized the anti-PPP campaign within the broader Mesoamerican resistance to "neoliberal regionalism." She identified four discursive themes of anti-CAFTA resistance: deceptive pro-market claims, market impacts on the most vulnerable, implications for sovereignty, and identification of alternatives (Spalding 2014, 238).

DIMENSIONS OF NETWORK POLITICS

The term "network politics" describes the anti-PPP campaign's organizing strategy. As defined previously in relation to organizations that draw principles from the Zapatistas (Swords 2005, 2007), network politics refers to modes of political action and meaning making that are not confined by the structures of traditional party politics, nor by identity politics. NGOs and grassroots organizations build commitments and identities that transcend the geographies, objectives, and narratives of individual organizations. They coordinate actions, continually assessing political challenges and opportunities and addressing new issues and changing demands. The following paragraphs describe and analyze four dimensions of the anti-PPP network politics: organization, education, leadership, and counternarratives.

Organization

The process of building opposition to the PPP in Mexico relied on local practices, communications pathways, leaders, and pedagogies that were established through Indigenous, *campesino*, rural development, liberation theology, and women's organizations and networks created decades earlier.[8] Many of these networks preceded and had been recently activated by the Zapatista uprising and subsequent struggles for peace, justice, and human rights in the face of the government's military response. Not all would have been considered progressive, since neopopulist governments created some to control and demobilize dissent (Leyva Solano and Ascencio Franco 1996). Nevertheless, they organized statewide and regional meetings, which established pathways for communicating, sharing analysis, and coordinating actions. They cultivated local leaders, including *promotores,* catechists, and peasant leaders. At regular meetings people facing similar issues met regularly to share experiences, articulate demands, address material conditions together, and mobilize.

Opposition to the PPP was forged in a context of emergent transnational coordination and protest. The World Social Forum, first held in Brazil in 2001, created a space for information sharing among NGOs. The 1999 protests in Seattle at the ministerial meeting of the World Trade Organization (WTO) brought global attention to coordinated protest, and the Zapatistas themselves invited international visitors to join them in solidarity with the 1996 Intergalactic Encounter against Neoliberalism and for Humanity. Yet as Harvey (2006b) affirms, there was no Mesoamerican network of popular organizations prior to the PPP. The fact that the PPP included development projects across an entire region created a target, which motivated organizations to coordinate regionally. Coordination by the anti-PPP network took shape at forums *(foros),* educational and political gatherings sponsored by NGOs and grassroots organizations for participants from urban and rural communities. The forums were intentionally statewide, regional, and transnational. From 2000 to 2005, the transnational Mesoamerican Foros were held in Tapachula, Mexico (May 2001); Xelajú, Guatemala (November 2001); Managua, Nicaragua (July 2002); Tegucigalpa, Honduras (July 2003); San Salvador, El Salvador (July 2004); and San José, Costa Rica (December 2005) (Spalding 2008). Attendance increased from 106 organizations in 2001 to 350 organizations in 2002 (Harvey 2004). Individuals attending increased from 250 in 2001 to 1495 in 2003, and 1747 in 2004 (Spalding 2008). Statewide and regional forums, including a series of Chiapan Forums against Neoliberalism in San Cristóbal (October 2002), Nuevo Huixtán (February 2003), and Huitiupán (March 2003) increased discussions about the PPP.

At the forums, participants made agreements that transcended individual organizational agendas, including commitments to convene upcoming forums and mobilizations. For example, at the Managua forum in July 2002, participants agreed to coordinate to block highways throughout Mesoamerica on October 12, 2002. Tens of thousands participated in highway blockades, temporarily paralyzing the Guatemalan border and twelve strategic crossings in Chiapas in the network's first coordinated actions (Pickard 2003; Henriquez and Mariscal 2002). At Nuevo Huixtán, Chiapas, in February 2003, the final agreements included the commitment to mobilize on significant dates including International Women's Day, the Global Day against Dams, and the anniversary of Emiliano Zapata's death (Alianza Cívica 2003).

Education

Forums explicitly emphasized mutual education, and sought to eliminate inequalities in knowledge and leadership. While teaching grassroots people about the threats of the PPP was one goal of the conveners, forums were not for top-down transmission of political rhetoric, nor simply to plan future mobilizations. To create spaces for participants to listen to, learn from, and gain inspiration from each other's experiences, testimonies were invited at thematic roundtables, working groups, and cultural celebrations. Roundtables focused on themes including militarization, transgenic seeds, and food sovereignty. There were workshops about the WTO and the Free Trade Area of the Americas (FTAA) and speak-outs about hydroelectric dams and women's rights. Even the logistical planning of the forums reflected pedagogical logic. For example, at a February 2003 planning meeting in San Cristóbal, those who had prepared logistics for the most recent Chiapan Forum against Neoliberalism in Huixtán were asked to help train the new organizers in Huitiupán.

Educational spaces contributed to building shared counternarratives, as we examine later in this chapter. Facilitators compiled and collectively edited testimonies and experiences with resisting the PPP. These were published for public distribution and diffused through networks as printed minutes, summaries, and final declarations. For example, the first Forum on Biological and Cultural Diversity (June 2001 in Xelajú, Guatemala) produced its conference proceedings as a popular education manual with large print and lively illustrations.

A series of roundtables about hydroelectric dams at the second Forum against Neoliberalism in Nuevo Huixtán, Chiapas in February 2003 demonstrates how forums' education spaces combined research with experiential knowledge. Communities affected by dams shared evidence about impacts of dams with participants from throughout the PPP region.[9] The delegation from Marqués de Jalapa in Oaxaca described the damages caused by the Benito Juárez dam, begun in 1954 and finished in 1960:

> People began to be displaced and lost their fruit and corn production. . . . They were relocated in areas with no potable water where they spent 15 years . . . with sandy and rocky soils where cultivating food is impossible. . . . The government offered to pave the streets and build schools for the displaced people [but] still today, they still don't have paved streets; they only have water for an hour a day, and they have to pay high fees for water and electricity. . . . Some of the elderly died of sorrow.

To add to this narrative, the roundtable facilitator summarized effects of dams citing NGO research: displacement of residents; the loss of lands, herds, and subsistence; loss of places of worship, schools, and lands; increases in costs for electricity for residents; and militarization. Building on both testimonies and research, roundtable participants created an "action plan" that included speaking with the National Human Rights Commission about the effects of dams; meeting to plan anti-PPP protests including highway blockades, a march, a rally, and teachers' strikes; and sending delegates to the next forums.

A year later, at the third Chiapan Forum against Neoliberalism in Huitiupán in March 2004, observations and interviews suggested that the 2003 Huitiupán forum and subsequent actions contributed to inform residents about the connections between the PPP and hydroelectric dams, particularly in communities where dams were sited. Félix, a young man from Huitiupán, taught about his community's experiences opposing a dam believed to be included in the PPP: "The Itzantún dam has been proposed in our community. It would flood our community, more than 11,000 hectares. We refuse to let that happen." The pedagogical objectives of the forums include giving grassroots leaders like Félix the opportunities to teach and share their expertise so as to develop their oratorical capacity and identity as leaders.

The 2004 Huitiupán forum also involved emotional, visceral, and relational learning. Forum participants rode in pickup trucks to the site of the proposed Itzantún dam and listened to stories from community members about the river. Several participants described being in the valley that would be flooded as a transformative experience that cemented their anti-dam sentiments. Though one can only speculate about the impacts of these educational processes, there is ample evidence that multiple forms of education were employed at network gatherings, that education involved mutual learning, and that such learning was a core objective of the network in building robust resistance to the PPP.

Leadership

Observations at anti-PPP forums reveal that power dynamics based on political-economic and social differences shaped interactions among participants, but did not preclude some mutual benefits. Leaders and participants referred to forums as spaces for horizontal interaction, as places for "equal participation" for "all voices to be heard," and for the Zapatista-inspired practices of *mandar obedeciendo,* rule by obeying, and *caminar preguntando,* or asking questions as we walk. Roundtables invited "open discussion," and often each roundtable contributed statements for the final declaration. Positions or hierarchies were not explicit in activists' language. They typically called each other by first name, or used *cuate* (buddy); *compa* for *compañero, compañera* (comrade); or *comadre, hermano,* or *hermana,* all affectionate terms for confidants, near-family, and friends.[10] Yet participation was not as equal and horizontal as these terms implied. Practices for effectively including monolingual speakers of Indigenous languages varied, for example. As Andrews concluded in her study of north-south dynamics in Zapatista solidarity organizations, the appearance of equal participation can "obfuscate power dynamics" (2011, 141). Indeed, scholars have documented that NGO funding can shape agendas, or professionalize and depoliticize social struggles (see Incite! 2007). A closer look reveals that the divisions of labor at forums did not erase power relationships, but rather reflected differences based on race, ethnicity, language, class, gender, religion, generation geography, political philosophy, experience, formal education, and funding access.

Grassroots participants included mainly Indigenous and *campesino* men and women who traveled to forums from rural areas. Their organizations received little or no outside funding, sporadic funding, or supported their work through agricultural or craft cooperatives or similar activities. Speed and Forbis (2005, 1) suggest that the Zapatista movement "generated a process in which a multiplicity of local-level 'everyday leaders' has emerged," often poor, Indigenous women from communities with little access to education. Those who participated in anti-PPP forums often had leadership roles in their communities, churches, in health or education, or with the system of *cargos* or communal responsibilities.

Campesino and Indigenous leaders were most visibly in the role of participants and learners. In spite of comments reflecting internalized beliefs about their own ignorance, some *campesino* and Indigenous people gained significant authority within the anti-PPP network. Their knowledge about social and ecological realities was central to planning. They were invited to give ceremonial welcomes and conclusions, to tell communal histories, and to describe current events. Josefina explained, "I attend because I like to learn and develop. It helps us improve the communication among organizations, and within organizations. Although we're organized, we're missing some things." Josefina also acknowledged that she enjoyed traveling, and that taking part in workshops "improves our self-esteem." She added, "What I like best is that there's a lot of comraderie among the participants, and lots of respect, because they listen to you."

NGO leaders set agendas and coordinated local, state, and regional events with other Mesoamerican NGOs. They exercised bureaucratic and administrative forms of authority in network activities. In Chiapas, most NGO activists were *mestizo* or did not speak Indigenous languages, and lived mainly in the urban hub of San Cristóbal. Because NGO work had come to be relatively well remunerated,[11] they could be considered middle class, although contracts were frequently short-term and unstable. Most had higher-than-average formal education, or were educators by profession. In interviews, NGO activists described gaining political consciousness through humanitarian work with Guatemalan refugees in the 1980s and after the Zapatista uprising (See González Figueroa 2002; Swords 2005). Many regularly traveled to visit Indigenous communities, and Mesoamerican activities required travel beyond Mexico, which strengthened social bonds. Tensions sometimes ran high due to competition for funding and personal conflicts.

In interviews, NGOs activists demonstrated deep convictions about organizing against the PPP. As Andrews (2011) concluded about northern activists who adopt zapatismo, involvement with anti-PPP networks gave NGO leaders an identity, ways to reflect on their privilege, and legitimate ways to see themselves as part of a larger struggle. As well, for NGO leaders, the forums were a space for self-criticism. A feminist NGO leader reflected on an anti-PPP workshop, "At the workshops, we aim to learn from what [Indigenous women] have lived, maybe help them locate their reality within a larger reality. We have great revolutionary discourses, but in practice, we all end up imposing our views and reinforcing dependent participation. It's a challenge we have to change—these vertical, authoritarian imposing structures that inhibit women from thinking and developing and really being agents of our own reality" (interview, 2003).

Forums, therefore, were neither leaderless nor vanguardist. While they were not conflict-free, relationships were also not stuck in neocolonial dynamics. NGO and grassroots activists each benefited in different ways from participating. For some, the benefits included self-reflection about how to create meaningful relationships in the context of inequalities.

Counternarratives

In network spaces, including forums, *encuentros*, coordinating meetings, and mobilizations, one outcome was to create counternarratives about the PPP. Research including technical-rational information (statistics, description, and analysis of the government plan) combined with testimonies to create moral counternarratives, or collective stories that define what is socially accepted as moral, good, right, and wrong, and that are used to guide action (Leyva Solano 2006). Social movement theorists have paid attention to narratives (See Ganz 2010; Polletta 2006), and now in the context of the post-9/11 counterterrorism war, military analysts are also studying counternarratives of opposition groups (see Kessels 2010). This research employed narrative analysis of observations, interviews, and written materials, including declarations, political education materials, agendas, and notes from network events from 2000 to 2003.[12] This analysis found counternarratives that consistently rejected the PPP; they portrayed it as an anti-democratic, as a foreign invasion, and as especially harmful to Indigenous people and women. These narratives were produced, repeated, and diffused at network events.

A primary counternarrative was to completely reject the PPP with no negotiation. Within a matter of months of the PPP's announcement, organizations in the emerging networks agreed to reject the PPP. Total rejection was reiterated after proponents began to intensify their public relations campaign, as in the final declaration at the 2002 forum in Xalapa: "We denounce the campaign of cooptation and divisionism by the IDB and World Bank to buy out farmers organizations and NGOs with credits so as to legitimate the imposition of megaprojects and the PPP. We reject any simulacrum of consultation or of manipulated dialogue by governments and multi-lateral institutions that does not take into account the interests and opinions of our communities." This narrative emphasized the PPP's nondemocratic nature, accusing its proponents of spending public resources to generate private profits and not considering the needs of local people.

The PPP's opponents frequently emphasized that despite its rhetoric, the plan was a particular threat to Indigenous peoples. Although NGO leaders often planned and facilitated network events with some input from Indigenous and grassroots leaders, written materials were frequently written in the voice of an Indigenous collectivity. In educational materials, the PPP was portrayed as an "attack on our Indigenous way of life." It was described as an attempt to "incorporate Indigenous people into global development." In this way, anti-PPP narratives used strategic essentialism (Warren and Jackson 2002), or employed an Indigenous voice and identity to challenge the PPP's discourse on Indigenous development.

The plan's gendered impacts were also criticized. An educational booklet about "Women and the PPP" from *Mujeres para el Diálogo* in Mexico City (circa 2002) suggested that women and children would suffer the most. The PPP would deteriorate women's rights by privatizing public enterprises, cutting public spending, expanding *maquilas*, requiring women to work a "double shift" (i.e., working outside the home in addition to domestic labor), and increasing violence against women.

At forums and in educational materials the PPP was frequently associated with national or cultural memories of defeat by foreigners. The PPP was called a "project of the powerful," a military invasion, *saqueo* or sacking, and a "second conquest." Illustrations caricatured "voracious foreign companies." The PPP was described as serving transnational interests or foreign companies who want to "spread maquilas" (sweatshops), "take ownership of our rivers and natural resources" and "extract the wealth of our biodiversity." An anti-PPP slogan in this vein was "The Isthmus is not for sale."

As a variation on this theme, the PPP was described as an "evil threat to the *pueblo*" by associating it with "neoliberal policies and projects" imposed from outside Mexico already understood as harmful, such as the North American Free Trade Agreement (NAFTA), FTAA, the International Monetary Fund, the World Bank, and foreign debt. For example, a flyer distributed at the October 12, 2003 anti-PPP protests in San Cristóbal stated:

No patents on medicinal plants, on corn and on life! No transgenic seeds and agro-industry! Yes to food sovereignty. Long live the milpa [small-scale agriculture]. Get out Maquilas. Yes to dignified and just labor. Get Coca-cola, Nestle and Grupo Modelo away from our water. No privatization of education. . . . Not one more hydroelectric dam. No PROCEDE [land titling program]. Respect the ejido. No to the Plan Puebla-Panamá. No FTAA.

Counternarratives were transmitted through poetry, songs, and other artistic media. At an August 2002 women's gathering in Oaxaca, the Oaxaca City delegation shared a poem with several rhyming stanzas about the PPP, along with critiques of transgenic corn, the failure of government programs, and of foreigners buying up land: "*Al Plan Puebla-Panamá queremos bien conocer/ Para que sus construcciones no las lleguemos a ver/ No queremos corredores ni aeropuertos en el pueblo/ La lucha se hará compañeras, ya ven el ejemplo de Atenco.*"[13] The popular victory in July 2002 against the airport proposed at Atenco was held up as an inspiration. NGO leaders also distributed popular education comic books and recordings of *radio-novelas,* soap operas for radio. With creative media, counternarratives "traveled home" and diffused beyond the forums.

Ethnographic observations, life histories, and interviews are useful for revealing how participants in anti-PPP networks connected the counternarratives they heard at network events to their own lives. Tzomé Ixuk, a Tojolabal women's organization from the municipality of Las Margaritas, Chiapas, participated regularly in network events. In their life stories, the women described their opposition to the PPP as part of a long history of standing up to injustices. After describing leaving her job as a domestic worker for an abusive boss, Teresa explained she got involved with Tzomé Ixuk "so I would never have to work with that terrible man again." When asked about her involvement in anti-PPP efforts, Anita of Tzomé Ixuk explained her opposition to government initiatives in this way: "In this neighborhood, we were a group of Indigenous people who lived on a ranch in slavery for twenty-five years. It was a long and oppressive slavery for our parents and grandparents. We bring that history, which is why we decided to be against the government because they always support the *mestizos* and the caciques."

The Tzomé Ixuk women connected their anti-PPP involvement to injustices they experienced after supporting the Zapatista uprising. Militarization affected them daily. As scholars have documented (see Olivera 1998), the Mexican military and paramilitaries used sexual violence as a tool for social control. Anita explained that soldiers stopped her at checkpoints, searched her home for political propaganda, and threatened her:

They [the Public Security Guards] came to look for me because I was a catechist, because there were men, PRI-istas,[14] who didn't like me. One time they stole everything from our cooperative store and accused my parents of having stolen from us. . . . They were going to open their beaks and talk badly about what we did because we were organized.

At the anti-PPP rally on October 12, 2002 in San Cristóbal, Anita declared,

> With this movement, we're on the state and international level because there are movements in other countries against neoliberalism. . . . We will protest the Plan Puebla-Panamá, telling them that we don't want to die. We want to transform people. Even if you don't leave your house, struggle! Even if you don't leave your community, organize! Let's organize within our municipalities, because the government system is there too. In our organization of struggle, we are women in resistance.

Anita and Teresa's life histories reveal that after the anti-PPP forums, they came to see the PPP as a threat in a long history of abuses of power from sexual abuse and domestic violence, to state violence and violence from international institutions. They saw the PPP as oppressive, humiliating, and violent, like slave owners, abusive employers, soldiers, and PRI-istas.

The strength of this counternarrative is that for Anita and Teresa, their very notion of who they are includes the fact that they are "in resistance." Besides aligning Tzomé Ixuk with the Zapatista communities in resistance, being "in resistance" defines their collective identity (Melucci 1995) as in opposition to the PPP, the government, the PRI, the military. This identity connects them with others who oppose neoliberalism, as Anita expresses in her call to organize.

ACHIEVEMENTS AND LIMITS OF NETWORK POLITICS

Assessing the success of anti-PPP network politics is complex,[15] especially because its target is mobile—global capital, a transnational investment plan that moves and changes form. In the short term, a primary goal was to prevent social displacement and dispossession by discrediting the plan and blocking the completion of projects. The campaign indeed created a public relations challenge for the PPP. But investors responded by repackaging the PPP as the PM.

With the PPP's rebirth and expansion as the PM, the IDB has learned from the public relations debacle of the PPP and has not provided transparent public information about what projects are included (Carlsen and Collins 2010). Resistance to specific projects continues (see for example Bellinghausen 2014; Pickard 2006). A variety of organizations continue to produce critical writings and political education materials, extending the anti-PPP counternarratives to the PM (see for example Otros Mundos 2011). Yet in interviews conducted in 2013, grassroots and NGO activists described resistance as significantly weaker and less coordinated than it was between 2001 and 2004.

Even so, in longer-term measures, the anti-PPP campaign may be assessed more positively, particularly since the networks developed capacities for future struggle. These outcomes are better viewed by studying ethnographic social processes in addition to policy studies because policy-level studies may overlook cultural outcomes (see Giugni 1998). Long-term outcomes include the creation of transnational social networks and forums as practices for mutual education, a self-reflexive division of labor among grassroots and NGO leaders, capacities for ongoing knowledge production and communication about development plans, and counternarratives opposing "megaprojects" and collective identities of resistance. As practices for mutual learning, forums created spaces for people to meet, discuss, create common language, and develop shared values. The anti-dam roundtables demonstrate the capacity to combine research with experiential knowledge about flooding and displacement to communicate the threat of the PPP. Grassroots leaders like Félix, Anita, and Teresa gained opportunities as teachers and experts. While anti-PPP forums were not free from unequal leadership dynamics among NGO and grassroots activists, these relationships were not unexamined; the forums served as sites for reflecting on structural inequalities. Even as the regularity and frequency of these forums falters, the practices and skills the networks created remain as tools that can be reactivated. Another long-lasting achievement was the creation of counternarratives that shape participants' collective identities in opposition to governments and megaprojects. In the words of the Tzomé Ixuk women, many participants see themselves as living "in resistance." These cultural tools outlast the PPP and remain as resources for future struggles.

The need for information about shifting development plans suggests a role for NGOs that have resources for research, notwithstanding the challenges of NGO-grassroots relations. Understanding the trajectory and timing of the financing and political processes of a development plan, as well as its profit structure, is critical for opposition. For example, as Gallardo suggested in an interview, knowing when the highest profits are made during the life course of a development plan might suggest new points of intervention.

The PPP's disappearance reflects its contradictions. The plan's discourse on sustainable development is in contradiction with the lack of impact assessment of the transport and energy programs; the discourse on democratic participation was in stark contrast with the plan's disregard for Indigenous rights (Harvey 2006). There were also contradictions between development rhetoric and gendered impacts. Another set of contradictions included the financial challenge the PPP faced as a result of the global economic downturn, and the reality that multinational funding was less forthcoming than national government funding. In the IDB's evaluation, the main source for financing the PPP (US$4.5 billion as of December 2007) was regional governments, totaling 38 percent, with remaining amounts from international institutions and private donors (Linhares Pires 2008, 35). The plan's proponents admitted their challenges in solidifying political leadership and consensus and achieving effective implementation. Learning from the contradictions identified about the PPP could help activists identify weaknesses of future development plans.

As Plan Mesoamérica looms, along with other transnational agreements such as the Trans-Pacific Partnership, the strength of opposition networks may be in their resilience and longer-term consequences. Anti-PPP networks have created individual and organizational capacities that might persist beyond the short term. Future research should continue to examine the durability and significance of horizontalism and network politics in social struggles, including practices of organizing forums, studying development plans, identifying contradictions, mutual education, creating counternarratives, supporting new forms of leadership, and building collective identities. Even as citizen groups confront the power of transnational capital, cultural skills, identities, and capacities may not be easily obliterated.

NOTES

1. Harvey's (2003) concept of "accumulation by dispossession" illuminates the expropriation that opponents of the PPP fear. Yet the PPP does not represent "new imperialism" (Harvey 2003) in terms of advancing U.S. imperial interests, but rather the interests of transnational investors and capitalists, in which the United States plays a leadership role (see Robinson 2008).

2. Given the history and reality of power imbalances in research, counterinsurgency war, and concerns about biopiracy and intellectual appropriation, I found it key to communicate my commitment to shared values and reciprocity in research. My involvement with the University of the Poor, a network of U.S. organizations that some local organizations had encountered at international Zapatista gatherings, often opened doors for me to take part as a participant-observer in gatherings, forums, workshops, and planning meetings and to interview activists. I took part in the June 2002 Forum for Cultural and Biological Diversity in Xelajú, Guatemala; the August 2002 Encuentro de Mujeres del Sureste in Oaxaca; the November 2002 Hemispheric Assembly against the FTAA in Havana, Cuba; the November 2003 Independent Women's Movement (MIM) Week of No to Violence against Women; and the March 2004 Forum against Neoliberalism in Huitiupán, Chiapas. I also took part in planning meetings for the Huitiupán and the MIM Co-property meetings. I conducted all interviews in Spanish; all translations are mine.

3. Neither the official IADB web page, http://www.iadb.org/ppp, nor the Mexican government PPP page, http://ppp.presidencia.gob.mx, have been available since 2003. The official PPP site (2001 to 2007) is archived: http://web.archive.org/web/20071029105130/http://www.planpuebla-panama.org/. Official documents are available on the IDB website http://www.iadb.org/.

4. The eight initiatives are energy, transportation, telecommunication, trade and competitiveness, sustainable development, human development, natural disaster prevention, and tourism.

5. An analysis of the Plan Mesoamérica is beyond the scope of this paper. For further assessment of the plan, see Pickard (2006), Zunino (2010), Wilson (2008), and Sandoval, Álvarez de Flores, and Fernández (2011).

6. See Harvey (2004, 2006b), Stahler-Sholk (2008), Call (2002, 2003a, 2003b) and Swords (2007).

7. See Call (2002, 2003a, 2003b), Harvey (2004, 2006a, 2006b), Kalny (2010), McElhinny and Nickinson (2004), Spalding (2008), as well as Center of Economic and Political Investigations of Community Action reports, including Pickard (2003, 2004, 2006), Wilson (2008), and Zunino (2010).

8. For more background on preexisting organizational networks, see Swords (2005, 2010).

9. Alianza Cívica's newsletter, *Poder Ciudadano*, number 21 (2002) describes this roundtable's results. I received reports from February 2003 and observed from August 2003 to June 2004.

10. The term *comadre* literally is the relationship between a mother and her child's godmother.

11. NGOs in Chiapas rely on funding from multilateral agencies, government aid agencies, large NGO cooperation organizations, church-funded agencies, and private foundations (Benessaieh 2011). Organizations in the anti-PPP networks described rejecting funding from international institutions, the U.S. government, and other entities they believed would manipulate their agendas for control or counterinsurgency. As Benassaieh (2011, 82) documents, NGO funding decisions involve both "strategic acquiescence and reluctant accommodation" to funders' priorities.

12. These included the Encuentro Sur-Norte (San Cristobal, Chiapas 2000); the weeks on Biological and Cultural Diversity in Xela, Guatemala, and San Cristóbal, Chiapas (2001 and 2002); the Forums against Neoliberalism in Nuevo Huixtán and Huitiupán, Chiapas (February 2003 and March 2004); anti-PPP meetings in Xalapa, Veracruz, and Managua, Nicaragua (June and July 2002); and the eighth Southeast Mexico Women's Encuentro in Oaxaca (August 2002).

13. Translation: "We'd like to get to know the Plan Puebla-Panamá well so that we don't ever see its projects. We don't want [biological] corridors, or airports in our towns. We will make this struggle, brothers and sisters, following the example of Atenco."

14. PRI-istas are members of the *Partido Revolucionario Institucional*, the political party that governed for more than seventy years.

15. On social movement outcomes, see Gamson ([1973] 2003) and Giugni (1998). Giugni addresses the importance of examining both short- and long-term outcomes, and of cultural consequences of movements.

Chapter Seven

Honduras

*Refounding the Nation, Building a New
Kind of Social Movement*

Suyapa Portillo Villeda

On November 24, 2013, at the Escuela Normal Mixta Pedro Nufio in Colonia Kennedy, the largest voting center in Tegucigalpa, enthusiastic Libertad y Refundación (LIBRE)[1] supporters turned out to vote throughout the day. But as late afternoon turned into night, so did the hopes for LIBRE fade, as a host of inconsistencies in the election process gave way to serious errors in the scrutiny and tabulation of the votes.[2] These days were not too far removed from the National Popular Resistance Front (FNRP, Frente Nacional de Resistencia Popular) assembly in 2011 (Portillo 2013a), when an eager populace gathered to represent their municipalities, towns, and collectives in a festive day of speeches to usher in a new era of democratic participation in Honduran politics. But on this election evening the mood was somber, as it became apparent that democracy had been thwarted by the appointed custodians of the tally sheets engaging in illegal transactions for their interested parties. LIBRE would be shut out this night from the high echelons of power, and from the presidency, by the right wing. Despite thousands of falsified ballot tally sheets, the Supreme Court of Honduras and the Electoral College turned a blind eye—throwing their support behind the extreme right-wing candidate. This would not be the year for Honduras to see the democratic election of a progressive leader to power. Despite the corruption, the falsification of tally sheets, the erroneous count, and the compromised Supreme Court and Electoral College, the Honduran people and delegates in the FNRP assemblies are confident that LIBRE actually won the vote count by a landslide. While many feel that LIBRE was robbed of the presidency, the party

121

did earn a host of *diputados* (congressional representatives) and some mayors in municipalities. Moreover, LIBRE won in the minds of resisters who had been organized since the 2009 coup d'état.

No one could have predicted that in November 2013, Hondurans would be deciding to vote on candidates from not two, but nine parties. Even more surprising was the sharp departure from the bipartisan past, and naming for the first time a powerful socialist, leftist candidate—a woman, Xiomara Castro de Zelaya—for a new party, the LIBRE party.[3] Given the history of Honduras within the Central American region, for some that seemed a historic, profound, and welcome change from politics as usual. Still other groups dissented and argued for a move away from electoral politics, instead advocating for strengthening the nascent wide-open (*amplio*) movement. Ultimately, all proved to be overpowered by a growing right wing, with larger connections to the organized right in Latin America.[4] But the new political dynamics created out of the ashes of the coup d'état are still unparalleled in Honduran history. This chapter looks at this movement and its origins, not just as a response to the coup but also as a response by a constellation of preexisting movements of labor unions, *campesinos*, political organizations, collectives, and even some nongovernmental organizations (NGOs) that came together in what we now know as the FNRP, a body that emerged in response to President Zelaya's forced removal from office.[5] People from all corners of the country took to the street in protest every day, withstanding the heat, police batons, the blood-red spray of a special peppery tear gas, illegal arrests, snipers, and even rape.[6] The coalition of sectors that would eventually become the FNRP, as broad and diverse as it was, and rooted in varied histories of organizing, also challenged the old conceptions of social movements and the left that Hondurans held about themselves.[7]

Most significantly, it must be noted that the path of Honduran social movements has rarely been free of U.S. influence; for decades the United States has loomed large in the domestic affairs of Honduras. Both the coup d'état and the elections of 2013 resemble an all-too-familiar Honduras, a twentieth-century Honduras that lived under the domination of the U.S. State Department and, before that, the United Fruit Company and the Standard Fruit Company. But what could be different now? In this chapter, I link three seemingly unrelated sectors within the resistance movement in Honduras in order to engage the contradictions, points of unity, and frameworks used to cross political and ideological borders to get to the work of *refounding* (*refundar*) Honduras. When do the collaboration and confrontation between older and newer sectors within the social movement provide opportunities for or curtail change? What are potential intersections and possibilities? The diversity of the FNRP—la Resistencia—gives it a dynamic position within the new social movements in the region. It is a viable means by which the resistance can confront acts by the right wing, which turned the people's vote into mockery by fraudulently crowning as president the Nationalist party candidate (who really came in third, if not fourth, place in most voting polls) (Portillo 2013a). This chapter deals with the organized resistance movement and its historical antecedents, and provides a look at the sociopolitical map of the resistance movement and a historical context for the development of the FNRP, which was consolidated during the 2009 coup d'état. The resistance movement was not spontaneous, situational, or temporary, but rather a product of a long history of social movements in the country. I contend that the resistance movement is different from what has been seen in Honduras before because of the involvement of new sectors, which challenge and compete for space along with other marginalized actors now at the center of mobilization (i.e., women, ethnic groups, and LGBTTI[8] communities). Moreover, the FNRP overall has demonstrated its coalitional character, allowing for participation of multiple sectors with very South-South transnational dimensions; for instance, solidarity comes from countries in South and Central America, as opposed to only the United States.[9] By looking at the new actors in this context of social mobilization, we can appreciate the diversity of strategy and tactics that aim to subvert the imposition of modern-day dictatorial rule by neoliberal technocrats and business.

UN GOLPE ANUNCIADO: THE AWAKENING OF A PEOPLE

On June 28, 2009, at 5:00 in the morning, the Honduran military broke through the front door of democratically elected president Manuel Zelaya Rosales, detained the president in his pajamas, and put him on a plane to Costa Rica, first stopping to refuel at Soto Cano Air Base, the U.S. airbase formerly known as Palmerola in the 1980s.[10] That very same day the *Consulta Popular*[11] was slated to take place during the special election, where people would answer a nonbinding poll from the executive branch of government asking them if they agreed to have a fourth ballot box installed for the general election that upcoming November. The vote never happened. Here is where most of the confusion about the process among the international community lies, a confusion propagated by the media and conservative sectors. The *Consulta Popular* was no more than a poll, an inquiry to the general citizenry, to get their opinion about having a fourth ballot that would then allow them to vote on the possibility of a national Constitutional Assembly. The Honduran people would have had two opportunities to voice their opinion on the issue, first in an informal poll that would ask them if the actual vote on the Constitutional Assembly should take place later that year, and the vote itself that November. The *Consulta Popular* galvanized civil society, and the campaign for that additional vote in November was dubbed the fourth ballot box. The right claimed that Zelaya wanted to change the constitution to remain in power indefinitely—but the reality was that he wanted to call a Constitutional Assembly to change the constitution for the benefit of disenfranchised sectors of Honduran civil society and social movements. What gets lost in the memory of the *Consulta Popular* campaign is that this was one of the first times that a president had used this tool in Honduras with such high stakes for the rights and livelihood of so many. The possibility of engaging their government and even changing the constitution was not just about Zelaya wanting to stay in office, but also about addressing a series of social inequalities imposed on the Indigenous and Afro-descendant populations, LGBTTI groups, women, and working-class Hondurans, all excluded from the protections of the state. The 1982 constitution was written as a top-down constitution in the worst year of atrocities in nearby Central American countries, under the Cold War world of Ronald Reagan and U.S.-backed Nicaraguan *contras* (counterrevolutionaries) operating out of Honduras. The constitution lacked basic rights to recalls and referendums, and lacked a "bill of rights" with race and ethnic protections, gender equity, protection of the environment, and rights to land for *campesinos* and Indigenous groups.

The *Consulta Popular* concept proved threatening to the elite and businessmen, the conservative military sectors, and Zelaya's competitors within his own Liberal Party because it was perceived to be a vehicle to change the constitution in ways that would not benefit them either financially or politically. The collusion of these powers orchestrated the coup, and effectively shut down any suffrage. Moreover, in response to mass public outcry, these powers imposed a state of siege and opened the doors for the military to exert control in the streets and beat protesters in widespread violation of civil and human rights. Despite the repression, Hondurans marched every day from June 28, 2009, to early January 2010, seeking to restore democracy.[12]

It is important to understand the coup d'état as a rebuke to progressive movements in Honduras. The coup d'état was executed with the collaboration of the Liberal Party elite, businessmen, the military, and the conservative and hierarchical Catholic Church—all of whom had been loyal to Zelaya in the past, before he underwent a transformation from a neoliberal president in a failing economy to a president who engaged the growing left in Latin America. At the outset of his presidency, sectors of Zelaya's cabinet had been leftist in the past, but for the most part Zelaya's cabinet belonged to the Liberal Party's landed elite. He showed some populist tendencies but could hardly be called a leftist. Zelaya had supported a fairly neoliberal agenda. Honduras before the coup was (and still is) the largest exporter of immigrant bodies (and given the remittances immigrants send home, more profitable than the export of coffee and bananas) to the United States and other countries (Barahona 2008). The country faced growing lawlessness and a poor economy where only the rich benefited.

Yet according to Father Ismael Moreno of the Jesuit Society, one of the biggest problems that has loomed large for Hondurans was the two-party rule system:

> The two traditional parties [National Party and Liberal Party] have governed the last 27 years that we have had of democracy. Just as elections have been the vehicle for both parties to distribute the three powers of state, political reforms have been converted into instruments to strengthen and consolidate the power that the Nationalist Party and Liberal Party exercise on the state and the rule of law. (Moreno 2008, 17)[13]

Father Moreno's essay, "Gobierno Formal/Gobierno Real: ¿Qué movimiento social frente a esta contradicción?" written in 2008 for the Honduran journal *Envío*, eerily describes the forces that would become the coup plotters in 2009 and also offers an interesting analysis of the emerging social movement, a mixture of old and new:

> The model of Honduran democracy is hostage to the two-party rule; it is exhaustive in formalities and deep in social inequity. Up to today, the popular and social movement is trapped within the nostalgia of past struggle and the dispersion of an uncertain present; while in the communities and territories, something is beginning to move. (Moreno 2008, 16)

These two political parties for decades traded political power between each other and also created an impossible system for any other party, aligning their fortunes with the business elite who anointed the elections and or became the candidates themselves. The suffrage process had become perfunctory, a routine that convinced many that they were actually selecting a candidate. Once elected, the candidate of the elite would be consecrated as democratically elected, as if the elite at the beginning of the process had not chosen them (Moreno 2008, 16).

Zelaya was expected to follow the path set out by the elite businessmen, and for the most part he did. But in 2008, his last year in office prior to the coup, Zelaya and his cabinet took two significant actions. First, Zelaya raised the minimum wage. Due to free-trade laws, this minimum wage law would only apply to domestic producers and not the foreign *maquilas* and exporters and other free-trade sectors. This enraged local domestic producers and landowners, who had become accustomed to having an open-door policy and powerful influence with Honduran presidents and their cabinets. Second, he entered Honduras into ALBA (the Bolivarian Alliance for the Americas, sponsored by then president Hugo Chávez of Venezuela) (Harris and Azzi 2006).

In order for Honduras to be competitive in the larger Latin American market, and enter ALBA, it would have to respond to the social and political changes initiated by more developed nations, such as those in South America. Zelaya's government had to confront this situation: how to enter into a more egalitarian relationship with the Honduran people in order to have cooperation in his social programs. Civil society would need to be integrated, and not just the richest oligarchic sectors but also the middle classes and the working poor; in ALBA, countries aspired to a successful economy measured not only by the richest sectors, but by its middle classes and labor sectors. Opening up a dialogue with civil society, and in particular social movements, built support for Zelaya (Lara 2010). He met with sectors that had been his opposition—coalitions of labor unions, and women's groups, among many others; this was notably the first time that disenfranchised groups had the opportunity to express their issues and desires for their sectors to a welcoming executive.

Zelaya's growing relationship with social sectors threatened the Liberal Party elite who may have felt he was straying from their reach. The orchestrators of the coup, once loyal to Zelaya, viciously turned against him. Immediately after the coup d'état, Roberto Micheletti, the president of congress (a presidential appointee of Zelaya), presented a fake resignation letter purportedly from the president to congress and the Honduran people—justifying the coup. The business elite and the post-coup government in control colluded in the largest media blackout the country had ever seen. In fact, beyond the blackout, news outlets were found to have doctored images and intentionally skewed the news by changing the facts.[14] Chanting, "*Nos tienen miedo porque no tenemos miedo,*"[15] in response, the Honduran people, in the largest protests ever seen in the history of the country, took to the streets. The people protested daily.[16]

While in the United States, the U.S. Embassy and the State Department ignored/refused to call it a coup d'état, the people formed la Resistencia, which would later be consecrated into the FNRP. The resistance began a long process of building a nonviolent movement that would be representative of a large section of the population, and that would address the needs of all those who took to the streets—from the grandmother, to the transgender woman, to the leftist union leader, to the youth. The process, an ongoing one, remains one of the largest challenges ever to confront Hondurans—that of building a movement that speaks to all and for all, a "movement of movements" (Asociación Colectivo Violeta, Asociación Kukulcan, Asociación LGTB Arco Iris de Honduras, APUVIMEH 2012, 27).

HISTORICAL ANTECEDENTS OF HONDURAN-U.S. RELATIONS

Honduras has been a key geopolitical outpost for the United States, historically and presently. Centrally located in the heart of Latin America, it is prime territory from which the United States can monitor Latin America, and Honduras's bicoastal sea access makes it key for trade and military operations in both the Caribbean and the Pacific Ocean. The systematic domination of Honduras by North American commerce and culture dates back to the late 1850s, starting with the efforts to build an interoceanic canal through Honduras.[17] Later the interests of the mining sector and banana producers raised the country's profile as a U.S. region of concern. The U.S. State Department guarded American business interests in the lands to the south (Barahona 1989, 1–6). These business interests quickly became military concerns, as the United States sought to protect potential routes and new investments in a relatively "open" country still mired in regionalism from recent civil wars and political strife (Barahona 1989, 6–10).

Honduras's relationship to the United States dates back to the nineteenth century, when an unequal relationship was forged with the North American Rosario Mining Company, the United Fruit Company, the Standard Fruit Company, and other small banana companies and North American business adventurers. By the first decades of the twentieth century the power of these companies in Honduras was unparalleled, leading historian Marvin Barahona (1989) to deem the relationship hegemonic and totalitarian within the region. This unequal and problematic relationship led to the development of an elite class that is closely linked to the export economy model and comfortable with a neocolonial economic and cultural relationship with the United States (Dunkerley 1988). So paternalistic has been the economic and cultural relationship between Honduras and the United States, with Honduras as the stereotypical "banana republic," that historian Dario Euraque (1998; 2003) documented the existence of a Ku Klux Klan in the 1930s North Coast banana region, among the most radical examples of U.S. omnipotence in the country (see also Barahona 2005). The extremity of the case makes it stand out, but it is clear that the cultural, political, and economic reach of the United States in the region has been steady and ongoing.

During the first half of the twentieth century, the U.S. preoccupation with Honduras centered on protecting their business interests, those of the United Fruit Company and Standard Fruit Company, which often required U.S. support for authoritarian rulers, such as Tiburcio Carías Andino, founder of the modern day Nationalist Party and prototypical *caudillo* (Portillo 2011). While this ensured the best production of bananas for export, the people stagnated under a repressive regime that granted national land to foreigners, favored large landowners, and created a system of debt peonage that led to starvation and misery. Dissenters were crushed for speaking their minds or simply voting for the opposition Liberal Party. Entire generations either organized underground or migrated to nearby countries such as Guatemala in the late 1940s and early 1950s, where more democratic presidents were in power. There, organizers learned about organizing, but also about the ways in which government could be run to empower people and what could be done in their home countries. The many engaged in the organizing of the Partido Democrático Revolucionario Hondureño in 1944, and others in the formation of the second Communist Party in Honduras in 1954. All at some point in history engaged in the organizing around the great banana strike of 1954, which was seen as an option for liberation for Hondurans (Portillo 2011).

When Carías left power in 1944, finding himself no longer under the protectorate of the United States as it was occupied with World War II, he chose his successor, a lawyer for the United Fruit Company, Juan Manuel Gálvez (Barahona 1989, 2004). Free and fair elections continued to be an issue and in 1954, Ramón Villeda Morales won the presidency, though he was not allowed to transition into the presidency until 1957 (Dunkerley 1988). By the time the United States and Honduras signed a bilateral military agreement in 1954, the United States was clearly and openly entrenched in Honduran everyday politics and culture.[18] Connections between *criollo* (creole) Honduran families and U.S. companies date back to this period, influencing a generation of Hondurans with U.S. loyalties and understanding of world politics and especially Latin American politics.

Shortly after, in 1962, Villeda Morales was deposed, and since 1963 a series of military juntas took control until 1979. The U.S. State Department found that the "free" elections of late 1970s would lead to "democratic" governments—again, with hand-picked leaders, like Roberto Suazo Córdova, under whose presidency heinous human rights atrocities were committed, including the disappearances of students and *campesinos*.[19] The significance of this period lies in the history of the Cold War, and its best exemplified by the Constitutional Assembly of 1982, which produced an iron-clad constitution that basically did not allow the people of Honduras the right to question their government, or even to protect civil rights. This era of "national security" was typified by the hunting down of presumed communists or leftists, Hondurans seen as "internal enemies."[20] The constitution served the interest of the U.S. government—providing a safety net for counterinsurgency against the leftist movements of the era. Against the backdrop of the 1982 constitution, the political will of Honduran people continued to stagnate, as they were rushed from authoritarian rule into the neoliberal era—one laden with more corruption and instability.

During the 1980s, Honduras was again useful to the United States in their invasion of Grenada and the formation of the counterrevolutionaries (*contras*) to fight the Frente Sandinista de Liberación Nacional (FSLN) in Nicaragua as well as the military campaign against the Frente Farabundo Martí de Liberación Nacional (FMLN) in El Salvador.[21] While Honduras did boast a small radical and revolutionary group of leftists during the period, they were hunted down, disappeared, or had to flee the country; many would join ranks with the FMLN and FSLN, because they saw it as a regional leftist struggle for all of Central America.

The geopolitical location of Honduras, both for U.S. interests and regional Latin American elite interests, creates an interesting stage for the United States to demonstrate its power and for Latin American right wing groups to exercise their agenda (Grandin 2006, 3, 19). The right wing in Latin America during this current neoliberal period encompassed both conservatives and former liberals—an example clearly seen in Honduras. The U.S. Embassy, President Barack Obama, and Secretary of State Hillary Clinton refused to even acknowledge the Honduras coup d'état as a coup; their actions and presence were complicit in destabilizing the country, as would be revealed in the Wikileaks memos in 2011.[22] The leaked documents on Wikileaks proved to many Honduran resisters that not only did the United States know what was happening, but also stood idly by, watching the coup plotters break the rule of law and violate the constitution and their rights as citizens.

THE FORMATION OF THE NATIONAL POPULAR RESISTANCE FRONT (FNRP)

The outcry that developed in the streets of Honduras against the political military coup and the ousting of the president was consolidated as la Resistencia, the National Front of Resistance against the Coup d'État.[23] While large numbers of Hondurans reacted immediately and in unity against the coup d'état and oppression of civilians, it is important to understand that the resistance that persevered over the immediate eight months following the coup was not purely spontaneous and has roots in a history of organizing in the country. Previous organizing campaigns, collaborations, and coalitions among the different sectors of society created the infrastructure necessary to sustain such a prolonged response from the Honduran people.[24] The high degree of unity and cooperation among various actors within the resistance movement, though sudden, is best understood as a product or outgrowth of past work by many social actors. Yet the resistance and the coming together of so many organizations far superseded the plans or expectations of any single group or progressive agenda in Honduras. The *"Honduran Spring,"* to take inspiration from Egypt during the same summer, was marked by over 190 days of daily protest, daily meetings of la Resistencia, and the formation of resistance collectives throughout the various disenfranchised neighborhoods, small villages, and every nook and cranny of working class neighborhoods in the cities, and also in small hamlets, villages, and pueblos.[25]

Father Moreno (2008, 19) documented what the social movement looked like in Honduras, which he named "five expressions." First is the traditional popular movement, made up of labor unions and labor federations, focused on their sectoral interests and rarely participated with other sectors. The second is the emerging popular movement, which was still developing its identity but for the most part was supported by nonprofit organization funds, largely provided resources to "Indigenous groups, Garífunas, women, youth, environmentalist and gay communities." Third, Moreno described the movement of "territorial community organizations"—groups based locally and linked to protecting and defending their land, such as local neighborhoods and territories (*patronatos*). These organizations were a different model of organizing, one that returned to a preoccupation with the rights to land and life, including such movements as the Western Regional Neighborhood Organization (Patronato Regional de Occidente), Social Forum of the Valley of Sula (Foro Social del Valle de Sula), Environmentalist Movement of Olancho (Movimiento Ambientalista de Olancho), and the organization on the banks of the Ulúa river in the Bajo Aguán. Moreno calls the fourth expression "groups of political action," which engaged with the government around one particular issue or theme. These could be nonprofit groups or private development groups—which are so broad that some are on the side of private enterprise. Fifth and last, the "fronts of political struggle" are the large coalitions that bring together organizations both regionally or nationally—for instance, the Bloque Popular (Popular Block) in the center of the country, Coordinating Body of Organizations in the Aguán (Coordinadora de Organizaciones del Aguán), and Popular Permanent Assembly of El Progreso (Asamblea Popular Permanente del Progreso). The largest body is the National Coordination Body of the Resistance (Coordinadora Nacional de Resistencia) that can be said to encompass the first three "expressions."[26] This last body was perhaps the best functioning body, from which actors provided leadership to the resistance after the protest against the coup d'état broke out.

The FNRP is really a conglomeration of three diverse political sectors that work in a coalitional formation: 1) the Zelayistas (Liberal Party members loyal to Zelaya), 2) the National Front of Popular Resistance, and 3) the everyday citizen and marginalized communities—the neighbor who perhaps had not been involved before; the young people from marginalized neighborhoods or small hamlets who defied the imposed curfew and came out at night to protest, take pictures of their protest, or sign and post them on Facebook or YouTube, defying the media blackout.[27] Most Zelayistas are Liberal Party members; some are part of the *criollo* elite families. The Liberal Party members are for the most part political centrists, and have historically held close elite and institutional ties to the United States. While Liberal Party members have never staged a coup d'état, until 2013 they were traditionally allied to U.S. interests, and for the most part have remained right of center and great proponents of free trade and privatization. In several significant historical moments, however, they have had trysts with the leftists. Namely, the early formation of the Great Banana Strike of 1954 saw such a connection, only to see the Liberal Party ally with U.S. interests in the end, effectively truncating the initial efforts of the strike (Barahona 2004; also see Portillo 2011). Zelaya has retained support from a portion of the Liberal Party; loyalty to the democratically elected president has helped maintain firm opposition to the coup. The alignment of Zelayistas at this time with the progressive left sector is notable.

The progressive left, which makes up part of the FNRP, is a conglomeration of different political left-leaning movements with a variety of historical connections to the later 1960s and 1970s leftist political battles, as well as some new currents of leftist politics. Included here are different militant federations of labor, such as the Unitary Federation of Honduran Workers (FUTH, Federación Unitaria de Trabajadores de Honduras), along with nonprofit sectors that work on issues of gender and sexuality, ethnicity and race, other collectives, and the progressive media, Radio Progreso, Radio Uno, Radio/TV Globo. Also traditionally forgotten in Honduras social struggles are *campesino* organizations, such as Unified Farmworker Movement from the Aguán Valley (MUCA, Movimiento Unificado de Campesinos del Aguán), in the Aguán valley and other cooperative organizations, and *campesino* organizations of the western and southern regions. *Campesino* and Indigenous movements are aligned in groups, such as Civic Council of Popular and Indigenous Organizations (COPINH, Consejo Cívico de Organizaciones Populares e Indígenas de Honduras) and the Black Fraternal Organization of Honduras (OFRANEH, Organización Fraternal Negra de Honduras).

The wide-open (*amplio*) nature of the FNRP allowed for community members to engage at various levels—on the local neighborhood level, at the regional representative level, and at the national level during larger assemblies. This dynamic convergence has set a new path for future social movements and has created an opening for the inclusion of previously marginalized social actors. While there are parallels with past organized movements, I suggest here that Honduras is entering a new period of organizing, marked by a realignment of national left, progressive, and liberal movements and an openness to previously marginalized sectors and communities.

The National Popular Resistance Front was formed in 2009 in the capital city of Tegucigalpa with representatives from the major regions of the country: the North Coast, the west, and the south. By November 2009 organizers were set to tighten and/or formalize the grouping created by the FNRP, and sought to pursue as a strategy a boycott of the illegal election planned for November. The boycott strategy worked, people effectively did not vote, and it also demonstrated to the FNRP just how deep their reach was. Ultimately, nearly 60 percent of the population did not vote—yet Porfirio Lobo Sosa was imposed on the populace as president. The FNRP needed to figure out where it would go from there. While the older leftists expected a long and arduous path, based on experiences from previous struggles, other sectors would be tested.

The FNRP has come about as a response and opportunity for unity among sectors that had not coalesced before, for example, the feminist groups and the traditionally male-dominated labor unions. Another example is the collaboration among the LGBTTI sectors and many of the leftist groups and labor unions. But the FNRP also has successfully agglomerated the regular uninvolved—at least up until this point—community members or common citizens.

Tensions Within and Without: Social Movement versus Electoral Strategy

In 2011 the FNRP called a National Assembly, this time not only including the national sectors but also the "Nineteenth Department" comprised of Hondurans living in the United States, Canada, and other countries. At this meeting the discussion centered on the formation of a political party that would be inspired by the FNRP but would participate in the next electoral campaign. This assembly was an important moment for Hondurans; it is here where the decision to create the LIBRE political party was voted on by delegates. The decision also caused controversy, as many people, particularly from the women's movement and Afrodescendant and Indigenous organizations, stated their claim to maintaining the National Resistance Front as a wide-open (*amplio*) social movement. The dialogue and debate took place in Tegucigalpa, with President Zelaya present as well as the elected members of the FNRP. Zelaya's attempted returns and finally his successful clandestine return and refuge in the Brazilian Embassy allowed him to be elected as the coordinator of the movement, a position he still holds today.

The assembly brought to light multiple agendas in the larger movement, but two strong competing agendas gained traction: one, the wider social movement's call to remain a social movement and make demands of the state from below; and the second, to convert the movement into a political party that could guide the wide popular support into an election. While some believe that both proposals won—after all, the political party (LIBRE) was created out of the FNRP, which continued as the popular social movement—others felt that the creation of the political party thwarted the continued growth and power of the popular movement.

Although the movement changed in 2011 with the decision to enter electoral politics, there were a lot of external factors also influencing that change, including rising human rights violations and state repression. I claim here that it was not solely internal tensions that led to what is perceived as a split in the movement between the "refounders" (wide-open social movement proponents) and the "electoral camp" (the proponents of an electoral party);

external factors, such as state violence, murders, death threats, human rights violations, and U.S. involvement in Honduran domestic affairs also influenced the direction of the resistance movement. It is these external factors that have been more divisive and profoundly damaging to internal group organization than anything else. Even as groups have been contributing to a broader movement and electoral effort, individual sectors have had particular challenges to contend with. It is in these struggles that we can see both the creativity and hardships of organizing in the face of particularized oppression in the post-coup environment, as well as the ongoing commitment to resistance and widening of opportunities to expand the movement.

GENDERED HUMAN RIGHTS VIOLATIONS: LGBTTI COMMUNITIES

A young female lawyer with the At-Large Movement for Dignity and Justice (Movimiento Amplio por la Dignidad y Justicia—MADJ), who had been in touch with me in Los Angeles after a speaking tour, sent me a spreadsheet that documented 3,033 illegal arrests and 4,344 human rights violations during the coup and leading up to illegal elections of November 2009. The spreadsheets took account of everyone who was beaten, gassed, or arrested during daily protests leading up to the elections. The human rights toll continued to rise, and soon the first and most affected group was the LGBTTI community that saw fifteen execution-style murders within the transgender community alone.[28] A Human Rights Watch report released in 2009 calculated seventeen transgender women murders from 2004 to 2009;[29] in the span of a few months after the coup, the number nearly doubled. Most of those killed were transgender women and gay men. While the rise in the numbers of deaths of transgender women, many of them sex workers, went unnoticed by the larger resistance movement, it is this community's ability to effectively advocate internationally that brought much-needed attention to Honduras and to the extrajudicial murders and ineffective courts. During the first months of coalescing of the resistance, small marginal groups had a lot of room to include LGBTTI communities. At the same time, these small organizations and collectives would have to compete with larger and more established organizations on the wide-open stage for attention to their agendas and for leadership positions. Representation of the LGBTTI community was important and was taken into consideration when formulating plans for the FNRP and even in public events—the microphone was openly available. In fact, LGBTTI groups first formed coalitions against the coup that engaged directly with the FNRP, such as the Coalition of LGBTTI against the Coup d'État (Coalición LGBTTI Contra el Golpe de Estado) (Portillo et al. 2011). Like every group in the FNRP, the LGBTTI community had its specific demands and their very own structural problems in their organizing. Both the superficiality of the FNRP's representation model and the structural divisions within LGBTTI groups failed to meet the promise of deepening the agenda for both. Seeing themselves as concerned citizens and loyal supporters of the resistance but marginal to the leadership structure of the FNRP, LGBTTI groups and individuals began to organize fundamental and important international ties abroad with groups in the United States, Germany, Spain, Argentina, and other Central American countries. A good example has been the human rights reporting of the collective Red Lésbica CATTRACHAS,[30] among other organizations, and activists like Walter Tróchez, a human rights worker killed in December 2009. The international work of transgender women and their international networks, such as the work of Colectivo Violeta in Tegucigalpa and the Colectivo Color Rosa in San Pedro Sula within the transnational Latin-American and Caribbean Network of Transgender REDLACTRANS, were also significant.[31]

It was not the fact that the LGBTTI community was particularly well organized that made them visible during coup protests and organizing meetings; in fact they remained marginal to large social movement organizing up until then. What made them visible was their recent experience of belonging and working within transnational networks beyond Honduras. LGBTTI organizations, at the time of the coup, had already been engaged in human rights work around issues of HIV/AIDs, seeking NGO status for their organizations and addressing gender identity issues with regional and national governmental offices and society at large. These organizations were able to translate their ongoing efforts, effectively demonstrating their intersectionality (multiple dimensions of oppression and discrimination) as a unifying factor in the post-coup resistance, and for the first time became visible as potential allies to the traditional left. Two particular international networks provided avenues to denounce the situation during the media blackout: 1) the HIV/AIDs networks of organization and health promoters, and 2) the Latin American feminist networks. Both of these acted as funnels to denounce and disseminate news about the illegality of the coup, the human rights violations, and the unprecedented resistance on the streets despite the imposed media blackout.

While LGBTTI representation has not translated to an end to homophobia within the traditional leftist sector, nor within the solidarity movement or the transnational Central American people's movements, it has created an opening that did not exist before. A collection of these moments throughout the years, particularly since 2009, have opened some channels and closed others. Visits by Honduran LGBTTI activists Indyra Mendoza, Erick Vidal Martinez, and Pepe Palacios to Los Angeles, California and other U.S. cities led to the construction of transnational ties with communities and individuals, as well as issues, among people of color. CATTRACHAS has maintained an effective network to communicate the domestic situation internationally when the local and national Honduran government does not listen or act:

> The organizations of sexual diversity have managed to position themselves as resource to international organizations and human rights institutions that use our information for their reports and recommendations to the Honduran government. The international community and specially Human Rights organizations have repudiated the murders of LGBTTI community members, have expressed concern upon seeing the impunity against the violent crimes and have asked the Honduran government to adopt effective methods to sanction the guilty perpetrators. The Inter-American Commission on Human Rights in their report *Honduras: Derechos Humanos y Golpe de Estado* of December 2009, documented the violence and discrimination against the LGBTTI community (Portillo 2013b).

Disseminating their own communiqués and reports, groups like CAT-TRACHAS managed to obtain international attention and have been able to provide an archive of the deaths that would not be recorded anywhere as LGBTTI. Furthermore, they determined the needs and the strategies in critical ways that allowed for a clear connection, and generated a "boomerang" effect that has placed pressure on the Honduran government of Pepe Lobo from international sectors, adding strength to the well-articulated national demands of the LGBTTI community (Keck and Sikkink 1998, 36, 258–59) . This demonstrated not only agency from Honduran actors, but also an intentional use of international networks to do the work that the state should have been responsible for—demonstrating once again the lawlessness/ungovernability and chaos of the presidencies that would follow the coup d'état. To many LGBTTI folks, Honduras is incapable of protecting them, and they choose to migrate—both to Spain and the United States (Portillo 2006).

Upon the creation of the LIBRE Party, a group called the Movement of Diversity in Resistance (MDR) was formed by college-educated gay men who work on human rights advocacy, under the banner "*Socialismo Sí, Homofobia No.*"[32] This group has yet to demonstrate its ability within the larger movement, and its future holds potential, but to date the group has exhibited the same problems that most LGBTTI nonprofit organizations present—an absence of lesbian and bisexual women leaders and participants. MDR's work has taken root in the capital city, and one of their first major campaigns was to work for the candidacy of the first gay man to run for congress, Erick Vidal Martínez. The MDR, however, has not expanded to the rest of the country, such as the North Coast where there is a large population of LGBTTI members. The preponderance of gay male leadership in a country where the left has been marked by male and masculine domination—from unions to the ballot box—is not surprising. It seems imperative, however, that the work of lesbians and transgender women should take special priority.

Two important things came out of the post-coup struggle, besides the creation of LGBTTI collectives and groups, large and small. For one, the LGBTTI community was able to formulate a political slate to run the first transgender woman, Claudia Spellman, in San Pedro Sula, and an openly gay candidate, Erick Vidal Martínez, in Tegucigalpa, for congress in the primaries under the LIBRE Party. Although these candidates did not get past the primaries, their public profile and the discrimination they faced allowed for a public discussion in certain sectors of the LIBRE party.[33] Their images graced the newspapers and local TV news where they would be able to get important information out to the nation. Secondly, groups like CATTRA-CHAS, along with other organizations such as MDR and APUVIMEH in a coalitional effort, and with international pressure, forced the administration to pass Article 321 of the penal code, which protects the LGBTTI community (and women and other marginalized and vulnerable communities) from hate crimes.[34] This was a historic battle that is now threatened and people fear will be rolled back by the new regime of President Juan Orlando Hernández and the Nationalist party, which has ties to evangelical pastors such as Evelio Reyes, who is famous for asking the Honduran people in his sermons and on TV to not vote for the gay and transgender candidates because it was a sin. Thanks to Article 321 of the penal code, the slandered candidates were able to put him on trial; though the case was not resolved in favor of the transgender woman and gay man, the fact that a pastor was brought to trial for hate crimes is truly historic in the context of Honduras.[35] Unity however is hard to achieve under threat of a constant and unrelenting rate of murders and homicides of transgender women, gay men, and lesbians. In 2013, CATTRA-CHAS reported twenty-six murders of LGBTTI community members.[36]

Feminists in Resistance

The chasm between feminist groups and LGBTTI groups in Central America exists due to both ideological and structural issues (Berger 2006). This is not to say that lesbian feminists or LGBTTI feminists do not exist, but rather that there are two camps. Ideologically, some of the feminist groups have waged important battles against free trade in Central America, violence against women, rights to fair wages for women, and more importantly, legislation to protect the rights of women and children. It is feminist organizations that provided a sharp analysis on feminicides, the intentional homicides of women and young girls.[37] Many of the organizers of feminist groups come from a long history of activism in the 1980s, and organized in collectives and organizations during that era, many times under male-dominated organizations where women's rights usually came second to revolution. Over the years, younger generations engaged and a rich productive group of organizations such as the Center for Women's Rights (CDM) and the Center for Women's

Studies (CEMH), among others, formed a strong network of advocates for women's rights.[38] The LGBTTI organizations came about in a different context and initially as a response to the growing HIV/AIDS epidemic worldwide, which was (and is) mercilessly affecting Hondurans. These organizations tend to be gay male–dominated, with lesbians and bisexual women and transgender women absent from decision-making positions. Although this is changing, with more transgender women organizations formed in the early 2000s, during the growth of LGBTTI nonprofit organizations in the 1990s, the goals were different—leading the organizations to work separately, perhaps only coming together in coalitional projects. The HIV/AIDS epidemic brought groups together with international networks that advocated for dignity and respect as gay and lesbian groups. But the two camps existed in separate realms.

The first bodies to take to the streets to protest the illegal coup d'état were women and some of the LGBTTI organization members, perhaps because they had been organized into a group known as Feminists in Resistance, who articulated the violations against women clearly in the report *Human Rights Violations against Women after the Coup d'État* produced in November 2009.[39] The report is important because to date, it is the only report in existence that deals with women's issues in the immediate aftermath of the coup, linking the violence against women to police and military presence in the streets. The report also includes one paragraph on transgender women as victims of the police; again, for the first time, transgender women are included in a report about women in Honduras.[40] In a country where turf has been fought and gender norms heavily policed even by the progressives, the Feminists in Resistance movement allowed for common ground. The paragraph, which details that there have been fifteen transgender women killed between June 28, 2009 and the elaboration of this report in November 2009, is a demonstration of collaboration in the streets and in actions on the ground between Red Lésbica CATTRACHAS and the diverse veteran feminist groups. The collaboration and intersection of these two agendas strengthened a discussion on women and violence by the state. The powerful unity of historic feminist and lesbian groups can be a cross-fertilization of history, ideologies, and resistance to gender norms, which have kept both groups from justice.

The connection between LGBTTI groups, Feminists in Resistance, and *campesinos* may not have been readily apparent before the coup, but after the coup their marginal status to the traditional leftist sectors, as well as their intersectional identities and the real-life experiences of violence, have brought together these important new actors.

"We Made Life Out of Death": Campesin@ Land and Life in Guadalupe Carney, Colón

"We made life out of death," says D, a *campesino* from western Honduras.[41] He had relocated to the Bajo Aguán on the North Coast in 1999 after Hurricane Mitch left him and his family homeless in 1998. He refers to the more than 500 families who have made a home on the 5,000 hectares in the community of Guadalupe Carney, which once belonged to the Regional Center of Military Training (Centro Regional de Entrenamiento Militar). In the 1980s, this area was where the *contras* were housed and trained to fight against the revolutionary FSLN government in Nicaragua. My conversation with D was cut short that hot and humid day in August 2011 by news that two young men and minors from the community were picked up by the police, erroneously accused of killing a taxi driver while on their way to claim paychecks from the local African palm processing zone owned by wealthy landowner Miguel Facussé. Although their families were cooperative partners at Guadalupe Carney, the young men themselves worked in the large African palm plantations to help ends meet, and were recognized as residents of the Guadalupe Carney community. The next thirteen hours would be spent outside the local jailhouse in Trujillo, Colón, assessing the situation, determining their charges, finding legal help, and keeping vigil outside the jail to ensure they would not be beaten or tortured. One of their community leaders, José Isabel "Chavelo" Morales López, was already in jail and at the time had been held for over two years without being charged formally.[42]

The struggle for land for *campesinos* in the Bajo Aguán has been ongoing, however, for much longer than just since Hurricane Mitch. This community is an indication of this, as it bears the name Guadalupe Carney, the Jesuit priest who fought for agrarian reform beginning in 1962 (Carney 1985). Carney was "disappeared" while organizing with *campesinos* in 1983. The community's name not only honors the Jesuit priest's contributions, but also references a time when the land and the people were fertile territory for radical organizing.

Established in 2000 post–Hurricane Mitch, this community is the result of a land recuperation campaign by homeless families. After finding out that this land was available from government officials, they set out to move. The first time they attempted to recuperate the land, in May 1999, they discovered that private security forces of rich landowners of the African palm plantations were waiting for them, armed and ready to shoot upon their arrival. They made another attempt in May 2000 and found again barbed wire and all kinds of obstacles to their settlement—yet however they could, families set up camp. Later, President Flores Facussé at the time granted them land titles in a show of pomp and circumstance. But the rich landowners and their security forces constantly threatened people in their current community and in their travel to and from their parcels of land. The *campesinos* persevered and set up a cooperative, obtained land titles in this way, and begin to work the land.

The biggest threat to the *campesinos* is the expansion of African palm production, which requires extensive tracts of land, few workers, and pays low wages. Producers of this commodity seem to be hoarding the land and making life harder for smaller cooperatives by creating multiple challenges. Private security forces harass and intimidate people traveling to and from work on their small plot of land; their harvests are limited if they cannot work the land. The African palm production plant owned by Facussé, for instance, creates such contamination of the air and water sources that often times small farmers do not see a good harvest. Ninety people have been killed in the Aguán Valley since the coup, and the number keeps growing; there have been no investigations by local police nor by any court in the area. For these men and women, who migrated to the North Coast after losing everything to Hurricane Mitch and who arrived there looking forward to a fresh start living off their crops, their lives have been turned into a perpetual nightmare. Despite their resiliency and peaceful organizing, the Honduran government has continued to side with the large elite landowners.

The coup d'état affected *campesino* communities by allowing private landowners to hoard public lands and resources for commercial use, thereby destroying long-term sustainability for the cooperatives and traditional forms of farming the land. The situation has escalated to such a degree that people can no longer rely on the state to make their claims, but rather use a combination of national and international solidarity strategies to pressure local and national authorities to respect the rule of law.

But the harassment from the rich neighbors has continued to this day, the situation even more acute after the coup d'état. Since then ninety *campesinos* have been killed in the region. *Campesinos* from the Movimiento Campesino del Aguán Guadalupe Carney continue to organize but are constantly under fire; many of them have been arrested for defending their newly acquired lands and wrongfully accused.

Tolupanes in Locomapa, Yoro

Driving through a dirt road nestled within majestic mountains, criss-crossed by a river that winds so much it must be crossed at different places numerous times when traveling through the area, the lawyers and human rights workers of the At-Large Movement for Dignity and Justice (MADJ) made their way into the Tolupan community of Locomapa, Yoro. Winding up these shimmering dirt roads and passing river crossings, the delegation noted measuring bars and rulers used to measure the water in the region. The measuring sticks and marked boulders all alerted community dwellers to surveyors' work in determining if the river and the water levels are sufficient for building a hydroelectric plant and dam in the area where the Tolupan people have held land titles since the second half of the 1800s. Facussé and Wasser, the company of wealthy, notorious Honduran businessman Miguel Facussé, is interested in developing a dam and hydroelectric plant in this region (Moreno 2008). Similarly to Guadalupe Carney, and perhaps with a unique historical context, the Tolupan people in the tiny community of Locomapa, Yoro, engaged in claims of rights to land. This community can trace a long tradition of struggle to sustain and survive on the land granted to them in the 1850s with the help of Father Manuel de Jesús Subirana.[43] This community is not new to struggle; in times before the coup d'état in 2009, they had been actively fighting against the illegal felling of trees. Though much of their land is protected by the state, illegal loggers and rogue companies penetrate this forest continuously without accountability. To put a stop to the destruction, several of the seventeen Tolupan communities in this particular region of Yoro have organized. Indigenous men like C have been arrested and processed; C still faces charges for fighting the chain saws on his own land.[44] The coup exacerbated the conditions for Tolupanes by making it easier for landowners to acquire lands for development, including using forceful tactics and deception with Indigenous communities. Now Indigenous lands are not just targets for loggers, but also private domestic companies interested in building dams and mining the lead- and mineral-rich lands.

The coup allowed businessmen such as Miguel Facussé to have not only an extensive reach throughout the country, but also access to obtaining land, legally or illegally. As early as 2005 Father Ismael Moreno (2005) wrote in reflection for the Nicaraguan magazine *Envío*:

> Miguel Facussé has a foothold in all the different regions of Honduras. It's no secret that a very important part of the African palm cooperatives in the Aguán Valley is now in his hands. The same is rumored of his presence in the beaches between Trujillo and Sangrelaya, on Honduras' northeastern Caribbean coast. Others say he has a powerful presence in other geographically important valleys, such as the Leán, Sula and Comayagua valleys.

Now it is more than evident that Facussé and his son-in-law have a reach into the Bajo Aguán and the mountainous regions of Yoro, where he has set up private security forces that operate outside of the law, terrorizing civilians. Facussé and other businessmen have been empowered locally, regionally, and nationally in the country so that the violent crimes committed in the past in covert ways are now happening in the light of day. No criminal investigations have been pursued against any of the businessmen. The worst violence is the rupture of everyday life and work for survival, bringing fear and apprehension to the community. Women and children, young men and young women, fear working alone in the fields where they face harassment from paramilitaries, kidnapping, torture, and death.[45] Many young people end up migrating to alleviate their families' hunger. Their fellow community members who have been killed serve as examples that Facussé's men are to be taken seriously.

In Locomapa, Yoro, Indigenous peoples are being swindled out of their land. Through false promises and lies, just as in the colonial and early independence times, the elite landowners lie to, swindle, and extort land from Indigenous people. A Tolupan woman who is president of her *patronato* explained how she was invited to a rich landowner's house, where there was food and lots of talk. In the end, all the presidents of the *patronatos* (neighborhood/small community representatives within the various communities) nearby signed a document that she then felt pressured to sign: "They even took my thumb print," she explained in a local meeting to discuss what to do about the surveyors coming around to measure the water levels of the river. Destroying natural resources often implies destruction of life for the poorest of the poor. Without this land, Tolupanes from the region would not only be without land to cultivate and survive, but also without a forest, traditional use of land and plants, and without a future. The threat is real for both of these communities and primarily for their youth; both community leaders and members speak of having something to leave for their children in the end.

In light of threatened extermination, *campesinos* are beginning to communicate their demands to the international world. The lack of government accountability of the outgoing Pepe Lobo government has made the situation dire, and they fear their demands will not be heard. Human rights entities have witnessed the violence and the destruction of the communities. In El Aguán between August 13 and September 13, 2011, there were more than eleven murders of *campesinos*. Over 600 operatives of the military moved in, and the violence continues today.

Both of these communities have been persevering to address land rights issues since long before the June 28, 2009 coup d'état. A few conclusions may be drawn about *campesino* organizing in the Bajo Aguán. First, one of the most detrimental outcomes was the rupture of constitutional order and the ensuing egregious circumstances of the coup: lawlessness, rampant violence, and violence with impunity. The extremity of the situation not only affects people's access and rights to land, but also the very basic survival of the community. Second, the hoarding of land and resources for commercial use by Honduran elite landowners who, in conjunction with U.S. interests, utilize the post-coup weak state system to obtain land by extortion and brute force, strangles the possibility for long-term sustainability of the communities' cooperatives and their traditional forms of life and work. Thirdly, in the current struggles for survival, people fighting for land rights no longer rely on the state to make their claims, but rather look to the international community to pressure their governments and local authorities to respect the rule of law and constitutionality. Historically disenfranchised, Comunidad Guadalupe Carney, Colón and Locomapa, Yoro, have learned that the only way to overcome the great obstacles facing them is through organization and movement building that goes beyond electoral politics and campaigns. They engage in this struggle for their land and survival, even as they work intentionally toward the refounding of Honduras. Their predominant work, however, at this time, is to confront the daily strife of unmitigated human rights violations, crises, and violence.

Honduran history has been contested territory, between the landless and the elite, and continues to be. The Honduras of today, contrary to the picture that President Lobo painted for President Obama in a May 2013 visit to the United States, is not the haven of reconciliation and peace, but rather an ungovernable state where the business elite rule, perhaps even from behind the presidency.

LA CONSTITUYENTE: BRINGING IT ALL TOGETHER

The disparate and diverse sectors, both those Father Moreno analyzed in 2008 and those that surged after the coup d'état, have one goal ahead: the Constitutional Assembly, *La constituyente*, which would allow people—common people—to participate and insert themselves in the country's constitution. The dream of being part of this, truncated by the robbed suffrage of June 28, 2009, is still alive. Numerous organizations want to get to this goal, and all have multiple strategies and tactics that at times coincide with and at other times strain against each other and the system. *La constituyente*, as the FNRP/LIBRE propose it, is perhaps a dream still. The loss of the elections was a big blow to certain sectors, primarily the smaller collectives and groupings that may have put the entirety of their resources behind the party effort. As it was with the earlier days of the resistance, people had to restrategize about how the coup would be reversed—and get creative. Now once again with the setback for LIBRE in the elections, the groupings and collectives, large and small organizations, are restrategizing in new ways, reworking dreams, learning from mistakes, collecting experiences, and remapping a road. They all knew it would be a long road, and though they did not count on all the murders and death, they continue on.

The FNRP/LIBRE is a social movement, one in process of formation—where many contradictions internally and externally are forming it. The days after the coup d'état brought together diverse sectors of the population in immediate response, diverse sectors that marched shoulder to shoulder, sharing the streets, getting to know each other through the work. The fervor of the movement in those days, the impassioned meetings, and the coalition work demonstrated to the various sectors that coalitional work was possible. The outpouring of protest also demonstrated to the everyday citizen that they can and should have a role in their government, and with this acknowledgment and action they began a long process toward social change. More importantly, once the process started toward social change, it could not be turned back—the loss of fear could not be turned back, the knowledge of collaboration and possibility could not be turned back, consciousness could not be turned back.

What *campesinos*, feminists, and transgender women have in common is not just that they are targets of state violence, or that they have a long trajectory of exclusion. These groups also have all evinced moments of coalitional work, brought on precisely by their own groups' intersectionality, that was easily transformed into action and organization against the backdrop of the extremely violent stage that is the neoliberal state. A book that documents the history of LGBTTI in Honduras calls the FNRP "the movement of movements," perhaps because of its broad and diverse nature that makes it unprecedented in Honduras (Asociación Kukulcan, Asociación Colectivo Violeta, Asociación LGTB Arco Iris de Honduras, APUVIMEH 2012, 27). Those same characteristics mean that the movement that coalesced in the wake of the 2009 coup is open-ended, and its path continues to be forged.

NOTES

1. The LIBRE or Libertad y Refundación Party, created in Honduras after the 2009 coup d'état; registered with the Electoral College on March 13, 2012 and published in the government newspaper, *La Gaceta*, on March 28: "Tribunal Supremo Electoral Certificación," *La Gaceta Diario Oficial de la Republica de Honduras*, March 28, 2012.

2. There were high-profile interruptions, such as a visit from the U.S. ambassador and her entourage of multiple police forces and secret police, and the leader of the Organization of American States delegation. All stopped in for minutes, assuring themselves that this was an example of peaceful participation.

3. Honduras has been dominated by the Liberal and Nationalist parties since the turn of the twentieth century. Doña Xiomara Castro Zelaya is the wife of Manuel Zelaya, the deposed democratically elected president. Doña Xiomara stayed in Honduras and attended the protests with many Hondurans supporting the return of her husband. She grew as a candidate in the eyes of many Hondurans due to her willingness to march with the people, even in protests where there was a lot of police and military repression.

4. For a study of the right wing in Latin American today, see Bowden (2011).

5. Berta Cáceres, interview by author, Tegucigalpa, Honduras, October 2009. Carlos H. Reyes, interview by author, Tegucigalpa, Honduras, October 2009.

6. A total of nine women were raped in the aftermath of the coup d'état—usually attacked after protests.

7. Berta Cáceres, interview by author, October 2009.

8. The acronym commonly used in Honduras is LGBTTI (Lesbian, Gay, Bisexual Transsexual, Transgender, Intersex). This paper uses LGBTTI in accord with the common practice in Honduras.

9. The FNRP has an international commission that works with people in solidarity in Central, South, and North America.

10. The Palmerola (or Soto Cano) base is notorious in Honduras and Central America because it was used as a U.S. airbase during the 1980s, the years of the counterinsurgency campaign waged against the Nicaraguan FSLN and Salvadoran FMLN by President Ronald Reagan. Today the airbase serves as a station for the U.S. military's Joint Task Force Bravo. See "Honduras: Human Rights and the Coup d'État" (Inter-American Commission on Human Rights, Organization of American States, December 2009); Lara (2010).

11. Also known as the *Cuarta Urna*, the "Fourth Ballot" box. In most elections, Honduran voting precincts have three boxes per voting stall, one box to collect votes for president, one for those to be elected to congress, and one for mayor, and their substitutes. The Zelaya poll would be the mechanism by which it could be determined whether people wanted to include a fourth ballot box in the November general elections. If the poll had been affirmative, then people would have voted in the November 2009 elections for the three main elected offices, and additionally, in a fourth ballot box, they would have deposited their vote for a referendum on the following question: Do you agree to have a fourth ballot box in the next general elections of 2009 where people will decide whether or not to convene a National Constitutional Assembly?" ("¿*Está de acuerdo que en las elecciones generales del 2009 se instale una cuarta urna en la cual el pueblo decida la convocatoria a una asamblea Nacional Constituyente?*").

12. Berta Cáceres, interview by author, Tegucigalpa, Honduras, October 2009.

13. "Los partidos políticos tradicionales han cogobernado en los 27 años que llevamos de democracia, y así como las elecciones han sido vehículo para que ambos partidos se repartan los tres poderes del Estado, las reformas políticas se han convertido en instrumento para fortalecer y consolidar el control que liberales y nacionalistas ejercen sobre el Estado de Derecho."

14. Isis Obed Murillo was killed at Toncontín Airport in Tegucigalpa as President Zelaya attempted to return on July 6, 2009. After being shot by a sniper, blood spilling from his head, he was carried by protesters to a first aid station. A picture was taken by the protesters and posted in social media, and when his picture was published in major newspapers they photoshopped the blood out. Examples such as this one were rampant during the coup (Portillo 2009).

15. The chant, which quickly became a motto for the Honduran resistance movement, is taken from the chorus of a song by Liliana Felipe, an Argentinean song writer and singer. The chorus translates to "they fear us because we are not afraid."

16. "100 Días en Resistencia," *Resistencia: Organo de divulgación del Frente Nacional de Resistencia Contra el Golpe de Estado*, October 5, 2009. Author's collection.

17. Ephraim George Squier, a New York businessman, attempted to fund the building of an interoceanic route in Honduras between the Atlantic and the Pacific oceans, devising an elaborate journey by land and water in the 1850s. E. G. Squier Papers, Huntington Library and Archives, Pasadena, California.

18. For a history of military collaborations, see Holden (2004).

19. "Los Hechos Hablan Por Sí Mismos": Informe Preliminar Sobre Los Desaparecidos En Honduras, 1980–1993" (Tegucigalpa, Honduras: Comisionado Nacional de Protección de los Derechos Humanos, 1994).

20. "Los Hechos Hablan Por Sí Mismos; "Violaciones a Los Derechos Humanos De Las Mujeres Después Del Golpe De Estado En Honduras: 'Ni Un Golpe De Estado, Ni Un Golpe a Las Mujeres'" (Tegucigalpa, Honduras: Feministas en Resistencia, 2009).

21. For more information, see Holden (2004).

22. http://wikileaks.org/wiki/Category:Honduras.

23. Renamed the National Front of Popular Resistance after the November 29, 2009 elections. See: http://contraelgolpedeestadohn.blogspot.com.

24. Coalitional organizing has occurred throughout the 1990s and 2000s on a variety of issues between the two waves of social movements: "old" social movements, those focused on material and immediate needs, with a larger working class membership, unions, and campesino land rights organizations; and the "new" social movements that, for example, work on environmental issues, feminist movements, lesbian, gay and transgender rights, as well as ethnic and racial rights. See Rose (1997).

25. "100 Días En Resistencia," *Resistencia: Organo de divulgación del Frente Nacional de Resistencia Contra el Golpe de Estado*, October 5, 2009.

26. I have cited and paraphrased from Father Moreno's (2008) analysis and added numbers for emphasis.

27. Father Ismael Moreno, Radio Progreso, Guest Lecture, California State University, November 2009 (author's translation). Also see Portillo (2009).

28. Summary of human rights violations in Honduras, June 28, 2009 to present: "'Cifras y Rostros de la Represión' Violaciones a Derechos Humanos en el Marco del Golpe de Estado en Honduras," Committee of Relatives of the Disappeared in Honduras (COFADEH), Tegucigalpa, Honduras, October 22, 2009; "Honduras: Reporte de violaciones a derechos humanos después del golpe de estado político-militar del 28 de junio de 2009," Center for Research and Promotion of Human Rights (CIPRODEH), Tegucigalpa, Honduras, July 17, 2009; *Human Rights Violations against Women after the Coup d'État*, Feminists in Resistance, November 25, 2009; and Indyra Mendoza and Gabrie Mass, "Asesinatos en el Marco del Golpe de Estado de la Comunidad LGBTTI en Honduras," Red Lésbica CATTRACHAS, Feminists in Resistance, and Coalición LGBTTI Contra el Golpe de Estado, Tegucigalpa, Honduras, November 17, 2009. Information also gathered from interviews with human rights representatives and organizations in Honduras conducted by the author, October 7–10, 2009 (COFADEH, COPINH, Coalición LGBTTI Contra el Golpe de Estado, Radio Progreso, Frente Nacional Contra el Golpe de Estado, Tegucigalpa y San Pedro Sula, Coordination of Banana and Agroindustrial Workers Unions of Honduras, MADJ). All translations are mine.

29. "'Not Worth a Penny': Human Rights Abuses against Transgender People in Honduras," Human Rights Watch, 2009.

30. A feminist lesbian and Trans-led team of human rights defenders and watchdog group that documents LGBT murders and hate crimes (http://www.cattrachas.org).

31. See http://redlactrans.org.ar/site/.

32. See their blog at http://resistediverso.blogspot.com/2011/03/actividades-mdr-honduras.html.

33. One big issue was that they did not let the transgender woman, Claudia Spellman, use her name; she was forced to campaign with the male name she was given at birth.

34. Article 321 will ensure that the forms for intake of discrimination and hate crimes claims will document LGBTTI complaints. Unidentified informant, interview conducted by author, San Pedro Sula, August 6, 2013.

35. The Reyes case is the first to be processed under this new law. As of August 15, 2013, his court audience was cancelled and he considers this a victory. It remains to be seen if the courts will hear this case in the near future. *Diario El Tiempo*, August 15, 2013. See http://tiempo.hn/portada/noticias/suspenden-la-audiencia-del-pastor-evelio-reyes.

36. "Informe Anual Sobre Muertes Violentas De La Comunidad LGBTTI," CATTRACHAS, 2013.

37. "Mapa de Las Violencias Contra Las Mujeres, Honduras, 2012," Centro de Derechos de Mujeres (CDM), 2012.

38. Some of the disciplined decisions they take include not accepting money from U.S. foundations or the U.S. State Department. See http://www.derechosdelamujer.org/observatorio.html. For more information on feminisms in Honduras, see Mendoza (1986) and Villars (2001).

39. *Violaciones a los derechos humanos de las mujeres después del golpe de estado en Honduras.*

40. *Violaciones a los derechos humanos de las mujeres*, 19.

41. Campesino D, interviewed by author, Comunidad Guadalupe Carney, Trujillo, Colón, August 13, 2011 (name omitted to protect safety of interviewee).

42. Morales was arrested in 2008 and was held for over four years without being charged. He was convicted of homicide with faulty evidence in 2012 despite his absence and the absence of his legal counsel, and is now sentenced to twenty years in prison.

43. Indigenous man C, interviewed by author, Locomapa, Yoro, July 24, 2011 (name omitted to protect safety of interviewee).

44. Indigenous man C, interviewed by author.

45. Indigenous man C, interviewed by author.

Chapter Eight

Brazil

Popular Feminism and Its Roots and Alliances

Nathalie Lebon

August 16 and 17, 2011: 70,000 women rural workers and small farmers from across Brazil gather in the heart of the capital, Brasilia, to participate in the fourth convocation of the *Marcha das Margaridas* (March of the Daisies). Every four years, some of this country's most marginalized citizens come "marching" to meet and share their experiences, debate and firm up their political platform, and make their voices heard by the powers that be. In 2011, President Dilma Rousseff addressed the women and listened to their demands.

March 8, 2010: International Women's Day, where 3000 women hailing from all corners of Brazil, in a lively and colorful cortege with dominant purple hues, initiate the first of their ten-day trek to São Paulo. They will be marching about 12 km each day, to share, chant, sing, and drum, their call for action against poverty and violence against women. A 16-minute video[1] records the journey and interviews women rural workers, neighborhood association members, Indigenous women, union leaders and rank-and-file members, Black women activists, students, journalists, professors, and many others, as they share their experience. This is the Brazilian contribution to the World March of Women's third International Action, joining marches of various types in some sixty other countries around the world.

These remarkable expressions of working-class women's activism, unheard of in the United States, illustrate the organizational strength of popular feminisms in Brazil in the new millennium. This chapter seeks to unfold the story of the consolidation of this sociopolitical actor over the course of the last four decades, through the development, accomplishments, challenges, and failures of its forbearers and allies: urban middle class feminism, rural

and urban trade unionism, urban popular movements, Afro-Brazilian political and community organizations, and sexual rights movements, among others.

Telling this story matters, because popular feminism (activism, mostly
among women from the popular sectors, which questions the many expressions of social relations of power with regards to masculinity and femininity)
is currently a stronghold of organizing for Brazilian feminist and women's
movements. Even then, and after two decades of presence, activists and
scholars agree that it has not received the scholarly attention it deserves
(Bonetti 2007; Faria 2006). In addition, this new stage in the development of
women's activism is particularly vital for social change and social justice
since it involves such large sectors of the Brazilian population—the working
class and working poor sectors—and strengthens their political awakening,
including awareness of their rights and agency as women, as citizens, and as
workers.

Until recently, the shared narrative of the birth of Brazilian women's
movements in the 1970s focused largely on middle-class feminists originally
active in opposition political parties on the left, in connection with working-
class women organized in urban popular movements during the military
dictatorship. Other collective actors were left out; their contribution deserves
to be rescued, especially given their influential role today: I will thus chart
here, albeit briefly, the course of organized women in rural and urban trade
unions and organized Afro-Brazilian women. Indeed the mid-1980s onwards,
marked by the return to formal democracy in the country, have often been
interpreted as a lull in women's movements organizing, when in reality, it
was a foundational period for autonomous organizing for Afro-Brazilian
women and for women in urban and rural trade unions, although they may or
may not have originally claimed a feminist identity.

Relations between middle-class and working-class women activists were
never easy, but nonetheless valued and sustained then (Saporta Sternbach et
al. 1992). By the 1990s, as the self-identified middle-class feminist movement both diversified and institutionalized, and took advantage of opportunities for change under new national and international political scenarios, it
turned to promoting and implementing gender equity legislation; set up research and women's studies centers, nongovernmental organizations
(NGOs), and policy think tanks; or worked as consultants for international
organizations. In this new context, most middle-class feminist organizations
became increasingly formalized and professionalized, thus facing mounting
challenges in working across class lines.[2] As such, the political expressions
of popular feminism presented in this chapter are partly a result of the efforts
of historical feminisms to be inclusive in terms of class, as well as partly a
response to the challenges encountered by these very same historical feminists in making inclusion and horizontalism work, that is, to be inclusive

across differences among women and promote horizontal social relations of power in their organizations and movements.

The contemporary face of popular feminism is highly multifaceted. The second half of this chapter will thus focus on two particularly successful experiences of self-identified feminism among the working class/working poor: the network of Promotoras Legais Populares (PLP, women legal advisors), and the Brazilian chapter of the World March of Women. This last example further illustrates the role of trade union women in today's popular feminism. It also highlights the role played since 2000 by alter-globalization alliances, since they clearly helped propel networking efforts among popular feminists in Brazil to a new level. The alter-globalization movement is a worldwide confluence of social movements that seek to promote a more people and eco-friendly form of globalization. This new global context has altered power dynamics among various sectors of the Brazilian feminist movement, and has helped movement claims for redistribution of resources among social sectors and other class-inflected gender equity claims find their rightful place on the feminist agenda again.

Nancy Fraser's (1997) distinction between social movements' redistribution claims to resources and their recognition claims to group identity and rights, even if imperfect, is particularly helpful to make sense of the tensions between organized women from different social classes. Redistribution claims provide greater attention to the class-inflected gender needs of working-class and poor women than do recognition claims. Both seem equally essential to working-class women, while middle-class women can afford to minimize class-related redistribution claims due to class privilege. Yet it does not mean they always do; in fact, all movements generally combine both redistribution and recognition claims. I would argue, however, that the emphasis on that combination in Brazilian women's movements has shifted back and forth with evolving political opportunities and economic contexts over the past forty years. In particular, organizing and coalitions around class-inflected gender issues have been negatively affected by the neoliberal focus on individual human rights and restrictive macroeconomic policies of the 1980s and 1990s. Cutbacks on subsidies for food and/or on already limited health, education, and other social spending, and the privatization of such services, have dominated much of Latin America until recently, making it especially hard to argue for a change in government spending in favor of economically marginalized sectors of society. The rise to power of left-leaning governments in Brazil, as elsewhere in the region over the past decade, has signaled citizens' increasing discontent with such neoliberal policies, offering new opportunities and challenges for popular feminism.

SHARED NARRATIVE OF ORIGIN: MIDDLE-CLASS FEMINISTS AND URBAN POPULAR MOVEMENTS

The shared narrative relating the birth of second-wave[3] Brazilian women's movements in the 1970s revolves around the confluence of middle-class self-identified feminist groups with organized women in urban popular movements during a politically and economically repressive military dictatorship (1964–1985). Feminism here refers to activists, generally women, explicitly and consciously organizing to fight the oppression and subordination of women. As the story goes, such feminist groups brought together mostly middle-class women experiencing and questioning gender discrimination as they entered the labor force in greater numbers, and/or joined left-wing opposition parties (most of them illegal at the time). These political parties' discourse was strongly focused on a return to democracy in the country, while the political role of women members was often restricted to menial tasks, such as making coffee or cleaning up after meetings. Such contradictions between discourse and practice were not lost on women members who sought to broaden the internal practice of democracy. The international attention to women's issues fostered by the United Nations' decision to designate 1975 the "International Women's Year" and to hold the first International Conference on Women in Mexico City spurred additional feminist activity, notably the creation of consciousness-raising groups. In these, participants discovered that their experience of gender inequality was shared by many and was not just an individual situation, thus uncovering its social roots, and hence the need for collective action to address it. The conference itself provided Latin American feminist and women's movements with an early opportunity to share experiences and perspectives at the regional level in 1975. By the late 1970s, as the dictatorship eased its grip, these groups were also strengthened by the return of women who had lived in exile, most often in France or Italy, fearing for their lives due to their political views.

Participatory models of decision making and horizontalism have been present—some would say central—to most early middle-class feminist political projects in Latin America and elsewhere: they sought alternatives to hierarchical forms of organization which they considered masculine forms of power (Maier 2010). In fact, for many, there was no feminist organization or movement if not one that was horizontal and consensus-based. These organizational principles reflected early feminist understandings, at times essentializing, of "women" as naturally, indeed biologically, inclined to consensus building, collaboration, and cooperation, rather than competition and hierarchy. They also grew out of the desire to avoid replicating prior experiences of exclusion and silencing in political parties and other organizations, and out of the understanding of the key role of active participation (actually speaking up and sharing one's experience(s) of oppression) to promote empowerment and self-esteem for individual members. This understanding was born out of the very experience of consciousness-raising groups, where for example participants pass around a token to ensure that all would get a chance to share.

As feminist organizations moved from consciousness raising to seeking to eliminate sexism from social, cultural, and political systems around them (for example, raising awareness and effecting actual changes in the medical world about women's health), many worked hard to maintain these principles of horizontality internally. Horizontalism was then implemented through a limited or nonexistent chain of command, rotation of tasks to avoid role specialization, absence of "gatekeepers" to ensure the free flow of information, and consensus-based decision making. Maintaining these practices proved difficult as tasks became increasingly specialized and, in some cases, technical. Even in these early, fairly homogeneous social movement organizations, that is, in mostly urban, educated, "white," middle-class, heterosexual, cisgender,[4] politically left-leaning, all-female groups, the challenges to maintain horizontalism led to many a heated discussion in the face of "the tyranny of structurelessness" (Freeman 1973). In the mid-1980s, the availability of foreign aid for women's organizations allowed a number of them to remunerate their members for their activities, thus leading to professionalization and to even stiffer challenges to maintain horizontalism in the face of, again, an increased need for specialized knowledge and activities, with at minimum a secretary and an accountant. Horizontalism, a much-cherished goal, was proving exceedingly challenging, even in the face of little else but individual differences of opinion, ability, and knowledge.

With time, increasing numbers of middle-class, self-identified feminists thought their political praxis of horizontalism should also involve social, racial, and sexual inclusivity; as awareness of racism, heterosexism, and more recently transphobia grew in Brazilian society, feminists increasingly sought to work horizontally across differences of race and sexual and gender identity among women. Activists and scholars have denounced and documented historic feminists' arduous journey in this matter: Afro-Brazilian women underscoring expressions of racism in the movement (Gonzalez 1982); sexual minorities decrying its homo- and lesbophobia (Mogrovejo 2010); and more recently, the exclusion of individuals with nonnormative gender identity and expression.

Working across class boundaries, with women from the working-class and working-poor sectors, was the first challenge tackled by middle-class feminists in the 1970s, given most of their origins in left-leaning political parties and the reality of class in Brazil. These middle-class women showed much interest in the women participating in the broad range of popular movements then emerging in Brazilian cities.

As the standard narrative of the origins of Brazilian women's movements continues, a broad range of urban popular movements in the 1970s and 1980s saw the involvement of large numbers of women on the outskirts of Brazilian megalopolises (Alvarez 1989; Caldeira 1990; Corcoran-Nantes 2000). Recently settled rural migrants in search of a better life were encouraged in their collective action efforts by the very existence of state social policies, even if ineffective and insufficient. They protested the dictatorship's political and illegal imprisonment activities (Movimento Feminino pela Anistia, for the amnesty of political prisoners), its policies leading to a high cost of living (Movimento Custo da Vida), the lack of public daycare centers (Movimento de Luta por Creches) and demanded minimal infrastructure for housing, sanitation, and health care in their recently settled neighborhoods. They received organizational support from the strong Liberation Theology branch of the Brazilian Catholic Church; from the new trade unionism, which was soon to give rise to the Partido dos Trabalhadores or Workers' Party today in power with presidents Lula and Dilma Rousseff; as well as from progressive intellectuals. In some cases, they were also organized by political parties for electoral purposes (Caldeira 1990).

In what came to be referred to as "militant motherhood"[5] in the scholarly literature (Alvarez 1989, 210), community-based women highlighted the contradictions of state rhetoric, which called upon them to be good nurturing mothers and wives while making it materially impossible to fulfill that role, either by "disappearing" family members or through exclusionary economic policies. Some observers have argued that women were intrinsically motivated by their social responsibilities as mothers and came down to the streets to demand what had been expected of them. Others, such as Caldeira (1990) and Corcoran-Nantes (2000), have argued that organized women had not so much internalized their duties as mothers and wives, as used them strategically to legitimize their transgressing of "proper" feminine gender roles on entering the public sphere of politics. Corcoran-Nantes, echoing anthropologist Lynn Stephen's (1997b) later call for attention to organized women's multiple identities, also emphasized that these women's struggles also involved their identities as workers and as citizens, not just as wives and mothers. Based on research done in 1983–1985, Corcoran-Nantes (2000, 84) writes that "women have created a political role for themselves based on their social status as wives and mothers but through which they have struggled for recognition of their roles and rights as workers, residents and citizens." This analysis points to a much more porous boundary between the public and private spheres than originally envisioned, and between feminist and feminine struggles.

Indeed, debates among academics over the nature of these movements, and in particular over which ones qualify as feminist, have taken many shapes over the years. In the Latin American context, a distinction has often been drawn between feminism and the larger women's movement: feminism referring to women explicitly and consciously organizing to fight the oppression and subordination of women, the women's movement referring n. inclusively to women organized to defend their interests, most often, thoug not always, through their role as women. This distinction resurfaced in the concepts of strategic gender interests and practical gender needs, ably formulated by Maxine Molyneux (1986). Examples of strategic gender interests feminists have organized around are equal pay for equal work, domestic violence, or the right to legal abortion. Practical gender needs have been understood as those concerns that women experience as a result of their gendered roles and duties (generally as mothers and wives) often in their daily life, such as the need for child care or access to fuel and clean water to feed their families. However, most scholars today recognize that it is often difficult to disentangle the strategic from the practical: for example, child care needs, as most others, reflect both a practical daily need for working mothers, but also a failure on the part of society to recognize the value of women's reproductive labor (hence it challenges women's subordination). Also, what seems practical to some may be strategic to others. Often what was seen as practical were the needs faced by working-class women, while what was defined as strategic were the concerns of middle-class white or mestiza heterosexual women. Indeed, in Latin America as elsewhere, the general tendency has been to equate feminism with its white or mestiza, educated, urban, middle-class manifestation of women's struggle against subordination. Finally, no organization is homogenous enough for all women to share the same motivations. Ultimately, these distinctions lead to the divisive question of "who is feminist enough."

These women's early transgressions into the public sphere, whether or not as a result of their internalized expectations as mothers, opened the door for other women to challenge "proper" women's roles, and facilitated the emergence of a different form of feminism: popular feminism. They also provided the organizational network necessary. With time, popular women's groups started to form and organize autonomously from the mixed organizations many of them had been involved with to that point. In some cases they did so in conjunction with middle-class feminist (support) groups and in others without such direct connection. However, they certainly were influenced by the public debates promoted by feminist ideas, practices, and visions (Stephen 1997b). In Brazil, the process of autonomous popular feminist organizing started in the late 1980s. We witnessed, for example, by 1992 the first feminist *encontro* of the Eastern Zone of São Paulo with the direct support of "historic" feminist organizations. *Encontros* are loosely themed gatherings offering a plethora of workshops, exhibits, and other political activities.

Today, social justice, citizenship, and the expansion of rights, along with redistribution claims, are essential to contemporary understandings of popular feminist activism in Brazil, as elsewhere in the region (Bonetti 2007; Di Marco 2010, Richards 2004). It means that whatever the nature of "militant

have been, it has undoubtedly now morphed into "popular
xample, research on urban low-income women, such as
ın Pernambuco State in northeast Brazil in the new millen-
their activism goes well beyond militant motherhood and
) motivated by "*gusto pela militancia*" (the appeal of acti-
vism) and expectations of opportunities for upward social mobility. It is interesting to note in Bonetti's (2007, 196) work the influence and the appeal of professionalized activism of middle-class feminist groups on working-class women, who see it as an ideal way to bring together a way to make a living and their desire to be active politically. Yet, a crucial difference with "historical feminists" is that popular feminists tend to focus on collective rights issues and on issues that bridge women's specific concerns and extend to those that affect both men and women of the popular classes (Citeli 1994). In other words, redistribution issues are essential to them (Cappellin 2000; Thayer 2001; Caldwell 2010).

A REVISED NARRATIVE: NEGLECTED COLLECTIVE ACTORS

Historian Becky Thompson (2002) brought to our attention the way our common narrative of the history of the second wave of women's movements in the United States obscured the participation and (especially early) contributions of women of color, indeed distorting our record of the ebb and flow of the movement. Analysts erroneously identified the 1980s as a lull in U.S. women's movements, while that decade was in fact a foundational moment for women of color feminism. Similarly, in the Brazilian case, the years following 1985 and the return to formal democracy have been regarded, according to Brazilian anthropologist Miriam Grossi, by "researchers of the movement, as uninteresting because it seemed that 'there were no longer a movement in the country,' due to the disappearance of a major part of the autonomous groups born in the redemocratization period" (1997, 290, my translation).

As we will see, this period was foundational for trade union feminism—and popular feminism more generally—as well as for Black feminism (the two are not mutually exclusive, since Afro-descendants are overrepresented among the poor). "Historic feminists," or middle-class, educated, self-identified feminists started being active in a wider variety of spaces following the formalization and institutionalization of their movement: establishing NGOs, lobbying for gender equity legislation, working for the state or for the United Nations, among others.

Organized Afro-Brazilian Women

The Afro-Brazilian women's movement is by now arguably one of the most dynamic sectors of the country's women's movements. Black women activists were first active in a wide variety of mixed-gender organizations, such as the Movimento Negro Unificado (MNU, Unified Black Movement), Afro-Brazilian religious and cultural institutions, residents' associations, trade unions, political parties, as well as in women's organizations and in the broader women's movement (McCallum 2007). For example, the women's division of the MNU participated in the coordination of the second São Paulo Women's Congress as early as 1980 (Alvarez 1990, 120).

However, sexism in the Movimento Negro and racism in the women's movement led Black women to experience marginalization in both and to search for their own collective political expression. Racial divisions within the Brazilian women's movement were first formally acknowledged by "the presentation of the *Manifesto das mulheres negras* during the Brazilian Women's Congress in July 1975" (Caldwell 2007, 151). By the mid-1980s, Afro-Brazilian women were moving to create their own collectives in Rio in 1983 (Nzinga/Coletivo de Mulheres Negras), and São Paulo in 1984 (Coletivo de Mulheres Negras) (Caldwell 2007, 157–58; Ribeiro 1995; Roland 2000). By 1988, the informal network of Black women collectives, individuals, and other entities was sufficiently dense to call for the first National *Encontro* of Black Women. This multiplicity of collective action experiences along with a focus on the constructed nature of their multi-pronged identity as "*mulher negra*" at the intersection of gender, race, and class has meant that the Black women's movement has presented remarkable openness toward, as well as strong skills for, coalition work (Caldwell 2007, 181).

Both Black feminism and, to a lesser extent (given the reality of homophobia), lesbian feminism,[6] have been reinvigorating and strengthening popular feminism in São Paulo's poor neighborhoods in the new millennium. In São Paulo we now find the recently established Mulheres de Keto, an organization of and for Black lesbians located in the very poor neighborhoods on the outer eastern edge of the city. Additionally, a popular feminist activist, a woman of color and a member of the Association of Women of the Eastern Zone, whom I met again after many years in 2009, mentioned another Black women's group that was organizing a Black cultural festival that summer. She was for the first time expressing to me her understanding of her own identity as Afro-Brazilian.

Trade Union Women

Organized women in trade unions have generally been overlooked in the standard story of the building of women's movements in Latin America and the Caribbean. Feminist scholars Marva Philipps and Lynn Bolles's (2006) review of trade union feminisms in the region shows how women's participation and political organization within trade unions have often been discussed separately from the literature on women's movements. This is no less true in Brazil, where, with rare exceptions, we had to work with two sets of literature until the turn of the millennium.

One important reason for this lack of integration of trade union women in the literature on women's movements is that, early on, autonomy from male-dominated institutions was considered to be key to feminist organizing. Trade union women, like party women, were seen as pawns in the hands of their respective institutions. Early manifestations of union feminism were therefore often mentioned only briefly, if at all, in most accounts of the birth of women's movements or feminism. This started to change after 1990 (see for example Teles 1993 and Soares et al. 1995). Confirming Phillips and Bolles's argument about the existence of separate bodies of scholarship on trade union women's organizing, trade union women were the key focus of the work of important Brazilian feminist researchers, such as Elizabeth Souza Lobo (1991), Lena Lavinas (1991), Paola Cappellin (1991; 1994; 2000), and Mary Garcia Castro (1999).

Upon closer examination, we see that trade union women held women's conferences as early as 1977 for women metalworkers (Teles 1993; Cappellin 2000). In fact, the first wave of feminism saw working women organizing as early as the 1920s, when the Union of Seamstresses and Hat-makers organized as part of the anarchist factory workers movement (Pinto 2003). By 1986, women trade unionists were establishing the National Women Workers Commission within the large, recently created Central Única dos Trabalhadores (CUT, Unified Workers' Central) (Castro 1999). Rural women workers first had to fight for the acknowledgment of their status as workers and to be accepted by trade unions. But as early as 1982, with the prodding of the Catholic and Lutheran Churches' Comissão Pastoral da Terra and in response to aggravated drought and dangers of expulsion, women workers came together in the remote region of the Northeastern Sertão arguing that women were indeed workers and could be trade union members, thus clearly challenging power relations between men and women (Cappellin 2000; Thayer 2001). The Movimento de Mulheres Trabalhadoras Rurais (MMTR) was born. Since then we have seen the recognition of the status of women as rural workers in one of the largest unions in South America, the Confederação Nacional dos Trabalhadores na Agricultura (CONTAG, National Confederation of Agricultural Workers). CONTAG now has a National Commission of Rural Working Women as well as a Secretariat of Rural Working Women. Its webpage uses gender-sensitive language, referring to rural workers as *trabalhador(a) rural*.

THE MANY FACES OF CONTEMPORARY
POPULAR FEMINISMS IN BRAZIL

According to Brazilian feminist sociologist Mary Garcia Castro (1999), a "class-based feminism" had emerged from organized trade union women, along with women from parties on the left and some "historic" feminist organizations, by the mid-1990s. Castro aptly argues that this new feminism was insisting that leftist political parties and trade unions change from within to shed their sexism. I define popular feminism even more broadly, including a more diverse range of organizations.

The contemporary face of popular feminism in Brazil is multifaceted. It includes a diverse array of community-based women's organizations in working-class and poor neighborhoods on the outskirts of Brazil's megalopolises, including Afro-Brazilian women's groups (Perry 2013); organized women in trade unions both in rural and in urban settings, as discussed above; and peasant and rural workers' movements, such as the Latin American-born but now global Via Campesina and the Brazilian Landless Rural Workers' Movement (MST, Movimento dos Trabalhadores Rurais Sem-Terra). The MST's results for women members have been mixed at best, giving rise to their Gender Sector (Bhattacharjya 2013; Caldeira 2009; Deslandes 2009) and the autonomous Movimento de Mulheres Camponesas (Peasant Women Movement). Also included are two groups to which I will dedicate the remaining pages of this chapter, namely, the Brazilian network of women paralegals known as Promotoras Legais Populares (PLP, translated alternatively as "popular women legal advisers" or "popular legal promoters"), and the Marcha Mundial das Mulheres (MMM, World March of Women), a broad international socialist-feminist coalition with an exceptionally strong Brazilian chapter. In addition, a few "historic" class-conscious, membership-based feminist organizations, such as União de Mulheres do Municipio de São Paulo (hereafter União de Mulheres), or the União Brasileira de Mulheres (connected to the Communist Party of Brazil), and an even smaller number of feminist NGOs, such as SempreViva Organização Feminista (hereafter SOF) also belong to this loosely defined field of popular feminism.

Promotoras Legais Populares

The PLP legal training course provides a remarkable example of an exercise in the deepening of democracy and citizenship for women through democratizing the law. These courses are specifically designed for women from marginalized neighborhoods, with little formal education, to learn about their rights, the law and the state, and the mechanisms by which they can claim their rights. Furthermore, this capacity-building course is meant for the trained paralegals to act in defense of others' rights and to serve as references in their neighborhoods on a range of human rights issues related to race, sexual orientation, and class, as well as gender.

The first Brazilian PLP courses were organized after two Brazilian feminist organizations discovered their existence in other Latin American countries, such as Argentina and Chile, at a seminar organized in 1992 by the then recently established Latin American network of feminist lawyers, CLADEM (Latin American and Caribbean Committee for the Defense of Women's Rights).[7] Two years later, both the NGO Thêmis-Assessoria Jurídica e Estudos de Gênero (in the southern State of Rio Grande do Sul) and the União de Mulheres had organized their own training courses (Cartilha Thêmis 1998; Fonseca 2012; Teles 2012). The first União's course trained thirty-five women in 1994 in collaboration with the Instituto Brasileiro de Advocacia Pública (Brazilian Institute of District Attorneys) and associations of judges and lawyers interested in promoting greater access to justice. Since then, PLP projects have spread to all regions of the country. In the state of São Paulo alone, where the União de Mulheres is gearing up to celebrate the twentieth anniversary of its PLP course, about 5000 PLPs have successfully completed the nine-month weekly training (Amelia Teles, *União de Mulheres*, personal communication). A charter sets the basic principles by which all PLP projects should abide, notably the fact that the courses should aim to transform the law into an instrument for the empowerment of women participants and a tool for social change. The course design favors a multidisciplinary approach, drawing on legal studies as well as on public health, critical studies, and the social sciences among others, and hands-on activities, taking advantage of on-site visits to legal institutions and partnerships with human rights organizations and NGOs. Women's Empowerment Centers (Serviços de Informação á Mulher) have been established to provide support to graduates in their work in their neighborhoods, and a network was created. Websites and Facebook pages facilitate communication and mobilization for joint action by course participants state- or country-wide. The São Paulo website can be found at http://www.promotoraslegaispopulares.org.br/. It helps promote events, share experiences, record key decisions, and celebrate accomplishments. Statewide *encontros* or meetings have been organized in the state of São Paulo, in Brasilia, and elsewhere, which helps cement PLP collective identity and their platform of action as a social change agent. For example, PLPs monitored the dissemination of information about the new Brazilian law against violence against women, known as Lei Maria da Penha, and how the law was implemented locally (Fonseca 2012, 108). In Brasilia, where the PLP project is housed in the University of Brasilia's extension center, clear tie-ins have been made to the University's law school: the First and Second Week on Gender and the Law at the University of Brasilia were organized by PLP participants, both students and contributors, in 2010 and 2011 respectively (Duque et al. 2011).

The PLP legal training projects, although crafted by Latin American feminist lawyers, embody the principles of popular legal education for democracy, a branch of legal studies influential in Brazil, known as "*o direito achado na rua*" or "law from the street." Brazilian legal scholar Roberto Lyra Filho (1982) coined this phrase to refer to social movements' consciousness-raising role with regards to people's rights under the law and to democratize access to the law. Valuing exchange among all legal actors rather than the sole expertise of law scholars and professionals, the goal is for the law to no longer stand as a mere instrument of the state but as a tool for raising consciousness and empowering citizens, particularly women, who have been not only excluded from writing the law, but also subject to discrimination by it. In other words, PLP projects exemplify yet another way in which social movements in the region have been putting horizontalism into practice.

Many PLP centers, forums, and individuals belong to a much larger feminist-socialist coalition: the Brazilian chapter of the World March of Women that will be the focus of the last section of this chapter. This section illustrates the importance of organized women in trade unions and in leftist political parties in the establishment and vitality of this remarkable millennial expression of popular feminism. It also foregrounds the role played by new transnational alliances in the context of the alter-globalization movement in the emerging post-neoliberal era, given the breakdown of the Washington Consensus, in propelling networking efforts and the viability and visibility of redistribution claims among popular feminists in Brazil to a new level.

A Marcha Mundial das Mulheres

Since 2000, the Marcha Mundial das Mulheres (MMM), as the Brazilian chapter of the World March of Women against Poverty and Violence is known, has been bringing together popular feminists and consolidating popular feminism in São Paulo and indeed throughout Brazil. The MMM's sheer size, 488 entities strong, second in size only to the Quebecois chapter, along with its innovative and transnational character and its success at attracting young activists, make it a political force to reckon with.

The World March of Women was originally launched by feminist organizations in Quebec Province in 1995 to bring attention to the increasing poverty women experienced as Canada was integrating into NAFTA, the North American Free Trade Agreement. Seizing on the symbolism of the new millennium, a worldwide initiative was launched to march to the United Nations headquarters in New York in 2000 to ask that concrete steps be taken against poverty and violence against women (Dufour and Giraud 2007).

First contacts between Brazilian feminists and the World March of Women were established when Québécoise activists contacted the Women's Department of the progressive trade union, Central Única dos Trabalhadores

(CUT). In 1998, these union feminists were invited to participate in a preparatory meeting for the organization of the 2000 march on New York. So were members of a class-conscious, feminist, professionalized NGO called Always Alive Feminist Organization (SOF, SempreViva Organização Feminista), based in São Paulo. While the trade union women initially did not choose to prioritize this transnational connection, SOF, which valued transnational connections but was dissatisfied with the United Nations-centered processes of Brazilian feminist organizing and what they saw as their focus on individual rights and lack of attention to redistributive issues, found in the World March of Women the transnational movement-centered partners it had been hoping for. It saw in the World March of Women the outlet (*"a possibilidade de desembocar"*) for all the training and movement-building activities it had been actively fomenting since the early 1990s. When European and Latin American organizers of the 2000 march argued in favor of pursuing networking and awareness-raising activities beyond the march on the United Nations headquarters, SOF members took it upon themselves—as a volunteer activity distinct from their "professionalized work" as SOF paid staff members—to organize the World March of Women's presence at the very first World Social Forum in Porto Alegre, southern Brazil, in 2001 (the World Social Forum has since then brought together a broad spectrum of social movements worldwide to promote a more people- and eco-friendly form of globalization). By 2006, Brazil was chosen to host the International Secretariat of the March, following the efforts of Quebec feminists. Miriam Nobre, a SOF staff member, then became the International Executive Coordinator of the Word March of Women until 2013.[8]

Beyond SOF's twenty-year experience of organizing the grassroots in the eastern zone of São Paulo, I attribute SOF's unwavering commitment to movement building around class-inflected gender concerns to its solid anchoring, ideologically and organizationally, in trade unions, left-wing political parties, and popular movements. Ideologically, SOF is organically connected to the democratic-popular project of the Democracia Socialista, a political faction on the left of the Partido dos Trabalhadores. Several key SOF members are longtime and active leaders of the Worker's Party National Women's Secretariat (Secretaria Nacional das Mulheres). Equally important to maintaining SOF's commitment have been its organizational ties to popular and workers' movements, in particular with CUT and, to a lesser degree, the larger Brazilian feminist and women's movements.

Indeed, SOF, unlike many professionalized feminist support groups, had been holding on to its movement-building political vision despite the pressures of professionalization since the early 1990s, likely thanks to the strong ideological commitment and organic connections mentioned above. It has continually envisioned its role as strengthening feminism among workers' and popular movements in order to build a mass feminist movement, building ties to, and promoting a feminist consciousness among, organized women in local, state, and national trade union federations, as well as among organized women in the Popular Movement Federation (Confederação dos Movimentos Populares), which brings together Brazil's popular movement leadership. In the mid-1990s SOF scaled up its activities toward the national level and drastically reduced its support work at the local level with organized women in São Paulo local popular movements. As I found out while doing fieldwork for my dissertation, much tension arose as a result, as local organized women expressed feelings of abandonment.

More pragmatically, SOF's resources and connections, as a formalized and professionalized social movement support group, were put in play: its "feminist training" activities; its publications, namely the *Folha Feminista* and the *Bolletim*, which spread awareness of the MMM's agenda and activities; its permanent administrative staff, particularly its accountants, well-versed in the intricacies of nonprofit accounting to financing agencies.

While some detractors argue that SOF "is the March" in Brazil, the MMM includes a broad variety of organizations and groups. One category, however, deserves attention: trade union women are essential to the success of the MMM, both numerically and in terms of resources. The MMM counts approximately 450 registered entities: of these, 113 (hence a full quarter of the total) are entities connected to urban or rural trade unions. Some of these registered member entities are the whole trade union, while others are their women's departments at the national or state level, or from a local.[9] These entities generally have large membership themselves, much larger memberships than other types of March members such as community-based women's groups, and even larger than NGOs or university gender research units, so they represent a very large constituency that also provides much visibility to the MMM. For example, the *Marcha das Margaridas* (March of the Daisies), a crucial moment of mobilization for rural women workers and their unions, was originally organized as one of the activities of the 2000 World March of Women. Since then, tens of thousands of women march to remind congress of their existence, their wishes for sustainable rural development, and their important economic contribution to the country, during these quadrennial marches and gatherings in Brasilia (in 2000, 2003, 2007, 2011) (Mascena 2000). The latest gathering, in 2011, was 70,000 to 100,000 strong, bringing together the organized women of various trade unions (CUT, CONTAG) along with a few class-conscious feminist/women's organizations such as the União Brasileira de Mulheres and, of course, was done with strong support from the MMM. The name, *Marcha das Margaridas*, refers to Margarida Maria Alves, a rural union leader from the northeastern state of Paraiba who was brutally assassinated in 1983.[10]

Horizontalism, especially at the local level,[11] and active empowerment of individual participants are strong principles for the MMM, as for the March globally, which makes sense given its desire to raise feminist awareness to generate a mass movement. This movement-building character of the MMM, interested in pressuring state institutions from the streets rather than through lobbying, translates into reduced need for specialization and expertise. In fact, auto-organization and rotation of tasks among participants of the entire logistics of the actual marches, encampments, and gatherings are intentionally used as an important tool to promote empowerment. This is no small feat when thousands of women participate. Activities are specifically designed to energize the group and promote emotional connection and active participation at the beginning and throughout meetings. Drawing on dance, song, and artistic expression, these activities also valorize popular (including Afro-Brazilian and Indigenous) women's cultural heritage and generate feelings of solidarity. This shared experience and emotional connection provide a fertile ground for the positive resolution of the negotiation of differences in the political debates to follow, all the more so because the activities chosen intentionally bring in joy and beauty through music/dance and other generally unappreciated women's arts. These activities, along with "women's craft fairs," also provide an opportunity for women with talents other than traditional political and intellectual skills to feel valued. Allowing enough time for decisions to be debated and consensus to be built across difference is a challenging proposition: encampments and gatherings are scheduled for extended periods of time, often a whole week, to facilitate this process. Shorter decision-making meetings are likely to be less participatory, but less formal venues and language are chosen to make those with little formal education feel at ease, and whenever possible, seating is arranged to avoid symbolically displaying hierarchy in space (chairs in circle, no podium, etc.) and thus facilitate the participation of all. Providing for meals to be taken together is another way to facilitate interpersonal communication and ensure the presence of those who cannot travel at their own cost. Clearly these practices (shared with other feminist movements) cannot immediately eliminate entrenched, often embodied, power differentials across class or race, but are designed to chip away at them by empowering the more marginalized.

The success of this international socialist-feminist initiative worldwide and in Brazil is, I argue, one manifestation of the renewed political strength of redistribution claims for socioeconomic justice at the global level. After two decades of neoliberal policies and of wrestling with the limitations of the UN-centered "women's rights"–focused feminist activism, people are voicing their discontent (Harcourt 2006). The World March of Women contributes to the alter-globalization movement, notably the World Social Forum. In turn, such global initiatives have contributed to redrawing power relations among women's movement segments within the Brazilian national context, bringing renewed strength to a thoroughly class-informed or popular feminism, and bringing back redistribution claims to the feminist agenda.

For example, in 2004, assured of their national and transnational alliances with trade union women and with the World March of Women, while dissatisfied with the lack of attention to public health issues and difficulties in participating in decision making, SOF decided to continue its affiliation with the larger Rede Nacional Feminista de Saúde, Direitos Reprodutivos e Sexuais (Rede Saúde—the Brazilian Feminist Health and Sexuality Network) but no longer participates in any meetings. In 2007 SOF's coordinator told me that they did not seem to be able to shake what she called the Network's "framework of individual reproductive and sexual rights," which she sees as an agenda borrowed from the United Nations.[12] Instead, SOF is a staunch advocate of public policies that ensure universal access to quality public health care facilities and frame women's health within this context. A few community-based women's organizations in São Paulo similarly have left the Rede Saúde and joined the MMM, where they find greater affinity in terms of collective identity and agenda priorities.

Riding right on the connecting line between class and gender, even though it may be dissatisfied with what it sees as the lack of attention paid by the "historical" Brazilian feminist movements to the ways working class and marginalized women are affected by gender subordination, the MMM is also strongly feminist. For example, contrary to earlier popular feminist initiatives, the MMM feels just as strongly and speaks just as loudly about core second-wave feminist issues such as abortion rights, and more recently, lesbian rights, as it does about core redistributive demands such as better wages and working conditions for working people. The MMM has become a powerful counterpoint to other feminist coalitions when it comes to representing the key concerns of working-class women with a mass-movement expression.

CONCLUSION

I hope to have demonstrated the diversity, as well as the vitality and strength, of women's contemporary popular feminist movements in Brazil. In fact, the very sectors that bring diversity to the movement today, namely Black women, trade union women and, to a lesser degree, for now, sexual minorities, are in large part to be credited for its vitality and strength. In particular, rural and urban trade union women provide much visibility and build up the movement's roots among large swath of the Brazilian population. I was able to ascertain in person the strong presence of union women in the Brazilian chapter of the March at the national *Encontro* of the MMM in 2007 and at the Ninth International *Encontro* of the World March of Women in August 2013 in São Paulo. Since social movements are not immune to the power dynamics within the larger society from which they are born, more research is needed to evaluate just how horizontal decision making and agenda setting in the MMM are for trade union feminists. Similarly, if racial discrimination in the wider society is denounced and Black and Indigenous women's presence celebrated, racialized power dynamics within the MMM still deserve attention. Innovative forms of feminist popular education, such as the Promotoras Legais Populares, generate a deepening of democracy at the community level through the empowerment of women, buttress horizontalism in the teaching and practice of law, and build a pressure movement for the implementation of laws which would otherwise just remain on the books.

In terms of alliances, if transnational, especially Latin American alliances have played an important role for both the PLP project and the MMM, the worldwide alter-globalization movement has clearly provided popular feminists not only with an enabling context, but even with the very organizational framework to pull all interested parties together. My current research on the World March in Brazil and France indicates that knowing that women around the world are "marching" along with you toward similar goals is proving to be a most powerful galvanizing and mobilizing force.

NOTES

1. "Seguiremos em marcha até que todas sejamos livres! - Video documentário da MMM," http://www.youtube.com/watch?v=myXa1JFSZ9Y (in Portuguese; accessed January 27 2014).

2. I have examined these processes elsewhere (Lebon 2013).

3. In Brazil as in many other countries, the "first wave" of feminist organizing in the early twentieth century was strongly, although not exclusively, centered on political rights, such as the right to vote. Already some trade union women were then fighting not only for better working conditions but also for the recognition of the structuring role of gender in labor relations (Pinto 2003).

4. Individuals whose gender expression and gender identity line up with their sex at birth, in contrast to transgender.

5. "Supermadres" in Elsa Chaney's work and "female consciousness" in Temma Kaplan's work (Stephen 1997b, 10)

6. Lesbian feminism deserves a more extensive treatment for which I am ill-equipped at this point. I will point out that, with the establishment in 2003 of the Liga Brasileira de Lesbicas, another sector of the movement is starting to grow in influence and to make its voice heard. The São Paulo feminist movement has always counted with a strong presence of lesbians in its midst. Some organized in lesbian-identified organizations, many working within feminist organizations, "without bringing lesbianism into their agenda" (Soares et al. 1995, 309). Sexuality issues did not mobilize much in Brazil in the 1980s and 1990s (Grossi 1997). In Brazil as elsewhere, women's organizations' fear of corroborating accusations of the "lavender menace" have long muted the concerns and interests of lesbian women (Mogrovejo 2010). The new millennium is bringing greater acceptance of the legitimacy of the claims of discrimination suffered by sexual minorities, as well as a much greater understanding of the effects of what is often viewed as a "deviant" sexuality or gender expression on the class status of sexual minorities. New studies, in the United States at least, have shown the staggering overrepresentation of lesbian, gay, bisexual, transgendered, questioning (LGBTQ) youth among high school dropouts and the homeless for example.

7. In Spanish, Comité de América Latina y el Caribe para la Defensa de los Derechos de la Mujer; see www.cladem.org.

8. Information on SOF and the World March of Women was obtained ⟨ interview with Nobre on September 16, 2008 and through content analysis of pɪ als (newsletters as well as web content).

9. This data was gathered from the World March of Women's internationaɪ wᴇᴜ ᵧ _ which lists all the member groups for each country: http://www.marchemondiale.org/structure/ cn/groupes/ameriques/bresil/fr?b_start:int=450 (accessed January 7, 2013).

10. For more information, see http://delubio.com.br/blog/2011/08/marcha-das-margaridas/.

11. Horizontalism is practiced at the local level. For national and international level decision-making meetings representatives are selected by each Brazilian state's chapter, and by each country's National Coordinating Committee, respectively. However, selection criteria encourage rotation among members for a chance to participate in higher levels of decision-making.

12. SOF coordinator, interview by author, July 9, 2007, São Paulo.

Chapter Nine

Brazil

The Contradictions of Black Cultural Politics in Salvador da Bahia

Kwame Dixon

This chapter examines Afro-Brazilian social movements and the rise of civil society in Brazil from the middle of the 1970s until the present. It analyzes the burgeoning rise of *blocos afros* (carnival blocks or clubs) as horizontal Black social movements as they burst onto the scene in Brazil and, more specifically, Salvador in the 1970s and 1980s. Many of these movements were deemed "cultural" as they emphasized Afro-diasporic music, religion, identity, and Black consciousness. At the same time, similar, more politicized Black movements arose in Rio de Janeiro, São Paulo, and Salvador with a discourse explicitly framed around questions of racial equality, social discrimination, and citizenship. These various formations, that is, *blocos afro*, Black social movements, and the rise of Black electoral politics, have their early foundations in the emergence of Brazilian civil society during the transition to democracy in the mid- to late 1980s. They were central to not only expanding concepts of citizenship but also developing new means of participation that were more horizontal than vertical in nature. In this context the *blocos* in the early days (1970s to 1980s) represented grassroots, horizontal structures organized alongside Brazilian political structures and civil society.

I argue that Afro-civil society in Brazil and more specifically in Salvador emerges as a specific response to a broad set of complex issues and conditions deeply embedded in Brazil's unequal vertical social relations, political institutions, and cultural formations. These issues include the harsh and unequal administration of justice (police, jails, and prisons); differential educational inequalities; lack of access to the university system; stark discrimination in the political economy and labor market; negative, one-dimensional and highly racialized images in the media; and a hierarchical political culture. And this is reflected in a legal system devoid of any real or deep understanding of the unique status of Blacks as racialized second-class citizens and their position in the social and political hierarchy (Goldstein 2003; Beato 2004).

Afro-cultural social movements in Brazil, while difficult to label, do mirror the horizontal nature of new social movements common across the Americas. Afro-Brazilian social movements emerged from below and outside the frame of traditional political institutions; they were not part of traditional political parties, nor were they interested in capturing state power. Afro-Brazilian social movements have sought to redefine relations of power by challenging the state's normative assumptions regarding race relations and by placing the politics of racial inequality on the table as a serious political issue. Specifically, since Brazil was under a military dictatorship when some of these movements arose, they were by definition horizontal as they emerged from below as legitimate grassroots movements with new forms of organization. As horizontal movements, they had to fight for space within the new democratic institutions in the post-dictatorship period as well as fight for space within emerging civil society institutions. In what Hardt and Negri (2001) refer to as "constituent power," Afro-Brazilians had to not only reshape and challenge outdated notions of Brazilian identity, but simultaneously fight for social space within the newly emerging democratic institutions and civil society. Therefore, Afro social movements in Brazil had to do the following:

a. Challenge and interrupt hegemonic notions of Brazilian identity as mainly white and Christian
b. Challenge vertical political structures that excluded or marginalized Blacks, while creating new forms of social movement participation from below
c. Challenge, critique, and transform racialized categories that had been de-racialized
d. Challenge and overturn the notion of racial democracy
e. Reposition the state and civil society views on racial inequality, and force the state to recognize that racial inequality is a legitimate political and social issue
f. Challenge and fight within leftist formations, traditional parties, and movement regarding issues of racial discrimination
g. Create space within newly emerging civil society structures to challenge white vertical hegemony in order to allow for more open and thorough discussion of racial exploitation.

CULTURAL POLITICS AND THE RISE OF *BLOCOS AFROS*: THE 1970S TO THE CURRENT PERIOD

During the Brazilian military dictatorship from 1964 to 1985, open discussions on key issues and grassroots mobilization was censured and denounced as subversive. Even some of the opposition groups could be characterized by authoritarian decision making and vertical structures. However, the reconstitution of formal democracy following military rule, and the emergence of Afro-Brazilian social movements during the final years of the dictatorship, presented new forms of organization and propelled a series of burning questions into Brazil's national discourse. Opposition to military rule peaked in the early 1970s, and by the end of the decade the country had begun a process of liberalization that enabled a large cross-section of diverse groups to challenge political and economic inequality through social movement action. During the transition from military to civilian rule, Brazilian social movement groups sought to connect their struggle for democracy with their struggle for social justice (Andrews 1996, 483). Issues of racial equality, as well as gender, emerged as important rallying cries for these new movements. Afro-Brazilians across the country joined labor leaders and church officials, as well as the rural and urban poor, and began an unprecedented dialogue on the role of race and gender and how they structured opportunities and rewards in Brazilian society (Lovell 2000, 85).

Starting in the 1970s, Black movement groups, labor leaders, church officials, political exiles, and the international media applied an unprecedented amount of pressure on the Brazilian military dictatorship to release the hundreds of detained political prisoners and end widespread torture; during this time, there was a call by these groups for an immediate transition to democracy (Green 2010). In fact these new social movements reengineered civil society, expressing democratic aspirations and broadening the experience of citizenship. Afro-Brazilians, as well as other key social actors, were central to these new democratic impulses. Specifically this chapter examines the rise of these horizontally structured Afro social movements and many of the issues and debates they tackled during this time.

Alvarez, Dagnino, and Escobar (1998) as well as Dellacioppa and Weber (2012) provide some important theoretical markers for understanding exactly what is meant by cultural politics and its relation to Latin American social movements. Dagnino posits that cultural politics is important for assessing the scope and nature of these struggles as social movements for the broader democratization of society and for highlighting the less visible and tangible implications of certain struggles (Alvarez, Dagnino, and Escobar 1998, 7). Cultural contestations are not simply by-products of political struggles but instead constitutive of social movements to redefine the meanings and inherent limitations of the political system. Cultural politics therefore is seen as both enactive and relational, and refer to processes enacted when sets of social actors shaped by and embodying different cultural meanings and practices come into conflict with each other. Conceptually this suggests that meanings and practices—particularly those theorized as marginal, grassroots, oppositional, minority, residential, emergent, alternative, and dissident, are conceived in relations to the dominant cultural order. As grassroots movements emerging outside the traditional structures they represented new expressions and forms of grass roots participation. Culture, therefore, by definition is political because such meanings are constitutive of processes that implicitly or explicitly seek to redefine social relations of power (Alvarez, Dagnino, and Escobar, 1998, 7). Thus when movements deploy alternative conceptions of woman, nature, race, identity, economy, democracy, power, or citizenship that unsettle the dominant institutional setting and challenge the language of the hegemonic structure, they are enacting cultural politics.

Cultural politics is at the core of most Afro-Brazilian social movements and aesthetics, and in order to best understand *blocos afros* and cultural politics in Salvador, it is necessary to trace the rise of the *blocos* as social movements starting in the 1970s as a unique cultural and political force. There has been a steady stream of rich literature and critical insights on the rise, significance, and relevance of *blocos afros* and carnival in Salvador, and much of the writing underscores four key areas: first, the founding of and the conditions paving the way for the rise of *blocos* and their re-Africanization of carnival in 1970s; second, their performative and identity aesthetics as cultural signifiers; third, the racialized Black body (both male and female) as sites of resistance, folkorization, and co-optation; and lastly, the process of commodification and commercialization (Risério 1981; Stam 1988; Dunn 1992; Butler 1998; Junior 2007; Pinho 2010; Conçeicão 2010; and Sterling 2012). Building on these important insights, this chapter expands the conceptual lens by examining the early role of *blocos* in articulating new forms of grassroots activism and cultural politics rooted in horizontal structures, and how these processes created new social and political spaces: By placing *blocos* within the frame of social movements, a new layer of understanding is presented on their evolution and early contribution to grassroots activism as well as insights into emergent cultural politics unfolding in Salvador from the 1970s to present.

The modern-day *blocos* are contemporary versions of the first African Clubs that formed in Salvador around the turn of the twentieth century. As cultural phenomena of the 1970s, *blocos* were influenced by "Black Rio," a cultural movement that flourished in Rio de Janiero and later spread to other parts of urban Brazil (Pinho 2010). Black Rio or the "Black Soul" movement was in turn influenced by North American soul music and the U.S. Black power movement. Theoretically, while the soul movement had no means to organize politically, its powerful articulation of transnational identity politics served to unite Afro-Brazilians from different class backgrounds and was a powerful cultural force. Black Rio or Black Soul served as an important marker of identity and was a catalyst for identity-based politics that were emerging in Brazil at this time (Turner 1985, 79).

ILÊ AIYÊ AND OLODUM: THE FIRST MODERN *BLOCOS*

Ilê Aiyê, the first modern *bloco,* began as a movement of young people known as Zorra who were from the neighborhood of Liberdade (Liberty), which is a predominantly Black community in Salvador. On November 1, 1974, a member from Zorra founded Ilê Aiyê with the idea of honoring and affirming Black identity. Roughly a year later, in November 1975, Ilê Aiyê paraded the streets of Salvador as an official *bloco*, dressed in colorful African garb and playing African influenced rhythms. This was important for several reasons: first, we witness the re-Africanization of carnival; second, Blacks previously excluded from carnival now had an all-Black *bloco;* and third, Ilê Aiyê with this new bold act ushered in a new period of Black social justice activism rooted in strong Afro-referenced consciousness in Salvador (Jones de Almeida 2003, 49). Equally important as a new grassroots movement from below and from the margins, Ilê Aiyê offered new forms of participation in the cultural arena (carnival and identity politics) for Blacks locked out of Salvador's highly discriminatory social structures.

The founding of Ilê Aiyê as one of the first *blocos* in 1974, and the re-Africanization of carnival in 1975, set the stage for a new era of heightened Black consciousness and social justice activism, and served simultaneously as a platform for the newly emerging Black power movement in Salvador. At this historical juncture Brazil was still ruled by a military dictatorship characterized by vertical authoritarian politics, but political liberalization was slowly unfolding and civil society groups were becoming more and more politically active and organized. Afro carnival groups like Ilê Aiyê were at the vanguard, emerging as a radical platform to project a new form of Black identity, social consciousness, and a new stage of Afro Brazilian political participation. A radical new social and political landscape arose that altered traditional carnival practices by actualizing a specific Black performative aesthetics, centering the Black body as a key point of reference while using music, dance, and polyrhythmic structures and Afro-diasporic cultural symbols rooted in African-inspired traditions. A revolutionary cultural shift was occurring, given that Brazilians still lived under a military dictatorship and Blacks had been historically excluded from carnival. Ilê Aiyê and the *blocos* that followed established a new framework for modern Afro-centric referenced identities and participation, based on reconstructing the past through the use of provocative body aesthetics while using music and dance as a form of sharp social commentary, an act which was unheard of at the time.

As the first modern *bloco*, Ilê Aiyê is central to contemporary Afro-Bahian culture, modern Black consciousness, and social identity, as it is considered the guardian of African traditions, the "most beautiful of all," the most African *bloco,* and of course, the oldest (Pinho 2010, 79). While *blocos* were opening new cultural spaces, they were also providing a direct challenge and critique of Brazil's and Salvador's racial classification system and white-dominated political and social institutions, in which Blacks were classified as *pardo* (black), *prêto* (brown) and *mulatto* (light-skinned). In this system, dark-skinned Blacks were placed at the very bottom, and white as well as light skin was idealized and worshipped. Ilê Aiyê is a direct repudiation of this racial classification system, and in the early days restricted its participation to only dark-skinned Afro-Brazilians. In other words, Ilê Aiyê reinvigorated and rescued the idea of "dark-skin Blackness," reaffirmed African-ness, and by definition, Pan-African and Black identity, concepts that had been severely distorted in Brazilian racial discourse, which reaffirmed whiteness. Ilê Aiyê set the tone and reflected a rising new Black social consciousness and new Black politics flowering in Brail and Salvador. Ilê Aiye was not only the first *bloco* to re-Africanize carnival, but it was one of the first to simultaneously mobilize Blacks and to denounce racial discrimination during the years of military dictatorship when such activities were strictly prohibited. In doing so it developed new forms of political and social organizations that would foreshadow other social groups that were soon to follow. Ilê Aiyê was in fact engaged in early radical cultural politics and acts of resistance, which had deep political and social overtones. Soon thereafter other *blocos* would follow in its footsteps.

Five years later, on April 25, 1979, prostitutes, homosexuals, drug users, bohemians, and lawyers founded Olodum. It started out as a grassroots, horizontal resistance organization in the historic neighborhood of Pelourinho and was born in the context of social marginalization to fight racial inequality and widespread social discrimination (Rodrigues 1999, 47). João Rodrigues, the current president, argues that Olodum was born to defend and articulate Black culture and argues that the defense of Black culture is "political" in Salvador and Brazil (Rodrigues 2000, 47). Olodum is currently the most famous *bloco* in Brazil. Building on the success of Ilê Aiyê, the members were catapulted to success and became famous for their pulsating drumming sessions held on Tuesday nights in Pelourinho, when it was then a run-down drug-infested neighborhood. In the beginning, the social base of its membership came from the masses and it was an organization with open and direct forms of participation.

In contrast to Ilê Aiyê, Olodum early on decided to admit whites and mestizos as members and made a conscious decision to involve itself in the political struggles in Salvador in the 1980s. It has carefully cultivated its image as a diverse cultural *bloco* that reaffirms Black identity within a broad multicultural framework. It was Olodum's commercial collaborations, first with Paul Simon's 1990s "Rhythm of the Saints" album, and later Michael Jackson's now-famous music video, "They Don't Care about Us" (1996) that firmly established the group's international credentials and allowed it to be referred to as the best-known *bloco*. The members have also collaborated with Jimmy Cliff, Ziggy Marley, and other reggae singers from the Caribbean. Other *blocos* of course would soon follow as many sprang up in neighborhoods across Salvador: included were Muzenza, Ara ketu, Puxada Axé, Malês and Debalês.

Olodum's rehearsals and drumming sessions soon became famous and the foci for local activists, poets, musicians, and tourists from all over the world. Its legendary Tuesday night rehearsals reinvented the tradition of benediction, a six o'clock evening mass at the Church of Rosário in Pelourinho, which became a common gathering point for Afro-Bahian youths (Butler 1998, 170). And, this new space was a vehicle for politics and a new form of grassroots community activism. Olodum's music, much like Ilê Aiyê's, fuses social and political commentary as a form of cultural politics that brings fragments of Afro-Brazilian history together and links them to a transnational Black identity. Olodum's Tuesday night rehearsals, along with the powerful percussions and the wail of music, became its signature trademark.

Through horizontal structures such as grassroots organizing, open membership, community service, and advocacy structures with links to poor communities, the *blocos* were able to mobilize their constituencies and deliver powerful messages to Salvador's dispossessed urban poor masses: issues of Black identity rooted in a multicultural Pan-African frame spoke to the lethal hand of the law and police brutality, social cleansing by death squads, lack of respect and dignity, and unemployment—only to name a few. Such themes were articulated with airtight clarity by the *blocos* and resonated deeply with the poor Black youth scattered across the urban peripheries and favelas in Salvador. The *blocos* were in fact creating a radical new social and political grammar and constructing new ways of communicating the language of marginality, which underscored how Brazil's highly unequal social system had kept Blacks permanently peripheral and locked out. It was within this social context that the *blocos* were born as militant Black organizations to denounce racial discrimination as well as reaffirm positive Black identity, personhood, and citizenship. Organizing from below and from the margins, the *blocos* were uncovering new terrain and operating from a new cultural angle as well as opening new sociopolitical spaces to talk about and critique racialized oppression and class inequality. Their creative production was articulated in a language that Salvador's urban masses could readily understand.

Simultaneously, on the transnational level, the early *blocos* like Ilê Aiyê and Olodum connected to Afro-Portuguese national liberation movements and other Black movements across the globe. According to João Rodrigues, president of Olodum, they were deeply influenced by the national liberation movements of the Portuguese colonies of Mozambique, Guinea Bissau, and Angola during the 1970s (interviewed by author, Salvador Bahia, July 8, 2013). African books and literature written in Portuguese circulated widely in Salvador's neighborhoods. In particular the ideas of Amílcar Cabral of the African Party for the Independence of Guinea and Cape Verde in Guinea-Bissau, Samora Michel of the Mozambique Liberation Front in Mozambique, and Agostinho Neto of the People's Movement for the Liberation of Angola in Angola influenced their views on culture, politics, identity, and struggle.

Blocos arose therefore as a direct reaction and challenge to very specific social and political conditions that kept Blacks locked outside the official channels of public discourse. Historically, Blacks in Salvador and across Brazil have had limited options for effecting change through established political networks and the traditional bureaucratic order. Afro-Bahians through *blocos* and other cultural productions have established alternative institutions that have accorded them some degree of political leverage (Butler 1998, 158). The *blocos* offered new structures for cultural and political participation in their organizations to Black and poor people who had been excluded from carnival and locked out of official political discourses. By opening new spaces and creating new participatory opportunities, the *blocos* were early precursors to many social movements that would soon follow in other parts of the Americas.

According to Butler, the creation and construction of new power bases through Afro-Bahian cultural institutions in the late twentieth and early twenty-first century must been seen as an attempt by Afro-Bahians to create alternative structures to correct and counteract centuries of political and cultural exclusion and social devaluation. Over the last forty years—until the present—the *blocos* in Salvador have grown in power, number, and prestige, and through their social and cultural activities they have been very effective in recruiting and maintaining a hard-core and dedicated cadre of supporters, mostly from the ranks of Salvador's urban poor and middle classes. Currently in Salvador the *blocos* are the main venues for the creation of strong Afro-referenced identities and Black cultural symbols. Many *blocos,* along with having strong followers in Brazil, are also well known and have an international following.

According to Walter Altino, an intellectual activist and expert on the *blocos* from Salvador, the rise of the *blocos* mirrored two sides of a simmering debate on the proper role and intersection of culture and politics in the Afro-Brazil social movement's circles in the 1970s (interviewed by author, Salvador Bahia, July 1, 2013). Each side had a distinct view on the role of culture and politics as vehicles of grassroots mobilization. One wing was represented by the cultural groups that emphasized music, dance, and religion; they did not consider their organizations as expressly political. On the other side were political activists, who wanted more concrete action based on grassroots organizing, political education, and promoting Black consciousness. The genius of the *blocos*—on some level—is that they were able to synthesize these tensions as they addressed or at least spoke to this dilemma by creatively deploying Afro-Bahian cultural formation, that is, song, music, and dance, to address a whole range of complicated political and social issues while creating new participatory structures. And at the same time they were able to amplify a social message that catered to and resonated widely with thousands of poor, disenfranchised citizens in Salvador and across Brazil.

WHAT IS THE PRICE OF SUCCESS?
COMMODIFICATION AND CO-OPTATION

Since their founding *blocos* created new forms of identity representation and political participation, served as a platform for political contestation and grassroots education and mobilization, established social justice activist networks, community outreach programs, and primary educational schools, as well as musical and technical training programs; engaged in politics by supporting political candidates, and established small lucrative businesses. Currently Ilê Aiyê and Olodum both have established what appear to be very successful businesses and earn revenues through lucrative business and licensing deals. Over the last two decades some *blocos* have entered local politics and engaged in politics from below as they have endorsed and campaigned for politicians, negotiated deals, and accepted the support from corporations while they have become for-profit businesses. Some *blocos* now charge for their concerts by performing in special shows; they sell music (CDs, DVDs) as well as T-shirts, caps, pants, coffee mugs, key chains, and an assortment of other goods. Their concerts, both free and paid, continue to draw large crowds of loyal fans from across Salvador, Brazil, and the world. The key question is: to what extent do such programs serve as a base of social and political empowerment? And, do their new commercial ties undercut or enhance their Black social agenda?

Michael Hanchard in his book *Orpheus and Power* (1994) raised an important point regarding the construction of hegemonic power and the intersection of culture with respect to Afro-Brazilian cultural articulations. Building on Gramsci's notion of hegemony, Hanchard (1994, 20) poses the following question: how do subordinate individual/groups forge counterhegemonic values out of existing, reactionary ones without reproducing the latter in new forms? This fundamental question, according to Hanchard, is relevant to most struggles over domination on a national scale and therefore key to understanding how Afro-Brazilians have attempted to create alternative political discourse and organizational forms regarding the reproduction of racial inequality and the creation of new forms of positive identities.

Blocos were born as Black militant organizations to challenge the dominant hegemonic patterns of racial inequality and promote positive Black identity and participation, as well as to serve the interests of Salvador's urban masses. However, these newly established political relationships and business ventures raise a series of thorny and difficult questions: has the power of the market, tourism, and mainstream clientele politics diminished the emancipatory logic of the Black struggle? Does the "cultural marketing of Blackness" or the "folklorization of Blackness" devalue or undermine the positive Black identity the *blocos* sought to reconstruct? Do these ventures undermine their grassroots structures and diminish the horizontal forms that Afro-Brazilians developed in these movements? To what extent have the *blocos* as nontraditional political actors been effective in local politics by electing individuals to office who might implement a progressive democratic vision that serves the needs of the poor urban masses? Has the cultural power of the *blocos* and their business and political relationships led to a better material situation for Blacks in Salvador and Bahia? Simply put, have the *blocos* strengthened Black consciousness and organization or have they sold out, and if so, to whom?

In order to best understand the evolution and contradiction of *blocos* it is important to narrate a series of events that unfolded in Salvador in the late 1980s and early 1990s. The United Nations Educational, Scientific, and Cultural Organization (UNESCO) declared Pelourinho—a historic neighborhood and Olodum's main site of operation—a world heritage site in 1985. The official declaration as a world heritage site unleashed and set in motion a powerful set of cross-currents and conflicting interests. At the time, Pelourinho was a dilapidated, run-down and crime-infested neighborhood, but the new designation by UNESCO meant that, if the area could be revitalized, then lots of money could be made. After years of delays and negotiations with local residents and community groups, the government implemented a program of restoration to refurbish many of the historic buildings which were literally falling apart. In 1991 O Patrímonio Artístico e Cultural (The Institute of Artistic and Cultural Heritage), a state-funded operation, led a massive revitalization program to modernize Pelourinho.

Olodum, which had been involved in the revitalization plans and negotiations, now found itself caught in the treacherous cross-currents of local grassroots advocacy, that is, support for poor Blacks—one of their key constituencies—on one side, and powerful state-led developmental interests on the other. Olodum, of course, shared the interest of the state as it wanted a revitalized Pelourinho, but in order to do this, local residents would have to be expelled. Many of these residents thought of Olodum as their advocate and not their adversary. Olodum's long-term interest, that is, to revitalize and rebuild Pelourinho into an important tourist site, directly conflicted with the interests of some of the longtime residents who were poor and Black. But what was termed "revitalization" for some was "ethnic cleansing" for others. In order to move forward with the revitalization plans, scores of poor and Black people were forcefully removed from their homes, some at gunpoint. It is estimated that roughly 600 families were "relocated" and the compensation for their removal was between US$400 and $800 (*A Tarde*, 1992). While there were consultations with many local residents, the best strategy was not mutually agreed upon, as some chose to accept the money while others refused. The process was deeply divisive, resulting in many longtime residents being forcefully relocated.

This messy situation underscores the sharp tensions and problems of urban developmental renewal initiatives: In this scenario, commercial "success" and "development" were translated into implementing a series of urban renewal projects, which only served residents who were allowed to stay (not all were removed) and the interest of local businesses, but the trade-off was that some of the poorer residents were expelled and forcibly removed. The renovations, which were desperately needed, did however benefit Olodum and other *blocos* and some artists as well as retailers, hotels, and restaurants. The revitalization brought fancy restaurants, art galleries, and expensive shops, but many of the residents who currently live in Pelourinho cannot afford to shop or eat in these establishments. There exists a silent but sharp tension between the residents and the some of the businesses, and these tensions, while not obvious on the surface, are prevalent. As one long-term resident of Pelourinho and member of the Association of Residents and Friends of the Historic District (a grassroots community groups fighting gentrication) said, "It's now a shopping mall for rich tourists" (Simone Pereira, interviewed by author, February 21, 2013).

Ilê Aiyê has received generous support from the mega-construction firm Odebrecht and the Brazilian oil company Petrobras. In its early years, Ilê Aiyê chose not to play a role in electoral politics. However, over the last couple of decades it has entered the electoral fray by openly supporting candidates. The 2000 mayoral reelection campaign of Antônio Imbassy received support from Ilê Aiyê. Carlinhos Brown, the famous singer and promoter of carnivals, and Gerônimo, a local singer and cultural hero, saw their voices and images used extensively throughout the campaign (Pinho 2010, 200). The ads used in the electoral campaign were based on carnival images six months prior, which meant important Black cultural symbols were used to add muscle and deliver political campaign ads to Salvador's urban masses. The new relationship between some *blocos*, corporations, and traditional ruling parties at least on the surface, appears to directly contradict their earlier missions as they were founded as independent autonomous agents of social change free from the influence of patronage, conservative political forces, and white hegemonic rule. It is difficult to see how such relationships confer or advance the broad interest of Salvador's urban poor. Ilê Aiyê, much like Olodum, was born as a grassroots resistance organization to articulate new ideas about citizenship, positive Black identity, and social inclusion.

Along with the *blocos* there are other Black cultural groups (none were social movement groups) that have formed strategic alliances with local and state government officials as well as with business and tourist interests to "promote roots tourism" or the cultural marketing of Afro-Bahians (Pinho 2010). This cultural marketing includes tours to visit *quilombos* (Maroon communities), to see *candomblé* ceremonies (Afro-Brazilian religion) and *capoeira* performances (martial arts), and, of course, *bloco* performances. State forces, business interests, the *blocos*, and Black cultural groups have entered into strategic relations and transformed Afro-cultural productions into a form of symbolic Black cultural capital. In doing so, some argue that Black cultural capital becomes overly commodified, thereby losing its emancipatory logic and its counterhegemonic positioning. Against this backdrop questions arise: Is the cultural capital of Afro-Bahians being crassly exploited and thus working against Blacks? Have these advances expanded citizenship and direct participation?

Within the larger hegemonic matrix and despite attempts by the *blocos* to create positive images, a series of complicated distortions continue to unfold and are at play in Salvador. Despite the attempt by *blocos* to create a more positive and nuanced Black identity, Blacks in Salvador are constructed via processes of commodification through the media, popular culture, and tourist images; they are constructed as "happy," "obedient," extremely musical, gifted singers, and exceptional athletes. And the image of the immaculate Black body—both male and female—which is a key site of contestation, co-optation, and exploitation, is central to the hegemonic positioning; from the *capoeiraista*, to the *acarajé* seller (the Bahian women dressed in white who sell traditional African dishes), the Black body is always on full display and is the main site of the social production of performance (song and music), exploitation (selling food in streets or on the beach) and gratification (sexual). In fact the wholesale commodification of the Black body and culture may have become an impediment to social and political power. Gilroy argues that the super-affirmation of the Black body in the realm of culture as a set of symbols creates a comfort zone that becomes more artificial as dissident culture becomes increasingly ever more spectacle-like and aestheticized. Thus, according to Gilroy, Black culture becomes "revolutionary conservative" since it is revolutionary in appearance but conservative in content (Gilroy 2000, 270). Pinho points out that as a consequence of commodification, Bahian Afro-cultural productions runs the risk of becoming an arena that allows little concrete resistance against a hegemonic system that reproduces racial dominance and race and class inequalities (Pinho 2010, 213). Against this backdrop and returning to Hanchard, we are led to ask, how do subordinate individuals/groups forge counterhegemonic values out of existing, reactionary ones without reproducing the latter in new forms?

Fernando Conçeicão, an intellectual and social justice activist from Salvador, argues that cultural commodification by the *blocos* and Black cultural producers has "repackaged" Blackness and distanced the culture from its revolutionary agency. The depth, texture, and the political substance of Black identity and urgency of critical issues have been severely undermined by market forces through alliance with the traditional ruling elements of Bahia. He believes that Black cultural capital that was accumulated in centuries of struggle is now being undermined by the same people who claim to defend it. The cultural power of Afro-Bahia and the formation of *blocos*, according to Conçeição, have not led to a better material situation for most Blacks, resulting in symbolic Black consciousness devoid of depth (Reiter and Mitchell 2010, 21). Along these lines, cultural commodification, according to Hanchard (1994), Pinho (2010), and Conçeicão (2010) freezes or hypostatizes cultural practices and participation, divorcing them from their histories and attendant modes of consciousness that brought them into being, and limiting the range of alternative articulations and movements by Afro-Brazilian groups.

The marketing of Afro-Bahia is now part of official discourse. The Brazilian state (regional and local), Black cultural groups, the tourism industrial complex, and some U.S. universities and colleges have entered into various alliances to package, market, sell, and present Afro-Bahian culture or "folkore" as uniquely Brazilian on one hand, and African on the other, that is, "milking mama Africa," in the words of Pinho (2010, 84). These processes, which are regional, national, and transnational, raise some important questions. According to Josélio Teles dos Santos, through carefully hegemonic construction of "folklore," the state—now in conjunction with other actors—manipulated the symbolic realm of culture to first gain political control, and second, realize economic gains. State cultural initiatives therefore have serious political meaning; they did not simply recognize the existence of Afro-Brazilian cultural expressions, forms of political participation, and their contributions to Brazilian society. Rather, the state sought political control and what might be termed symbolic surplus value for economic development, in particular the reproduction of national and regional identities that could be marketed by Bahia's tourism industrial complex (Teles dos Santos 1999, 123). The state via the commodification of Black cultural productions is therefore able to engage in the following hegemonic theatrics: first, commercially exploit Black culture; second, keep Blacks marginal to economic and political power; third, apply extremely harsh and at times disproportionate violence through the criminal justice system in the name of law and order.

Today in Salvador the *blocos* are still very active across the city, and they have grown in size and prestige as they are able to project their power across Salvador, Brazil, and the globe; their message, rhetoric, and image represent the projection of Afro-referenced social identity and Black cultural capital. More importantly the *blocos* have built important social institutions like their schools and after-school educational programs, which have served thousands of poor school children over the years. Given their central role in carnival and tourism, they will continue to construct and form an integral part of Salvador's cultural and social identity. Carnival and the *blocos* are now synonymous with each other and central to Salvador's and Brazil's image and ever-expanding tourism industry. However, their business ventures and new commercial ties have called into question their ability to continue to challenge Salvador's ruling hierarchies. And while they still continue to serve poor and often forgotten constituencies, their grassroots participatory horizontal structures have eroded and been replaced with top-down, personality-driven, vertical styles of operation. Both Ilê Aiyê and Olodum now operate with corporate style structures with boards of directors and are run by strong personality-driven individuals with lots of power. In short, the power of the market, questionable political alliances, and ties to mega-corporations like Petrobras and Odebrecht and their corporate style have severely compromised their previous horizontal decision-making structures. Yet at the same time, they have continued to promote their grassroots Afro-referenced social identity.

More disturbing is the fact that roughly forty years after the rise of *blocos* and cultural politics, Blacks have made only modest progress in local and municipal politics, and despite 80 percent of the population being Black, with strong Afro-referenced identity and cultural capital, neither the city of Salvador nor the state of Bahia have ever elected a Black mayor or governor, and Blacks currently occupy very few seats on the city council. But, as informed readers are well aware, formal Black political power and the election of a Black mayor or governor will not address or offer a panacea to four centuries of extreme social and political oppression and structural marginalization. History has been cruel to Black people in Salvador and Brazil, as reflected in these knotty contradictions in Black cultural politics in Salvador da Bahia.

Jornada de Lucha Contra el ALCA, Quito, Ecuador, 31 October 2002. Peasant, Indigenous and student organizations protesting a meeting of Latin American finance ministers to negotiate the Free Trade Area of the Americas (ALCA). (Peter Rosset)

III

Dealing with the (Reconstituted) State

Grassroots mobilizations against neoliberalism in the 1990s laid the ground-work for a remarkable shift leftward in electoral contests at the beginning of the twenty-first century. Soon, left-of-center governments that seemingly would advocate for the interests of social movements that placed them in office governed almost all of Latin America. Despite an apparent congruence of interests, grassroots movements that operated according to horizontal forms of organization quickly ran into conflicts with progressive govern-ments that utilized vertical mechanisms to implement their agendas. These conflicts ran the gamut of ideological and strategic differences that played out on a variety of levels.

The authors in part III examine through a variety of different lenses how activists have responded to new challenges that state structures present to social movements. We start with two of the clearest challenges to emerge to electoral systems in Latin America, the 1994 neo-Zapatista uprising in Chia-pas, Mexico, and the *piquetero* movement in Argentina, spawned by the 1998–2002 economic crisis. In chapter 10, Richard Stahler-Sholk examines how Zapatista communities practice de facto autonomy in their everyday lives as a method of challenging electoral systems and formal government institutions. As a result, the movement remains resistant to co-optation by outside forces or domination by a small cadre of leaders. The Zapatistas represent one end of a continuum of movement-state relations, practicing a strategy of resistance involving rejection of all government aid and pro-grams, with community members assuming responsibilities for self-govern-ance as well as autonomous education and health care. The radically democratic aspects of this model have helped consolidate a distinctive collective identity for the Zapatista movement, but there are also challenges in sustaining this horizontal orientation in the face of government counterinsurgency programs and the global market forces that are disintegrating *campesino* communities across Mexico.

The *piquetero* movement provides a second clear example of a social movement that deemphasizes hierarchical and institutionalized structures. Drawing on innovative organizing strategies that emerged in Argentina in the aftermath of economic crisis and the collapse of neoliberal governing structures in 2001, Marina Sitrin explains what it means for activists to create alternative autonomous models of people power. She examines worker takeovers of factories and innovative civil disobedience campaigns. This rejection of traditional forms of political power and the maintenance of autonomous political agendas has become synonymous with the central ideas and organizing practices of horizontalism.

In Argentina, debates over horizontalism flourished in the context of attempts by the progressive Kirchner governments to rebuild a political consensus based on progressive notions of social justice. A similar story played out in Brazil with the Landless Rural Workers' Movement (MST) as they ran into conflicts with the ruling Workers Party (PT), first under the administration of Luiz Inácio Lula da Silva and then Dilma Rousseff. Initially the MST and PT were strong allies, and social movements provided direct input into the policy-making processes of the party and government. Indeed, the MST endeavored to rule from below by pushing for the radical agenda that the PT initially championed. Once in power, however, the PT faced intense pressure from corporate agriculturalists, Brazilian financers, and São Paulo industrialists. In response, the MST became increasingly critical of the economic policy and priorities of the government, arguing that the consumerist neoliberal model that the PT government championed was leaving too many ordinary Brazilians behind. In his chapter, Harry E. Vanden analyzes how social movements in Brazil attempted to gain the attention of the government and the Worker's Party leadership to change the neoliberal economic model that concentrated wealth in the hands of the better off while leaving the marginalized rural and urban masses behind. Vanden critiques the government for squandering scarce government resources on stadiums and megaprojects while neglecting schools, health care, and employment for the newly trained sons and daughters of workers and other sectors of the population. This message dramatically emerged into the national consciousness after massive June 2013 street demonstrations.

The Kirchners in Argentina and the PT in Brazil represented moderate-left governments, whereas a triad of governments in the Andean countries of Venezuela, Ecuador, and Bolivia epitomized more radical alternatives to neoliberalism. Hugo Chávez's 1998 electoral victory in Venezuela ushered in this dramatic leftward shift in Latin American politics, and he was followed by Evo Morales's victory in Bolivia in 2005 and Rafael Correa's in Ecuador in 2006, both of whom attempted to emulate Chávez's political strategies. In all three countries, social movements have attempted to retain a certain amount of autonomous distance from the elected governments that they helped place in power.

George Ciccariello-Maher presents an innovative interpretation of the emergence of the Bolivarian Revolution in Venezuela. He argues that "Chavismo," a political ideology associated with the late president Hugo Chávez Frías, does not represent the entirety of the revolutionary movement, and the movement is not simply one aimed at seizing state power. Rather, the political changes that emerged in Venezuela over the last several decades represent a negotiation between grassroots movements and centralized governmental structures. As Ciccariello-Maher argues, the success of the Bolivarian Revolution is built on walking a fine line between horizontalism and government structures that allows for political changes to surge forward through pressure from below.

In Ecuador, Correa followed Chávez's lead in convoking a constitutional assembly in order to remake the country's governing structures. Although social movements supported the new and progressive constitution, activists questioned whether the new document would benefit social movements or enable Correa to occupy political spaces that they had previously held. As Marc Becker explains, although social movements shared Correa's stated desire to curtail neoliberal policies and implement social and economic strategies that would benefit the majority of the country's people, they clashed over how to realize those objectives. Correa's relations with these movements point to the complications, limitations, and deep tensions inherent in pursuing revolutionary changes within a constitutional framework.

Similar to electoral triumphs in Venezuela and Ecuador, the left cheered when Evo Morales won the Bolivian presidency in 2005. It was the first time an Indigenous person was elected president in this country, whose majority Indigenous population was not allowed even to walk outside the presidential palace some years ago. But that was not the only reason. As Leonidas Oikonomakis and Fran Espinoza explain, the formation of the first government cabinet of 2006, with its strong participation of labor union and Indigenous leaders, made evident that Morales was bringing to the political frontline the movements that helped him grasp state power. Vice President Álvaro García Linera famously argued that "the MAS [Movement Toward Socialism] represents a new form of government, one which is run by and for Bolivia's social movements" which "are now in control of the state apparatus." But, Oikonomakis and Espinoza question, what has happened to this "government of movements"? How has this relationship developed? Adopting a process-tracing approach, they analyze what social and political alliances helped form the government in 2005, and how these alliances have developed during the course of time. They argue that not only has the participation of people with a grassroots and social sector background dropped steadily in Morales's government, but also that the party's structure has imposed a top-down control over the very groups that conceived it as a political tool.

As viewed through these different lenses, these studies highlight the promises and expose the limitations of state-centered paths to social change. How to confront the new challenges that pink tide governments present to grassroots activists remains a key issue that Latin American social movements are currently facing.

Chapter Ten

Mexico

*Autonomy, Collective Identity, and the
Zapatista Social Movement*

Richard Stahler-Sholk

Twenty years after the 1994 Zapatista uprising in Chiapas, Mexico, that derailed celebrations of the implementation of the North American Free Trade Agreement (NAFTA) and galvanized the alter-globalization movement, the Zapatistas inaugurated the Escuelita Zapatista (Little School). Students of "freedom according to the Zapatistas" were invited to participate in week-long study sessions, live with a Maya Zapatista family, and discuss texts consisting of narratives by community members reflecting on their experiences of autonomy, resistance, and processes of social transformation such as gender equality. Students, mostly from around Mexico but also internationals, swung a machete or ground corn with the family in the morning, then sat with members of the family and an assigned "guardian" (usually a young person from another community) to ask questions based on the community narratives. The main lesson was that emancipatory change is a participatory process, not a grant from someone in power.

This chapter will explore the implications of the Zapatista strategy of rejecting engagement with the state to implement de facto autonomy. I argue that the distancing from party-electoral logics and state institutional structures opened space for more horizontal forms of organizing. By exercising autonomy rather than negotiating it as a concession from above, the Zapatista communities empowered themselves, practicing new ways of doing politics through their everyday lives. Less hierarchical and less institutionalized movements are perhaps more resistant to co-optation or decapitation, to the extent that the movement is embodied by the experience of its participants rather than by a small number of irreplaceable leaders who could be targeted to control or derail the movement. On the other hand, decentralization may present special challenges for maintaining coherence and for presenting a common agenda that can form the basis for alliance with others.

The Zapatista rebellion began on January 1, 1994, as an armed uprising confronting state power, but the military phase of the conflict lasted only twelve days. Images of the coercive power of the state deployed against poor Indigenous peasants provoked mass mobilizations of Mexican civil society demanding a ceasefire and negotiations. The rebellion morphed from an assault on the state to a prolonged struggle to carve out an autonomous space in which to reorganize society around the eleven Zapatista demands of work, land, housing, food, health care, education, independence, freedom, democracy, justice, and peace (EZLN 1993). Beyond the armed insurgency, with its necessarily hierarchical character, is the social movement consisting of the support base of Indigenous communities[1] and wider networks of supporters (Diez 2011). The impact of the movement extended to the way the everyday practices of its participants influenced the wider society, nationally and internationally. Zapatismo was one of the inspirations for the formation of the National Indigenous Congress (Congreso Nacional Indígena, CNI) in 1996 and a myriad of Indigenous and other mobilizations across Mexico, as well as a galvanizing force for alter-globalization protests including the watershed 1999 showdown in Seattle at the World Trade Organization ministerial meeting (Dellacioppa 2009).

CONCEPTS AND CONTEXT OF AUTONOMY

The demand for autonomy from the state and from conventional political institutions has long been a defining characteristic of social movement organizing (Hellman 2008a). The concept of autonomy has historically been used in a somewhat different sense by neo-Marxist and poststructuralist thinkers to explain the circumstances under which the state itself may sometimes act, not exactly as the executive committee for the bourgeoisie (in Marx's classic description of the capitalist state), but rather with a degree of independence from at least the short-term interests of the ruling class, exhibiting what has been called "the specificity of the political" (Laclau 1977). In the case of Mexico, the Institutional Revolutionary Party (PRI) that governed Mexico for seventy-one years under what the conservative Peruvian novelist Mario Vargas Llosa once famously called "the perfect dictatorship" built an elaborate corporatist and clientelist apparatus that sustained itself more often through ideological hegemony than by blatant coercion (Hamilton 1982). Using strategies that Adam David Morton (2011) called "passive revolution," including a mixture of some redistributive reforms and symbolic nationalism, postrevolutionary governments in Mexico managed to reconstitute social relations in ways that blended the illusion of progressive change with restoration in order to preserve the capitalist order.

The long postwar "pax priísta" was actually something of a myth, as twentieth-century Mexico saw a series of agrarian rebel movements (Padilla 2008) that were repressed, co-opted, or covered up. The model started to come apart with the shifting political economy of the 1970s–1980s, marked by the oil boom and bust followed by the 1982 foreign debt crisis that ushered in neoliberal policies of austerity, privatization, and opening to the global market (Collier 2005). Some peasant organizations had begun to stake out positions independent of the PRI, but this limited notion of autonomy (institutional separation from the party) proved insufficient as the PRI evolved more pluralistic forms of co-optation of groups nominally independent of the party (Hellman 2008b). In 1992, as part of the structural reforms paving the way for NAFTA, the Mexican government "reformed" Article 27 of the 1917 constitution, ending the land redistribution that had been a hallmark of the revolution and allowing communal *ejido* lands to be broken up into individual private parcels. This eliminated the last hope for many Indigenous and other peasants in Chiapas, one of the poorest states with the largest share of unresolved land reform claims (Harvey 1998). The blow had been preceded by the elimination of agricultural price supports (including the 1989 collapse of the coffee marketing board INMECAFE) and the opening of the floodgates to U.S. corn imports, devastating small producers. The Zapatistas had been organizing clandestinely since 1983 among poor Indigenous populations, who by the end of the 1980s had grown weary of begging for land and credit and basic services. The ending of agrarian reform was one of the final triggers of their uprising on January 1, 1994, the day NAFTA took effect. In the words of a longtime Zapatista from one of the canyons of the Lacandón Jungle of Chiapas,

> We would go shout in their palaces and they ignored us. The ejido commissioner even spent more than 20 years petitioning for land, with no resolution. We asked for potable water, housing materials, electricity, schools, but the government did not pay attention. It enraged us. (interview cited in Stahler-Sholk 2011: 418)

The Zapatistas broke with the historic Mexican tradition of vertical negotiations and petitioning of state officials for a quota of power and resources. They proposed instead a radically democratic model—like the long-standing practice in the liberation theology of Catholic "base communities"—in which fundamental change would be made in a horizontal fashion, not by reforming state institutions but by reorganizing social relations. They began that process without waiting for permission, in poor Indigenous communities in the

remote southeastern state of Chiapas. That process of what they called autonomy "from below and to the left" has often been criticized by sectors of
Mexico's institutional left, some of whom argued that although the center-
left Party of the Democratic Revolution (PRD) had been cheated of electoral
victory in 1988, the party could have made a subsequent electoral comeback
if not for the extrainstitutional activism of groups such as the Zapatistas.
They also drew criticism from some older currents of Indigenous activists
and their supporters (many from the old left), who believed that the native
peoples who made up 14 percent of Mexico's population[2] could best claim
rights by negotiating a kind of regional devolution of powers with the central
government (Burguete Cal y Mayor 2000, Mattiace 2003). The Zapatistas in
turn pointed to the long history of opportunism, manipulation, and co-optation by political party and Indigenous bosses. Their alternative model of
community-based autonomy resonated far beyond Indigenous villages of
Chiapas, sparking debate about whether and how it was possible to "change
the world without taking power" (Holloway 2002), and inspiring activists
from diverse corners of the alter-globalization movement who sought to
reclaim the commons (Hardt and Negri 2003).

The Zapatista rebellion occurred in a Latin American context of popular
mobilizations against the military authoritarian regimes that had ruled from
the 1960s to the 1980s, and against the devastating impact of neoliberal
globalization on the poor in the world's most unequal region (Stahler-Sholk,
Vanden, and Kuecker 2008). This cycle of protest in recent decades has
notably included a resurgence of Indigenous movements that asserted collective rights, criticizing the myth of formal political and economic equality of
individuals espoused by the liberal state (Yashar 2005). These were not
narrow identity movements harkening back to a romanticized past, but rather
mobilizations that combined cultural markers of community with class-based
organizing against concrete effects of neoliberal globalization (Nash 1993,
Otero 2004). Indigenous groups in Mexico, Bolivia, Ecuador, and elsewhere
were continuing the decolonizing project, calling for a refounding of the
nation-state to recognize its plurinational character.[3] The incorporation of
non-market values reflected in various Indigenous concepts of *buen vivir*, or
living well, posed what some refer to as a *crisis civilizatoria*, in opposition to
predatory capitalism and political exclusion (Santos 2007, Mora Bayo 2008,
Goodale and Postero 2013).

For Indigenous and non-Indigenous movements alike in this era, the prospect of democratic opening led many to form or ally with political parties and
seek electoral change, fueling a "pink tide" of elected left governments in the
2000s. However, the logic of electoral politics and institutional compromise
often overshadowed the movements that originally backed these governments, creating strategic dilemmas for grassroots organizing coming from a
more horizontal tradition (Van Cott 2001, 2005; Dangl 2010; Prevost, Oliva

Campos, and Vanden 2012; Webber and Carr 2012). On the spectrum of choices, the Zapatistas opted for a greater degree of distance from party-electoral politics and governments, in a national context of discredited conventional political institutions. The following section will examine their practices of de facto autonomy, variants of which Indigenous communities in Chiapas had long been exercising over time, which is distinct from negotiating permission from the state. This approach to autonomy as a participatory process (including the Zapatista variant), rather than an outcome negotiated with elites, forged evolving new collective identities that shaped the long-standing struggles of Indigenous peoples in Chiapas. This historical background helps explain why many Indigenous people recognized and joined the Zapatista project of self-governance, made public with the 1994 uprising.

FREEDOM ACCORDING TO THE ZAPATISTAS

Following the initial armed takeover of towns in Chiapas on January 1, 1994, and the government's military response (which shifted from direct counterattack to low-intensity warfare), the Zapatistas essentially slipped out and surrounded the military encirclement with the declaration in December 1994 of thirty-eight civilian Zapatista Autonomous Rebel Municipalities (MAREZ). Each MAREZ comprised a constellation of Indigenous support base communities in the central highlands, northern zone, eastern Lacandón Jungle, and southeastern border zone of Chiapas, with communities choosing council members of the self-proclaimed autonomous municipalities. A third level of autonomous government was added to the communities and municipalities in August 2003 with the formation of five *caracoles*, regional centers governed by Juntas de Buen Gobierno (JBGs), or Good Governance Councils.

Various autonomous governing structures had been functioning in Chiapas (especially in the settlements in the Lacandón Jungle) for decades, including those organized under the influence of the liberation theology catechists of the diocese of San Cristóbal under Bishop Samuel Ruiz, the Jesuit mission of Bachajón, and peasant organizations formed outside the corporatist structure of the ruling PRI party (Harvey 1998), though many of the latter were frustrated by the PRI's well-honed mix of co-optation and selective repression. The Zapatista structures of authority after 1994 were established without recognition by the Mexican government, drawing lines of jurisdiction distinct from the official municipalities. The Zapatistas rejected political parties and the authority claims of "elected" government officials, instead invoking Article 39 of the Mexican Constitution, which gives the people "the inalienable right to alter or modify their form of government" (EZLN 1993). They also grounded their practice in international law, including Convention 169 of the International Labor Organization (which Mexico ratified) recognizing the right of Indigenous and tribal peoples to exercise their own forms of social organization, laws, and customs in their native lands. In contrast with traditional leftist/electoral engagement with state structures, power was to be constructed through the learning experience of ordinary people participating in decision making. Rather than authority flowing from representatives in centralized institutions, in competition filtered through parties, the *caracoles* serve as networks for collective decision making by assembly in the communities (González Casanova 2005).

The Zapatistas entered into talks with the Mexican government that led to the signing of the San Andrés accords on Indigenous rights and culture in February 1996, but meanwhile they proceeded to implement what they considered to be their rights without waiting for recognition. The spirit of San Andrés went far beyond a mere federal decentralization of state functions, recognizing community-based rights to organize governance as they saw fit through *usos y costumbres* (practices and customs), such as making decisions by assembly, and to control the resources in their territories (Aubry 2003; Esteva 2003). More importantly, rather than being a pact negotiated at the top, the San Andrés accords reflected a process of participatory assemblies and discussions in the communities; a pattern begun in 1974 with the first Indigenous congress in Chiapas convened by Bishop Samuel Ruiz in the former colonial capital of San Cristóbal de Las Casas, and continuing with a participatory process of defining the conceptual complexities of autonomy in each of the Indigenous languages spoken in the state (Aubry 2011).

When the government stalled on passing implementing legislation, the Zapatistas organized a "March of the People of the Color of the Earth" to Mexico City, where supporters camped out until Commander Esther was allowed to make an historic address to the national congress in March 2001. Afterwards the government passed an Indigenous Rights law that completely reneged on the spirit of San Andrés,[4] designating Indigenous peoples as "subjects of public interest" rather than "public rights" and subordinating their governing bodies to the official state structures. Suddenly the government was eager to embrace what Hale (2002) calls "neoliberal multiculturalism," acknowledging cultural diversity but not collective rights. The law was passed with the complicity of all the major political parties, and denounced by every major Indigenous group in Mexico—including the National Indigenous Congress, CNI—reinforcing the resolve of those whose autonomy strategy did not focus on parties or the state. In any event, the Zapatista model of de facto autonomy relied on legitimacy rather than legality; they did not ask for the right to have rights, but simply exercised them. So the participatory process of conceptualizing and implementing autonomy created the basis for what Gandhi had once called "being the change you want to see in the world," or what social scientists have referred to as "prefigurative politics" (Breines 1979, Maeckelbergh 2011). Rather than engaging in a struggle for power as defined by the existing political system, the Zapatistas are part of a growing number of movements choosing to redefine politics in terms of everyday practices in society, and power as something constituted through the actions of ordinary people (Motta 2009, 2013a; Nail 2012; Ross and Rein 2014).

Practicing Autonomy

Within the Zapatista communities, autonomy has been a work in progress. All autonomous authorities and *cargos* (tasks) are unpaid, a tradition in many Indigenous communities, and service on the Juntas de Buen Gobierno (JBGs) rotates for periods ranging from ten days to a month from a pool elected for three-year terms. The idea is to avoid bureaucratization, entrenched interests, and distancing from community life, and to make everyone responsible to the collective. This alternative to the professional politician means there is a slow but broad-based process of socializing the experience of governance (Starr, Martínez-Torres, and Rosset 2011). The evolving governing practice has included developing their own administration of justice, enacting a de facto agrarian reform through the occupation or "recovery" of lands, new practices of production and exchange, community-based social services such as education and health, and promoting change in gender and other social relations. In each of these areas, the emphasis is on praxis rather than following an ideological formula, and a decentralized approach has meant considerable variation across communities, autonomous municipalities, and *caracoles* (Baronnet, Mora Bayo, and Stahler-Sholk 2011). Key to the process has been the development of new subjectivities or collective identity, how movement participants see themselves, constructed on an ongoing basis through everyday practices.

Scholars of subaltern groups (Scott 1985) and social movements (Polletta and Jasper 2001; Fominaya 2010) have noted the importance of the subjective experience of struggle from below, in generating bonds of solidarity as well as a narrative in which participants envision themselves building a better future (Selbin 2010). Today's Zapatistas began forging their collective identity through successive waves of clandestine organizing in Chiapas beginning in the 1970s, alongside a number of parallel and partly overlapping initiatives that included liberation theology catechists of the Catholic diocese of San Cristóbal under Bishop Samuel Ruiz, Maoists promoting rural credit and marketing cooperatives independent of the PRI, as well as "Indianist" groups (some initially linked to the Communist Party) advocating for Pluriethnic Autonomous Regions led by local power brokers (Harvey 1998, Burguete Cal y Mayor 2000, Mattiace 2003, Leyva Solano 2005). An offshoot of one of the Maoist groups from northern Mexico began organizing a guerrilla nucleus called the Fuerzas de Liberación Nacional in the Lacandón

Jungle in the 1970s. A later wave of organizers formed the EZLN in 1983 (including the eventual military leader/spokesman, Marcos), and in the process of recruiting Indigenous leadership, the composition and philosophy of the nucleus was significantly transformed. Growing numbers gravitated toward "the Organization" during its ten years of clandestinity, as the combination of co-optation and repression thwarted the progress of other groups (Harvey 1998, Cedillo-Cedillo 2012). Liberation theology catechists played a crucial role, as what Gunderson (2011) calls "organic Indigenous-campesino intellectuals," in the synthesis of ideological and cultural strands that became the Zapatista movement.

Practices of participatory decision making by assembly grew out of Indigenous communal traditions, as well as the grassroots "Christian base communities" of the liberation theology Catholic Church, and the *ejidos* or self-managed peasant communities created after the Mexican Revolution (which provided a legal model of assemblies that in practice barely functioned in Chiapas). In addition, tradition was constantly being reinvented, particularly in the *cañadas* or canyons that traversed the Lacandón Jungle, which were colonized by a growing stream of migrants from the central highlands and northern zone that began as a trickle in the 1950s and accelerated significantly after the mid-1970s. Many of these settlers on the agricultural frontier were escaping from landlessness and/or the strict political-religious hierarchies of local Indigenous caciques (bosses) who were closely tied to the clientelistic structures of the PRI (Rus 1994). Settling on national lands or seeking employment on the *fincas* and cattle ranches that followed the settlers clearing lands in the jungle, where the effective presence of the state was sparse, many communities developed a concept of the *común* (Leyva Solano 2003) or collective sense of territoriality, understood not just as land use but also the cultural, social, and decision-making practices that bound them together. This shared experience and outlook became an important reserve for Zapatista organizing, but transcended the specific Zapatista project and influenced many Indigenous communities that did not join the rebellion (Rus, Hernández Castillo, and Mattiace 2003). Zapatistas and non-Zapatistas were interspersed in the primarily Indigenous northeast half of the state of Chiapas after the 1994 uprising, often inhabiting the same *ejidos* and communities, with varying dynamics of coexistence and influence across political lines. In this sense the Zapatista model of autonomy was not based on legal recognition of an exclusive geographic jurisdiction, but depended on establishing the legitimacy of its local practices.

The Zapatistas initiated a number of changes related to land, production, and political economy that were part of a reconfiguration of space, in more than just a physical sense. Latin American social movements in recent decades have been creatively redefining social spaces. For example, in response to the military authoritarian regimes of the 1960s–1980s that shut down the institutions of politics, movements politicized a variety of cultural and social spaces such as gender and motherhood, religion, neighborhoods, and music. In response to neoliberal policies of private enclosures of the commons, movements have evolved strategies including factory takeovers in Argentina, land occupations in Brazil, cooperatives, and fluid networking through transnational social movements, with similar reappropriations of space extending to the global North as well (Kohn 2013). These new spatializations of power (Featherstone 2008, Zibechi 2012, Hesketh 2013) reject state-centric demarcations of territory and sovereignty, seen in the Latin American context as exclusionary legacies of the colonial era (Reyes and Kaufman 2011).

In the first couple of years after the 1994 uprising, landless and land-poor Zapatistas invaded or "recovered" commercial *fincas* and ranches, in effect restarting the agrarian reform that the government had canceled in 1992 as part of the neoliberal program. The recovered lands became *nuevos poblados zapatistas* or *nuevos centros de población*, which along with historic *ejidos* and some scattered *rancherías* or independent multifamily settlements formed the three main social and productive structures in Zapatista territories. In the recovered lands, like the *ejidos*, families had access to the land they needed to work with household labor but did not have individual ownership titles. In addition to this "individual collective" allotment of land, each *nuevo poblado* designated lands for the "general collective," with decisions made by assembly as to how the labor obligations would be distributed and the proceeds used in these general collectives (Stahler-Sholk 2011). That participatory process helped build social bonds and collective commitment in the *nuevos poblados*, as communities invested the fruits of their labor in new productive projects or locally controlled social programs such as health and education.

Living in Resistance

In all three forms of settlement, the Zapatistas declared themselves to be "in resistance," by which they meant they refused to participate in any official government programs or receive government assistance. The government took the opportunity to shower the previously neglected Indigenous communities with aid to undermine the autonomy project. Counterinsurgency strategy also involved sponsoring paramilitary groups to intimidate Zapatista support base communities. The government also paid compensation to landowners for Zapatista land recoveries and then encouraged competing Indigenous and peasant organizations to reinvade recovered land, with promises of official recognition of ownership. While these strategies had some of the intended effect, they also had the reverse effect of reinforcing unity and pride among those who remained "in resistance." Zapatistas compared their own self-sufficiency with the dependency of their neighbors, some of whom had even ceased to work their *milpas* (cornfields) and therefore essentially lost their Indigenous-*campesino* identity. In the recovered lands, in contrast to *ejidos* which were often divided between Zapatistas and non-Zapatistas, occupiers were expected to abide by the principles of the movement, contribute collective labor, and defend the lands against other claimants. While reinforcing the in-group sense of belonging to a common project, this was also a source of tension with some who shared the movement's overall outlook but chose not to join (such as those philosophically opposed to armed struggle), or who left, often for personal reasons or exhaustion with being "in resistance" (Aquino Moreschi 2013).

Other distinctive practices that evolved in the spaces carved out by Zapatistas included banning alcohol—also a norm among many evangelicals—which had a distinct impact on community dynamics (particularly appreciated by the women, as it helped reduce domestic violence and improve the domestic economy). Gender relations in general changed slowly, with a discourse of gender equality and some new opportunities for women in the autonomous structures, but also some reluctance to impose sudden change in the Indigenous communities by decree (Speed, Hernández Castillo, and Stephen 2006). The emergence of Indigenous feminist perspectives was complicated on the one hand by essentialist views of Indigenous "tradition" that either glossed over gender inequality or misunderstood the gendered division of labor established historically among Indigenous peoples resisting oppression; and on the other hand by urban mestiza feminism that did not always connect with the experience of Indigenous communities (Hernández Castillo 2006). Twenty years after the uprising, Zapatista self-assessments acknowledged candidly that progress toward gender equality was slow and uneven. For example, one woman noted the continuing impact of education gaps and gender roles in limiting women's participation in taking on responsibilities outside the community:

> If a woman is married she knows there is no way to leave her child, maybe she feels bad about leaving her husband because he doesn't know how to take care of the animals, he doesn't know how to cook his food, he doesn't know how to make his tortilla . . . When a woman is finally selected . . . before saying anything else she just looks at her husband and the compa is already making a face. So she looks at her husband and then says "no, I can't because I don't know how to read." (EZLN 2013, Vol. 4: 35).

Yet as women moved into nontraditional roles, the experience gave many the self-confidence to begin changing expectations in the communities, and also to retake control over how they are represented by researchers and other outsiders (Mora Bayo 2008; 2011).

The Zapatistas also launched workshops to promote agro-ecology, perhaps making a virtue of necessity (as in Cuba since the "Special Period" of the 1990s), since they lacked resources or government support to purchase fertilizers and pesticides. In a larger sense, the economically and politically driven migration of poor subsistence cultivators into the Lacandón Jungle since the 1950s was ecologically problematic. The government had historically used a shifting discourse of "development" of untapped resources in some eras and environmental protection in other periods, to reward allies with lucrative resources and undercut radical organizing in the jungle. An example is the renewal of lumber concessions and the designation of the Montes Azules Biosphere Reserve in the 1970s, which overlapped with a vast territory awarded to the small Indigenous group of Lacandones who were pitted against other Indigenous settlers in the region.[5] In more recent times, "conservationist" language was used to rationalize government-promoted "ecotourism" investment and to evict Zapatista communities. A combination of awareness of this politicization and a desire for self-sufficiency led the Zapatistas, particularly in the jungle region, to evolve their own notions of sustainable coexistence with nature and to enact corresponding regulations in their territories (Gómez Bonilla 2011). This often led to conflict with government officials who claimed a monopoly of technical expertise, and with investors and local community members who were persuaded that they would benefit from externally driven "development" schemes. Throughout the hemisphere, communities resisting mega-projects are often accused of opposing progress, while the poor who are forced to migrate to remote regions to eke out subsistence are blamed for the resulting environmental damage. Grassroots alternatives, such as the movement launched in the Brazilian Amazon by rubber tapper Chico Mendes, take time to develop and are often targeted for repression by beneficiaries of large-scale projects.

The de facto restarting of agrarian reform launched by Zapatista land recoveries highlighted the complicated dynamics with other Indigenous/*campesino* groups that did not share the specific Zapatista project of autonomy. While some clashed ideologically and politically with the Zapatistas, others were major indirect beneficiaries of the uprising. Some took the opportunity to recover lands themselves, or received government handouts and services showered on regions of the state after 1994 (Harvey 2005b). For some, the whole point of resistance was to win official recognition and assistance, a de jure status that defined movement success (Burguete Cal y Mayor 2005); while for the Zapatista model of de facto autonomy, settling for such concessions meant falling into a demobilizing trap. This difference was often a source of conflict among Indigenous groups in Chiapas and elsewhere (Gledhill 2004), and the government was quick to exploit such conflicts by offering to "regularize" land claims by cooperating groups (Stahler-Sholk 2011).

To address the politicized conflicts stemming from these competing Indigenous projects, the Zapatistas developed their own judicial procedures.
Each MAREZ and JBG had an Honor and Justice Commission, with investi-
gative and judicial functions to deal with criminal and civil infractions, and
the Zapatistas claimed legal authority to implement Indigenous customary
law according to local *usos y costumbres*. This normative framework sometimes clashed with the liberal-individual framework of jurisprudence and
rights, which became entangled with the political conflict between government and rebels (Speed 2008, Mora Bayo 2013). Research in the jungle
region of La Garrucha Caracol in 2005–2006 (Stahler-Sholk 2007) found that
non-Zapatistas often preferred to take their legal disputes to the Zapatista
JBGs.[6] Studies in other *caracoles* found similar patterns (Mora Bayo 2008,
161–63; Cerda García 2011, 194). They saw this parallel justice system as
offering advantages of not charging fees or bribes, hearing cases in the Indigenous language, and meting out restorative justice such as community service rather than punitive jail time. This horizontal model of a kind of community peer judiciary was imperfect, but in its everyday practice it won a measure of legitimacy and reinforced collective identities that sometimes crossed
the lines of Zapatista affiliation.

    In one Tsotsil community on the outskirts of San Cristóbal that was an
historic *ejido*, a group of twenty-two families who had been clandestine
supporters of the Zapatistas before 1994 formally became *bases de apoyo*
(support base members) after the 1997 Acteal massacre by government-
sponsored paramilitaries.[7] This angered the other seventy-two families, who
tried to expel them from the *ejido* and take their lands. As the conflict
escalated, the government jailed one of the Zapatistas on trumped-up
charges. After attempts by human rights lawyers to intercede, the case was
taken to the JBG. Realizing that the minority Zapatista faction was part of a
larger movement, the rest of the community relented and came to a working
accommodation.

    Given the porous character of Zapatista dispersion in the territory, the
practice of autonomy involves a delicate balance between negotiating and
attempting to preserve the norms that imparted a distinctive identity to members of the movement. For example, government infrastructure projects such
as roads and electricity, intended to benefit non-Zapatistas, often had to
traverse Zapatista territory. While the Zapatistas were "in resistance" and did
not directly accept government programs, the contractors installing such
works typically negotiated with the JBG of the communities en route, agree-
ing for example to leave behind equipment, or hire local community labor, or
acquiesce to the Zapatistas connecting themselves to the grid without payment. When government programs gave gifts such as roofing material to
non-Zapatistas, the beneficiaries often monetized this largesse by selling the

goods at steep discounts to the Zapatista communities, undermining the government's intent to accentuate divisions.

Social policy was another area in which the Zapatistas carved out separate social space based on separation from officialdom. They rejected government schools and clinics, arguing on the one hand that these services when offered had historically been disrespectful of Indigenous culture and priorities, and on the other hand that they were only offered conditionally and instrumentally to divide communities and reinforce dependency. The decision was a trade-off, since some people on the government payroll made a positive contribution, and starting over again with limited resources was difficult. At the same time, this allowed innovation and a shift in priorities. The Zapatistas chose health and education "promoters" from the communities, who were unpaid, but the community assemblies could decide to use funds from collective projects to cover their expenses (such as travel to training workshops), or to pitch in to work on the promoter's cornfield when she or he had to be absent on community business.

This reconceptualization of education and health work as a collective responsibility reinforced the sense of collective identity that sustained the movement. As with judicial process, the deprofessionalization of these roles brought them back into the community, where educational content became a matter of public discussion and the community's economic support created an organic relationship between the community and promoters (Baronnet 2008; 2012). In contrast to the official schools, classes in the autonomous schools were held in Indigenous languages (with Spanish taught as a second language), and lessons were generated based on local experience. The role of promoter also served as a kind of cadre school, preparing a new generation of Zapatista youth who often moved into responsibilities in the autonomous governing structures. In the Escuelita Zapatista launched in 2013, many of the guardian-tutors were young education or health promoters, and the experience of preparing for and assuming the task of explaining the movement to outsiders functioned as internal reflection and training.

Dilemmas and Challenges of Zapatista Autonomy

The Zapatista model was not secessionist, nor was it predicated on exclusive authority over their territories of influence (which were politically heterogeneous, except in the "new population centers" on recovered lands). Therefore it depended on winning the voluntary adherence of its members and a measure of legitimacy beyond the ranks of the support bases. This created some tension between winning support by claiming rights as Indigenous peoples and peasants and Mexican citizens, but rejecting government aid and resources; in other words, how to sustain the movement both in terms of economic reproduction and political viability (Stahler-Sholk 2007, 2010). In a broader sense, this was part of the dilemma of defining spaces of autonomy within the larger structures of the state and a global capitalist system (Böhm, Dinerstein, and Spicer 2010).

At the economic level, within their Indigenous communities in Chiapas, the Zapatistas faced the same crisis confronting rural Mexico in the neoliberal era, while rejecting government social compensation programs. Part of their alternative strategy for sustainability rested on the land recoveries, which allowed for not only family subsistence agriculture but also a slowly expanding number of collective production projects that generated community-controlled funds for social and productive investment (Stahler-Sholk 2011). As these projects developed, one challenge was how to prevent regional inequalities from generating internal conflict. With the government encouraging other groups to reinvade Zapatista recovered lands, the Zapatistas often resettled their own supporters who had been displaced due to conflicts or government repression from distant territories. This created new inequalities between different waves of settlers, with tensions sometimes aggravated if they were of different ethnicities.

In one divided *ejido* in the jungle region, for example, some of the offspring of the original Tseltal *ejido* members moved onto nearby recovered lands in 1996, but they entered into conflict with Tsotsil Zapatista families who settled there after the initial land recovery.[8] When the Zapatista judicial authorities in the region ruled in favor of the newcomers, some of the earlier settlers dissented and left in protest, returning to inadequate land on the original *ejido*. Interestingly, though no longer formally members of the Zapatista support base, they voluntarily remained "in resistance" against government programs and considered themselves Zapatistas in spirit. In that same community, a trainer from Mexico City who wanted to start a program for education promoters in the *ejido* and the surrounding new population centers was denied permission, on the grounds that it could create inequality since the program would not extend to the entire autonomous municipality. This example, with the goal of equity seemingly in tension with innovation, illustrates some of the challenges of finding an economically and politically sustainable way of implementing autonomy with limited resources.

Aside from land recoveries, the collective projects were another way of trying to create alternative spaces with more egalitarian social relations within a larger capitalist framework. These were mostly at the community level, but there was some effort to try to socialize investment and development at a regional level. This often involved support from solidarity collectives and nongovernmental organizations (NGOs), which created a different set of dilemmas (Barmeyer 2009). In 2003 the Zapatistas created the larger governing structure of *caracoles*, in part to shift more decision-making authority away from the hierarchical structures of the insurgent forces to the civilian bases, and in part to ensure regional equity in development plans; and also so

NGOs that brought resources would not be determining priorities (EZLN 2003). In one illustrative case in the *caracol* of Roberto Barrios, for example, a Basque solidarity group bringing in funds began to assume decision-making functions and installed its own offices in the *caracol* (EZLN 2013, Vol. 1: 73). The Zapatistas shut down that operation, and after 2003 the JBGs (composed of representatives of all the constituent autonomous municipalities) screened and revised all proposed NGO projects, taking a 10 percent tax which they used to rebalance the allocation of resources within the zones of each of the five *caracoles*.

The limited resources in poor communities, and the strict "resistance" requirement of rejecting government programs, created some pressure to exit. One route was temporary labor migration, either to the traditional construction and service jobs around the Cancún resort area or to the United States. The motives were often economic necessity, but another factor was the natural curiosity of youth in the communities about the world beyond the closed circuit of Zapatista rules and norms (Aquino Moreschi 2009). The dilemma was how to allow some flexibility for individual circumstances without abandoning the collective labor requirements and other community-building aspects of the Zapatista project. The JBGs in effect dealt with this on a case-by-case basis, granting some permissions and negotiating postponement or replacement of the labor obligations. Migration from Zapatista communities to the United States was probably much less than migration from non-Zapatista communities of Chiapas, which surged in the mid-2000s for a variety of reasons, including the government's Oportunidades "conditional cash transfer" program to poor women, which had the effect of freeing men for labor migration (Rus and Rus 2014). Another exit route was to stop being a Zapatista support base member, which except for those on recovered lands did not mean physically moving anywhere. The motives varied from local conflicts within communities to exhaustion with "the resistance," but interestingly those who left generally did not do so out of ideological differences with the movement (Aquino Moreschi 2013). There is not sufficient evidence to measure the net number of those leaving versus those joining, including new generations coming up in the communities.

Defining alliance strategies and relations with the world outside their communities was another challenge for the movement. The rebellion had captured the imagination of a broader alter-globalization movement, illustrated for example by the thousands who attended the July 1996 "Intercontinental Encounter for Humanity and Against Neoliberalism" held in the *caracol* of La Realidad. The Zapatistas defined themselves explicitly as anticapitalist, but they did not propose to overthrow global capitalism from one corner of southeastern Mexico. Rather, they called on like-minded activists around Mexico and the world to find their own place in a transnational network of struggle. In their Sixth Declaration of the Lacandón Jungle (EZLN 2005) they invited supporters to form a global alliance against neoliberal capitalism and become "adherents" to the principles of the Sixth Declaration (Harvey 2005a). Within Chiapas, this offered an alternative collective identity (Gómez Carpinteiro 2013) for those who found "resistance" (refusing government aid) and other requirements of the support base communities too onerous. Outside Chiapas, it represented another in a long series of outreach initiatives (Harvey 2005a, Mora Bayo 2007) to address the dilemma of a direct participatory, locally rooted movement proposing global systemic change (Stahler-Sholk 2010). Rather than building an "International" in the old left, centralized sense, they called for a kind of autonomy of autonomies.

While zapatismo with a small "z" served as an inspiration for many movements (Zibechi 2004, Swords 2008, Dellacioppa 2009), this loose network strategy posed a number of dilemmas. The Zapatistas were wary of establishing links to groups that worked with parties and states, which ruled out many. Left groups themselves were fractured and sometimes competed with each other for the use (or misuse) of the Zapatista "trademark." The Mexican government learned that they could wreak havoc by sporadically repressing adherents to the Sixth Declaration rather than directly hitting the Zapatistas. North-South power dynamics did not entirely disappear in the formation of transnational social movement networks (Andrews 2011). Outside groups were intrigued by the Zapatista "imaginary," the prefigurative aspects of the radically democratic promise of community empowerment embodied in the slogan *mandar obedeciendo*, to lead by obeying (the grassroots), which was necessarily a work in progress that developed unevenly (Khasnabish 2008, Mora Bayo 2008, Cerda García 2011). Yet, if the example practiced in the autonomous communities of Chiapas was to be at the core of the transnational neo-Zapatista networks, then the intermittent opening and closing of access to the communities by the Zapatistas—albeit for perfectly valid reasons—posed a challenge for sustaining the wandering attention of the outside world. The ongoing challenge for the Zapatistas was how to focus inward enough to reduce dependencies and foster development of capacities and consciousness in the communities, while at the same time creating possibilities for a "scale shift" in the movement that would connect to networks that could challenge larger power structures (Young and Schwartz 2012). The Escuelita Zapatista, launched twenty years after the 1994 uprising, heralded a new generation of Zapatistas as well as a further effort to balance these goals and to be equal participants in a process of global change.

BEYOND ZAPATISMO

The core of the Zapatista movement might be thought of as the thousand plus Indigenous communities in some thirty to forty autonomous municipalities, grouped into the zones of five *caracoles* in Chiapas. Alongside these geographically porous support base communities, there are wider layers of those who are not formally members but may voluntarily follow the movement norms, some of whom are adherents to the Sixth Declaration, and international supporters. Zapatista influence also extends in varying degrees to non-Zapatista organizations, as well as many individual ex-Zapatistas, so the movement is somewhat amorphous at its margins. In principle the structure is horizontal, in the sense that the emphasis is on modeling new relations within society rather than negotiating power with the state, although the horizontal dimension is in tension with the continuing existence of the EZLN insurgent structure, as well as the periodic need to respond to state policies and actions. The movement is not delimited by strictly geographic boundaries, but it is territorial in the sense of territory defined not only by land but also by the sociocultural, political, and economic practices and relationships of the inhabitants.

In thinking about the impact of the Zapatista movement, it is useful to consider briefly the comparative context of other models of autonomy. The Zapatistas are only one of many movements and organizations that have proposed autonomy as an organizing principle, within Mexico and throughout Latin America (Burguete Cal y Mayor 2000, Ceceña et al. 2011, Gabriel and López y Rivas 2005, Gasparello and Quintana Guerrero 2009). Some predate the Zapatistas, and others followed, sometimes aligning with or incorporating elements of zapatismo. The drive for autonomy had long roots in Chiapas, in some ways going back to the colonial-era Repúblicas de Indios, through the Sindicato de Trabajadores Indígenas of the 1930s, groups trying to push the margins of independence within the corporatist structures of the long-ruling PRI, and the Plural National Indigenous Assembly for Autonomy (ANIPA), which emphasized Indian national identity within a given territory and a regional layer of government that would be linked to the national state (Díaz-Polanco 2000, Leyva Solano 2005). This model of regional, de jure autonomy was a different approach from the Zapatista community-based, de facto model. It had been implemented in Nicaragua in the 1990s, where autonomous regions were created in the sparsely populated North and South Atlantic, and elements of it can be seen in the autonomy proposals in Bolivia under Evo Morales.

Critics of negotiated regional autonomy argued that it set up a layer of authorities who were distanced from the base and dependent on the central government. It was also less participatory and transformative, and limited the political agenda by ethnicity and geography. Some of these shortcomings can be seen in Bolivia, where the government claimed the right to define a "neo-extractivist" development model—what David Harvey (2003) called "accumulation by dispossession"—and to set the terms of prior consultation with Indigenous groups. Meanwhile reformulation of the Bolivian state as "plurinational" in a way that recognized four different types of autonomy (departmental, regional, municipal, and "Indigenous/native/peasant") created ambiguities exploited by right-wing mestizo sectors, who demanded "autonomy" to control hydrocarbon wealth in the eastern Media Luna departments of Santa Cruz, Beni, Pando and Tarija (Santos 2010b, 98–140). The Zapatistas had declined to send a representative to the inauguration of Bolivia's first Indigenous president, and once in office, Evo Morales proved subject to electoral logics as well as pressure for "development" projects that could finance social programs and maintain his party's popularity.[9] Groups such as the Guaraní in the lowlands felt marginalized from the inner circle of Aymara in the Altiplano and Morales's coca growers union in the Chapare. The Guaranís' own Indianist vision (including their self-identification in opposition to *campesinos*, who aspired to individual land ownership) limited the possibility of forming alliances for the kind of national political strategy needed to negotiate autonomy within the legal-constitutional framework of the state. Also with politics defined as taking place in the realm of the state, the focus was not on social transformation, and as Santos (2010b, 120) noted, "the Indigenous communities constitute undemocratic enclaves where, for example, women are systematically discriminated against." Yet perhaps in the historical context of the exclusion of Indigenous peoples in Bolivia, Indianist identity movements might be seen as a step toward overcoming invisibilization.

If the internal process is crucial to developing new social relations in order to sustain a movement, a key question that remains open is whether more horizontal and participatory practices can occur without a total disengagement from conventional political institutions. In several Nahua communities in the Sierra Norte region of the state of Puebla,[10] the population had begun acting as though they were autonomous since the 1970s but without rejecting government programs. They were in effect resisting without direct confrontation, using "weapons of the weak" (Scott 1985) that were part of the diverse repertoires of contention employed by Indigenous peoples of Latin America since the European invasion. Some young government teachers, mestizos sent to the region decades before, realized that they would need to learn Nahua and listen to the community if any real education were to occur. Without waiting for permission, and with support from academics and activists from Puebla and working collaboratively with the community, they changed the class schedule to fit local rhythms, incorporated organic agriculture into the curriculum, replaced school uniforms with Indigenous dress, offered educational content in Nahua, and started a school breakfast program to address the main obstacle to learning (Sánchez Díaz and Almeida Acosta 2005). Related activities that emerged in the region included a community radio station, an Indigenous judicial system that won grudging recognition from the authorities (Chávez and Terven 2013), and more recently a movement to oppose mining projects in the region owned by billionaire Carlos Slim.

While not autonomous in the Zapatista sense of refusing engagement with the government, local activists in this part of the Sierra Norte of Puebla became enthusiastic adherents of the Sixth Declaration and hosted the Zapatista caravan when it passed through the region in 2001. In Chiapas too, there were groups that were influenced by the Zapatistas, but had a different local history of demanding local control and independence in the use of government resources. Some community-controlled education projects, for example, persisted after 1994 and sometimes received government support (Baronnet 2012, 72–87). In the neighboring state of Oaxaca, where some communities juggled a historic alignment with the PRI's revolutionary legacy and sympathy for the Zapatistas (Stephen 1997a), I visited one Zapotec community on the isthmus of Tehuantepec that had separated from the PRI decades ago to align with an independent local party, COCEI (Coalition of Workers, Peasants, and Students of the Isthmus). However when a Spanish transnational corporation moved in to start a wind-energy farm that threatened local fishers without consultation, with complicity of COCEI (which had since allied with the national PRD party), the community in 2013 organized to throw out the transnational and all political parties, invoking their right to choose their leaders according to Indigenous custom.[11] Their actions and discourse were strikingly similar to the Zapatistas, though they had little direct contact and at that point were not adherents to the Sixth Declaration. In April 2014 they hosted a regional meeting of the National Indigenous Congress, with a concluding declaration that included accepting an invitation to visit Zapatista territories. Perhaps their intensely negative experience with the state and foreign capital had been compressed into a shorter time frame, but like the Zapatistas they drew organizing strength from collective identity; in this case reinforced by their Zapotec traditions, the mythology of postrevolutionary local hero General Heliodoro Charis, the experience of standing up to the ruling party initially through another party alternative, and the economic bonds of a close-knit fishing community.

The question of whether and how to engage with the state remains a central dilemma for social movements. The Zapatistas are an important reference point for strategies that emphasize social transformation rather than negotiation of power, highlighting both the possibilities and the challenges of that approach. If we understand social movements in the prefigurative sense, then outcomes are measured not in concessions made by the state, but in the process of changing the everyday practices, social relations, and consciousness of their participants.

NOTES

The author is grateful for a 2013–2014 sabbatical research leave from Eastern Michigan University, and a visiting researcher affiliation at the Centro de Estudios Superiores de México y Centroamérica (CESMECA) of the Universidad de Ciencias y Artes de Chiapas (UNICACH), Mexico. This chapter draws on field work conducted in 2005–2006 in the four autonomous municipalities of La Garrucha, with the permission of the Zapatista authorities of the Junta de Buen Gobierno, as well as lessons learned in the Escuelita Zapatista in August 2013. Thanks to Marc Becker, Melissa Forbis, Jan Rus, and Harry E. Vanden for helpful comments on an earlier draft.

　　1. Within Chiapas, the structures of the movement consisted of a) insurgents, a small group who were prepared militarily; b) militia, who lived in the Indigenous communities but could be called into action as a home guard; and c) *bases de apoyo del EZLN* (BAEZLN), or the much larger "support base" group of civilians in the communities who participated in the movement and abided by its collective decisions. Beyond Chiapas there were networks of national and international sympathizers; the Zapatistas' Sixth Declaration of the Lacandón Jungle in 2005 invited individuals and nonelectoral groups who subscribed to their principles to become "adherents" of the Sixth Declaration.

　　2. Based on language spoken and self-identification as Indigenous, according to the Instituto Nacional de Estadística, Geografía e Informática, *Censo de Población y Vivienda 2010*, statistics summarized in Mexico, Cámara de Diputados, "Situación de los indígenas," December 2011. http://www3.diputados.gob.mx/camara/content/download/271337/837099/file/Carpeta16_Situacion_indigenas.pdf (accessed February 6, 2013).

　　3. The 1991 reforms to Article 4 of the Mexican Constitution stopped short of using the term "plurinational," instead affirming that "The Mexican Nation is unitary and indivisible. The Nation has a pluricultural composition based originally on its Indigenous peoples." See http://www.diputados.gob.mx/LeyesBiblio/pdf/1.pdf (my translation, accessed February 6, 2014). For analysis, see De la Peña 2006.

　　4. The government had essentially repudiated the San Andrés accords almost immediately after signing them in 1996, and in 1998 interim Governor Roberto Albores Guillén presented state legislation he claimed would implement the accords, but in fact ignored them. For analysis of the April 2001 Indigenous Rights law, see, for example, "The Indigenous Law: A Mocking Step Backwards," *Revista Envío* 238 (Nicaragua), May 2001, http://www.envio.org.ni/articulo/1501 (accessed March 25, 2014); and Servicio Internacional para la Paz, "Update: Indigenous Rights Law, A New Obstacle to the Peace Process in Chiapas," *SIPAZ Report* 6 (3), August 2001, http://www.sipaz.org/en/reports/55-informe-sipaz-vol-vi-no-3--agosto-de-2001/146-actualidad-la-ley-indigena-frustra-otra-vez-el-proceso-de-paz-en-chiapas.html (accessed March 25, 2014); and De la Peña 2006. The law was rejected by the CNI and by the legislatures of the states with the highest Indigenous concentrations, but was upheld by the Supreme Court despite hundreds of constitutional challenges.

　　5. The last of the original Lacandones had actually been exterminated by the Spanish in the 1700s, but Maya peoples from the Yucatán Peninsula who migrated into the area called the Lacandón Jungle later became known as Lacandones. See De Vos (2002).

　　6. For similar findings in La Garrucha, see Melissa Forbis, "'Never Again a Mexico Without Us': Gender, Indigenous Autonomy, and Multiculturalism in Neoliberal Mexico," PhD dissertation in Anthropology, University of Texas at Austin, 2008, http://repositories.lib.utexas.edu/bitstream/handle/2152/18324/forbism09397.pdf?sequence=2 (accessed March 25, 2014).

　　7. January 19, 2014 visit to politically divided *ejido* near San Cristóbal de Las Casas, and interview with an Indigenous lawyer who had been involved in the land dispute case.

　　8. Visits in 2013–2014 to a divided *ejido* in the one of the *cañadas* (canyons) of the Lacandón Jungle.

　　9. Based on a November 7, 2013 presentation in Tarija, Bolivia by Raúl Prada Alcoreza, researcher at Universidad Mayor de San Andrés, former member of the Bolivian Constituent Assembly (2006–2007) and former vice minister of strategic planning (Feb.–Sept. 2010); and November 8, 2013 meetings with the Asamblea del Pueblo Guaraní, Camiri, Bolivia. These

activities were part of a Working Group of the Consejo Latinoamericano de Ciencias Sociales (CLACSO) on "Indigenous Peoples in Struggle for Autonomy: Movements and Politics in Latin America."

10. Visit to the Sierra Norte region of Puebla, September 12–13, 2013. The trip included conversations with teachers in the bilingual primary school in Ayotzinapan, and with members of the Proyecto de Animación y Desarrollo, and a discussion in the community radio station Radio Tzinaca in San Miguel Tzinacapan, municipality of Cuetzalan.

11. Conversation with members of the Council of Elders and Community Police, Colonia Álvaro Obregón on the isthmus of Tehuantepec, Oaxaca, January 4–5, 2014, and attendance at the meeting of the Congreso Nacional Indígena-Región Istmo, March 29, 2014.

Chapter Eleven

Argentina

Against and Beyond the State

Marina Sitrin

It is the evening of December 21, 2001. Hundreds of thousands are in the streets of Buenos Aires, watching the helicopter holding the president and minister of the economy take off. They have resigned. Dozens of government officials and members of the judiciary have resigned and are hiding out; no one even knows the official number. If they appear anywhere in public they are followed and harassed. They fear for their safety. Despite the state of siege, the people dominate the streets. In fact, because of the state of siege even more people come out into the streets. They are singing and greeting one another. They are helping each other escape police repression. Many cafes and restaurants open their doors to everyone in the street. Food, water, and refuge are provided. Many thousands of people are in the square in front of the Pink House, the same square where the Madres of the Plaza de Mayo have been walking twice a week since the dictatorship of the 1970s, bravely demanding the appearance of their children. These protestors, now both young and old, are survivors of the dictatorship and children of the dictatorship, they are all in the same square. All children of the same history. They are proudly and bravely demonstrating. In a flash, seemingly out of nowhere, police move in on a few hundred protesters . . . the protesters run, they jump over the fence to the Pink House and get close to the doors. There is no one blocking the doors. There are hundreds of thousands in the street. The president has fled. Who is the government? What is the government? Should they go in? Should they take over? Is that where power is? . . .

They stop.
They turn around.
They go to back to the neighborhoods . . . look to one another . . . and
begin . . .[1]

This chapter examines what movement participants in Argentina mean when they say they are rejecting power, creating alternative power, and doing so autonomously. It then explores the relationship between the state and the autonomous movements that emerged post-2001, examining the question of cultural hegemony. It delves into how the movements have been relating to the state by first rejecting it, then sometime engaging with it, while always attempting to maintain their own agenda and tempo. The movements discussed in this chapter are not the numerical majority in Argentina, but are the focus of this work due to the innovative nature of their organizing. By innovative I am referring to the ways in which people are organizing and where they see power located. Rather than organize a political party or group with forms of representation or hierarchy, as has generally been done in the past, people formed nonhierarchical and directly democratic assemblies and networks, looking to one another as the source of power and possible change, rather than institutions of power such as governments, banks, or other agencies. These movements are also the focus because so many movements around the globe have since been organizing similarly, such as Occupy Wall Street, the 15M in Spain, the assembly movements in Greece, Brazil, Turkey, and Bosnia, often even using the same language, such as horizontalism.[2]

FROM POPULAR REBELLION TO HORIZONTALISM

A growing economic crisis came to a head in Argentina when on December 19, 2001, the government froze all bank accounts. This was on top of a deepening crisis that had already left many thousands without work and hungry. The state provided no possible way out. In response, first one person, and then another, and then hundreds, thousands, and hundreds of thousands came out into the streets, banging pots and pans, *cacerolando.* They were not led by any party, and were not following any slogans; they merely sang, *"Que se vayan todos! Que no quede ni uno solo!"* (They all must go! Not even one should remain!). Within two weeks, four governments had resigned, the minister of the economy being the first to flee. The institutions of power did not know what to do. On the evening of December 19 a state of siege was declared, reverting back to well-established patterns of state power and violence. But people broke with the past, with what had always been done; they no longer stayed at home in fear, they came into the streets with even more bodies and sounds. *Que Se Vayan Todos!* was sung, and sung together with one's neighbor. It was not just a shout against what was, but it was a song of affirmation—a song of collective power.

The wake of the rebellion witnessed a massive wave of movement organizing, from the unemployed to the formerly middle class to workers and Indigenous peoples. Many movements were born of the rebellion of December 19 and 20, such as neighborhood assemblies, art and media collectives, and collective kitchens, while others existed previously in incipient forms, and blossomed after the rebellions, such as the recuperated workplaces and unemployed movements.

NEW MOVEMENTS AND SOCIAL RELATIONSHIPS DEFINED

This section of the chapter will briefly outline the movements discussed as well as describe the new forms of social organization created. The movements are: neighborhood assemblies, unemployed workers movements, recuperated workplaces, HIJOS (children of the disappeared), and the social relationships: *horizontalidad, autogestion,* and affective politics. [3]

Neighborhood Assemblies

The neighborhood assemblies are in many ways the most similar to what has been seen with Occupy! and similar movements in the squares around the world. When people are fed up with an ever-increasing crisis, including a crisis of representation, they use public spaces to create assemblies and counter power. For this reason the people in the neighborhood assemblies in Argentina first met to explore new ways of supporting one another and meeting their basic necessities. Many explain the organization of the first assemblies as an encountering. People were in the streets, began talking to one another, saw the need to gather, and began, street corner by street corner, intersection by intersection. Pablo, a participant in the neighborhood assembly of Colegiales in Buenos Aires, explained:

> This did not obey an ideological decision, people simply met on a street corner in their neighborhood, with other neighbors who had participated in the *cacerolazo*s. For example, in my assembly, in the neighborhood of Colegiales, and I know many other cases, someone simply wrote on the sidewalk, in chalk, "Neighbors let's meet here Thursday night" period. Who wrote this, no one knows. In the first meeting there were maybe fifteen people, and by the next week it was triple. (quoted in Sitrin 2006, 41)

In each neighborhood the assemblies worked, and some continue to work, on a variety of projects, from helping facilitate barter networks, creating popular kitchens, alternative medicine, planting organic gardens, and sometimes taking over buildings, including the highly symbolic creation of community centers in abandoned banks. These occupied spaces house any number of things, including kitchens, print shops, day care areas, after-school help for kids, libraries, micro-enterprises, free Internet access and computer usage, and one even has a small movie theater.

Hundreds of neighborhood assemblies emerged in the first year after the rebellion, each comprising anywhere from one to three hundred participants. This number began decreasing in 2003, and in 2013 there were a few dozen assemblies in the greater Buenos Aires area. There are many reasons for this decrease, but the fact that the number of assemblies has decreased does not mean that the horizontal form of organizing in assemblies has changed. In fact, there are many dozens of assemblies in the north of the country, in provinces such as Corrientes, La Rioja, and Cordoba, where people have been coordinating defense of the land from mining and land grabbing[4] as well as creating self-sustaining projects.[5]

Unemployed Workers Movements

The *piquetero* or Unemployed Workers Movement (MTD) in Argentina arose in the north and south of the country in the 1990s when unemployed workers, as well as broader-based popular movements, organized against local governments and corporations in the context of a growing economic crisis. Generally led by women in the provinces of Salta, Jujuy, and Neuquen, thousands took to the streets, blocking major transportation arteries to demand subsidies from the government. In a decisive break with the past, this organizing was not done by or through elected leaders, but directly by those in the streets, deciding moment to moment what to do next. In some places neighbors came together first, tried to discover what needs existed in the neighborhood, and from there decided to use the tactic of blockading roads—*piquetes*—to leverage their demands since job actions were not possible because they did not have places of work. Many of the neighborhoods in which the MTDs are now located are on the outskirts of cities, in areas that some might refer to as slums. These are neighborhoods that often do not have paved roads, sometimes no electricity or water formally connected to the homes, and have a level of unemployment that is not so much an occurrence as a state of being. One is unemployed, likely to be regularly unemployed, and one's children face similar prospects. The *piquetes* are not only spaces of protest; once there is a blockade people create assemblies, make sure there is food for all, and often when they go on for days, begin to create mini alternative societies (Zibechi 2008). This tactic has now extended to the environmental movement where blockades have been set up over the past few years to prevent strip mining, water damming, toxic fumigating, and the construction of a Monsanto plant. In these spaces, as with the unemployed movements, an alternative political construction opens up as the *piquete* shuts things down.

From the *piquetes*, after 2001 many groups became movements, expanding their strategies and tactics. The movements created autonomous areas upon which they have built housing and gardens, raised livestock, create alternative education and health care, along with many other subsistence projects. These projects are organized geographically in different neighborhoods, with some working together in network formations. For a number of years there was coordination amongst the autonomous MTDs in the network of Anibel Varon. It later split, then was dissolved and in its place the Frente Dario Santillan[6] was organized, which is a network of autonomous MTDs as well as supporters from the broader left.

Recuperated Workplaces

The recuperated workplace movement is the most globally influential in form, tactic and strategy, as well as the movement expanding the most numerically. The process of recuperation generally comes about when workers are faced with the possibility or reality of a workplace closure. Rather than face unemployment, which in the context of an economic crisis can mean years of no income, they organize using a form of horizontal assemblies, and decide that they will take over and take back their source of work, thus the Spanish word *recuperar*, to recuperate. This is a very different process from, say, cooperatives or other collectively and cooperatively run projects, as it begins with a group of people challenging the issue of ownership and private property, and from the position of direct action the workers begin the process of taking back their workplace—something they see as theirs by right (Azzellini, forthcoming).

As the post-2008 global economic crisis worsens, workers from Argentina are increasingly being invited to speak with other workers and movement participants all over the world, from the United States and Canada to other parts of Latin America, Europe, and Asia. For example, in 2013 workers in the small factory of Vio.Me in Thessaloniki, Greece, decided to occupy their workplace rather than see it closed. They were unsure of whether or not to recuperate, and in the process of deciding, movement participants from other parts of the world fundraised so workers from Argentina could go to Greece and help them decide what to do. As a result, the workers of Vio.Me recuperated their factory and have been running it in common, with the support of the movements. Not only did Argentina directly affect the decisions of these workers, but the experience in Greece has now influenced other workers in Europe; at a gathering on economic solidarity in February 2014, workers from almost a dozen recent recuperations in Europe met to share experiences and challenges.[7] All were inspired directly or indirectly from the process in Argentina.

The dozen or so occupied factories that existed at the start of the 2001 rebellion grew in only two years to include hundreds of workplaces, taken over and run by workers, without bosses or hierarchy. This movement also continues to grow numerically, with over sixty new workplace recuperations between 2010 and 2014.[8] Almost every workplace sees itself as an integral part of the community, and the community sees the workplace in the same way. As the workers of the Zanon ceramic factory in Patagonia say, "Zanon is of the people." Zanon, like many workplaces. has renamed itself and is now called FaSinPat—*Fábrica Sin Patron* (Factory Without a Boss).[9]

Workplaces range from printing presses, metal shops, and medical clinics, to cookie, shoe, and balloon factories, as well as a four-star hotel, schools, restaurants, grocery stores, and a daily newspaper—this is why they are referred to as *empresas*, workplaces, and not factories. Participants in the movement explain everywhere they go that what they are doing is not very complicated, with the exception of the financial challenges, quoting the slogan they have borrowed from the Landless Movement in Brazil: "Occupy, Resist, Produce."

The recuperated workplace movement continues to grow and gather support throughout Argentina, despite threats of eviction by the state and political and physical intimidation by the previous owners. So far, each threat has been met with mobilization by neighbors and various collectives and assemblies to thwart the government's efforts. In the example of Chilavert, a printing press, the elderly in the retirement home across the street came out and not only defended the factory from the police, but insisted on being the front line of defense, one of many stories reflecting how popular the recuperations are. Many outside the movements explain them quite simply, saying that there is a lack of work and these people want to work.

Over time, recuperated workplaces have begun to link with one another, creating barter relationships for their products. For example, a medical clinic will service members of a printing factory in exchange for the free printing of their material. Some of the workplaces have organized community centers in spaces that are not being used, or when the factory is closed. There are workplaces that have space that alternative video collectives can use, where political prisoner support groups meet, where there is Internet access, as well as social events organized in some in the evenings, such as art classes, salsa lessons, concerts, and tango nights.

HIJOS

HIJOS (Hijos por la Identidad y Justicia Contro el Olvido y Silencio, Daughters and Sons for Identity and Justice against Forgetting and Silence) is a group begun in 1995 by the children of the disappeared, the victims of state terrorism during the dictatorship that governed the country from 1976 to 1983. The name HIJOS resonates with the names of other related human rights organizations like "Mothers of Plaza de Mayo" or "Grandmothers of Plaza de Mayo." The acronym HIJOS becomes the word that spells out their agenda. HIJOS emerged from the human rights movement but has transcended it in several ways. It is comprised of the children of those who disappeared during the dictatorship and their contemporaries as well as the relatives of the children of the disappeared. With 30,000 disappeared, the number of children, grandchildren, nieces, nephews, cousins, and so on who could be a part of HIJOS could easily reach many hundreds of thousands. All were touched directly by the dictatorship.

HIJOS is significantly different from the Madres of the Plaza de Mayo, who continue to demand that the government return their children and that those responsible are punished, or even the Abuelas, the grandmothers, who continue to look for those children stolen and "adopted" from the prisons and torture chambers during the dictatorship. HIJOS is not placing demands upon the government, but rather speaks to society as a whole. Its members address society as a way of consciously breaking with the silence around what took place during the dictatorship—what they call a social silence.

As discussed later in this chapter, most members of the military dictatorship were left untouched by the transition to "democracy."[10] This protection was legislated with the Ley Punto Fina (final end law) that was passed at the end of the dictatorship. The law prohibited not only the prosecution, but also the investigation of people accused of political violence during the dictatorship. There was no public outcry at the Ley de Punto Final, nor at the fact that military officials and torturers from the dictatorship were living, seemingly happily enough, among everyone else in society. People were afraid. People were silent. HIJOS organized to speak specifically to this silence. Many in HIJOS have and had little confidence in the government, whether "democratic" or otherwise. When HIJOS formed in 1995 there were hundreds to thousands of known *genocidas* (those who committed genocide) living in society.[11] Unpunished. Free. But not only unpunished by the state; they were living in peace in society as a whole.

The form that the HIJOS protest took was more of a public outing than a protest and is part of a serious and long campaign. It became known as the *escrache*. An *escrache*, or to make an *escrache* (*escrachar*) in slang means "to put into evidence, disclose to the public, or reveal what is hidden" (GAC website, http://criticalspatialpractice.blogspot.de/2006/09/grupo-de-arte-callejero.html). *Escrache*s begin with research. The person who is "outed" has been researched in great depth. There are often people who can testify directly that the accused person tortured them, or that they witnessed this person carrying out torture. Once the person's actions have been confirmed, the education in the neighborhood begins. Maps are made, based on the city maps for tourism or the subway system, and they have a location pointed out marked "*AQUÍ*" (HERE), as many maps indicating where one is, and then it says "*Aqui vive un genocida*" (here lives a person who has committed genocide). The map contains footnotes that go into detail as to who the person is, what atrocities they have committed, and so on. These maps are pasted over local maps, on street lamps, newspaper stands, store fronts, walls, and throughout the neighborhood.

HIJOS and their supporters distribute informational leaflets to the people who live in the neighborhood, asking if they know that a *genocida* lives there. Flyer distribution continues for a few weeks and then the action is scheduled. Actions take on different forms; most often they are in front of the accused person's home. The intention of HIJOS, however, is not to attack the house. They instead perform street theater, sometimes acting out what the person did, the horrors they committed. Sometimes it is more informational, and HIJOS members state what the person has done and then at the end the throw red paint "bombs" at the door and the house or apartment. One of the main chants at an *escrache* is "*Si no hay justicia, hay escrache!*" (If there is no justice, then there is an *escrache*!).

The point of this action, however, is not for justice—meaning social justice or judicial action; the point is that there is no justice by the very nature of the person living freely in society without any social outcry. HIJOS makes that outcry. HIJOS speaks to neighbors, to society, and makes people uncomfortable. HIJOS makes noise in the silence.

Horizontalidad

One of the most significant things about the social movements that emerged in Argentina is how generalized the experience of *horizontalidad* was and is. *Horizontalidad* is a word that encapsulates most directly the ideas upon which the new social relationships in the movements in Argentina are grounded. It is a word that previously did not have political meaning. It emerged from a new practice, from a new way of interacting that has become a hallmark of the autonomous movements. People speak of the newness of the relationship as it relates to the movements, and as a break from previous ways of relating and being. When interviewing people for the oral history I compiled I would ask, again and again, what does *horizontalidad* mean, as it is a term that did not exist in a political context earlier. Person after person would respond that it was "this" moving their hands back and forth horizontally, palms down, and when I would ask if they could describe it more, they would show that it is not "this" and make their hands into the two sides of a triangle—the point being that it was not a pyramid, but a flat plane. Later, after the first year of organizing, came the more elaborated descriptions about hierarchy and direct democracy.

Horizontalidad implies the use of direct democracy and the striving for consensus, processes in which attempts are made so that everyone is heard and new relationships are created. *Horizontalidad* is a new way of relating, based in affective politics and against all the implications of "isms," despite it often being translated as horizontalism. What this means is that it is not an ideology or set of principles that must be met so as to create a new society or new idea, such as with forms of socialism like Trotskysim or Maoism. It is a break from these sorts of vertical ways of organizing and relating. For example, the neighborhood assemblies were formed when neighbors came together on a street corner, looked at one another, and began to talk. They did not elect a leader, spokesperson, or president, but each began to talk, while others listened.

And still, thirteen years later, as people come together to organize, the assumption is that it will be horizontal. As Emilio, a former neighborhood assembly participant and now an environmental organizer in the north, argued:

> But yes, sure, one can go to Buenos Aires today and not find a neighborhood assembly in every neighborhood, or on every corner as it was in 2002. But it is no less true that today if you went around the whole country to all the provinces, in many you will find horizontal assemblies organized in territorial defense—there are endless struggles taking place in the form of direct assemblies with strong horizontalism and where the discussion of the role of the State or unions or institutions is strong and permanent, that is, the discussion about the autonomy of these experiences is permanent—the experiences of 2001 and 2002 in Argentina had become something permanent in the population. (quoted in Sitrin 2014)

Autogestion

Autogestion is how most in the movements discussed here describe what they are creating, and how. *Autogestion* has generally been translated as self-management and linked to workers' control of factories, but in Argentina there is now the implied horizontal forms in the process of self-organization, as well as the use of *autogestion* for all sorts of projects, from autonomous schools and media to farming, and if one were to ask workers in a recuperated workplace, unemployed movements, or assembly participants how they do what they do, the most likely reply is that they *autogestionarlo*, and with *horizontalidad*, thus making any translation less than adequate. For this reason I continue to use the word in Spanish.

Affective Politics

The politics of affection, or affective politics, is a term that came about when people in the movements were looking for ways to describe the place from which they were organizing. Using the language of love and trust, they came upon *política afectiva* in Spanish—affective politics. As with *horizontalidad*, it is not seen as something finished, but rather as a goal and a tool, something that one aspires to, wanting to have more care, trust, and love; at the same time it is something that is a foundation for organizing so as to create even more possibilities for deeper relationships, and so becomes a tool for more affective relationships.

POWER AND AUTONOMY

After the 19th and 20th of December power was no longer located in the Pink House or with the state. Power was being created in and amongst people in the autonomous social movements. No matter what tactics people were choosing in a particular moment, the consensus was clear: power, the sort of power they desire, the power they are creating, is not located in the state or formal institutions of power. What they are creating and theorizing are new and different forms of power. It is living and changing power, it is power as potential and capacity. Some people have come to call it *potencia*, distinguishing the relational and active interpretation of the word.[12] Others simply put it that power is a verb and not a noun. The state holds power as a thing, something to wield over others, when really power is a verb, something one creates, uses, and shares.

Power-over, or power as a thing, is a form of power that has been the most widely discussed in the social sciences. It is the power of a subject, or institution, over another subject or institution. Steven Lukes (1974, 23) defines three dimensions of power: "A may exercise power over B by getting him to do what he does not want to do, but he also exercises power over him by influencing, shaping or determining his very wants. Indeed, is it not the supreme exercise of power to get another or others to have the desires you want them to have—that is, to secure their compliance by controlling their thoughts and desires?"

There are countless theories of power, many quite interesting and nuanced. But for the purpose of this chapter, placing arguments and articulations on power in slightly more generalized categories is useful for an understanding not just of power, but of the ways in which it can be used, especially with regard to its potential relation to the state.

For a common definition of this widely articulated view on power as a thing, I use the definition by Max Weber (1962 [1990], 117): "By power is meant that opportunity existing within a social relationship which permits one to carry out one's own will even against resistance and regardless of the basis on which this opportunity rests."

In addition to the examples of those social movement actors creating alternative forms of power through the new social relations, a few social scientists and movement thinkers have also been developing concepts of power to help explain these new ways of being. One of the most well known is John Holloway, author of *Change the World without Taking Power: The Meaning of Revolution Today* (2002, 15). He explains power:

> Power-to, therefore, is never individual: it is always social. It cannot be thought of as existing in some pure, unsullied state, for its existence will always be part of the way in which sociality is constituted, the way in which doing is organised. Doing (and power-to-do) is always part of a social flow, but that flow is constituted in different ways.
>
> Power-over is the breaking of the social flow of doing. Those who exert power over the doing of others deny the subjectivity of those others, deny their part in the flow of doing, exclude them from history. Power-over breaks mutual recognition. . . . History becomes the history of the powerful, of those who tell others what to do.

Argentina—Power as Verb

In Argentina the creation of other power exists in pockets throughout the entire country. As Neka from the MTD Solano explained,

> The issue isn't just the physical confrontation with the system. Everyday we're forced to confront a system that is completely repressive. The system tries to impose on us how and when we struggle. The question for us is how to think outside this framework. How to manage our own time and space. It's easier for them to overthrow us when we buy into concepts of power based on looking at the most powerful, based on something like weapons or the need to arm the people. We're going to build according to our own reality, and not let them invade it. I think this idea of power as a capability and a potential, not a control, is a very radical change. (quoted in Sitrin 2006, 163)

This is seen with the movement creating various means for self-sufficiency, from building their own homes on occupied land, to growing their own crops and raising livestock, to creating alternative medicine, health care, and education, as well as workers taking back workplaces by the hundreds and running them in common—and not only are these things being done together, but they are done while creating new relationships based in horizontalism and affective politics. This involves a break with capitalist value production, and creating new solidarities with different concepts of power and new ways of being. As described in the conversation with participants from the MTD Solano,

Neka: We want to take power [everyone around the table laughs].
Alberto: What we believe is that transformation occurs when one begins to
relate differently to one another, and begins to have other values. . . . Our
principal struggle is this, the generation of new subjectivities, new relationships, and ones that have to do with the new transformations. We don't think
this will come about because of a revolutionary president or a revolutionary
group like we've seen historically, in Russia and China for example, where
they fought for values and ideals, but ended up continuing the same oppression, and freedom remains absent from their lives. (quoted in Sitrin 2012, 110)

There was never a desire to create a revolution like that of Russia in 1917,
and in fact, it is precisely this vision of change to which the movements were
responding, while simultaneously creating another path to change, power,
and revolution. Raul Zibechi, in his book *Geneologia de la Revuelta*, discusses the daily changes taking place in the Argentine movements, and
breaks down the dichotomy between reform and revolution: "The State cannot be a tool for the emancipation since one cannot structure a society of non-
power relations by means of the conquest of power. Once the logic of power
is adopted, the struggle against power is already lost" (Zibechi 2003, 21).

AUTONOMY

Autons-nomos, the Greek for autonomy, means "self-governance and self
legislation." Autonomy as used by the movements in Argentina is an evolving term, based in practice. The core of the meaning is the same, though now
infused with *horizontalidad*. Autonomy as discussed by contemporary social
movement scholars is posed in a number of ways: as a positive process of
self-valorization, as discussed in the writing of Antonio Negri (Negri and
Fleming 1996); another, also positive, is in the creation of spaces "beyond
capital," as described by Massimo De Angelis (2010). Third, it is seen as a
negative reaction, or negation that then creates the positive, as is the case
with the movements in Argentina with the rejection of state and hierarchical
power.
    Ana Dinerstein (Dinerstein, Bohn, and Spicer 2009), a scholar of the
Argentine movements, explains:

Recently we have witnessed the emergence of autonomy as a central demand
in political struggles. Autonomy is usually defined as self-determination and
independent practices vis-à-vis the state. Autonomy asserts itself as organisational self-management. It is also based on the assumption that autonomous
practices can actually offer an alternative to economic and political capitalist
practices and relations.
    Emilio, at the time a neighborhood assembly participant reflected,
    "What is it that we want? What is our project?" The good thing is we have
no program. We are creating tools of freedom. First is the obvious: to meet our

basic necessities. But, the process of finding solutions to meet our basic needs leads us to develop tools that make us free. For me, that's the meaning of autonomy. If you start to think about what constitutes autonomy, and you then discuss notions of *autogestión*, self-sufficiency, web-like articulations, non-commercial exchange of goods, horizontal organizing, and direct democracy, you eventually end up asking yourself, "If we achieve all these things, will we then be autonomous?" Autonomous from what? No. If one day we achieve true autonomy, we will not be autonomous, we shall, in fact, be free. (quoted in Sitrin 2012, 117)

Ten years later, Emilio, now an organizer in Corrientes in the north of the country, where he is participating in the defense of the land from international corporations and helping develop autonomous networks of self-sustaining communities, put forward:

Our vision of autonomy is based on the strong territorial presence and strong political independence of the organization in the sense that the sovereignty of our decisions is the people in each village assembly. We will not allow the State or political parties or businesses, nor the church or anyone to violate the political sovereignty of our assemblies, therefore our organization. Now that does not mean we cannot have a dialogue or relationship with the Church or the State, because they exist, they are real, because they interfere in our lives and so we can set up specific issues, and in the case of the State, the state exists and captures the workers' money so I do not think there is any contradiction in obtaining financing for our projects provided they do not violate our policy decisions. (quoted in Sitrin 2014,)

While the movements began the construction of autonomy, with all the different meanings, the state did not sit idly by. This is a bit of a contradiction, since one would think that the state would be happy enough if people began finding ways to live without demanding support, yet at the same time, this very ignoring by the state also can create a crisis of legitimacy. If people are ignoring those who supposedly govern, how do those governing claim any legitimate place in power?

REGAINING LEGITIMACY THROUGH INCORPORATION, CO-OPTATION, AND REPRESSION

"We take from the state all that we are able, as long as it does not get in the way of our sovereignty" (El Vasco, quoted in Sitrin 2012, 123).

The "*que se vayan todos*" (they all must go) sung in the streets on the days of the popular rebellion really meant *todos* (everyone); it meant a rejection of the government and the judiciary. Many people spoke of how government officials were afraid to go out in public for fear of ridicule or even violence. While I do not know of any reports of physical violence, I did hear many accounts of people yelling and throwing things at officials when they were seen in public.[13] Without a doubt, the state and government of Argentina lost legitimacy.

Not only had the state lost its legitimacy in terms of people "believing" in it, but many people were no longer looking to the state to resolve their problems. They began to look to one another, form horizontal assemblies, and decide how to run their lives together. This was a moment of crisis for the state, which of course began to construct solutions.

The election of Nestor Kirchner in 2003 provided a starting point for the process of relegitimizing the state. Initially, the neighborhood assemblies had organized for a no vote, and many in the unemployed movements had no intention of voting (which in Argentina is illegal, as voting is mandated by law). However, Carlos Menem then announced his candidacy for president, and the situation changed. Menem is rightly blamed for the continuation of the process of neoliberalism, which had begun during the time of the dictatorship. He sold off most of the country though the privatization of almost all resources, from the airlines and the post office to water and the zoo. He also is responsible for the accumulation of tremendous national debt, which grew from US$8 billion at the end of the dictatorship in 1983 to US$180 billion at the time of the rebellion in 2001 (Salbuchi 2006). Menem also publicly announced that he would use direct repression to prevent the movements from mobilizing and growing (Dangl 2010). Needless to say, Menem was not a popular figure with the movements, and the prospect of his election, which was a possibility considering the movements' plan to not vote, shifted the decision of most movement participants to vote tactically. While the voter turnout was still exceptionally low, and hardly the reflection of a popular consensus, it was higher than initially planned by the movements and Kirchner was elected with 23 percent of the vote.

From the time of the election began the process of the state working to regain its legitimacy in multiple ways. Government funding was passed to the movements, former leftists were brought into office, and a human rights discourse, long absent from the state's repertoire, began. These tactics proved quite effective in disorienting and often demobilizing the neighborhood assemblies and autonomous unemployed movements.

Economic Stabilization?

It is argued that the main reason for the demobilization of many in the movements, particularly the neighborhood assemblies, was a new-found economic stability. And while it is true that the Kirchner government began all sorts of economic reforms as soon as it was elected, it is also true that the type of reform depended on toward which class it was geared. For example, for those who identified as middle class, real jobs were created so as to make for longer-lasting reforms, but for the unemployed, jobs were never creat-ed—only more subsidies were distributed. Thus the stabilization was for the middle class, while the unemployed and working classes were kept depen-dent, and the working class generally left out as well. Because history is not written by the underclasses and the unemployed, nor are the statistics for unemployment taken from those already in a perpetual state of unemploy-ment, the lack of economic recovery for those most excluded is not generally a part of the writing on the "recovery" in Argentina.

For segments of the middle class, while the partial economic recovery was real, it was not the only factor leading to a decline in activism after the elections. The active incorporation of middle-class activists into the new government led to disorientation of many neighborhood assemblies. For ex-ample, almost all assemblies had a position of not working from within the state. But when the new government invited former radicals and even Monte-neros and the People's Revolutionary Army, the former revolutionary guer-rillas, to join their ranks, some saw this as an opportunity to make change. Some of these individuals had previously played important roles in their neighborhood assemblies. These participants leaving the assembly and join-ing the government created tensions and discord within the assemblies, re-sulting in less of a unified and clear path with regard to how to engage, or not, with the government. Additionally, the new government offered many of the neighborhood assemblies food and shelter, as it did with the unemployed movements. During the assemblies in which I participated, when there was a government offer, hours and hours of discussion and debate ensued. General-ly offers from the state were rejected, but such lengthy debates frustrated many participants by derailing the agenda. Often people would stop taking part because of this derailing of the movement agenda.

Together the economic recovery, the incorporation of community leaders into the government, and the division of the neighborhood assemblies led in large part to their steady decline. Thus, with fewer assemblies, there were less-structured relationships between and among the unemployed, the recu-perated workplaces, and the middle class. Some critics have argued that the middle class no longer supported the struggles of the unemployed or recuper-ated workplace movements, but this is less the case than the fact that there were fewer structures facilitating these relationships.

Hegemony and Social Consensus

Prior to the election of the Kirchners there had been no prosecution of those who participated in the military dictatorship, a dictatorship that ruled with terror, "disappearing" 30,000 people who were often tortured and raped be-fore they were murdered. Not only were those responsible not prosecuted; those who participated in the atrocities were forgiven under the guise of creating peace in society. This left open a huge collective wound, and meant that none of the governments were fully legitimate with respect to human rights. With the election of Nestor and then later Christina Kirchner, laws began to change and a human rights discourse was adopted. It became a priority to find and punish those military and even nonmilitary personnel who participated in the disappearances and murders. A highly symbolic act, soon after Nestor Kirchner was elected in 2003, was the removal of the photographs of Jorge Rafael Videla and Reynaldo Bignone, the leaders of the military dictatorship, from the Military College. At the time Kirchner stated, as quoted in the *Los Angeles Times*, "I come to ask for forgiveness on behalf of the state for the shame of having remained silent about these atrocities during twenty years of democracy" (quoted in Wright 2007, 171).

Nestor Kirchner also replaced numerous members of the Supreme Court of Argentina, which many argue led to the overturning of the Punto Final laws in 2005, meaning that amnesty would no longer be granted to those who participated in the military dictatorship. This step was hugely significant in that it has led to the prosecution of dozens of military leaders and collaborators.

In addition, whether intentional or not, the human rights project of the Kirchner governments[14] has led to profound divisions within human rights movements, including, not insignificantly, splits within the Madres of the Plaza de Mayo, the Abuelas, and HIJOS. Each of these splits was based on how much to support, or even if they should join, the government in the pursuit of human rights, and how much to continue to remain autonomous.

Here, Antonio Gramsci's concept of hegemony, as well as the notion of political legitimacy and domination, become useful analytic tools (Haugaard and Lentner 2006). The state requires at least some form of support or consensus from the population, and it is this part of Gramsci's concept of hegemony that is most applicable (Gramsci 1971). It is precisely through the implementation of human rights discourses that this support is born. While economic and political hegemony are important, it was the state's tremendous sociopolitical shift in perspective with regard to the military dictatorship that permeated all levels of society. While many were and continue to be critical of how the government is carrying out the prosecutions (for example, many people criticize the lack of direct participation from and by human rights organizations), no one is overtly critical of the fact it is taking place. Following Gramsci's concept, for the state to rule, particularly in a context of "*que se vayan todos*," some semblance of consensus and support was necessary.

Divisions Fostered in the Movements

Hegemony is not just about creating a consensus in the populace. It is also about political domination of the more direct sort, which is often done through the creation of discord within movements—a simple form of divide and conquer. This is what the Kirchner government did quite brilliantly. The two most important areas of division were with human rights organizations and the unemployed workers movements.

There is considerable support for the Kirchner government when it speaks out against the military dictatorship and prosecuting some of those who were involved. However, within this support there emerged disagreement regarding the question of whether to support the government absolutely, or to support the human rights policies but remain an outside force and not join any government agency. Unfortunately this resulted in a more profound split. The Madres of the Plaza de Mayo now not only have two offices, one located in the large, well-known school and bookstore and the other in a small upstairs location a few blocks away, but they hold two separate marches in front of the Pink House every Tuesday and Thursday—marches that have been taking place since the beginning of the dictatorship. The Association of the Madres, the one in the larger location, led by Hebe Bonafini, absolutely supports the Kirchners. So much so, that groups and movements that are organizing in opposition to the government cannot use the Madres school or bookstore for events. Bonafini (2011) is now one of the most visible supporters of the Kirchner governments, regularly saying things such as, "Nestor gave us our country back" and "I am so proud of Christina."

This is quite different than the message from the Madres de Plaza de Mayo Linea Fundadora (2006), who in a letter to the president wrote,

> We support the positive steps you have taken to move the country forward, a country that you received in ruins and with tremendous suffering of the people. Still today there is so much more that needs to happen so as to advance, and that the Argentine people can live in dignity, justice, equality and solidarity, as our children dreamt and for which they gave their lives. . . . Unfortunately there are still unacceptable violations of human rights . . . and the situation of extreme poverty persists, which makes it necessary to change the unfair distribution of wealth.

Similar divisions have taken place in the *Abuelas* and *HIJOS*.

The other main area where divisions have occurred is within the unemployed workers movements. While political and tactical disagreements existed before the election of Nestor Kirchner, they were magnified and exacerbated by the government's new policies. Before the election in 2003 the unemployed movements were generally in one of two categories: autonomous or political party–centered. Those that had relationships to political parties continued this form of organizing, and many joined together to support the new government directly, including mobilizing people in the streets as a show of support, and are thus referred to as *Piqueteros* K (K for Kirchner). Divisions also emerged within the more autonomous movements, as will be addressed later, though this also was something that had begun to occur before the elections. The main reasons for these divisions were whether or not to have relationships to the government and/or receive financial support from institutions.

"To build a Latin American welfare state and bring about conciliation between social classes, centralizing power in the distributional state" (quoted in Lievesley and Ludlam 2009, 211): this is what the Kirchner governments put forward as one of their goals. While Argentina is no welfare state, the new governments have increased the number of people receiving benefits. These numbers rose under Eduardo Duhalde in 2002–2003 from 700,000 to 2 million, and then again under Nestor Kirchner to 2.6 million (Svampa 2008). While the amount of money did not increase for almost a decade, and considering inflation arguably decreased, the number of people receiving benefits increased so much that it created the illusion that the government was going to meet people's economic needs. So while the illusions increased, material conditions for the vast majority of the poor, the unemployed, and the more precarious working class changed very little (Svampa 2008). The situation of the poorest is not as desperate as it was at the time of the popular rebellion, when children were actually starving and the numbers of malnourished skyrocketed. But this is only in part due to the policies of the state in response to the mobilization of the population. It is these "gifts," even if temporary, that together with an antineoliberal rhetoric adopted by Kirchner helped shift some of the consciousness in favor of the government (Svampa 2008). As an MTD participant explained in 2005,

> *Compañera:* Right now, there are about five hundred to six hundred people involved in weekly movement activity in our neighborhood. At first there were around three hundred, but we kept growing until we were a bit over one thousand. Then when the electoral political campaigns began, there was a decrease because the political party apparatuses put up a lot of money to buy people into their campaigns. In the last electoral campaign in the neighborhood, they tried to buy *compañeros*. A sister said that someone who works for the government told her that political parties offer more money if a party broker can get someone who's involved in the movements, rather than someone who's not, and even more if they are a leader. It's more cost efficient to them to get a *compañera* because she is fighting. (quoted in Sitrin 2006, 104)

THE MOVEMENTS' DANCE WITH DYNAMITE [15]

I believe that the relations with the state have always been complicated. To put forward autonomy necessarily implies to not get caught up in the state agenda, but to look for ways to meet your concrete necessities that you have and take them from the state—and to do it in a way that does not harm our sovereign space most of all. . . .

It is a difficult relationship, but there are issues that we have clear in this regard, from the state we will take what we can get, and will not let the state condition our own practices or constructions. We start from the premise that everything the state has is ours, so then what we are doing is taking back what is ours, and always to serve in the construction of an autonomous area. . . . This does not mean that the state is not constantly attempting to co-opt what we are trying to do. But we don't take it. We won't accept it. (quoted in Sitrin 2012, 195)

The struggle to remain independent and create one's own agenda is common to all the autonomous unemployed movements. What this has looked like over the past decade or more has changed at various times for the movements. For example, the MTD Solano, Guernica, La Matanza, Cipoletti, and Allen decided in 2004 to no longer organize *piquetes* for unemployment subsidies. Their argument was that it forced too much of the movement's agenda into a constant relationship to the state, such as demanding subsidies, rather than focusing on autonomous and internal construction. In the few years since the MTD broke all economic ties to the state, there have been a number of different projects and forms of organization that the movement has experimented with, including taking over dozens of hectares of land upon which they have built homes and farmed. These projects, however, were not enough for the movement to become self-sufficient, and this contributed to the movement seeing a sharp decline in active participants. By 2009, the MTD Solano again began to think about their relationship to the state, and shift its position, though never looking to the state as the answer since deciding to find ways to take what they can from it.

In the meantime, there had also been a shift in some of the incentives offered by the state to movements, including a then new policy that resembled the cooperative laws of the recuperated workplaces. This new law grants money to collectives for specific projects. To receive this money a collective needs to register all of its participants with the state, create some sort of structure that demonstrates the active participation of all members, at which point they can request funds. As Emilio, an environmental organizer with movements in Corrientes that are developing self-sufficiency, explained in 2014:

I think there has been maturation in terms of how to obtain or not obtain financing by the government, to have an alternative that is one hundred percent

economically autonomous, without receiving government money that involves
a client relationship, and in that I think there has been maturity. One can
receive government money without generating a political condition. (quoted in
Sitrin 2014)

This relationship plays out in many ways in the movements. For example,
the Movement for Social Dignity in Cipoletti receives building material from
which it has constructed homes and a community center as well as the raw
materials with which the movement cooks food in their collective kitchens.
The coordination of what to do with the materials is done in working groups,
after the assembly of the movement as a whole has discussed it. Everything is
done collectively, and all receive the collective and individual benefits without a formal checking system. That said, however, there is an informal dynamic that many talk about, which includes forms of pressure on those who
are not seen as carrying their weight. This can take the form of teasing
someone, asking where they were, or sometimes a more formal conversation
between a longer-standing participant in the movement and a newer one,
describing the culture and what the group's ethic is about. This is quite
distinct from some of the other MTDs that continue to distribute subsidies
and base the receiving of the money on whether the person participated in the
piquetes.

This is a very new process, and only began taking effect in 2010, so a full
analysis has yet to be conducted. The movement of Solano speaks, as does
that of Cipolletti, of the relationship to the state as one of "permanent tension," and that they will continue the relationship as long as they can maintain their own agenda and continue to do so autonomously.

The recuperated workplace movements' relationship to the state in a certain regard is more straightforward, yet at the same time can be more nefari-
ous. Under the laws of cooperatives, written specifically for the recuperated
workplaces, once certain criteria are met the workplaces can apply for legal
status and loans from the state. At this point the law should protect the
workplace. What happens, however, is that sometimes the previous owners
file claims against the workplace, or the workplace does not fill out all the
proper paperwork on time, and there are then loopholes that are used to
rationalize attempted evictions. The sheer quantity of paperwork has been
found to be overwhelming for many of the workplaces, which find that they
have to spend so much time responding to inquiries from the government that
this gets in the way of their production and following their own agendas. In
addition, the state attempts to control all interactions related to commerce or
any wider regional and international global networks. With the example of
Chilavert, a printing press in Buenos Aires, Placido explained in late 2009:

The state is encouraging all workers to come together and form cooperatives
[like the MTD Solano is doing], though without any initial capital, and then

the state proposes that it will support this project with initial capital. This is a good program to help alleviate unemployment. But for us this does not help, since we need someone to sell to on the market. We are trying to continue to exchange things with other recuperated workplaces, and when this begins to go well, they [the state] then are there, always putting obstacles in our way, like inspections, permits, and right when you are going to get back to work, there is another bureaucratic obstacle that takes all your time and you end up doing nothing. (quoted in Sitrin 2012, 198)

And there is another example, this time with regard to international relationships between movements and left governments and the recuperated workplaces. Placido here explains what happened with Chilavert, but it is true for many of the workplaces:

The idea here was to strengthen the recuperated factories with the help of Venezuela through economic credit or financial aid but the state would not let it happen. It is that the state does not want to let this, what they call, public policy, out of their hands. . . . Because when people are in this desperate situation of not being able to decide their own destiny, which is what we have, we look for help on the outside, and that is where there is a block, where we get stuck, because the state is making policies that prevents that from happening. (quoted in Sitrin 2012, 198)

The above example is specific to one particular international gathering that took place in Caracas, Venezuela. Dozens of agreements were made among and between recuperated workplaces throughout the Americas, as well as with the government of Venezuela, although the Kirchner government would not permit these exchanges as they were outside the formal relationships of exchange between state and state. They also would allow the recuperated workplaces to create an international network of sustenance and survival, based not on the market but rather on the solidarity economy. The example of Chilavert is only one of many, and is indicative of the state's relationships with the recuperated workplace's attempts at international relations. Some have slightly different opinions of the state, but as a whole, there is no policy of "autonomy" or working within the state. The workplaces tend to use the state when necessary and however they can, and when it is an obstacle they look for other ways.

FaSinPat (Zanon) is a different scenario. The workers of FaSinPat have been calling for worker control through the state expropriation of the factory for a number of years:

We propose the expropriation of the factory, which is worker-controlled nationalization. The funds are then managed by workers, and the state provides the raw materials, energy, and gas for the workers to produce and generate resources, renew technologies and allocate those resources into public works

schemes. . . . Four hundred and fifty workers here can manage the factory and
it can progress. (conversation in Nuequen, Patagonia, 2009)

FaSinPat is the only workplace in Argentina to now function under this
new legal relationship. One thing is clear with FaSinPat, and I believe most
other workplaces from the countless conversations I have had over the years:
at their core they do not believe the state is on their side, but rather on the
side of the owners, as explained here:

> And governments govern for the employers that is why these factories are here
> in Argentina [recuperated factories] all policies that were carried out in the
> context of the international economic crisis were in order to guarantee the
> profits to the employer. (quoted in Sitrin 2012, 199)

Other Movements for Autonomy Relate to the State

> H.I.J.O.S. does not act against the state—nor with it. As with other movements
> in contemporary Latin America (the Mexican EZLN or the Brazilian MST), its
> interventions are rather independent from it. They are not anti-state in the
> sense of attacking it; they are anti-state because they build autonomy. Their
> radicalism and strength resides in the fact that they do not need the state. Even
> though, in turn, this produces a delegitimizing of the state, it is not the central
> point of the action. The *escrache* does not negate the power of the state to
> judge, it only points to its lack of action and its complicity with state terror-
> ism. . . . The discussions about the structure of the organization, horizontality
> for example, got to the fore as H.I.J.O.S. was discussing more its proposals not
> only for political action but also for a new democratic country. As the State
> was showing fissures, the main task was no longer just opposing the State but
> rather imagining, practicing, and building new forms of social organizing.
> Away from the State forms of social intervention that rely on autonomy and
> imagination were emerging. Practicing new socialities and creating new insti-
> tutions were ways to enact, to put in practice, concrete proposals for social
> change. (Benegas forthcoming)

The most serious challenge to HIJOS's autonomy and horizontal decision-making structures occurred in 2004 when the Punto Final law was re-
voked and the trials of the former military began. For HIJOS, the challenge
was how (and if) to participate in the trials without giving up on its deep
questioning of institutional justice; and how to get what it could from the
system without compromising the bigger long-term goals of social transformation and the creation of new social relationships. For example, practicing
*escrache*s is quite different from joining the state in trials of individuals,
which shift the attention somewhat away from society as a whole, and onto a
number of bad people held responsible by a handful of good people.

On a number of occasions HIJOS has been asked to participate formally
in the trials in collaboration with government agencies. This has raised seri-

ous debates as to what is the best role and place for HIJOS. It is based on these sorts of debates that HIJOS split earlier. HIJOS, the more autonomous part of the split, believes that direct and regular engagement with the state by representatives of HIJOS will break up the horizontal nature and spirit of the group.

In another area, however, similar to a number of the MTDs discussed above, the state has offered some HIJOS groups money for projects; for example HIJOS Cordoba accepted government funding and bought a printing press for the distribution of their material.

As with the unemployed movements, HIJOS is struggling with the question of how to maintain its autonomy, its own agenda, but at the same time get what it believes to be its own from the state. The dance is a very dangerous and tricky one, but now that the discussion is taking place, there are more possibilities for autonomous creation.

Two more examples, similar to HIJOS and the unemployed movements (though there are many dozens if not hundreds more as the numbers are increasing rapidly), are with the media collective, Lavaca, and the photo collective, Fotocoop. Both groups have become official under the state, but maintain their own agendas and do whatever work the collective decides. One of the ways that Lavaca has found to struggle with the relationship to the state is to make sure it always happens with at least a few participants at a time, and that these roles must rotate. As with the recuperated workplaces, whatever monies are made from the projects at both collectives are divided equally among all participants. While challenging, this is not contradictory, as "Social movements can struggle for autonomy in the sense of escaping state control, while still very much engaging in political action" (Foweraker 1995, 61–64).

CONCLUSION: IT'S A WAR, NOT A DANCE

"The relationship with the State will always be contentious, it will always be a sordid war, always" (Sitrin 2012, 202). The final section began a discussion of the "dance with the state." For the movements, the relationship to the state is more aptly described as a war, as described above by a participant in the Movement for Social Dignity in Allen in 2010. The incredible strategy, foresight, and planning needed to have a relationship at all with an institution that does not want you to exist is profound and constant. On the other hand, the movements also want to create something very different from the state, and by creating autonomously in the cities, towns, and countryside throughout Argentina they are creating bases from which the war is being waged. This is not a typical war with guns and battle lines, but one of two opposing forces, often working covertly to undermine the other; a war that on the one side is creating new value and values, new subjectivities, based in love and affect, and new people—and on the other, is destroying or co-opting these new social subjects. The future, as has been said, is yet unwritten, but for now the dance/war is gaining ground on behalf of the movements. Time has allowed for a much more sophisticated analysis of how to wage this war, and the participants are cautiously optimistic.

NOTES

Much of the material in this chapter, before 2010, is based in research for the oral history I compiled in 2005, *Horizontalism: Voices of Popular Power in Argentina*, and thinking and writing for the later, 2012, *Everyday Revolutions: Horizontalism and Autonomy in Argentina*.

1. This is one of many narratives I wrote based on descriptions and interviews with people who were present on the scene that day and continued to organize.

2. The new global movements, since 2010, are known for their use of direct democracy over representation and the striving for horizontal relationships. See Sitrin and Azzellini (2014) for a testimonial-based book of the new movements.

3. For a more thorough description of the movements that emerged post-2001 see Sitrin (2012) and Dinerstein, Bohn, and Spicer (2009).

4. Land grabbing is the purchasing or taking of large plots of land for private and for profit use, generally done by corporations.

5. For more information on the horizontal and assembly based environmental organizing see: Zibechi (2014) and Sitrin (2014).

6. Both Anibel Varon and Dario Santillan were *piqueteros* murdered by the police. There have been a number of murders of MTD participants, going back to the late 1990s.

7. www.workerscontrol.net.

8. For more information on recuperations in Argentina, see the regular reports on recuperations, including statistical information by the Facultad Abierta (2010). Also see Hirtz and Giacone (2013).

9. See the films *The Take* (www.thetake.org) and *Corazón de Fábrica* (http://vimeo.com/55379683).

10. Most people with whom I spoke would refer to the period after the dictatorship as a "democracy," making scare quotes with their fingers. When asked why, people were consistently clear that there was no real democracy just because military rule ended.

11. There is a long history of debate within the human rights field as to the "proper use" of genocide. While the 1948 Universal Declaration of Human Rights does not include political groups in the definition of genocide, that has been contested in the years since, particularly by some countries in Latin America (see http://www.hrweb.org/legal/). There is documented evidence that the military dictatorship of Argentina wanted to eliminate all political opposition, thus fitting into the definition now used by some human rights courts.

12. *Potencia* in Spanish means power, capacity, and ability—distinct from the Spanish *poder*, meaning power, might, and authority.

13. These actions were similar to the idea of *escrache*.

14. I refer throughout this chapter to the Kirchners, and while Nestor and Christina governed Argentina at different times, their politics and relationship to the movements as well as human rights have been fairly consistent and not worth separating out each time the politics or perspectives are described.

15. This phrase is taken from the title to Ben Dangl's 2010 book *Dancing with Dynamite* that discusses the relationship of social movements to the state in Latin America.

Chapter Twelve

Brazil

Taking the Streets, Swarming Public Spaces:
The 2013 Popular Protests

Harry E. Vanden

In middle of 2013 major cities in Brazil erupted in massive street demonstrations that saw more than a million Brazilians *"tomar as ruas"* (take the streets) over several nights in June in more than 100 cities. Tens and then hundreds of thousands of people swarmed major avenues and public spaces. The people would not be silenced, discounted, or ignored any longer. The political class and economic elites that had ignored their demands for so long had no choice but to listen. The locus of power and decision making was being moved from the halls of government, from corporate headquarters and boardrooms to the streets. The people would rule (from below)—at least for a while.

What started as a protest against a 10-cent (.20 real) increase in the fare for public transportation in São Paulo, Rio de Janeiro, and other major cities widened into a protest against general conditions and government action, if not against the whole neoliberal model of development that had made life in the cities (and countryside) unbearable for all too many (see Vainer et al. 2013, especially Maricato 2013). The principal areas of dissatisfaction included not only the rise in fares and the poor quality of the public health insurance system, but the poor quality of education in the public schools, the perception of massive public corruption, and the inordinate amount of spending on new stadiums and infrastructure for the 2014 World Cup and the 2016 Olympic Games that were to follow. The vast majority of Brazilians supported the popular demonstrations that registered growing anger with a system that collected relatively high taxes but did not use the funds to satisfy popular needs in health care, education, and public transportation. Instead public officials were allowed to profit from new construction, public funds were invested in mega show projects for the World Cup and the Olympics, the government sanitized and even tore down favelas (slums) and relocated their residents, and generally ignored popular expression of needs and wants.

The outpouring of dissatisfaction shook the political system and President Dilma Rousseff to the core; the PT (Workers' Party) government had to force the municipalities to cancel the fare hikes and the national government itself had to make concessions in regard to health care and public education at the national level while promising substantial political reform. Dilma Rousseff, her government, and the Brazilian elite generally were caught unawares by the breadth, depth, and intensity of the demonstrations. They were not expecting such vociferous political participation from below. Yet, for years there had been clear signs and indicators of what was to come. Many social movements in Brazil had registered their complaints, often vociferously, for some time. There had been much organization at the grassroots level and there was a significant sector of Brazilian society—including much of the left wing of the Workers' Party that had seen and protested against the conditions that motivated the protesters in June of 2013. Indeed, formally and informally they had registered many of the same complaints that resounded from the streets in June of 2013.

There had, for instance, been protests against increasingly expensive fares in public transportation for more than a decade. The largest social movement in Latin America, the million-strong Landless Movement (MST, or Landless Rural Workers' Movement) had been militating about the lack of social and economic justice and the need for land reform since its formation in the early 1980s. The Sem Teto (homeless movement) had been occupying buildings in major cities like São Paulo to call attention to the lack of affordable housing and an urban political economy that made it difficult for many to live. Similar complaints were made by a multitude of social movements and organizations that arose in the poor neighborhoods of these same cities. But, as we shall argue in this chapter, the people's pleas were not heard. The business and political elite just did not think it was necessary to listen. Even the former union leader (Lula da Silva, former president) and former guerilla (Dilma Rousseff, now president) were not hearing what the masses were saying. That is, while Brazil was developing into the world's sixth-largest economy, a BRIC (Brazil, Russia, India, and China) country and an increasingly active player in international affairs, much of what large segments of the domestic population were saying was not being heard. The political structures in the most populous Latin American democracy had ossified to such an extent that the masses could not effectively register fundamental popular demands.

In order to govern, alleviate some of the worst poverty through monthly stipends to poor families, get the minimum wage increased to 680 reales a month (about US$350), and get its legislation through congress, the PT had had to make compromises with the São Paulo industrialists, the São Paulo financial sector, agribusiness, and rightist politicians and parties (and evidently buy some congressional votes, as in the *mensalão* vote-buying scandal that erupted while Lula was still in office). Referring to the need to get its programs enacted without a legislative majority or its own friendly media outlets, one high-level PT official, Florisvaldo de Souza, noted that

> You have to remember this is a country that is profoundly unequal and contradictory, in that neoliberalism continued to be ideologically and economically hegemonic while the left appears to be politically hegemonic. This contradiction—almost a paradox—is at the root of a great part of our problems. [1]

That is, the progressive PT leadership and two PT governments felt they had been forced to be part of the acceptable or good left (see Prevost and Vanden 2012, 10–21; Webber and Carr 2012) in order to effectively govern and enact many of their policies to ameliorate some of the worst poverty and penury. They had, then, bought into and further developed what some have dubbed the post-neoliberal model—one that might be described as neoliberalism with a more human face (see, inter alia, chapters 1 and 8 in Veltmeyer and Petras 2014). More equitable growth—but economic growth as fundamental—will be fostered through increased exports of agricultural and mineral products, direct transfers to the poorest, more better-paying jobs, with better minimum wage floors, and the expansion of consumerism to not only all of the middle class but to a significant part of the working class. Indeed all or almost all would have cell phones, and more and more would be able to go to the malls to enjoy their consumption. In order to achieve the necessary economic growth and targeted redistribution, dynamic agribusiness, financial, and industrial (especially automotive) sectors would have to be encouraged and supported and a few concessions would also have to be made with right-wing politicians. Thus in order to implement the economic and social welfare policies that would significantly help the poor and lower middle class—originally the Workers Party's most solid base—agribusiness, financial sectors, industrial sectors like the automobile industry and some rightist political sectors would need to be privileged in their communication and input to the PT leadership while the MST, Sem Teto, and other social movements would be politely referred to, but their demands would not be listened to or implemented because to do so would alienate the newfound supporters of the Brazilian neoliberal model. Selective hearing was very much in vogue. Many would not be heard, and fundamental structural changes would be postponed until later, or would never happen at all.

And so it was that the traditional political system did not input growing demands from urban and even rural workers, and large segments of the middle class. Unable or unwilling to respond, it was challenged by a massive social movement that took advantage of its familiarity with social media and of Brazil's democratic openness to political participation to challenge the political class and its monopoly on effective political input. The massive mobilization of so many people from diverse backgrounds, their ability to use social media to obtain information, organize demonstrations, and disseminate information, and the media and social media coverage of their contentious actions to register their demands, made them a formidable force. Through their mobilizing actions they had demonstrated a powerful capacity to widely disseminate their views, messages, and demands and to challenge government rule when they mobilized their forces. As the protests continue into 2014, it remains to be seen if the nation's political institutions and economic system and those who control them can make the changes that are necessary to meet the challenges posed by an angry, politically conscious, and highly mobilized populace.

BACKGROUND

We believe that there is a profound realignment in Latin America that may well represent a sea change in politics and democratic practice itself (Stahler-Sholk, Vanden, and Kuecker 2008; Prevost, Oliva, and Vanden 2012; Dangl 2010; Webber and Carr 2012). This new social movement–based mobilization has continued to evolve. It is not only a movement toward wider political participation; it is a movement toward horizontal structures, and horizontal as opposed to vertical interactions and avenues of participation from below (Holloway 2002; Zibechi 2010).

In Brazil, the assertion of popular power that had been seen in popular mobilizations, like the pre-1964 coup Peasant Leagues in the poverty-stricken northeast, began to bubble up in new and different forms. By the time economic neoliberalism became more widespread in the 1990s, there were growing questions as to whether the extant political systems in Brazil and much of Latin America were proving unable to formulate economic policies that could provide some modicum of economic and social security for the vast majorities. The introduction of the monetarist Real Plan (1994) and the subsequent election of its intellectual author, Fernando Henrique Cardoso, as president in 1998 bought time for the traditional economic and political elites in Brazil. Yet there and elsewhere many wondered aloud if the much-touted democratization and free elections were not, in fact, new political mechanisms supported by the national and international economic and political elites to keep the masses subordinated (and not rebelling) and in an ongoing state of poverty—if not penury. And it should here be noted that then and now, Brazil has one of the worst distributions of wealth in the world. Further, the effects of the economic contraction of the 1980s and the unbalanced economic growth of the 1990s often left some segments of the middle class economically marginalized, along with large swaths of the lower classes.

As national political leaders felt increasing pressure to maintain national economic growth, they found that they often were being obliged to implement policies that did not alleviate and sometimes caused a further deterioration of living conditions for the masses and some segments of the middle class. Although some began to do better in recent years in Brazil, not all benefited equally, and the economic and political expectations of many grew more rapidly than economic benefits and opportunities for meaningful political participation.

As has been the case all too often in Latin America, the political systems have been unable to provide basic security in food, housing, education, employment, or monetary value and banking to wide sectors of the population. That is, the many are or have been marginalized from the nation project, and of immediate concern in this chapter, the governing institutions have been unwilling or unable to provide solutions to their situations, or even to hear their demands. Insecurity, dissatisfaction and unmet expectations thus drove many to new forms of protest and to seek new and different political structures that might better respond to their needs. Traditional parties and governments were increasingly seen as unable to respond or even comprehend their needs. These political parties, if not the political systems themselves, were often rapidly losing their legitimacy. Faith in the government, if not the system, was faltering. Satisfaction with Brazilian democracy had fallen to 26 percent by 2013 (see Latinobarometro 2013, 36). The perception of government corruption and the emergence of a corrupted political class that cared little for popular needs and desires exacerbated this phenomenon in Brazil. Though not always well or precisely articulated, new demands were being registered. Something different was being sought. Different groups were looking for new political and administrative structures that allowed for, if not encouraged, their participation. Civil society was becoming the new locus of conflict and contention. We note that this reality enabled the growth of the leftist Workers' Party in Brazil and the eventual election of party leader Luiz Inácio Lula da Silva as president (2002–2010). PT rule was continued with the election of Dilma Rousseff as president in 2010, but the party's movement to the right distanced it from large segments of the masses and social movements like the MST, and even many leftist supporters.

There was, then, a search for new structures or at least new avenues of participation that could respond to the perceived—and not always clearly articulated—demands being formulated from below by the popular and many middle sectors. Broad segments of the population (from the lower and middle

classes) had begun to mobilize and seek new and different political involvement and responses in parties, governmental structures, and social movements. They sought something that worked for them. Indeed, the increasing
promotion of democracy and democratization told them that their voices
should be heard and that the political system should somehow respond to
them. The Brazilians had fought to rid the country of military rule in the
1980s and had reinstituted a more vibrant democracy. However, when it is
unclear how, if at all, their votes counted, and whether the political class was
capable of responding to their hue and cry, many became disillusioned and
angry. This would eventually lead to more and different forms of actions that
contested the power of the state and the power of the powerful.

Traditional personalismo, clientelismo, and coronelismo, corruption and
personal, class and group avarice, became subjects of ridicule and anger, if
not rage.[2] The effects of neoliberalism and continued racism and classism
amidst ever stronger calls for racial and economic equality began to be felt.
They were cast against the background of corruption and clientelism and
increasing calls for a return to more effective democracy and honest government, if not new forms and modes of political engagement and participation.

Indeed, as background we believe growing abstention rates suggested a
general dissatisfaction with the political system. The 1998 national elections
in Brazil saw a manifestation of this phenomena, with 40.1 percent of the
electorate either abstaining, or casting blank or annulled ballots (Banco de
Dados Políticos 2002). This strongly suggests that a substantial segment of
the population no longer believed that the systems of governance that the
electoral processes had produced were adequate. There seemed little point to
electoral participation if the elected officials did not respond to the needs of
the electorate or the decisions made at the polls. It was, it turned out, the
calm before the raging storm of popular participation that swept Brazil and
Latin America.

Finally, the growing popular resentment of the political class, the failures
of economic policies to address the needs of all the public, the inefficiencies
and corruption of administrative institutions, and the distance of the governance processes from the majority of the people activated new social and
political movements noticeable in Brazil and in many countries in the region.

The new social movements in Bolivia, Ecuador, and elsewhere had been
able to take politics out of the presidential palace and halls of congress where
the traditional political class dominated into different spaces: the villages,
neighborhoods, rural highways, and popular councils that they could control
(Vanden 2008; Stahler-Sholk, Vanden, and Kuecker 2008; Zibechi 2012).
They had done so *from below*, through a broad coalition of social movements
with strong identities and deep, democratic ties to those who participated in
them. They had initiated a form of participatory governance that would radi-

cally alter decision-making practices in their Andean nations and suggest that government must indeed serve the people if it was to endure.

NEW SOCIAL MOVEMENT IN BRAZIL: THE MST

The radically different nature of these new social movements and the new politics of participation can perhaps best be seen in the largest of the new social movements in Brazil and Latin America—the MST, Landless Rural Workers' Movement. MST ranks exceed one million and in 1997 the movement was able to mobilize 100,000 people for a march on Brasilia. The organization believed that "popular movements must challenge this neoliberal conceptualization of our economy and society" (MST 2001a). The organization called for popular mobilizations, noting, "All the changes in the history of humanity only happened when the people were mobilized," and that in Brazil, "all the social and political changes that happened were won when the people mobilized and struggled" (MST 2001b).

The MST itself was formed as a response to long-standing economic, social, and political conditions in Brazil. Yet land, wealth, and power have been allocated in very unequal ways since the Portuguese conquest in the early 1500s. Wealth has remained concentrated. In 2001, the Brazilian Institute of Government Statistics reported that the upper 10 percent of the population averaged an income that was nineteen times greater than the lowest 40 percent.[3] Some of the worst of these conditions have shown some improvement in recent years and Brazil is considered one of the more successful developing countries as it has implemented its post-neoliberal growth model through general economic growth and the direct transfers to the poorest through programs like *Fome 0* (0 Hunger) and *Bolsa Familia* (Family Food Basket). Although there was a rising tide in urban areas, not all boats were lifted the same way. In 2005 the poorest 10 percent of urban households got less than 1 percent (0.9 percent) of income, while the wealthiest 10 percent got nearly half (49.8 percent) (ECLAC 2006). Elements of the middle class were also affected by increased taxation, lack of affordable health care, and deteriorating public education.

While the now-growing Worker's Party engaged in more traditional party activity, the MST response consisted of grassroots organization and the development of a new repertoire of actions that broke with old forms of political activity. Developing organization and group actions began to tie individual members together in a strongly forged group identity. The process led to direct actions such as land takeovers from large estates and public lands, the construction of black plastic covered encampments along the side of the road to call attention to their demands for land, and marches and confrontations when necessary.

The Landless Movement was well attuned to the international globalization struggle and its members considered themselves part of it, helping to organize and participating in the World Social Forums in Porto Alegre and sending their representatives to demonstrations and protests throughout the world. They were one of the new type of internationally connected social organizations that met together in places like Seattle, Prague, and Geneva as well as the World Social Forums. Struggles that were once local and isolated were now international and linked. The news media and growing international communications links, especially email, greatly facilitated the globalization of struggle, and the globalization of awareness of local struggles, and support and solidarity with them. This and the dramatic actions like massive land takeovers by the MST also generated considerable support at the national level, and helped to define what might have been considered a local problem as a national problem that required national-level attention and resources to remedy it.

In small classes, meetings, and assemblies and through their newspaper *Jornal Dos Trabalhadores Sem Terra,* magazine *Revista Sem Terra,* and numerous pamphlets, the MST carefully educated their base through a well-planned program of political education. The organization even established schools in their encampments, settlements, and cooperatives to make sure the next generation has a clear idea of the politics in play and the need for popular involvement and participation. The Landless Movement facilitated the organic development of highly participatory grassroots organization, beginning with groups of ten families organized as a base nucleus in each neighborhood. Local general assemblies are used frequently, and all members of the family units (including the children) are encouraged to participate. Leadership is collective at all levels, including at the national level where some 102 militants make up the National Coordinating Council (Coordinacão Nacional). The strongly participatory nature of the organization and the collective nature of leadership and decision making made for a dynamic new democratic, participatory political culture that challenged traditional authoritarian notions and vertical decision making structures (see MST 2000 and Rodrigues Brandão 2001).

Although the MST had significant public support in the 1990s, such support had declined in large part because of negative press coverage and flagging interest among university students and other more sympathetic groups. In recent years there had been fewer land takeovers and not as much enthusiasm in the settlements. The national government had chosen to facilitate financing for large agribusiness concerns and not small farmers. Intellectuals were no longer as interested in agrarian reform, and the movement did not feel it had as many allies as before.[4] By 2013 the MST was not as strong as it had once been. Its example of horizontal participation would still inspire, but the locus of organizing and direct participation would now move to the cities.

LULA AND THE PT

Meanwhile, the Workers Party (PT) was growing in influence and numbers as it began to campaign on a national scale. Former metalworker and union leader Luiz Inácio da Silva, affectionately known as Lula, led the party. The party had grown out of the successful union organizing of the metalworkers in São Paulo in the 1970s and early 1980s that also generated the new, linked militant labor organization, the United Workers' Federation (CUT). During the 1980s workers, former communists, progressives, and other leftists as well as labor militants, intellectuals, and legions of the MST also joined the party, brought more radical visions of democracy, and helped to contribute to its growing successes. By 1990 the party was able to field a presidential candidate in the person of Lula. Although he spoke to the impoverished masses, leftists, and many members of the middle class, he was perceived as too far to the left, especially by business and commercial elites. Even though the PT continued to enjoy electoral success at the municipal and state level, its representation in the Brazilian Senate and Chamber of Deputies was growing but never extensive. In the 1998 election the PT took a little less than a third of the Senate and had only 82 out of 187 seats in the lower house. Lula continued to run for president on the PT ticket, but lost in 1994 and 1998, in large part because of the view that he and his party were radical and dangerous to the economic interests of the upper class, if not much of the middle class.

BRAZIL GAINS ECONOMIC STRENGTH

Brazil's economy grew, exports flowed, and by the twenty-first century Brazil was one of the up-and-coming economies in the world, forming part of the newly classified rapidly developing BRIC countries. Yet, as suggested previously, this type of growth did not distribute wealth well or alleviate the persistent extreme poverty that characterizes the society. It did, however, help to develop a vigorous capitalist economy complete with a dynamic stock market (the Bolsa de Valores de São Paulo), the largest in Latin America; thriving industrialization and commercial agriculture; and a growing commercial and banking sector, all of which resulted in a well-off capitalist class that vigorously protected its interests. Indeed in the years that followed, Brazil would radically increase its production of soy (Brazil now exports more soy than any other nation) and gear up sugar production to produce ethanol (Brazil is now the world leader). This has led some scholars to include these activities in what has been termed the new extractivism, because so much of the economy was being geared to the export of grown crops or mined products (Veltmeyer and Petras 2014). This type of export activity

Harry E. Vanden

is comparable to the way other countries like Ecuador are allowing large capitalist companies to mine and export unfinished mineral wealth.

THE PARTY OF THE WORKERS MAKES FRIENDS WITH THE CAPITALISTS

In order to take and maintain power, Lula and his Workers' Party had to continue to appeal to the impoverished masses while reassuring the economic elite that they would respect their interests as well. After his three previous unsuccessful presidential runs, Lula and the PT mounted a different kind of campaign in 2002, forming an alliance with the more moderate Liberal Party and taking on a businessman as their vice presidential candidate. Lula now dressed in coat and tie and paid his respects to São Paulo state's dynamic capitalists. He even made a point of visiting the São Paulo stock exchange and also paid his respects to Wall Street on a visit to the United States so as to reassure U.S and other foreign investors. This calmed capitalist nerves and increased his appeal among more conservative Brazilians. This and Lula's strong support from the lower classes enabled him to win the presidency in 2002 and again in 2006, despite blowback from a PT vote-buying scandal (the monthly payments to opposition legislators or *mensalão*). It was also to define his rule and link him to the successful Brazilian growth model and the economic elites that were leading it. The model that was developing was what some have referred to as the above-mentioned post-neoliberal capitalist model because of attempts to reduce some of the worst poverty through direct transfers of income to those suffering the most persistent poverty.

The interaction between the MST and the PT is also instructive. Although relations between the two organizations were generally excellent at the local level, with overlapping affiliations, the national leaderships have remained separate and not always as cordial. The MST has maintained a militant line in regard to the need for structural reform and to taking over unused land and asserting its agenda, whereas much of the PT leadership wanted to be more conciliatory with the capitalist class. Thus, the MST backed and supported Lula and the Workers Party in most local campaigns and the national campaigns for the presidency. In this way they helped to achieve significant regime change in Brazil, where Lula was elected with 61.27 percent of the vote in the second round of voting in 2002. Indeed, realizing the PT's historic challenge to neoliberal policies and elitist rule, the landless turned out heavily in the election to join some 80 percent of the registered voters who participated in the voting in both rounds (International Foundation for Election Surveys 2002). However, once the election was over, the MST did not press to be part of the government. Rather, it continued to press the government for a comprehensive land reform program and a redistribution of the land and the wealth. However, the PT would push its 0 Hunger program and other social and economic initiatives, and the MST would push the PT government for the structural reforms that it considered necessary.

Lula's reelection in 2006 put MST and PT policies in even sharper relief. The second Workers' Party presidential term proved to be even more receptive to capitalist interests than the first. Agribusiness interests in the form of large soy producers and cane producers for the ethanol industry had good access to government. The Party of the Workers felt obliged to support such big capitalists because their production and exports were fueling Brazilian economic growth. The same was true for the industrial, commercial, and growing banking interests as well. The Landless Movement pushed land reform and economic redistribution, but the governmental response was not radical reform. Rather, the government further evolved their 0 Hunger program, so that a *Bolsa Familia*, a basic family "food basket" allowance of as much as $35 to $50 a month, would allow the poorest—particularly those with children—to buy the basic foodstuffs to survive and would also diminish some of their political fervor. These same policies were continued under Lula's successor, Dilma Rousseff, a former guerrilla who was closely associated with Lula in the PT. Indeed, it could be said that in the last few years Lula, Dilma, and the PT governments were pursuing a dual tract: working with the Bolsa of São Paulo (stock market) while distributing the *Bolsa Familia* to the poor. Radical change would not be forthcoming, the capitalist economy would grow, and prosperity would hopefully spread, but the hungry would not starve in the meantime. This was the essence of the post-neoliberal model that was developing in Brazil and which could be seen in sharp relief in the Brazilian cities, where the homeless slept in the streets and abandoned buildings and the wealthy lived in well-protected high-rise apartments and navigated the outside world in their posh cars, while the very wealthy flew to work in helicopters.

THE POST-NEOLIBERAL CAPITALIST MODEL

So the new post-neoliberal capitalist model of development was being implemented in Brazil. Wider credit, consumerism, massive purchase of new automobiles and motorcycles, and a growing real estate and housing market defined the new reality. In the cities, development was defined in terms of more cars and high-rise towers. Windfall profits and speculation were the order of the day. As noted by Ermina Maricato in her chapter, "It's the Urban Question, Stupid!," affordable housing was not on the agenda either (Maricato 2013, 23). The built infrastructure was being dedicated to individual vehicles rather than an extensive, rational public transport system. The public coffers financed the construction of roadbeds, viaducts, bridges, and tunnels

(Maricato 2013, 25) for those who had cars; meanwhile, many workers and even much of the middle class had to take several busses, trains, or both to go to and from work and home, paying more than a dollar each way, experience intense overcrowding, and spend as long as two hours in transit. While the municipalities were investing millions in new roads, bridges, and bypasses, those who were taking the busses, subway, and light rail trains were expected to pay more and more for inadequate public transport.

Supported by the growing financial sector, private companies built expensive high-rise towers packed with condominiums, and, taking advantage of the auto-friendly infrastructure, were able to develop new areas further from the centers of the cities. Real estate speculation was rampant and the cost of housing skyrocketed. The price of real estate grew 153 percent between 2009 and 2012 in São Paulo. In Rio de Janeiro the cost grew by 184 percent in the same period (Maricato 2013, 23–24). It was hard to afford decent housing in many of Brazil's big cities—even for the growing middle class.

This reality added to an increasingly difficult existence for the 86 percent of Brazil's population that lives in an urban area. The cost and quality of public transportation was emblematic of the problems the vast majority of the urban dwellers were facing, but it was not the only problem. The increasing cost of housing was discussed above. The quality of public health care also declined, forcing many—particularly from the middle class—to seek private insurance coverage, even though the premiums increased drastically to hundreds of dollars a month for a family of four. The public education system also was of generally low quality, was not improving, and was unable to prepare the vast majority of its graduates with sufficient knowledge or skills to pass the rigorous university entrance exams for the excellent state and federal universities, or to get a decent job in an increasingly sophisticated and technologically oriented modern capitalist economy. That is, public resources were not being invested in better public health care or better public education. Nor did public policy encourage the construction of affordable housing. Public resources were, as we shall see, going elsewhere.

RESISTANCE

Faced with the difficulty of urban transport almost every day, the transportation issue had been sparking public ire for some time. Urban fares for public transportation had increased close to 200 percent from 2000 to 2013 (Romero 2013a, 1). Protests were not new. In Salvador de Bahia there were major protests against an increase in transit fares in 2003. It was called "A Revolta do Buzo" (bus revolt) and lasted for a month. As many as 40,000 people were involved (Movimento Passe Livre 2013, 14). Students and youth were particularly active, and the Revolta do Buzo required newer ways of organiz-

ing and protesting. The street actions required a movement away from hierarchical models of action to new forms of protest. Organization, planning,
and poster making was done at schools and other decentralized locations.
The protesters did not use the political parties but engaged in direct action in
the streets, and developed horizontal assemblies. The documentary *Revolta
do Buzo* by Carlos Pronzato that was soon disseminated throughout the country and used by Passe Livre (Free Passage) committees in other cities captured the essence of the protests (Movimento Passe Livre 2013, 14–15). This
helped to spark a Passe Livre protest dubbed *Revolta da Catraca* (revolt
against the turnstile) in Florianapolis in 2004. Occupying the terminal and
blocking the walkways to the platforms, the protesters were able to force the
municipal authorities to revoke the fare increase. This served as a base to
organize a national MPL (Movimento Passe Livre) the following year at the
meeting of the World Social Forum in Porto Alegre (Movimento Passe Livre
2013, 15). From the accumulated experiences of this popular process, there
emerged "an autonomous, horizontal, nonpartisan social transport movement
whose local collectives although federated were not subordinate to any central organization" (Movimento Passe Livre 2013, 15). Major protests followed in Vitória (2006), Teresina (2011), Aracuju and Natal (2012), and
Porto Alegre and Goiânia (beginning of 2013).

Like the development of the Landless Movement in the countryside, this
was a rhizomatic movement in urban areas that had been building for years.
It and subsequent protests had an element of spontaneity, but were also
rooted in previous horizontal organization and preparation. As millions of
rural workers and small farmers were finding life intolerable in the countryside, many millions more were finding urban life under the new neoliberal
system alienating and equally untenable. Major structural reforms were
needed in both areas. But even the progressive Workers' Party was unwilling—if not unable—to make the fundamental changes that were necessary to
create a more humane environment in the country side and urban areas alike.
The PT, it seems, had made an accommodation with agribusiness in the
countryside and was now responding to the interests of large urban banks,
real estate developers, all parts of the automobile industry, and other domestic and foreign corporations. So while land reform was being called for in the
countryside, land was being concentrated in large commercial farms to produce soy in vast green deserts. In urban areas public monies were being used
to build roads, overpasses, and bridges and expensive high-rise condominiums were being encouraged, while public health and education were receiving marginal funding. The Free Passage Movement had been calling for free
public transportation, but the authorities had decided that public transport
was supposed to pay for itself (which it never does) through round after
round of increases in already expensive fares.

Matters came to a head in June 2013. While all of the above was taking place, more and more public officials (including some high-ranking members of Lula and Dilma's Workers' Party) were being found guilty of public corruption (though they seemed able to continually postpone serving their sentences). Taxes were high and there was now a big push to use large sums of public funds to improve—that is beautify and relocate poor residents—Rio de Janeiro for the 2014 Soccer World Cup and, in cooperation with FIFA, to build huge, expensive stadiums in Rio and other Brazilian cities. The cost for the six stadiums that would be used to inaugurate the World Cup would be US$2 billion. FIFA required Brazil to build or improve twelve stadiums in all, twenty-one new airport terminals, seven runways, and five maritime terminals. The total cost for these works was estimated at $15 billion (Zibechi 2013b).

To pay for this, Brazil had levied one of the world's highest tax burdens, estimated by the Brazilian Tax Planning Institute to be 36 percent of GDP (Latin American Weekly Report 2013). Further, there were persistent allegations that much of the money for the stadiums and new infrastructure was being siphoned off through corruption. After the *mensalão* scandal, there was increasing public skepticism about the probity of the government and government projects.

As local MPL organizations had spawned horizontal organization in urban areas across Brazil, the controversy around the World Cup and preparations for it also generated the creation of Cup Committees in cities throughout Brazil. Popular Cup Committees were organized with the participation of the Sem Teto, displaced favela (slum) communities, and university militants. A new horizontalism across popular organizations was also building. As one militant observed, there were direct links to Black and favela youth culture, which helped to bridge the growing urban segregation between the poor and the better off. There was a growing movement of horizontal organization.

TAKING THE STREETS

There was, then, a culture of horizontal mobilization that was embodied in the MPL and Cup Committees by the time the protests started in June 2013 (Adital 2013). Other social movements like the MST and the homeless (Sem Teto) had been developing this type of horizontal organization for some years as well. The World Social Forums in Porto Alegre, the extensive organization and publicity about the Landless Movement and how it functioned, and a general new orientation about the use of power (rule from below!) were creating a different political culture among many in Brazil. Some saw the transfer of ideas from rural to urban areas. In a an interview in the widely circulated electronic bulletin *Otras Palavras*, well-known MST leader and National Directorate member João Pedro Stedile noted that "people were living a Hell in the large cities" because of the time they had to spend on transport and other problems. He strongly urged people to join the protests and noted that some groups in the MST who lived near cities were already participating and that others would follow (Viana 2013). Another national MST leader[5] further noted that the movement had strongly supported the street protests and had even allowed organizers to use their headquarters.

As in many countries, the authorities had often successfully suppressed popular protests in Brazil. This was particular true during the military dictatorship, and some of this tradition was carried on by well-organized military police who were particularly present in Rio de Janeiro and São Paulo. For these and other reasons, the first reaction of public authorities in June 2013 was repressive once the first street demonstrations started after the 20-cent fare increase (20 cents of a real, or about US10 cents). The demonstrations were not massive when they started, and the Free Pass Movement was central. Many of the participants were now educated sons and daughters of workers who had come to the cities for a better life. The actions soon struck a chord with growing segments of the public. However, not only did São Paulo state's Social Democratic governor Geraldo Alckmin order the demonstration repressed, he was joined by the popular PT mayor of São Paulo, Fernando Haddad. Major media outlets like the right-wing weekly *Veija* and Globo television network encouraged the repression, painting the protesters as violent hooligans or anarchists. This proved to be a disastrous mistake; it only enraged the demonstrators and quickly garnered growing sympathy, empathy, and support. And the political class was not prepared to listen. As one Brazilian analyst noted, "They don't understand anything, don't hear anything, just don't get it at all" (Nepomuceno 2013). The masses who took to the streets shared this perception. They felt they were just not being listened to, and were not going to be. The parties were no better (author interviews in São Paulo, August 17–20, 2013).[6] The political class and even the governing PT elite had not responded to the demands registered by the MST, Sem Teto, and even the MPL and other organizations for years. They were supported in this by the conservative media like *Veija* and the Globo television networks, which had vilified the MST and treated the first round of protesters with equal contempt. It seems that many members of the elite and political class thought they could continue on this road. They were wrong.

Before, the Brazilian masses had engaged in massive mobilizations toward the end of the dictatorship with their resounding cry for "*diretas ja*"— direct elections now. A new generation was now capitalizing on this tradition. The protesters were not just working-class youth or favela residents, though there were many of these. Many professionals and members of the middle class participated. Further, the great majority had cell phones and were adept at social media. They had also followed what their counterparts had done in Egypt, Spain, and New York. Not only were Facebook, Twitter, and similar programs used to announce and coordinate events, cell phones were used to photograph the massive swarming of the streets and videotape the sometimes brutal police beatings of the original protesters in early June, and almost immediately disseminate them throughout the cities and nation. As Manuel Castells, the well-known student of the media and social movements, observed in the Brazilian edition of his widely read *Networks of Outrage and Hope, Social Movements in the Internet Age*, "the autonomous communication by the masses is the technological platform for the new culture of autonomy [self initiated individual communication and action]." He had studied such movements as those in Tunisia, Iceland, Egypt, the United States (the Occupy Movement) and Spain (the Indignados) as they developed in 2011. He found them to be movements that were using new communication networks to restructure political participation, stimulate direct forms of democracy and change governments and policies. In light of these movements, Castells commented on the protests in Brazil:

> It happened in Brazil too. Without anyone expecting it. Without leaders. Without parties or unions in its organization. Without help from the media. Spontaneously. A cry of indignation against the increase in the price of transport that was communicated by the social networks and was transformed into a project for a better life through demonstrations that brought the multitudes into the streets in more than 350 cities. (Castells 2013, 178)

The massive protests of June 2013 were not just a Brazilian phenomenon, not just part of the growing surge in social movement in Latin America; they were part of a worldwide movement that had started in Latin America, swept through parts of Europe, North Africa, and the Middle East, and even occupied Wall Street for a while. Some even saw it as a continuation of the popular mobilizations of 1968 (Wallerstein 2013). We even see a direct link to the popular direct democracy that the French *communards* practiced for a short time in Paris in 1871. In the present day, it is a form of radical direct democracy that emphasizes popular, horizontal communication and organization, the use of social media, and the massive occupation of streets and public places (swarming).

FINAL WORDS

By June 17 the people were swarming the streets and public plazas much the same way they had in Spain, Turkey, and the countries of the Arab Spring. Organization was decentralized and done in small groups, but general directions and images were transmitted by cell phone through the social media and also over the Internet. Initial attempts by local governments and the police and the media to repress the protesters were widely disseminated, engendering a strong surge of public support and causing the commercial media to change its coverage. The public backlash against police brutality and solidarity with the protesters and their goals created wide public support for the actions. By June 20, over a million Brazilians had taken to the street in massive actions in cities all over the nation. They were there to protest rising transit fares, poor public health care and education, the high cost of housing, widespread corruption, and the massive use of public funds for new stadiums for the World Cup and Olympics. They had said: Enough!

The force of the people was overwhelming and of such strength that the governments of São Paulo and Rio de Janeiro had to rescind the fare hikes and the national government, which had pressured the local governments to cancel the fare increases, had to listen to the protesters and promise political reform (Romero 2013b, A7). More money for public transportation and education was promised, and a plan to increase the number of physicians in poor areas (bringing in many from Cuba) was unveiled (Rohter 2013, 9). The immediate goals of the protestors had been realized, but there was still significant dissatisfaction with the precipitating conditions. The protests were supported by 75 percent of the population. Many thought that the national government had turned a deaf ear to the people and waited too long to act. President Dilma Rousseff's approval rating fell significantly, and many worried that the PT would do poorly in the next elections. And it did not stop there. The young began another kind of action where they began to swarm the malls. Protests against the stadiums, FIFA, and the World Cup continued into 2014 as the matches drew near, and—for a while—massive numbers of Brazilians seemed ready to once again take to the streets if they were not heard.

NOTES

1. Interview with Florisvaldo de Souza, National Secretary of Organization, Workers Party, by author. Workers Party Headquarters, São Paulo, August 21, 2013.

2. Personalism refers to personal rather than institutional rule; clientelism refers to patron-client relationships, and coronelismo refers to the Brazilian practice of allowing rural notables (usually large land owners not unlike the colonels in the old rural U.S. South) to have unwarranted local power and influence in the state government and legislature and the national legislature.

3. Brazilian Institute of Statistics. *Statistical Report 2001,* as cited from "Pais Termina Anos 90 Tão Desigual como Começou," *Folha de São Paulo* April 5, 2001 (Lewis 2001).

4. Interview with João Paulo Rodriguez, member of the National Directorate and Coordinating Secretary, MST, by author. MST Headquarters, São Paulo, August 13, 2013.

5. Interview with João Paulo Rodriguez, August 13, 2013.

6. Interviews by author of participants in the June protests on Avenida Paulista, São Paulo, August 18, 2013. Those interviewed included a young professional couple who worked in public relations, a lawyer, and a group of young high school age skate boarders.

Chapter Thirteen

Venezuela

Bolivarianism and the Commune

George Ciccariello-Maher

The Bolivarian Revolution currently underway in Venezuela sits at the overlapping intersection of a series of identities—the people, the class, revolutionaries, Chavistas, Bolivarians—and at the tense interplay of forces "from above" and forces "from below."[1] Despite an understandable emphasis on Venezuela's late president, Hugo Chávez Frías, who played a fundamental role in unifying and driving the Bolivarian Revolution forward, the process itself emerged long prior to Chávez the individual. Before Chavismo there was Bolivarianism, a concept that emerged out of the Venezuelan armed struggle to refer not only to the political legacy of the liberator, Simón Bolívar, but also encompassed a broad range of other figures and, more generally, the attempt to rediscover local inspiration for revolutionary change. As Venezuela's corrupt representative-democratic two-party power-sharing agreement known as *puntofijismo* entered into severe crisis in the 1980s, Bolivarianism gained force, helping to gather together the broad range of diffuse social movements that had developed to resist the regime (McCoy 1999). If these social movements provided the motor force for the Bolivarian process, however, this was nevertheless not simply a story of horizontalism, of the gradual accumulation of directly democratic and participatory practices.

Horizontalism, at least in the demand for a more participatory democracy, was indeed one historical horizon of the movements struggling against the corrupt, elite representative democracy. But radical and revolutionary movements in Venezuela have rarely limited the means at their disposal to the strictly horizontal, nor have they refused to engage the state a priori. Instead, the history of those movements coalescing around the Bolivarian process is a

251

history of armed vanguards, coups, mass revolts and riots, strikes, *and* horizontalism, with each of these subjected in turn to critical and strategic assessment. As a result, not all revolutionary or grassroots movements involved in the process could be understood as strictly horizontal in terms of their methods or practices (see Sitrin and Azzellini 2012, 36), but most nevertheless do aspire toward a revolutionized, antihierarchical society based on participatory and directly democratic principles.

In this sense, such movements are *horizon*-tal in the vein of Enrique Dussel's insistence that political postulates serve as *horizons* to orient strategic action. Central among these postulates for the revolutionary left is the "dissolution of the state," and Dussel writes: "We must operate in such a way as to tend toward the (empirically impossible) identity of representation with the represented, in such a way that State institutions become always increasingly transparent, effective, simplified," and, I would add, *unnecessary* (Dussel 2008, 96, 132). It is by aiming at such an impossible and utopian horizon—the total elimination of the gap between representative and represented—that we can "orient praxis toward its goals and to transform institutions, thus fixing a horizon of empirically impossible realization but one that *opens up* a space of practical possibility beyond the current system" (113). In the words of Venezuela's until recently commune minister and current cultural minister, Reinaldo Iturriza, to whom I will return at the end of the chapter, "the imperative is still the progressive reduction of the distance between the institutions and the organized people" (Iturriza 2013). Progress toward this utopian withering away of the Venezuelan state—while very real and inspiring—is both limited in its scope and tenuous, under constant threat both from within Chavismo and from without.

This chapter charts the historical relationship between the decades-long struggle for a Venezuelan revolution, one which eventually hoisted the banner of Bolivarianism, and the much more recent phenomenon that was the spectacular irruption of Chávez into politics. To do so requires disentangling the two threads: Chavismo is not the entirety of the Bolivarian revolutionary movement, and the movement is not simply one that aims at seizing state power. Rather, both Bolivarianism and the Chavista identity that would come to complement it are dialectical constructs that serve to unify and consolidate the popular will of grassroots movements. Chávez in life, and Chavismo after his death, have needed to walk a fine line between horizontalism in the state in order to allow the movement to surge forward through pressure from below, taking aim at the state not merely to seize but also to radically transform it. Gesturing toward the asymptotic extreme of this transformation—Dussel's "dissolution of the state"—in the post-Chávez era, we turn finally to the figure looming so large on the revolutionary horizon: the commune.

BOLIVARIANISM

The process of change currently underway in Venezuela is often referred to as the "Bolivarian Revolution," but this has never been strictly about the figure of the eighteenth-century liberator of Latin America, Simón Bolívar. While Karl Marx's acerbic comments on Bolívar have colored an entire legacy of Marxist derision toward his historical significance, the reemergence of Bolivarianism as an identity within the late stages of the Venezuelan guerrilla struggle in the 1970s was not reducible to either this caricature or the very real limitations of Bolívar, but instead represented an attempt to broadly rethink revolutionary change on the basis of local conditions.[2] While a popular upsurge against the dictatorship of Marcos Pérez Jiménez led to the establishment of formal representative democracy in 1958, this was a heavily mediated and buffered form of democracy whose early leaders were eager to prove their pro-U.S. and anticommunist credentials. When popular movements continued to press the regime, repression ensued, which in turn sparked a guerrilla war in the 1960s. Despite early optimism—fueled in no small part by the success of the Cuban Revolution in 1959—the armed struggle in Venezuela soon stalled, and a period of crisis and reflection ensued.

In the waning days of the guerrilla struggle, and in part due to its failure to resonate with the population, a generation of young revolutionaries, many of them Marxists, found themselves increasingly skeptical of Eurocentric theories of and strategies for revolutionary change, and turned toward more local sources of inspiration. These included religious cult figures like María Lionza, Indigenous groups and caciques renowned for ferociously resisting the Spanish, and rebellious Afro-Venezuelans—free as well as slave—who led resistance to slavery and colonialism, and played major roles in the independence struggle. On the theoretical level, José Carlos Mariátegui's foundational text *Seven Interpretive Essays on Peruvian Reality* was read and re-read as a model for rethinking Marxism on the basis of local conditions (Mariátegui 1971; Vanden and Becker 2011). Last but not least was Simón Bolívar himself, who revolutionaries sought to liberate from the dusty confines of the National Pantheon, reconnecting national liberation with the class struggle.

While widespread, this renewed emphasis on Bolívar and Bolivarianism emerged above all within the Party of the Venezuelan Revolution (PRV), a splinter group of hard-line guerrillas that had refused to leave the mountains when the Communist Party (PCV) withdrew its support. For the PRV, Bolivarianism came to refer to this broad process of breaking with European dogmas to rethink revolutionary change in Latin America in general and Venezuela in particular, and PRV members began to study liberation theology, María Lionza, Mariátegui, and the history of slave rebellions in Venezuela and elsewhere. Much like the syncretic cult to Lionza—whose pantheon encompasses Indigenous caciques, Catholic leaders, Afro-Venezuelan figures, and even Bolívar himself—this new Bolivarianism was transformed by its content to exceed its namesake.

Bolivarianism, moreover, fit well with the PRV's strategy for a "military-civilian alliance" that sought to draw together leftist members of the military with revolutionary social movements to overthrow an increasingly corrupt and violent representative democracy. Thus it was that, under the banner of this renewed Bolivarianism, the PRV connected with disgruntled mid-level officers who in 1983 had formed a conspiratorial grouping known as the Bolivarian Revolutionary Movement (MBR-200). Among others, this group included a young Hugo Chávez.

Chávez was not merely a soldier with a conscience who attempted an isolated coup before then emerging as a popular hero. Rather, understood in the context of the subterranean world of clandestine revolutionary movements, he was part of an organized response to economic crisis, corrupt democracy, state repression, and neoliberalism. When Chávez and others formed the MBR-200, the Venezuelan economy had just entered into a serious crisis marked by the severe devaluation of the bolívar on what is still known as *viernes negro*, or Black Friday (López Maya 2005). As the economy tanked and the state withdrew, revolutionary movements were expanding their reach and threatening to connect to the mass unrest developing in the rapidly expanding barrios. Especially important was the growing connection between a rebellious student movement—which was on the upswing with militant demonstrations in 1987—and the urban poor: many students abandoned the universities to test their street-fighting tactics in the popular trenches of the barrios.

When the state realized the danger of previously isolated revolutionary groups igniting the explosive kindling that had been stacking up around Venezuela's major cities, it responded in kind: to the expanding and broadening aspirations of revolutionaries, the government answered with the broadening of repression to ultimately engulf the poor as a class. On February 27, 1989, poor Venezuelans responded to the imposition of a neoliberal structural adjustment program by rebelling, burning, looting, and taking over cities for nearly a week in what was called the *Caracazo*, before a mass slaughter of up to 3,000 momentarily quelled the revolt (Ciccariello-Maher 2013, 88–104). Chávez, whose elder brother was a member of the PRV, was not ignorant of these developments, and when he and his coconspirators attempted to oust the government of Carlos Andrés Pérez on February 4, 1992, they did so both as a direct response to the *Caracazo*, and with the active support of a multitude of revolutionary movements.[3]

With the coup, and with his fateful words uttered on live television—that they had failed *por ahora*, for now—Chávez stepped consciously and decisively into the breach that the people, in the imagery of Walter Benjamin, had "blasted" open in the "continuum of history" (1968, 261). In his failure, his imprisonment, and later pardon, and above all his promise that the defeat was merely temporary, Chávez's irruption into Venezuelan politics strikingly parallels that of Fidel Castro in Cuba, and in particular Castro's similar insistence in his 1953 trial speech that "history will absolve me." The 1992 coup attempt was but one of many possible responses to this moment of rupture, and its success or failure was not predetermined, but once it did fail, Chávez and his *por ahora*—a promise to supporters and a threat to established elites—became indelible and inescapable focal points around which questions of power coalesced. But if Chávez emerged on the national stage as a political actor in the 1992 coup, Chavismo proper—as a political identity—would only emerge a decade later.

HORIZONTALISM

The guerrilla struggle and its aftermath saw revolutionaries grappling seriously with the limitations of vanguardism and engaging in new experiments in mass organizing. The revolution, as became increasingly clear, would emerge not from small and isolated *focos* of revolutionaries in the mountains, but instead from the participation of the poorest masses of Venezuelans, which had been gathering increasingly rapidly in the barrios surrounding the large cities. It was in part the threat of this fusion of revolutionary elements with the increasingly militant barrio population amid the economic crisis of the 1980s that generated the both the rebellion of 1989 and the slaughter that followed shortly thereafter, but this was not the end of the story.

The period following the repression of the *Caracazo* saw an organic blossoming of popular barrio assemblies, directly democratic and participatory institutions that became the most important expressions of a surging wave of demands for radical change whose spontaneous form had emerged in the *Caracazo*. The PRV was one group among many that participated in the development of these assemblies alongside its conspiratorial role within the military and the MBR-200, and a central figure in the development of assemblies, both on a theoretical and practical level, was PRV *comandante* Kléber Ramírez Rojas. An engineer-turned-militant, born in the Andean state of Mérida, Ramírez was among the first Venezuelan communists to take to the mountains in the guerrilla struggle, and among the last to leave: when the PCV withdrew its support from the armed struggle, he and others remained, establishing the PRV.

For decades, Ramírez was a central if unrecognized contributor to what had become an essential plank of the PRV's program: the establishment of a military-civilian alliance with the potential to carry out a leftist coup in Venezuela. It was this objective as well as Chávez's brother's PRV militancy that brought these soldiers and guerrillas together. Prior to the 1992 coup, Ramírez was even called upon to draft what would have become early government decrees in the event that Chávez and the others successfully seized power (these and other documents are collected in Ramírez Rojas 2006). Soon after the coup's failure, however, and with the seizure of the state momentarily blocked, Ramírez began to have doubts about the strategic usefulness of what he considered an exaggerated horizontalism among popular movements of the time.

In a 1994 essay, Ramírez conceded that horizontal modes of self-organization—which he rooted in the student movement of the mid-1980s—had emerged as a justified and necessary form of "self-defense from the disastrous mediatic, opportunistic, and anti-national influence of the political parties" and therefore represented "a well-deserved social and political accomplishment." However, he insisted that through the fetishization of these dispersed popular assemblies, this "triumph has been converted into its own defeat," by isolating barrio communities from national struggles. These participatory organs, whose horizontalism protected them from political parties, decisively weakening the party system in the process, had nevertheless failed to present an alternative, thereby leaving the political field open to those parties, however discredited.[4] Ramírez concluded that, "From a strategic perspective, horizontality will be necessary for the development of the commoner state; but tactically, at this moment it becomes a serious error because it foments the isolationism of the popular bases from national struggles" (2006, 203).

This was not an argument to abandon the horizontal—far from it. Ramírez was instead urging revolutionaries to think hard about how these dispersed and isolated forces, subsisting and maintaining their autonomy on the basis of horizontal and participatory practices, would be able to unify and coalesce into a new alternative power. No longer a task to be accomplished from above, Ramírez instead saw potential for these grassroots movements—unified and consolidated—to effectively devour the existing state from the ground up, "explod[ing] the straitjacket that the exhausted Gomecista state represents, creating a new state, a commoner state" (2006, 47).[5] This would be a "state" only in the loosest sense of the term: rooted in cooperative, socialist production and directly democratic decision making, Ramírez's "commoner state" would see a "broadening of democracy in which the communities will assume the fundamental powers of the state, electing and recalling their own authorities" (122).

The path toward such a broadening of democracy implied "install[ing] parallel popular powers" in the barrios and communities, thereby "beginning the construction of the new state" from below, from the popular and horizontal movements themselves (Ramírez 141). This was therefore not a call to abolish horizontalism but to *deepen* and consolidate the already existing popular assemblies, alongside the simultaneous development of self-defense structures like the grassroots militias already emerging in the Venezuelan barrios.[6] The result, for Ramírez, would in theory be "a new democracy led by a government of popular insurgency" (207). The tense relationship between horizontalism and the state is embedded within the very idea of the commoner state itself, simultaneously a "government" and its nominal opposite: an "insurgency" of the very sort that Kléber Ramírez himself had previously led against a rotten state. How to combine the two?

CHAVISMO

Suffice it to say that history did not follow the course proposed by Ramírez, at least not on the surface of things. Alongside the deepening of grassroots organs for popular resistance—the "parallel popular powers" of which Ramírez wrote—the Bolivarian movement eventually overcame its allergy to elections, propelling Hugo Chávez to the presidency in January 1999. Against the exaggerated picture common to the mass media and even most scholarly accounts, however, this movement was never strictly about a fidelity to Chávez. In fact, the movement was not even initially "Chavista," and was certainly not reducible to either personalism or verticalism. Rather, Chávez can be understood as playing a major role in the very same sort of political unification that Kléber Ramírez had advocated under the sign of the commoner state. While the existence of this centralizing force *within* the state introduces an undeniable tension and even threat to popular horizontalism, it has nevertheless also facilitated the emergence of a "communal state" that shares much with Ramírez's "commoner state."

As we have seen, the Bolivarian movement both *preceded* Chávez—in the four decades of struggle against the existing liberal-democratic order that paved the way for his appearance—but also crucially *exceeded* Chávez and "Chavismo" as well. The revolutionary movements that cohered around Chávez's presidency did not simply hand over authority to a "leader," but instead sought to use him as a strategic spearhead to break open an increasingly important political space for grassroots organizing that they continued to fill with autonomous practices. In this sense, Chávez played the role of what the philosopher Ernesto Laclau would call an "empty signifier," into which the movements and disaffected members of the population could simultaneously deposit their varying and shifting political demands and aspirations. For Laclau, such broad-based movements need a basis for unity, but any attempt to rigidly fix that basis would paradoxically undermine the movement by excluding its component parts. The need for an empty signifier thus "arises from the need to name an object which is both impossible and necessary," and for Laclau, the concept of "the people"—arguably *the* central identity for the Bolivarian process—is the paradigmatic example (Laclau 2005, 72).

Despite Chávez's unifying function, his ability to symbolically and practically unify diverse and dispersed movements and individuals, he did not accomplish this task single-handedly, but instead did so alongside a series of other such "empty signifiers." For longtime organizer and popular intellectual Roland Denis, the 1999 constitution—written shortly after Chávez's election through a process of popular participation—represents another such signifier:

> Here there was no revolutionary organization that assumed role of driving force. There were only insurrectionary movements—first of the masses (in the uprising of 1989), then of the military (in the coup attempts of 1992). These movements were heterogeneous, dispersed, fragmented. What united them was the project to develop a common foundation—that is to say the constitution. Nobody had been able to centralize this movement around a program, not even Chávez. His leadership is unquestioned, but his ideas were not sufficient to unite the movement. The constitution filled this emptiness. (quoted in Wilpert 2006, 253)

And it bears mentioning that it is not only the concrete content of the constitution that serves to unify, but also a sort of collective pride at having participated in its crafting, a sense by many that this is *our* constitution. Alongside Chávez and the constitution, moreover, the Bolivarian revolutionary movement crafted its unities in the overlapping interplay of a series of painful memories of the past and the *Caracazo* in particular, of identities—the people, the poor, women, Afro, and Indigenous—and aspirational demands like the loose idea that is "twenty-first-century socialism." Into each of these, hopes and dreams are deposited, but more than that, the movement itself is performatively drawn closer and stitched together in the process.[7]

Furthermore, the revolutionary movement *exceeded* Chávez not only in its attachment to these identities, these concrete and often horizontal grassroots practices, and the fact that it was clearly always about more than a single individual. The movement also exceeded Chávez because he was as much the product of the movements as the cause for their success. This was not only because the movements created a space into which Chávez was able to step, but even more so in the transformation of Chávez himself: the Chávez of 1998, a moderate reformer who spoke of a third way between capitalism and socialism, was nowhere to be found especially after the short-lived coup of 2002 and the turn toward socialism in 2006. That the movements exceeded Chávez is also visible, finally, in the nuanced progression of political identities, and specifically in the way that the very idea of "Chavismo" emerged and was filled dialectically with the content provided by the movements.

The former vice president of Venezuela, Elías Jaua, locates the recent origins of the Bolivarian movement in both "the rebellions of the people and the military in 1989 and 1992." But at first, the movement was precisely that: Bolivarian. As late as 2001, "very few people identified themselves as Chavista,"[8] but this all soon came to an end around the 2002 coup against Chávez and the constitution:

> The moment that the dominant elites decided to put an end to this revolutionary experiment, they used their entire arsenal of social hatred against the poor people who followed *Comandante* Chávez. That's how they added the new epitaph "Chavista" . . . to the long and historic list of adjectives used to criminalize the people (scum, hordes, bandits, black trash, thugs etc.).
>
> In reality it was an attempt to strip us of our identity as Bolivarian, it was the oligarchy's final effort to preserve the term Bolivarian within the moldy archives of the Academies of History. However, not only could they not steal from us the essence of the name "children of Bolivar," but we took on the name of Chavistas as well, resignifying it with dignity. (Jaua 2013, n.p.)

It was thus not Chávez and not the movements supporting him that identified as Chavista, but instead the opposition and elites who imposed that identity onto them. This was not, however, a one-way street, and rather than simply conforming to the personalistic contours of the identity, revolutionary movements effectively resignified and transformed the idea through their self-activity into a more direct expression of popular struggles. Just as Bolivarianism exceeded the limitations of Simón Bolívar the individual, so too did Chavismo "transcend" Hugo Chávez, and similar processes of reappropriation and resignification can be tracked with other pejorative terms on the "historic list of adjectives used to criminalize the people" (Jaua 2013). "Chavismo is," in the words of Iturriza, "a universe in which many worlds fit, many forms of recreating the popular world" (Iturriza 2014b).

THE COMMUNE

As the Bolivarian process became increasingly radicalized, demands for increasing the scope of popular power and direct democracy became increasingly vociferous. While the experience of the popular barrio assemblies had not faded, instead merging into a series of informal institutions from "Patriotic Circles" (around 1999) to "Bolivarian Circles" (in the early 2000s), the question remained as to how the popular participatory impetus enshrined in Article 184 of the 1999 constitution would be put into systematic practice. The first major step in this process was the formal recognition of communal councils—directly democratic assemblies with significant decision-making authority on the very local level—in 2006, in some ways making official and granting resources to decades of popular democratic practices.

While more than 40,000 such councils currently exist, today these councils face a challenge that is arguably similar to the limits of horizontalism that Kléber Ramírez had diagnosed in the mid-1990s, albeit on a shifted terrain. The task twenty years ago was to build an alternative power through the coordination and strategic unification of organic, horizontal barrio assemblies as the first step to replacing the traditional state from the outside and from below (Ramírez's "commoner state"). Today, this task has shifted from the realm of the constituent power of the people to the constituted power of state institutions, however decentralized, from the extrainstitutional to having at least one foot in the institutional sphere. The goal is to coordinate and unify the communal councils into a broader power that aims not to replace the state from the outside, but to devour it from within. As a result, if the task previously required the unification of the Bolivarian movement, today it demands in part the consolidation of a revolutionary sector *within* Chavismo, with this struggle within the movement serving as a point of leverage.

Strategically unified and endowed with a participatory political vision, these councils—in alliance with the persistent and pervasive organizations outside the state—can provide a fulcrum for the radicalization of the revolutionary process against more conservative sectors of Chavismo. If Chávez the individual is not present to serve as the unifying instance for this radical vision for Chavismo, radical sectors of the Bolivarian process are nevertheless currently coalescing around one crucial aspect of Chávez's political legacy: the dream, not his alone, of a "communal state." Shortly after his final reelection in October 2012, Chávez gave his last important speech in the form of a wide-ranging and critical televised cabinet meeting. In what has come to be known as his *golpe de timón* (roughly indicating a dramatic shift in direction), Chávez insisted only months before his death that communal power should be at the heart of the Bolivarian project as it moves forward (Chávez 2012). But for popular participation to play this role, the communal councils would need to both grow economic teeth and to gain broader competencies. The figure of the commune envisions both.

Dario Azzellini (2014, 217) describes the emerging communal structure as a "multilevel self-government" in which "nonrepresentative structures for local self-administration—based on assemblies, direct democracy, spokespeople, and higher levels of coordination (the communes and communal cities)" have become increasingly consolidated. This communal state, which is emerging through efforts both from above (from the state) and from below (popular organizations and direct participation), consists of three broad categories. On the most local level we find the communal councils, directly democratic and participatory political organs. Then:

> At a higher level of self-government there is the possibility of creating social-
> ist communes, which can be formed from various communal councils in a

specific territory. . . . These communes can develop medium- and long-term projects of great impact for their locales, while also the decisions concerning the commune continue to be made in the neighborhood assemblies of the communal councils that are part of the commune. Communes can develop projects and planning on a bigger scale. Various communes can form communal cities, with administration and planning from below, if the whole territory is organized in communal councils and communes. (229)

The economic aspect of this consolidation is central: a major limitation of the local councils is their dependency on state funding, which can both limit the ambitiousness of their scope but also subject them to sudden shifts in the direction of the political winds. At the commune level, councils interface directly with several forms of property and production: worker-run cooperatives, state-owned factories, and many forms of social property and comanagement in between. This integration can protect against traditional dangers of cooperatives and worker control when set apart from the local community, while more importantly granting the political claims of the commune more social weight. While the final step of this consolidation—the establishment of socialist cities—still has no basis in law, just as with the councils and communes themselves, these have leapt forward in practice nevertheless in experiments. The first socialist city, Ciudad Caribia, perched in the hills separating Caracas from the coast, was inaugurated more than two years ago; a handful of similar experiments have sprung up across the country, often pressed by social movements like the Ezequiel Zamora National Campesino Front (Azzellini and Ressler 2010).

While the process of building communal councils, communes, and socialist cities has emerged both from above (from the state institutions, or constituted power) and from below (from direct participation and social movements, or constituent power), Azzellini (2014, 218, 237) rightly argues that "the role of the state is deeply ambivalent" due to a "power asymmetry" in favor of the state. Not only do state administrators wield disproportionate political and economic influence in these processes and within the Bolivarian process as a whole, but there is a built-in tendency for such figures to adopt top-down approaches at best, and conservative policies at worst.

These profound and intractable tensions between the "from above" and "from below" have manifested in all instances of popular participation in Venezuela, be they cooperatives (Piñeiro Harnecker 2007), the communal councils (Fox and Leindecker 2008), and the nascent communes themselves (Azzellini and Ressler 2010). Venezuela's National Commoner Network, which was established by the government in 2008 only to declare its autonomy within a year, walks this fine line (Azzellini 2014). Despite the current coexistence between a nascent "communal state" and the liberal-bourgeois state, moreover, this tense relationship that I have elsewhere discussed in terms of "dual power" (Ciccariello-Maher 2013, 234–55) must ultimately be resolved in favor of a communal power that displaces the existing state: "Future Venezuelan socialism is thought to be built based on various council structures that cooperate and converge at a higher level so as to transcend the bourgeois state and replace it with a communal state" (Azzellini 2014, 219).

Despite his own position within the state apparatus, Hugo Chávez played a significant role not only in unifying popular movements against the old regime, but also often as a radical spearhead *within* Chavismo and *against* its more moderate and bureaucratic proponents. It is this space, which draws together the most radical sector of Chavismo as a fulcrum to leverage against governing inertia and the economic self-interest of elites, that has been left vacant with the death of Chávez, and it is this space that the communes must fill in both symbolic and practical terms. As Chavismo enters a phase of heightened contradiction between conservative and radical sectors of the process, there is an increasingly acute need for a consolidated counterweight to the wealth and power of moderate Chavistas and government bureaucrats. This is where the communes enter the picture, walking the fine line between constituent and constituted, power from below and power from above, a form provided by the latter to be filled with revolutionary content by the former. But this task cannot be accomplished as long as the communal councils remain dispersed.

Given this revolutionary affinity between the late Chávez and the communal project—one that he championed tirelessly until his death—it is perhaps unsurprising that Chávez first announced the idea of a "communal state" by referencing a quote from none other than Kléber Ramírez Rojas himself, stating: "The time has come for communities to assume the powers of state, which will lead administratively to the total transformation of the Venezuelan state and socially to the real exercise of sovereignty by society through communal powers" (Ramírez Rojas 2006, 146, cited in Chávez Frías 2010). But while it may seem natural and of course laudable for one late *comandante* to cite another, especially given their prior role as coconspirators, simply doing so does not mean that we have escaped the inherent tensions between the state and participatory social movements.

For Roland Denis, one of Ramírez's younger comrades, the state cannot build the commune that will be its own undoing: "It is not the law that gives the revolutionary Commune permission to enter into history." Against what he deems a "verticalist" and even "feudalist" legislation of the communes from above, Denis insists that communes necessarily emerge "without the law" (Denis 2010, n.p.). In other words, the communal state as a governing project is not simply Kléber Ramírez's commoner state under a slightly modified name. The commoner state, as I have explained, was Ramírez's attempt, from a position outside the state, to theorize the unification and consolidation of existing popular and horizontally organized movements. The establishment of the communal state, by contrast, while not a purely top-

down endeavor, is nevertheless an attempt from above to channel both resources and popular energies toward a communal infrastructure.[9] Neither of
these terms simply drops away faced with the other, however, and it is
instead between the two—and in reference to other forms of direct grassroots
participation—that we can best triangulate the coordinates for a radical popular power in today's Venezuela for which horizontal direct democracy and
what Dussel (2008, 131) calls the "dissolution of the state" operate as political postulates.

In the gaping space left by the death of Chávez, it seemed at least initially
that President Nicolás Maduro would maintain his predecessor's devotion to
the communal project. Maduro soon named a radical—Reinaldo Iturriza—to
head the commune ministry, promised increased attention and resources, and
even affirmed the most radical aspirations of the commune, suggesting that
"We've inherited the structure of the bourgeois government, the bourgeois
state. We need to erect a new structure" (Robertson 2013, n.p.). However,
much can change in Venezuela's complex political atmosphere, and after a
strong result for Chavismo in December 2013 regional elections, many opponents of the Maduro government took to the streets decrying economic hardships and insecurity to demand his ouster. In the context of this destabiliza-
tion effort, many worry that Maduro and his close advisors have opted for the
route of "treasonous pacts" with big business (Denis 2014). But the very fact
that the Maduro government has been caught in the double-bind of the import economy—in which confronting currency and import corruption leads to
empty shelves—only points more directly to the need for a communal economy capable of bypassing the import sector entirely.

It is in this sense that Iturriza, until recently commune minister, under-
stands the tense interplay between institutions and movements in the construction of a Venezuelan communism. Every commune—and there are now
hundreds registered—represents for Iturriza one of many "trenches" in the
struggle to build a peculiarly "toparchic" socialism emerging from a multitude of dispersed points, and indeed the same could be said of the communal
councils themselves (Iturriza 2013).[10] Despite this dispersal, however, those
struggling in these trenches are gaining new confidence every day, with their
claim for the scope of popular power expanding in accordance with—and
indeed ahead of—the establishment of institutions, pressing ever toward
what Iturriza calls the "territorialization of our socialism," and, quoting
Chávez himself, the construction of the "territory of the new" (Iturriza
2014a; Chávez Frías 2012, 16). "More than simply a new instance of participation," Iturriza (2014a, n.p.) argues, "the Commune is the organizational
advance guard of socialist democracy under construction."

As with any "advance guard," the experiences of Venezuela's communards of today are mixed. Many complain of resistance, lack of support, and
even sabotage from above, as well as the occasionally more deleterious dan-

ger of inertia and apathy on the grassroots level. According to one commune organizer in Mérida State, Antonio Portillo,

> There are still difficulties. Sometimes we call a general meeting and only 40% of the community attend, it's a lot of effort to get that many people, normally we just get 15%. There are people in my community who have a negative influence on the process, they tell people that the commune and the communal councils are useless, and the people have to listen to this every single day, and some of them start to believe it. (Pearson 2013, n.p.)

But difficulties aside, the dedication of many revolutionaries to the communal project is gradually growing and becoming consolidated in regional networks and national conferences designed to share experiences and formulate a new path forward. For Portillo:

> I want to build my commune because it's a totally different form of life. I dream about this, about building something with different values. I don't think "commune" is just a word, just another meeting, it's a lot deeper than that. Many of us still aren't clear about what a commune is, it's not an event, it's a new state of things, where there's no exploitation, there's equality, love, simpleness, well-being for all, not just for me and my pocket . . . that's why I fight for it. (Pearson 2013, n.p.)

The task of revolutionaries, for Iturriza (2013), is not so much to lead as to recognize the advanced status of popular movements, and—here echoing the Marx of *The German Ideology*—to "hurry up so that we walk at the rhythm of the real movement," a movement that is itself communism.

NOTES

1. For a recent collection analyzing participation in contemporary Venezuela, see Smilde and Hellinger 2011. For a more recent comparative view of the tension between "from above" and "from below," see Ellner 2014.

2. Among these real limitations, it is worth mentioning that for much of his early career, Bolívar stood on the side of the wealthy, white *Mantuano* elite and against the aspirations of Indigenous people, slaves, and the poor. The danger of Bolivarianism as an identity lay precisely in the obscuring of the real tensions within and beyond the independence movement around these questions, dangers that resonate in the current tension between national liberation and revolutionary socialism. This reemergence of Bolivarianism placed this *prócer* of independence alongside local religious cults, Afro and Indigenous leaders, and critical Marxists in the vein of José Carlos Mariátegui (see Ciccariello-Maher 2013, 48–50). For Marx's critique of Bolívar, see Marx 1858.

3. There is much debate over the balance between military and civilian actors in the February coup. According to some movement organizers, the soldiers did not trust or support the civilian side enough; according to some soldiers, the radical movements failed to live up to their promise of mass support in the streets.

4. Two parties in particular attempted to fill this space: first the Movement Toward Socialism (MAS) and later the more innovative Radical Cause. Both, however, suffered the fate of participating in a discredited political system, and lost support as a result, clearing the way for

Chávez as an "anti-party" alternative. On the MAS, see Ellner 1988; on Radical Cause, see Buxton 2001.

5. The "*Estado Gomecista*" refers to dictatorship of Juan Vicente Gómez, who ruled Venezuela directly or indirectly from 1908 to 1935. This period saw the modernization of the state and military apparatus and the centralization of authority, alongside an obedient openness to the interests of U.S. capital.

6. I have argued elsewhere that these assemblies and militias can be understood in terms of Lenin's discussion of dual power, which itself draws upon the example of the Paris Commune (Ciccariello-Maher 2013, conclusion).

7. Dussel (2008, 72) would call this, departing slightly from Laclau, a process of dialogue and translation.

8. A LexisNexis search would seem to confirm this, showing almost no news results for "Chavismo" or "Chavista" prior to 2002.

9. While it is true that Ramírez uses both "commoner state" (*estado comunero*) and "communal state" (*Estado Comunal*), he uses the latter only once and capitalizes it as a proper noun. Chávez, however, referred almost exclusively to the communal state, and given the prevalence of the term *comunero* among grassroots movements like the National Commoner Network, it seems justified to see *comunero* as referring *tendentially* to the "from below" and *comunal* as referring *tendentially* to the "from above." It is worth noting that the until recently commune minister, Reinaldo Iturriza, who has so consistently sought to immerse his work in popular struggles, also speaks of the "commoner state" (Iturriza 2014a).

10. According to Azzellini (2014, 221), Bolívar's mentor Simón Rodríguez introduced the concept of toparchy, which refers to "a confederation of local self-governed communities," as a counterweight to excessive centralization.

Chapter Fourteen

Ecuador

*Correa, Indigenous Movements, and the Writing of a
New Constitution*

Marc Becker

On September 28, 2008, voters in Ecuador approved a new constitution by a
wide margin. This was the country's twentieth constitution since becoming
an independent republic in 1830, almost matching Latin America's record of
twenty-six in Venezuela. Under the guidance of the young and charismatic
president, Rafael Vicente Correa Delgado, the constitution promised to bring
an end to neoliberal policies that had shifted wealth from marginalized peoples to elite corporate interests. "Today Ecuador has decided on a new nation," Correa declared. "The old structures are defeated. This confirms the
citizens' revolution" (Partlow and Küffner 2008). Supporters of this "citizens' revolution" hoped that the new constitution would lessen inequality,
foster social justice, and bring stability to the chronically volatile South
American country.

Whereas Correa wanted to usher in a citizens' revolution, Indigenous
organizations appealed for a constituent revolution that would embrace the
country's plurinational nature. They had long pressed for mechanisms to
make the country's social, political, and economic landscape more inclusionary and participatory. When Correa made a call for a constituent assembly a
central tenet of his 2006 presidential campaign, Indigenous leaders resented
his hijacking of one of their principal demands. Despite his leftist reputation
and broad popular support, social movements became concerned that Correa
was occupying political spaces that they had previously held, and would use
these spaces to advance his personal power rather than the broader interests
of society.

Correa had initially discussed forming an alliance with the Indigenous-led Movimiento Unidad Plurinacional Pachakutik (MUPP, United Plurinational Pachakutik Movement—often referred to as Pachakutik) in his presidential campaign. Some observers dreamt of a shared ticket between Correa and a historic Indigenous leader. Indigenous activists wanted to put their leader in the presidential slot, but Correa refused to consider running as vice president. This dispute quickly led to a breakdown in the dialogue. Correa subsequently resented Indigenous movements for their refusal to support his candidacy, and in response one of the most organized sectors of civil society always held the popular president at arm's length.

Indigenous movements gained strength by organizing on a participatory model that was designed to empower the grassroots rather than following a vertical, top-down command structure. The largest federation, the Confederación de Nacionalidades Indígenas del Ecuador (CONAIE, Confederation of Indigenous Nationalities of Ecuador), grouped the country's fourteen Indigenous nationalities into a recognizable force for social justice. In an attempt to maintain tight connections between leadership structures and rural communities, the CONAIE prohibited leaders from serving more than two terms in office or from simultaneously holding a government post. Over the previous two decades, the CONAIE had emerged as the leading force behind street mobilizations that repeatedly pulled down neoliberal governments. Although representing a minority of the population (estimates ranged from 7 to 40 percent of the country's inhabitants, varying according to the definitions and political interests of those who did the counting), as the best organized sector of society, Indigenous peoples gained political significance well beyond their limited numbers.

Correa, in contrast, emerged out of a liberal framework that emphasized individual rights. This was a citizens' revolution, Correa declared, not one built by social movements. CONAIE president Marlon Santi complained that Correa's emphasis on individual rights and the idea of a "universal citizen" excluded Indigenous peoples, with their communal-based societies. His citizens' revolution deemphasized social movements and reinforced colonial and liberal ideologies that oppressed and erased the unique histories of Indigenous nationalities. Indigenous activists forwarded instead a counterdiscourse that emphasized collective control over land and natural resources. The Indigenous intellectuals Luis Fernando Chimba Simba and Laura Santillán (2008, 4) called Correa's policies a new form of colonization. The sociologist Mario Unda said, "Correa wants his own social base and he is mistrusted by organized grassroots, especially those that have the most ability to mobilize" (Saavedra 2007a, 5). Correa and Indigenous leaders increasingly clashed over their competing attempts to organize the grass roots.

The 2008 constituent assembly provided a critical juncture for Indigenous movements by opening up a historic opportunity to decolonize the country's political structures. Could activists exploit the openings that the drafting of a new constitution provided to advance their interests and political agenda? "The democratic phase in which we have lived to this point," the CONAIE's regional affiliate organization Ecuarunari (2007, 4) argued, "has allowed that a few become wealthy while the majority are impoverished as a result of unemployment, migration, lack of access to resources and services. All of this," Ecuarunari continued, "has been aided and legalized by 19 constitutions written in 177 years of republican history." Eighty percent of the Ecuadorian population was poor and excluded from the political process. It was necessary to refound the Ecuadorian state on the basis of the people's collective force so that the government would respond to their needs. Assembly president Alberto Acosta echoed these sentiments with pledges that the assembly would be more inclusive than any previous government and would incorporate the concerns of Indigenous peoples, Afro-Ecuadorians, and others who lacked representation (*Latin American Weekly Report* 2007b, 2).

Correa's relations with Indigenous movements point to the complications, limitations, and deep tensions inherent in pursuing revolutionary changes within a constitutional framework. "A regime that limits and at the same time consolidates the power of the oppressors entails a great challenge for the left," the political scientist Claudio Katz (2007, 37) argues, "especially when this structure is seen by the majority as the natural *modus operandi* of any modern society." Activists noted the important role of civil society in advancing the constitutional process. "In order to realize governmental changes," the Indigenous leader Luis Macas emphasized, "it is necessary to have a mobilized social force such as we have that will guarantee these changes" (Comunicación Pachakutik 2006, 3). This strategy paralleled what the political scientist George Ciccariello-Maher (2013) observes in the Venezuelan case, in which the transformation of political structures required the simultaneous actions of a centralized state power from above and popular initiatives of organized social movements from below. Although Indigenous movements, as well as most social movements, shared Correa's stated desire to curtail neoliberal policies and implement social and economic policies that would benefit the majority of the country's people, they increasingly clashed over how to realize those objectives. The political outcome of the new constitution depended not only on the actions of the constituent assembly but also on whether organized civil society could force the government to implement the ideals that the assembly drafted.

THE CONSTITUENT ASSEMBLY

On April 15, 2007, over 80 percent of the Ecuadorian electorate approved a referendum to convoke a constituent assembly. In no small part, the success of the referendum was due to the support of Indigenous communities. "It is a victory for the Indigenous movement," Humberto Cholango (2007a, 3), president of Ecuarunari, declared, "the triumph of all of the accumulated histories of the Indigenous and popular social struggles in Ecuador." Cholango argued that political parties had failed, people were ready for a change, and now was the hour of social movements; the victory of the referendum represented a rejection of the neoliberal economic model that concentrated wealth and power in the hands of a few privileged people. Cholango (2008a, 61–62) urged the implementation of social policies to increase funding for education, fight illiteracy and discrimination, and improve health care. He embraced a political project to end inequality and discrimination. A new constitution represented the beginning of "a truly profound change." Hopes ran high among social movements that this was the political opening that they had long desired. Although the oligarchy, as in most of Latin America, maintained control over most of the country's political and economic mechanisms, the balance of forces definitely seemed to be shifting to the left.

In the subsequent September 30, 2007, elections for deputies to the constituent assembly, Correa consolidated his political control by winning a majority of seats, thereby ensuring that a new constitution would be to his liking. He had campaigned alone for the presidency, but now he built up a new political movement called Alianza País (AP, Country Alliance). AP won almost 70 percent of the vote for the assembly, far outpacing its nearest rival, former president Lucio Gutiérrez's Partido Sociedad Patriótica (PSP, Patriotic Society Party), with barely 7 percent. The AP was a very loose and diverse grouping of social-movement activists, academics, and nongovernmental organization (NGO) leaders, and holding the coalition together represented a challenge. In part, its margin of victory was due to some activists who broke from Pachakutik and joined Correa's party. Mónica Chuji, one of the more radical members of Correa's AP coalition, declared her allegiance to the CONAIE and the social movements out of which she emerged: "I owe the Indigenous movement, and my behavior in the assembly will be in that direction" (Saavedra 2007b, 2). Pedro de la Cruz, the president of the Confederación Nacional de Organizaciones Campesinas, Indígenas y Negras (FENOCIN, National Confederation of Peasant, Indigenous, and Negro Organizations), who had been an alternative congressional deputy for the Socialist Party from 1998 to 2003, also won election as a delegate to the assembly from the AP. Many Indigenous activists believed that they could most effectively influence the content of the new constitution by working within Correa's government.

Leftist parties and social movements did not fare any better than their conservative opponents in gaining seats in the assembly. Since its founding in 1996, Pachakutik consistently polled about 10 percent of the vote (Mijeski and Beck 2011). In elections for the constituent assembly, however,

Pachakutik won only four seats and together with the traditional parties was increasingly left behind as a marginalized and irrelevant political force. Even this showing was a bit of a surprise, as earlier polls had indicated that Pachakutik might not win any seats in the assembly (*Latin American Weekly Report* 2007a, 11). The public seemingly lumped Pachakutik together with the rest of the discredited political class as part of the country's problem. "Despite its scathing criticisms of the country's traditional parties and its goal to profoundly change Ecuador's politics," Mijeski and Beck (2008, 54) note, Pachakutik "has simply become another maligned party whose interest in patronage outweighs its commitment to social justice." Its previous promises to create a new type of politics seemed to be falling apart.

Correa's former energy minister, the well-known and highly regarded economist Alberto Acosta, led the AP ballot. He won the most votes in the September 30 elections and with this support was elected president of the assembly. In this role Acosta (2008, 17) sought "to construct a truly democratic society, underscored with the values of freedom, equality, and responsibility." His vision for a new society included spaces for both individuals and community concerns, where "economic rationality would be reconciled with ethics and common sense." Acosta pledged to work under the principle of *sumak kawsay*, the Kichwa concept of living well, not just living materially better. It included an explicit critique of traditional development strategies that increased the use of resources rather than seeking to live in harmony with others and with nature. Not only did *sumak kawsay* forward a radical critique of development strategies while endorsing alternatives based on the rights of nature, it also expanded conceptions of the community, plurinationality, and Indigenous cosmologies. It broke from a consumptionist model of material accumulation, and instead provided a new way of thinking about human relations that was not based on exploitation (Gudynas 2011; Walsh 2010). "Western development is concerned only with politics and economics," the Pachakutik delegate Carlos Pilamunga stated. "We are also concerned with cultural elements, plurinationality, and the environment." *Sumak kawsay* advocated modifying state structures in order to "search for harmony between people and nature" (*El Comercio*, June 29, 2008). Acosta's leadership in the assembly gained him a good deal of popular support even as social movements became increasingly alienated from Correa.

While these electoral victories represented major personal triumphs for Correa, they left the social movements feeling marginalized from the political changes sweeping the country. Even though Correa denied that he was engaging in a cult of personality, from the perspective of the social movements the consolidation of power in the hands of a strong and seemingly egotistical executive meant that they would lose access to the spaces necessary to press their own agendas (Lucas 2007, 232). Correa made it clear that he would not be held accountable to the corporatist social movements—that it was those who won elections, not those who mobilized street protests and toppled governments, who had the right to rule. Correa's leftist opponents complained that his approach privileged liberal, individualistic politics and that decision-making processes in the AP were highly centralized and even authoritarian. As political scientist Susan Spronk (2008, 43) notes, Correa "acted in a more strategic, although highly 'top-down,' fashion" than Evo Morales's Movimiento al Socialismo (MAS, Movement Toward Socialism) in Bolivia. While this approach may be more successful, Spronk cautioned, "any spaces opened by the new constitution are unlikely to foment true structural change unless they build upon the energy of organized forms of popular participation, that is, of social movements." Indigenous activists feared that Correa's victories would come at their expense.

Despite these concerns, Pachakutik's political coordinator, Jorge Guamán, pledged its support to Correa and the assembly. It would organize meetings in rural communities where its supporters lived to monitor the assembly's progress (*El Comercio*, October 28, 2007). Ecuarunari (2007, 4) declared, "We are fighting in the Constituent Assembly for a true democracy in which all of us have the rights to decent work, education, health with dignity, identity, and access to communal and individual property." Achieving these goals, the Indigenous federation contended, "would only be possible if as peoples and nationalities we are able to gain a broad representation of popular sectors in the Constituent Assembly but also maintain an organized struggle with everyone mobilized." Constituent assemblies could lead to positive changes, but only if people made this happen. The political commentator Guillermo Almeyra (2008, n.p.) calls a constitution "a piece of paper in the barrel of a cannon" that depends upon a relation of social forces to bring it into being. It is not sufficient to approve laws, Almeyra argues, unless there is appropriate pressure to force the government to implement them. This pressure comes not only from the electoral realm, but also from the presence of an organized and mobilized social movement.

INDIGENOUS AGENDAS

Indigenous leaders emphasized that the revisions they had proposed to Ecuador's constitution would benefit everyone in the country, not just Indigenous peoples. As Leon Zamosc (2007, 28) notes, "Indigenous struggles in Latin America falsify the basic tenets of the 'new social movements' approach." Rather than privileging the more limited and sometimes fundamentally conservative identity politics of cultural affirmation and ethnic rights, Indigenous organizations in Ecuador have embraced a class struggle that engages "broader battles over social issues and political power." First and foremost, Indigenous activists emphasized the importance of political changes, specifically the primary and continuing demand for acknowledgment of the plurinational character of the Ecuadorian state. This meant not only recognition of fourteen Indigenous nationalities but also acknowledgment that their systems of life, education, and economy were different from those of the dominant society. Being a nationality meant having one's own territory, language, history, and culture. Among their specific and concrete proposals, Ecuarunari and CONAIE (2007, 6–7) urged direct representation of Indigenous and Afro-Ecuadorian nationalities in the national congress, with each nationality internally selecting one delegate, and the renaming of the national congress as the "Asamblea Plurinacional Legislativa" (Plurinational Legislative Assembly).

In the economic realm, activists argued that the neoliberal model was not the proper one for Ecuador. The extractive economy was damaging to the environment and society. Mining, in particular, harmed local communities in their struggles for land, life, and biodiversity and their very survival. Production and resource extraction that did not serve a social function needed to be stopped (Kuecker 2008). Social movement pressure led to the inclusion in the constitution of the innovative concept of the rights of nature that extended beyond an anthropocentric vision of society. In addition, previous governments had ignored the domestic agrarian economy. Emphasis needed to be placed on small and medium-sized producers rather than on large corporate and agribusiness interests. Concretely, activists pressed for replacing the U.S. dollar as legal tender in Ecuador with a regional currency as a step toward reclaiming sovereignty over monetary policy. They also called for nationalization of natural resources, governmental support for microcredit, and equal rights for women. Access to water was a human right, and the new constitution should declare it to be a social good and a strategic resource whose commodification and privatization would be prohibited. Water should be used first to meet human needs and to guarantee food sovereignty before being apportioned for industrial needs. Similarly, land needed to be used for the common good, and large concentrated landholdings should be broken up. In addition to the political and administrative division of Ecuador into provinces, cantons, and parishes, Ecuarunari and CONAIE (2007, 7–11) proposed the addition of a fourth level, communal territories governed by local community governments.

Socially, the activists argued, Ecuador needed to rethink the way people were organized. Modernity had not benefited Indigenous communities. The country faced an extreme outmigration that needed to be addressed. Education through high school should be free, secular, obligatory, and bilingual in both Spanish and an (unnamed) Indigenous language. Universal health care should also be a right. The rights of community media should also be protected, including granting Indigenous peoples, Afro-Ecuadorians, and other popular sectors preference in acquiring radio frequencies (CONAIE 2007a,

21). Women should have full and equal rights, including provisions for maternity leave and the protection of young children. Social security, Indigenous activists declared, was an inalienable right. Finally, informal workers and domestic employees should be protected (Ecuarunari and CONAIE 2007, 11–12).

On an international level, Indigenous organizations wanted the country ruled according to the principles of peace, sovereignty, solidarity, and dignity. This would mean, in particular, evicting the United States from the Manta Airbase that it used as a forward operating location for intervention in the civil conflict in neighboring Colombia. The government should guarantee and protect the rights of immigrants. Finally, foreign debts should be declared to be illegitimate and unpayable (Ecuarunari and CONAIE 2007, 11–14). Many activists looked to what Hugo Chávez had done as president of Venezuela as a model for the type of political changes they desired in Ecuador. Indigenous leaders had long worked with the Bolivian social movement leader Evo Morales in their transnational organizing efforts, and when he won the presidency many in Ecuador applauded him as their Indigenous president.

Once the constituent assembly was in session, it became increasingly apparent that it would provide little possibility of fundamental societal change. The government engaged in much talk but very little action, and as a result positive reforms would largely be the result of social movement pressure. The delegates could have engaged pressing issues of mining and petroleum extraction, but they enacted few concrete proposals to deal with these concerns. During the 2006 presidential campaign, the CONAIE leader and Pachakutik presidential candidate Luis Macas said that, in contrast with Correa's, his was "not a three-month project." He went on to explain: "Our political project has a long history, built with years of struggle and humility, not with words, much less with vanity. Correa will pass as [Lucio] Gutiérrez passed, as all presidents and presidential candidates pass; the Indigenous movement will stay" (Saavedra 2006, 1–2). Correa was skilled at manipulating movements, and activists feared that spaces were closing for social movements. Strengthening the executive meant co-opting social movements. Increasingly, many leaders argued that they could organize more effectively as a social movement outside of the government than by joining Correa's project.

PLURINATIONALISM

Indigenous activists had long and repeatedly called for a constituent assembly that would rewrite Ecuador's constitution to create a more inclusionary political system. One of their primary and constant demands was to rewrite the first article of Ecuador's constitution to declare the plurinational nature of the country, something that previous constitutional assemblies had refused to do. Ever since the 1990 Indigenous uprising that launched Indigenous concerns onto the national stage, activists had complained that dominant sectors of society had drafted the current constitution to benefit their own interests to the detriment of those of the majority of the population (Ospina 2007). The 1998 constitution, similar to ones in Colombia, Mexico, and Venezuela, had defined Ecuador as "pluricultural and multiethnic" but stopped short of the more politically charged term "plurinational." Donna Lee Van Cott (2002, 60) notes that the CONAIE strategically backed down on its long-standing and highly symbolic demand to declare Ecuador a plurinational country in exchange for the "recognition of collective rights that effectively constituted their vision of pluri-nationalism." Instead of identifying Indigenous peoples as nationalities, the 1998 constitution stated that they "define themselves as nationalities." Van Cott (2003, 63) argues that "Indigenous delegates conceded on terminology in exchange for substantive and symbolic rights with which they could continue their struggle." But the 1998 constitution failed to deliver on its promises, and this led the Indigenous movements to return to their key central demand.

In October 2007, just before the assembly was to begin its work, the CONAIE (2007b) released a draft of what it would like to see included in the new constitution. The proposal began with the statement "Ecuador constitutes a plurinational, sovereign, communitarian, social and democratic, independent, secular, solidarity, unitary state with gender equality." The constituent assembly refused to lead its definition of Ecuador with the term "plurinational" as the CONAIE advocated, but for the first time it incorporated this word into its text. Article 1 now declared that Ecuador was a "constitutional state of rights and justice, social, democratic, sovereign, independent, unitary, intercultural, plurinational, and secular" (República del Ecuador, 2008). Indigenous movements had finally realized their goal.

Tucked into these debates were disagreements over what "plurinationalism" meant. The CONAIE wanted plurinationalism to empower Indigenous peoples, including granting them control over commercial enterprises on their lands. In making this demand, the CONAIE drew on international law as codified in the International Labor Organization Convention 169 that stipulated the need for prior consultation with Indigenous communities before commencing the extraction of natural resources from their lands. As Maximilian Viatori and Gloria Ushigua (2007, 15) note, activists embraced the discourse of plurinationalism "to stress the systemic discrimination under which Indigenous people suffer and to pressure the state to recognize Indigenous rights that would balance historical inequities in the distribution of resources." Theodore Macdonald (2002, 184) emphasizes that the goal of pursuing this policy was "inclusion as equals in a plurinational state." Conservatives feared that the doctrine of plurinationality would create "quasi-ministates in which the Ecuadorian state could not exercise its sovereignty" (*El Comercio,* July 6, 2008). AP delegates wished to leave the term vaguely defined, essentially ensuring that it would remain on the level of rhetoric without any significant substance or concrete implications.

Even among Indigenous activists the significance of plurinationalism was hotly debated, with those allied with the CONAIE most interested in pressing the issue. Pedro de la Cruz, an AP delegate and president of the competing FENOCIN, remained skeptical of the practicality of the concept of plurinationality, stressing interculturality instead (*El Comercio,* March 23, 2008). In contrast, for the CONAIE's regional affiliate Ecuarunari (2007, 4), "plurinationalism means building a strong and sovereign state that recognizes and makes possible the full exercise of collective and individual rights and promotes equal development for all of Ecuador and not only for certain regions or sectors." It denied that plurinationalism meant creating a state within a state. Rather, it was "a democratic rupture that permits the organization and social control over public goods and the state, in this way surpassing the neocolonial system that marginalizes and subjects people." The CONAIE (2007a, 5) contended that this communitarian form of government was not a mechanism for guaranteeing undue special privileges. Furthermore, the Indigenous federation emphasized that plurinationalism would be part of a unitary state. It would "strengthen a new state through the consolidation of unity, destroying racism and regionalism as a necessary prerequisite for social and political equality, economic justice, direct and participatory democracy, communitarianism, and interculturality" (Ecuarunari and CONAIE 2007, 5). Plurinationalism would benefit everyone in the country.

The Indigenous intellectual Luis Maldonado Ruiz (2008, 4-6) defines plurinationalism as "the legal and political recognition of cultural diversity," reflecting people with "differentiated historical entities who share common values, particular identities, forms of social and political organization, historical origin, and language." Plurinationalism challenged previous governmental attempts to divide Indigenous peoples, de-ethnicize them through labels such as "peasants," or denigrate them with racist terms such as "savages," "naturals," "tribes," "hordes," and "ethnics." For these reasons, Maldonado argues, "it was necessary for Indigenous peoples to look to the language and conceptual development of the social sciences of the dominant class for a concept that provides the best expression of their sociopolitical reality." Maldonado proceeds to define three key elements of a plurinational state. First is the recognition of the diversity of peoples and cultures, including respect for different visions of development and social and political organization. This would require "recognition of two political subjects and rights, that of citizenship and of nationalities or peoples." The second element requires the transformation of the state and hegemonic powers. "Incorporating nationalities and peoples into the new state implies the abolition of all forms of oppression, exploitation, and exclusion," Maldonado argues. Plurinational- ism "should have as its objective the decolonization of the country and the state, permitting a just and egalitarian participation." Finally, he argued that a plurinational state requires an interculturality that implies respect among different nationalities, peoples, and cultures. A plurinational state, Maldona- do concludes, would end systems of domination and replace them with rela- tions of equality.

Mónica Chuji (2008b, 14, 16) considered a plurinational state to be "a new form of a social contract that respects and harmonizes the rights of Indigenous peoples and nationalities with the judicial structure and political force to recognize their status as political subjects with clear rights." Such a state would "recognize and guarantee the exercise, application, and force of the fundamental rights" of Indigenous peoples and nationalities. She empha- sized that plurinationalism would not mean the dissolution of the Ecuadorian state or its fragmentation into autonomous groups. Rather, she stressed, pluri- nationalism proposes "unity in diversity" (Chuji 2008a, 55). Plurinationality is critical for Indigenous peoples, Cholango (2007b, 1) argued, because "we no longer want to speak only of democracy." Rather, he maintained, "we should decolonize democracy and get rid of the colonial obscurity that has lasted for more than 514 years." Only by shedding a "false democracy with folkloric characteristics" will a "real democracy" emerge (Cholango 2008a, 64). Embracing plurinationalism is necessary to realize a true democracy.

Was the inclusion of the term plurinational a symbolic or concrete victory for Ecuador's Indigenous rights movements? The CONAIE (2007a, 2) argued that plurinationalism should not remain on the level of a formal paper declaration, but instead contribute to a fundamental change in the structure of the state that would lead to the "decolonization of our nations and peoples." In the end, its importance would be determined by whether social movement activists could mobilize sufficient political pressure to make language rights part of a fundamental opening up of Ecuador's historically exclusionary state structures rather than simply a cultural advance.

INDIGENOUS LANGUAGES

In addition to plurinationalism, another struggle in the constituent assembly was whether Kichwa and other Indigenous languages would be granted offi- cial status. In laying out its proposals for the new constitution, the CONAIE (2007a, 21–22) argued that "it is impossible to promote those languages (and with them those cultures and their other ways of understanding the world) if there is not a national and collective effort." If this goal remained only an Indigenous concern, it would never be realized. "Interculturality is a matter for all Ecuadorians," the federation declared. "When a language is lost a vision of the world also disappears," and that would be a blow to the entire country. At 1 a.m. in the middle of a final marathon session on July 19, 2008, under instructions from Correa, the AP-controlled assembly voted against Acosta's proposal to grant Kichwa official status. In response, the Pachakutik delegates and AP ally Mónica Chuji walked out of the session (*El Comercio*, July 20, 2008). That vote against Kichwa faced an immediate and visceral reaction from Indigenous organizations. Ecuarunari's Cholango called the assembly's action racist, and the CONAIE's Santi called Correa a racist. Correa retorted that in much of the country learning English was more important than learning Kichwa (*El Comercio*, July 23, 2008). Indigenous languages became central to debates regarding what kind of country delegates wished to see developed.

At 2 a.m. on July 24, under the guidance of the FENOCIN's de la Cruz, the assembly revised the proposed constitutional text to say "Spanish is the official language of Ecuador; Spanish, Kichwa, and Shuar are official languages for intercultural relationships. Other ancestral languages are for official use for Indigenous peoples in the areas they inhabit and on the terms that the law stipulates. The State will respect and will stimulate their conservation and use" (*El Comercio*, July 25, 2008). To all appearances, the last-minute inclusion of Kichwa in the constitution was either a concession or a sop to the Indigenous organizations to gain their support for the document. Rumors swirled that Correa's allies wanted to include Shuar, the third most important language in Ecuador but one spoken largely only in the southeastern Amazon and neighboring Peru, in order to undercut Kichwa, the Ecuadorian variant of the pan-Andean Quechua language and the only Indigenous language that could legitimately be considered for use on a countrywide basis (Denvir, 2008). Even though the text recognized the importance of Indigenous languages, activists criticized it for stopping short of granting them official status equal to Spanish. These editorial revisions demonstrated that it was easier to make minor cultural concessions than to create more inclusive social and economic systems.

In reality, as with the wording with plurinationality, the constitutional text on Indigenous languages was largely adopted from the CONAIE's October 2007 draft proposal. That recommendation read, "Spanish and Kichwa are the official languages for intercultural relations. The other languages of the nationalities are official in the regions and areas of their use and comprise part of the national culture" (CONAIE, 2007b). Despite Indigenous complaints, the draft constitution did include precisely the same construction of Spanish and Kichwa as "official languages for intercultural relations" that the CONAIE had originally proposed and even took it one step further with the inclusion of the dominant language in the southeastern Amazon. Furthermore, this text was not significantly different from that of the 1998 constitution, which recognized Kichwa, Shuar, and other ancestral languages as official for the use of Indigenous peoples. Removing Shuar would have been a step backward, but retaining it was little more than maintaining the status quo rather than advancing Indigenous rights. In addition, the phrase "official languages for intercultural relations" remained very vague, and the specific ramifications of its implementation would only later emerge through the secondary legislation.

Why did the CONAIE oppose the constitution's constructions on Indigenous languages? Criticizing the text may have been an almost automatic response for an organization that had spent years working in the framework of oppositional politics. It also emerged out of frustration and deepening antagonism toward the Correa government, and raised questions of whether these statements were just ideological positioning or whether they were part of a serious political agenda. CONAIE's actions also highlight tensions between social movements and elected officials over what policies to implement and how they should be implemented. While on occasion these objectives and strategies coincided, often they pulled activists in two different directions.

COLLECTIVE RIGHTS

The CONAIE demanded that, in addition to acknowledging Ecuador's plurinational character and embracing Indigenous languages, the new constitution maintain and expand the collective rights for Indigenous peoples and Afro-Ecuadorians codified in the 1998 constitution. While that document referred to "Indigenous peoples who self-identify as nationalities of ancestral races," chapter 4 of the new constitution explicitly recognized the collective rights of "communities, peoples, and nationalities." Article 56 stated that "Indigenous communities, peoples, and nationalities, Afro-Ecuadorians, *montuvios* [poor coastal peasants], and *comunas* [Indigenous communities] form part of the unified, indivisible Ecuadorian state." The following Article 57 "recognizes and guarantees Indigenous *comunas*, communities, peoples, and nationalities in conformity with the constitution and agreements, conventions, and declarations and other international human rights instruments for the protection of collective rights." These rights include those of embracing an ethnic identity, being free of racial discrimination, holding communal territories, and protecting natural resources (República del Ecuador 2008). In arguing for these additions the CONAIE (2007a, 19) declared that it "was necessary to rethink Ecuador from an inclusionary perspective instead of one of subordination," and to remake a country in which "all have the right to live according to their traditional customs." Social movement pressure was necessary for the imple-

mentation of the constitution's promises of significant and dramatic gains for
Indigenous aspirations.

MINING

In November 2007, just as the assembly began its work on the constitution, a
simmering dispute at the biologically sensitive and diverse Yasuní National
Park boiled to the surface. In the town of Dayuma, local inhabitants protesting oil exploitation seized control of several oil wells, demanding support for
economic development and environmental protections for Indigenous communities. Correa responded in a heavy-handed fashion, deploying the military to stop the dissidents and accusing the protesters of being unpatriotic
saboteurs. He complained that "infantile environmentalists" were creating
obstacles to economic development. The government arrested forty-five people and charged them with terrorism for attempting to disrupt petroleum
extraction. After protests from human rights activists, Correa finally lifted
the state of emergency that he had imposed, though the government kept
twenty-three activists in detention. In March 2008 the assembly granted amnesty to 357 dissidents facing criminal charges for their actions in the defense of the environment from mining and petroleum extraction (INREDH
2008).

For some, this repressive response showed Correa's true colors. The Indigenous think tank Instituto Científico de Culturas Indígenas (Institute for
Indigenous Sciences and Cultures 2008, 8) criticized Correa for a betrayal
that showed "signs of subscribing to the most radical proposals of colonial
territoriality in recent years." This included his desire to open spaces to
mining, privatize biodiversity, and increase petroleum extraction. In response, Correa called on his opponents to respect the law. "No more strikes,
no more violence," he said. "Everything through dialogue, nothing by force"
(Saavedra 2008, 4). He indicated that he would not be swayed by social
movement pressure.

A hotly debated topic was whether local communities would have the
right to accept or reject resource extraction on their lands. In a May 2008
letter, the CONAIE (2008, 8) demanded that Indigenous communities be
consulted on any mining on their lands. The Indigenous organizations, of
course, wished to maintain control over their territory, while Correa wanted
to maintain the right to decide when and where mining operations would take
place. In the end, the constitution conceded that communities had the right to
consultation, but extractive endeavors would not be subject to their consent
or veto. This decision was a major blow to the aspirations of Indigenous and
environmental activists.

Debates over mineral extraction once again surfaced in January 2009, when the interim congress approved a new mining law. Correa believed that the law would create new jobs and help grow the economy. Opponents denounced the government for not requiring prior approval from rural communities before commencing mining activities on their lands. They also complained about a lack of adequate environmental safeguards, and argued that the law was unconstitutional because it contradicted provisions of the new constitution that protected the environment and Indigenous rights. Chuji denounced the law as a neoliberal imposition that allowed multinational corporations to hold majority interests in mining endeavors, and accused Correa of presenting "a rehashed neoliberalism with a progressive face." The CONAIE called his actions "neoliberal and racist" (*Latin American Weekly Report* 2008, 8). Correa denounced the dissidents as "criminals and subversive terrorists" and insulted Indigenous and environmental activists for blocking the country's progress. The CONAIE responded with nationwide protests against the law. Activists shut down highways in the southern highlands and the eastern Amazon. Some protesters were beaten and arrested, and even suffered gunshot wounds (*Latin American Weekly Report* 2009, 3). Social movement criticisms of the neo-extractivist policies of progressive governments were common throughout South America. In Bolivia, for example, anthropologist Bret Gustafson (2013, 61) argues that "this new 'progressive' extractivism is much like old extractivism—destroying the environment, generating intense social conflict, and eroding indigenous and citizen rights." More than any other issue, the conflicts over resource extraction illustrated the wide, growing, and seemingly unbridgeable gap between Correa (as well as other new left governments) and the social movements, and the erosion of the ability of social movement activists to influence government policies (Albuja and Dávalos 2014).

REFERENDUM

With all of the contradictions involved in advancing their political agendas, many on the Indigenous left viewed the new constitution as a mixed bag. In some respects it was a step forward, whereas in other respects it appeared to be a jump backward. Furthermore, if popular movements opposed the constitution because it did not have everything they requested, they would play directly into the hands of their traditional conservative enemies, while if they supported it they would strengthen the hand of a political force that did not embody their interests. How could they support the constitutional project without giving the appearance of allying themselves with the government? The Indigenous organizations felt that they had been placed in a very difficult position.

Facing this conundrum, the Indigenous movements decided to take what they could get rather than losing everything with a more principled stance. In a lengthy meeting on July 29, 2008, Ecuarunari (2008, 4) decided to support in a tepid and tentative manner Correa's project of rewriting the country's constitution in the upcoming September 28 referendum. Supporting the constitution, Cholango declared, was not the same as supporting a political party or an individual; they were not giving Correa a blank check. Rather, Cholango cast the gains of the constitution as the result of long struggles of diverse social movements (*El Comercio,* July 30, 2008). In the run-up to the referendum, Ecuarunari become even more vocal in its support for the constitution, calling on its supporters to vote for it. It published a special issue of its periodical *Rikcharishun* that pointed in detail to the gains that the new constitution embodied. In a lead editorial, Cholango (2008b, 2) argued that because of the organization's pressure, the constitution "incorporated fundamental demands for all Ecuadorians, particularly Indigenous nationalities and peoples," and that approval of it would "mark the beginning of a new plurinational state."

Other individuals and social movements who were critical of the government joined Cholango and Ecuarunari in a Frente por el Sí y el Cambio (Front for Yes and Change) (2008, 1) to campaign for passage of the referendum. They declared that "the new constitution is the result of decades of resistance and struggle of social movements, the Indigenous movement, and diverse sectors of the Ecuadorian people; it does not belong to any one person." They noted that the new constitution embodied very important social, cultural, political, economic, and environmental advances, including plurinationality, interculturality, collective rights, rights of nature, defense of sovereignty, food sovereignty, Latin American integration, expansion of education and health care, water as a human right, rights of migrants, respect for diversity, solidarity economy, and access to the media. They pointed out that the text made repeated reference to *sumak kawsay*, beginning in the preamble that called for a new form of citizenship that embraced diversity and harmony with nature in order to live well. It was a blow against neoliberalism and a step toward opening up democratic participation. All of these factors provided strong reasons to support it, and the activists hoped that it would lead to important advances in the country. To advance this agenda it was important to go to the polls to defeat the conservative economic forces that were campaigning against the constitution, and then maintain pressure on the government to implement the positive gains that the document embodied: "Only the popular ratification of the constitutional project will guarantee the realization of the changes for which we have long hoped."

On September 28, 2008, Correa won an overwhelming victory, with almost two-thirds of the electorate (including a majority of Indigenous peoples) voting in favor of the new text. Despite their disagreements with

Correa, the Indigenous movements embraced the triumph as their own. Cholango (2008c, n.p.) declared that passage of the constitution represented a new and historic stage in Ecuador's history. Latin America's first constitution to recognize a plurinational state was the culmination of two centuries of struggle for *sumak kawsay*. The wide margin of victory meant the "definitive burying of an exclusionary neoliberal system." But, Cholango cautioned, the Indigenous communities that had thrown their support behind the constitution now faced the most difficult and serious challenge—ensuring that the gains of the new document would actually be implemented. The Indigenous movements would need to maintain a protagonist role to prevent the country from sliding back into oligarchical control.

MOVING FORWARD

The role of the Indigenous movements in the writing of a new and progressive constitution in Ecuador points to the promises and limitations of social movements realizing their agendas through engagements with governing bodies. As part of a well-organized civil society, social movements can influence the direction of governmental deliberations, but engaging state structures requires compromises and tradeoffs. Perhaps most important, as the Ecuadorian case illustrates, it is not sufficient to draft new legislation; social movements need to remain ever-vigilant to ensure that the government follows through on its promises and implements its progressive policies. How to push a popular president to be more responsive to social movement demands without strengthening a common enemy to the right remained a key concern, especially as those who logically should have been allies locked horns over the best strategies to realize shared objectives of decreasing poverty and economic inequality. Achieving those goals required an ongoing struggle.

Chapter Fifteen

Bolivia

MAS and the Movements That Brought It to State Power

Leonidas Oikonomakis and Fran Espinoza

The question of how to deal with the state has been central for social movements and political philosophers preoccupied with bringing about (or blocking) social change. Theorists and revolutionaries ever since the times of Russia's October Revolution have tried to provide different responses. For Lenin and Trotsky (Lenin 1917; Trotsky 1930), during what they call "revolutionary epochs" we often notice the rise of an antagonist to state power (a kind of "constituent power"), "a power directly based on revolutionary seizure, on the direct initiative of the people from below, and not on a law enacted by a centralised state power" (Lenin 1917, n.p.). This condition is defined as dual power[1] (or dual sovereignty—*dvoevlasty*), and for Lenin and Trotsky it is temporary; ultimately, the rising people's power is expected to take over the state apparatus, establish the dictatorship of the proletariat through a vanguard communist party, and after an indefinite period of time dissolve the state in order to create the classless, stateless society that Karl Marx described as the ultimate goal of communism. According to anarchist thought, the problem of dual power has to be resolved the other way around, with the withering away of the state and its replacement by the autonomous, self-governing structures that will have been developed in the meantime by the people from below without the intervening "dictatorship of the proletariat" phase. The dictatorship of the proletariat is viewed as reproducing the same unequal power relations, differing only in regard to the fact that it is a vanguard communist party in power this time. The Marxist-Leninist view predominated among revolutionary movements of the past, especially in Latin America, which—inspired by the Cuban revolution and by the electoral success of Salvador Allende in Chile—tried to change the world by seizing the apparatuses of the state, either through revolution or through elections.

More recently, with the coming (or return) to power of "left-wing" political parties in Latin America (Argentina, Bolivia, Uruguay, Brazil, Venezuela, Ecuador, Paraguay, and Nicaragua) as well as with the wide resonance of movements that do not target state power (with the Zapatistas being the most prominent example), the question of the state is again generating a great deal of heated debate amongst activists and academics. Based on the aforementioned experiences, John Holloway (2010), Raquel Gutiérrez Aguilar (2008), and Raúl Zibechi (2012; 2010) maintain that the state is not the tool for emancipatory social change, precisely because by its nature it simply reproduces the vertical power relations of the past. For James Petras and Henry Veltmeyer (2009), on the other hand, controlling and restructuring the state apparatus in a revolutionary manner is the only way of bringing about social change; but it should not be done through electoral means because, they maintain, electoral politics is a game designed in a way that makes it a "trap for social movements," leading to their bureaucratization and institutionalization. George Ciccariello-Maher (2013), in a recent book on the Bolivarian Revolution in Venezuela, argues in favor of a dual power that exists in a tense and antagonistic relation with the state, which in its own turn enters a process of gradually self-dissolving from above and with its own initiative until it becomes a "non-state." Venezuelan activist Roland Denis (2014, n.p.) maintains, however, that the Bolivarian Revolution, contrary to its radical rhetoric, has become a "sustained petite-bourgeoisie in a massive popular mobilisation supporting the revolution, but totally contrary to the demand for power deconcentration, transparency and the people's movement's direct participation in public power," and has reinforced rather than dissolved state power. When it comes to the contemporary Bolivian case, it seems that what Vice President Álvaro García Linera at least is advocating for is a kind of dual power of a less temporary character, under which the state apparatus is subordinated to the movements that brought the Movement Toward Socialism (MAS, Movimiento al Socialismo) to power (Rockefeller 2007, 174) and socialism is deferred for the distant future, perhaps in 50 or 100 years (García Linera 2014). In the meantime, the "dual power situation" in which Bolivia has found itself has to reach its "bifurcation point that consolidates a new political system or re-establishes the old one (a combination of parliamentary forces, alliances, and changing government procedures) and reconstitutes the symbolic order of state power (the ideas that guide social life)" (García Linera 2010, 36). Additionally, García Linera argues in a Gramscian logic that it is the "Indigenous-popular pole" that "should consolidate its hegemony, providing intellectual and moral leadership of the country's social majorities" (García Linera 2006, 85).

This chapter will contribute to this discussion. Examining the relationship of Bolivia's MAS with the movements that brought it to state power, as well as the participation of people with a social movement background in Evo Morales's different cabinets, we argue that—at least in the Bolivian case—in this peculiar dual power situation, it is actually the movements that are being subordinated to the state and not the other way around, as the country's vice president claims.

In addition, during the cycle of protest of 2000–2005 that eventually brought the MAS to power, the protagonists of the mobilizations—the "multitude," as Álvaro García Linera refers to it, using Hardt and Negri's (2001) term—had practically rejected both representative democracy as a governing system, and the "party" as a form of organization. And the movement did so both in rhetoric and in practice, through the horizontal, assemblyist, direct democracy and communitarian organizational practices it adopted during the water and gas wars of Cochabamba and El Alto. Even the *cocaleros* of Chapare, who had a more trade union type of organization, with a centralized predominantly male leadership (Farthing and Kohl 2010, 199), governed themselves through a form of radical democracy "in which all members of the community meet to debate, decide, and enact their laws" (Grisaffi 2013, 3). All those radical democratic experiences seem to have been replaced by the vertical and at times authoritarian structures and processes of the government, while the party has returned as the main agent of change in Bolivia, replacing the movements and the peoples, as it has also happened in other "pink tide" experiences as Zibechi (2012) has analyzed.

THE SIX FEDERATIONS

September 28, 2013, Lauca Ñ, Chapare. In this small village a few kilometers from Chapare's main commercial town, Shinahota, among the small houses of the locals, something immediately captures the visitor's attention: the gigantic building and huge transmitters of Radio Kawsachun Coca (long live coca), the radio station of the coca producers of the Six Federations of the Tropics of Cochabamba. It was built in 2006, in the first year of Evo's government, to replace the older, more community-based wooden radio building that used to exist nearby. Today is a special day. The president of Bolivia—and still president of the Six Federations—is here to present the program, "Mi Agua III," which is intended to improve the access to potable water for the residents of the region. At the end of the presentation, the journalists and researchers who are present are asked to leave the room for Evo to have a private meeting with the *dirigentes* (community leaders) of the Six Federations. Even the presidential guards and the undercover policemen who accompany him are obliged to leave. The door is closed, and Evo remains with the *dirigentes* and the mayors of the region who are also prominent members of the movement. Bolivia's president was in fact holding a private meeting with a movement of which he is also the president, to discuss matters that need to stay outside the knowledge of the general public. But what is the relationship of the president, his government and his party, MAS, with the *cocalero* movement of the Six Federations? The answer, we believe, is summarized in a response that Asterio Romero, the secretary general of the Cochabamba Region's local government, gave to us in an interview we conducted together with Argentinean journalist Tomás Astelarra:

> Romero: For example, if our national government offers the capital for infrastructure, we put the raw material . . .
>
> Interviewer: When you say we? [You are talking] as provincial government? As Federation?
>
> Romero: As Federation . . . well, as both. . . . We, as government give the money for infrastructure, but at the same time I am also a *dirigente*, a coca producer, I have my property there.[2]

It is clear that we are talking about a double structure, especially in Chapare, which is also evidenced in "*compañero Presi*," Evo's double identity as both president of the country and president of the Six Federations of the Tropics of Cochabamba. As anthropologist Thomas Grisaffi (2013) has noted in a recent article, the *cocalero* structure views MAS (and therefore the government) as an extension of the union organization. To understand how this relationship has been established, we have to examine the history of the Six Federations, how and why the group decided to create MAS as a political instrument, as well as how—during Bolivia's turbulent years of 2000–2005—it managed to take the seat of government and elect the first Indigenous president in the history of the country, Evo Morales Ayma. The dynamics of this movement took place in the coca-growing region of Chapare.

CHAPARE

El Chapare (known to the Incas as *Ancha Para* [Ramos Salazar 2012, 20] or "the place where it rains a lot"), a province in Cochabamba Department, is a lowland region in the center of the country with dense tropical vegetation and difficult access. It is comprised of three tropical zones: Carrasco, Chapare, and Tiraque. It is generally agreed that the region's modern colonization began in the 1920s when the construction of the first road that would pass through the region began. The road built in 1938—thanks to the forced labor of the Paraguayan prisoners of the *Guerra del Chaco*—reached San Antonio (modern-day Villa Tunari, the principal town) (Spedding 2005; Albro 2005; Grisaffi 2013; Gutiérrez Aguilar 2008). In those years, Chapare became something like a "pirate island" where people from all over the country (mostly from Oruro, Potosi, Cochabamba, and La Paz) moved to settle. Migrants of diverse sociopolitical backgrounds moved to the region either to escape from the slavery of the *haciendas* of the lowlands, as was the case of the first colonizers[3] of the 1940s, or simply looking for a better life. They grew yucca, *walusa* (another starchy tuber), citrus fruits, and bananas that were mostly consumed for subsistence; coca was also produced in the region in those years, but its trade was minimal due to the absence of a road network that would facilitate market access. With the agrarian reform of 1953, the colonization of Chapare became a bit more organized and the state promised technical and infrastructural assistance to the new colonizers (roads, clinics, schools); however, that promise was never fulfilled (Spedding 2005) and colonization remained rather haphazard. When the colonizers returned to their places of origin, they recruited relatives and friends who joined them in the quest for a better life in the tropics. It was in a similar manner that Evo Morales's family also moved to Chapare in the early 1980s from the village Orinoca, near Oruro.

Between 1966 and 1969 some bridges were constructed over the main rivers (which until then were crossed with locally constructed zip lines) and access to the main coca market of Villa Tunari slowly developed. Here the *cocaleros* of Chapare could sell their coca leaves, which became their only viable means of survival and a very profitable industry, especially in the early 1970s in the time of the "coca boom" (Spedding 2005, 91; Gutiérrez Aguilar 2008). Due to the practical absence of the state in their region, Chapare's residents had to organize in an autonomous manner in order to meet their needs and obtain access to some social services (schools, hospitals, road construction).

When internal immigrants decided to move to Chapare, they first had to register with the agricultural *sindicato* (union)[4] that became the highest authority in the region. The *sindicato* was responsible for allocating land in parcels (*chacos*),[5] resolving local disputes (robberies, land disputes, etc.), and administering the coca commerce that was slowly emerging. In return, the new affiliated members (*afiliados*) had to pay the monthly participation fee of five pesos per month, participate in communal works (opening of roads, construction of bridges over the rivers, etc.), as well as commit to not treating their land as private property but rather as communal. If someone decided to abandon their land, then their *chaco* would be transferred to somebody else after a payment of a relatively small amount to the outgoing owner. In addition, the *sindicato* would be responsible for providing social services to the community, such as health and education, since the state remained absent from the zone. The current (as of March 2013) mayor of Villa Tunari, Feliciano Mamani, a legendary *dirigente* of the *cocalero* movement, confirms that the *sindicato* was the highest (self-organized) authority in the region when he arrived there in 1986. It built schools, clinics, and roads through community work, while it also assigned *promotores* of education and health, responsible for providing those services.[6] Later on, with the criminalization of coca and the entry of the state—and its army—in the region, the *sindicato* was also responsible for organizing the self-defense units of the *cocaleros*:

> In any case, it wouldn't be an exaggeration to say that the sindicato from its very start constituted the principal civil authority of the zone, practicing a de-facto autonomy, in permanent confrontation with the military and police authorities that were implementing the decisions taken by the government in regards to the war against coca. (Gutiérrez Aguilar 2008, 190)

A number of *sindicatos* composed a *central*, and a number of *centrales* formed a federation. According to a work published by Radio Kawsachun Coca in 2008 (Salazar Ortuno et al. 2008) the first federation established in Chapare was the Federación Especial de Colonizadores de Chimore, founded in 1964. According to Spedding (2005) and Salazar Ortuno et al. (2008), the Six Federations were then united under the name Federación Especial del Trópico de Cochabamba, which in 2000 was renamed Coordinadora de las Seis Federaciones del Trópico de Cochabamba, influenced by the success of the Coordinadora por la Defensa del Agua y la Vida, of the Cochabamba Water War (Spedding 2005, 297). At the time Coordinadora had around 50,000 families, who were producing almost two-thirds of the coca that was destined for the drug industry in the country (Farthing and Kohl 2010, 200).

FROM THE *SINDICATOS* TO THE
MOVIMIENTO AL SOCIALISMO (MAS)

While the federations of coca producers had managed to undertake all the responsibilities of the absent Bolivian state, run all the day-to-day activities in Chapare, and become a kind of de facto autonomous government, when it came to issues of political consciousness of their members they did not do a very sophisticated job, at least until 1985. Filemón Escobar, one of the founders of MAS and a former miner and union leader, argues that when he moved to Chapare in 1986 the *cocaleros* used to support one or another institutional party.[7] Fernando Mayorga, professor at the Centro de Estudios Superiores Universitarios of the University of San Simón of Cochabamba, who was also involved with the political and ideological formation of the *cocalero* leaders, suggests that "the Chapareños were not anti-imperialists ideologically; they became so when imperialism hit their door and came to find them,"[8] referring to the U.S.-conceived and led, violent coca eradication programs implemented in the region from 1988 onwards. We believe two developments contributed massively to the radicalization of the *cocalero* movement and its evolution into a political party:

1. The criminalization of coca production and the forced eradication programs that followed it; and
2. The gradual arrival of miners from 1985 onwards, who brought with them their union experience and militancy.

LAW 1008

The issue of coca is central in the process of change Bolivia has been undergoing in the past two decades. In order to try to regulate coca production, the government of Víctor Paz Estenssoro (MNR, Movimiento Nacional Revolucionario) approved Law 1008 (Ley del Régimen de la Coca y Sustancias Controladas) in 1988, which opened up Pandora's box for the country's coca producers. According to the law, the production of coca would be legal in the zones that the law defined as "traditional" (where coca has been cultivated ever since the times of the Inca Empire) and "illegal" outside of those limits. The "illegal" zones were subdivided into the "*zonas de producción excedentaria en transición*" (zones of surplus production in transition), where the cultivation of coca would be gradually replaced by other crops with the assistance of the state, and the "*zonas de production ilícita"(zones of illicit production)* where the coca trees would be simply uprooted without any kind of compensation (Gutiérrez Aguilar 2008). Chapare was categorized as *zona excedentaria,* while Yungas Vandiola, Yungas La Paz, and Apolo, as *zonas tradicionales.* Here it is worth mentioning that the coca reduction programs did not begin in 1988, but rather in the early 1980s, under both military and civil governments. As part of those policies, Chapare became a militarized zone where the regular army as well as special military/police forces were deployed to forcefully uproot the coca plants of the *cocaleros,* under the supervision of the U.S. government. Those special antidrug units were the Unidad Móvil para el Patrullaje Rural (UMOPAR—locally known as the *leopardos,* due to the color of their uniforms), the Unidad de Policía Ecológica, and paramilitary groups, such as the Fuerza de Tarea Expedicionaria. As a result, between 1982 and 2004, the *cocaleros* of Chapare suffered heavy repression and marginalization: 206 of them—including 8 babies— were killed either by the army or the special antidrug and paramilitary forces, 519 were injured, 121 tortured, 447 were whipped (including children), and 4,134 were detained (Salazar Ortuno et al. 2008). The implementation of

Bolivia's war on drugs was administered by the DEA, the U.S. Drug Enforcement Administration. The *cocaleros*, in an effort to resist and to defend their right to coca production, deepened their political organization, and created the Six Federations and the *Coordinadora*, and started a protest campaign that included marches, road blockades, and self-defense committees. However, the key to this radicalization of the *cocalero* movement was the arrival in the region of the "*mineros*," the ex-tin miners who lost their jobs under the neoliberal policies the Bolivian governments started to implement from 1985 onwards, causing many of them to move to Chapare and become coca producers.

LOS MINEROS

In 1985, the Bolivian government was unable to service its debts and started implementing neoliberal structural adjustment policies under the advice of Harvard professor Jeffrey Sachs,[9] who came up with a plan to "save" the country's economy, the infamous "Decree 21060." According to the decree, the country had to (neo)liberalize its international trade by removing any protectionist trade restrictions in place, freeze wages, and massively "reduce" the public sector by firing large numbers of public employees (Dangl 2007). As a result, 22,000 miners who used to work in the nationalized mines (a product of the revolution of 1952) became unemployed and had to look for an alternative livelihood elsewhere. Many of them moved to Chapare, sometimes as whole unions, to grow coca (Grisaffi 2010; Albro 2005; Dangl 2007; Gutiérrez Aguilar 2008; Spedding 2005). The reason why they chose Chapare and coca production is simple; one of the main markets (if one excludes the cocaine market) for the coca leaf in Bolivia has traditionally been the mines. In order to be able to work under the extreme conditions and temperatures of the mine, without sufficient oxygen, the miners consumed coca leaves. The *cocaleros* and the miners were so intertwined that at times the annual price of coca leaves was directly dependent on the price of gold or silver. Therefore, the miners knew that coca was a profitable crop and some of them already had family members in Chapare, a factor that made relocation a less risky business. They also knew that a big share of the country's coca leaf production was destined for the cocaine industry, since Bolivia was and still is the third largest coca producer worldwide, behind only Peru and Colombia (Grisaffi 2014; Farthing and Kohl 2010). The miners got the unoccupied—more distant—lands of Chapare, while some of them occupied whole regions. Those miners bore the union tradition of their sector, one of the strongest in Bolivia since the revolution of 1952, and were known for their militancy and activist experience, including leading resistance to successive military dictatorships. In an interview with ex-miner and veteran of the *cocalero* movement Dario Mendoza, he related that his federation—now called Mamore/Bulo Bulo—had so many miners who had seen their comrades killed and repressed, that when looking for a name for the federation the second most popular proposal was "*Sangre Minero*," Miner's Blood.[10] And of course these former miners carried a strong determination not to lose their livelihood for a second time. They politicized and radicalized the region's *cocaleros*, according to accounts provided by Feliciano Mamani, Dario Mendoza, and Filemón Escobar,[11] all of them miners who moved to Chapare from 1985 onwards. Dario Mendoza remembers that the *cocaleros* were less politicized and less militant, while the miners preferred direct actions and also possessed guns and dynamite which they would not hesitate to use. Gradually the *cocaleros* started looking for ways to react to state violence. At first they tried making demands on the state to stop violence and block anticoca proposals (including the "one *cato*," a proposal that would reduce their *chacos* to 1600 square meters), often through protests that were met with bloody repression; later on they established self-defense units that used wooden clubs and dynamite against the army and the special antidrug forces. According to Feliciano Mamani and Dario Mendoza, they even considered engaging in a guerrilla war. In 1995, *cocalero* leader Evo Morales had threatened that Chapare would become a new Chiapas in the heart of Latin America (Petras and Veltmeyer 2011, 104). However, the idea that prevailed was the one advocated by Trotskyist ex-miner Filemón Escobar, who became Morales's personal advisor. He organized more than 600 workshops in Chapare in order to "educate" the *cocaleros* about what he believed was the correct road: the formation of a political party and participation in local and national elections.[12]

Taking advantage of the 1994 Law of Popular Participation (Kohl 2003) that gave extended budgetary and planning powers to Bolivia's local municipalities (20 percent of the national budget rather than the previous 10 percent), the *cocalero* movement in 1995 went on to cofound a political instrument (Instrumento Político por la Soberanía de los Pueblos-IPSP) that would later become today's MAS. As Moira Zuazo (2009, 38) emphasizes, the decision to create a *political instrument* and not a party is related to the crisis of legitimacy of the *party* as an organizational form in those times, since it was perceived as controlled "by the elite" (Stefanoni 2003, cited in Postero 2010, 20).

The IPSP slowly started taking over the Bolivian state structure, starting from local administration, such that "mayors, *corregidores* and subprefects [were] de facto subordinated to peasant confederations," as Álvaro García Linera (2006a),[13] the country's vice president, confirms.

However, it should be noted that the MAS did not begin only as a project of the Six Federations of Chapare. It was first conceived as the political instrument of the Indigenous-*campesino*[14] movement of Bolivia, and its creation was approved in the Sixth Congress of the United Union Confederation of Peasant Workers of Bolivia (CSUTCB, Confederación Sindical Única de Trabajadores Campesinos de Bolivia) in 1994. A year later, in the congress on "Land, Territory and Political Instrument" that took place—ironically enough—in Santa Cruz,[15] the CSUTCB, the Bartolina Sisa National Federation of Bolivian Peasant Women (FNMCB-BS, Federación Nacional de Mujeres Campesinas Bartolina Sisa), the Union Confederation of Bolivian Colonizers, and the Indigenous Central of the Bolivian East established the Asamblea de los Pueblos (ASP) that would later become the MAS-ISP. After the elevation of Evo Morales to the leadership of the Six Federations in 1996, the *cocalero* movement would fight for the leadership of that political instrument, for which until then there were three candidates: Alejo Véliz Lazo, a Quechua ex-secretary general of the CSUTCB and first leader of the ASP; Felipe Quispe, the *mallku* (leader) of the Aymaras of the Altiplano; and Evo Morales, the leader of the *cocaleros* of Chapare. Thanks to the latter's electoral success in the municipal and national elections of 1995 and 1997,[16] Evo Morales and the *cocaleros* of Chapare managed to win the internal battle for the leadership and control of the MAS-ISP.

BOLIVIA'S TURBULENT YEARS (2000–2005)

With their political instrument in place, the *cocaleros* of Chapare started occupying local government positions and even parliamentary seats from 1997 onward (Mayorga 2007). As Raquel Gutierrez (2008) demonstrates in her book, *Los Ritmos del Pachakuti*, during Bolivia's turbulent years (2000–2005) MAS became one of the three main opponents of the state's sociopolitical strategies in a process that began with the 2000 Cochabamba Water War against privatization and ended with the election of Evo Morales as president in 2005. During that period the country experienced several serious social conflicts that had as the epicenter the exploitation of its natural resources; water, gas, and of course the coca leaf. The first rupture with the Bolivian governments' neoliberal policies came in 2000 with the Water War, which overturned the sale of Cochabamba's municipal water system SEMA-PA (Servicio Municipal de Agua Potable de Cochabamba) to Aguas del Tunari, a consortium of multinationals in which the Italian firm Edison SpA and the American corporation Bechtel controlled the majority of the shares. Two years later it was the turn of the so-called Coca War,[17] which intensified in January–February 2002 due to the government's decision to prohibit the production, sale, and transportation of the coca leaf and the closure of its main markets, especially the one in Sacaba, near Cochabamba. In 2003 there were the events of "Red October," a massive nationwide mobilization triggered by the government's plans to export the country's natural gas to the

United States through Chile, which evolved into a demand for the nationalization of the country's natural resources that had been hitherto exploited by
several multinationals.[18] Two years later, Bolivia's social movements fought
a second water war against the privatization of water in El Alto, and a second
gas war for the nationalization of gas and the other natural resources of the
country. During those five turbulent years, the main protagonists were the
autonomous self-organized Indigenous peoples, trade unions like the Bolivian Workers Central (COB, Central Obrera Boliviana) and the CSUTCB,
neighborhood assemblies such as Federación de Juntas Vecinales de El Alto
(Federation of El Alto Neighborhood Councils), and social movements such
as the *cocaleros* of Chapare and Yungas La Paz. Thus social movements, not
parties, were the principal organizational structures that fueled this upheaval.
The struggle led to the forced resignation of two presidents, and the overturning of privatization of natural resources such as water and gas. Throughout
that process, the representativity and the legitimacy of the country's political
parties was questioned, as was the efficiency of the neoliberal economic
policies the country's successive governments had been implementing since
1985. According to Fernando Mayorga (2012), two main proposals were
developed to counter the critiqued practices and policies: participatory democracy—direct or communitarian—for politics, and state economic nationalism for economic policy. Instances of horizontal direct-democracy forms of
organization appeared in Cochabamba, where the water war was coordinated
by the Coordinadora that assembled in the main square of the city, and where
spokespersons of the different neighborhood assemblies gathered to discuss
their strategy and future plans. Similar processes were experienced in the
mainly Indigenous city of El Alto, where the water and the gas wars were
coordinated on the squares of La Ceja and the other neighborhoods under the
communitarian organizational form of the *ayllu*.

If we accept Lenin's and Trotsky's theory that dual power is a condition
that appears in "revolutionary epochs," then we have to note that in the
Bolivian case, dual power took three different forms that were simultaneously antagonistic to the state and to each other, competing for the revolutionary
hegemony of the Bolivian "constituent power" of the time. Without doubt,
the most horizontal and directly democratic of those forms was that of the
Coordinadora por la Defensa del Agua y la Vida (hereforth: Coordinadora) of
Cochabamba, which in the words of one of its spokespersons, Oscar Olivera
(in *La MAScarada Del Poder* 2012, 85), was "a self-organized autonomous
instance made of urban and rural people that resisted to and reversed the
privatization of water in Cochabamba."[19] That horizontal experience of self-
organization from below, in which Evo Morales and García Linera played a
rather peripheral role (*La* MAScarada 2012) and in which the whole population of Cochabamba participated directly through popular assemblies, became one of the main tangible critiques of the inadequacy of Bolivia's repre-

sentative political system. The experience prefigured a possible way forward: a horizontal, direct-democratic, participatory way of decision making, which in turn demanded the socialization of formerly public/newly privatized enterprises, and the formation of autonomous municipalities (Gutiérrez Aguilar 2008, 51). Another political proposal was the revolutionary *indigenismo* of Felipe Quispe, which had a longer history,[20] and a more exclusionary character that focused mostly on the Indigenous question and itself evolved into a political party that took the electoral road to social change, but achieved little success. The third proposal was that of Evo Morales, his *cocaleros*, and MAS. With a strong militant basis in Chapare, and a strategy of coalition building outside of it (Anria 2013; Rockefeller 2007), in the elections of 2005 it managed to elect the first Indigenous president of Bolivia. But what was the new government like? And how has Bolivia's "dual power situation" evolved nine years later?

"CONTROLLING" THE STATE APPARATUS?

On the composition of the first ministerial cabinet of 2006, Xavier Albó (2007), wrote:

> With the formation of the new government even greater access has been given to the Indigenous peoples in key positions of the state than ever. The Ministers of Foreign Relations and Education are Aymaras. A Quechua cholita [woman of Indigenous ancestry] leader of the domestic workers is Minister of Justice, not because of her judicial specialization, but rather for her experience with the injustices that take place in the name of justice. Quechuas are also the presidents of the two Cámaras, one of them an urban syndicalist and the other an old rural mayor.

According to Mayorga (2012), ever since the rise of Morales to the presidency the unions and the Indigenous organizations, together with other popular sectors such as the *colonizadores*, the cooperativist miners, the female farmers, the Indigenous, the workers, the pensioners, and the neighborhood councils, formed new forms of organization and mobilization in favor of the government of MAS and its political project.[21]

> This participation in the political sphere also expresses an elite transformation with the massive presence of union leaders above all *campesinos* and Indigenous, within the instances of representation and government at a national and sub-national level. This result is part of a process that has the electoral victories of MAS in 2005 and 2009 as milestones and has as antecedent, in the mid-90s, the determination of the campesino unionism to form a "political instrument." (Mayorga 2011, 82)[22]

The first cabinet included local leaders who were active participants in the Water War, while women with a history in the human rights movement were also present, some of them belonging to the poorest and most vulnerable parts of Bolivian society (Cuba Rojas, 2006, 58). The cabinet was also composed of representatives of unions, neighborhood assemblies, and social organizations—sectors traditionally excluded from the political life of the past. The ministerial cabinet of 2006 consisted of sixteen ministers, twelve of whom were men and four women. There was also a small number of old technocrats with experience in public administration (sociologists, economists and lawyers) who were appointed as "invitees" (also known as "intellectuals"), even though they did not belong to any popular movement, but had however been identified with the government of Morales, and were offered only vice-ministerial positions (Zegada, 2008, 47–49).

The first ministerial formation was a demonstration of symbolism and a claim of power on behalf of the representatives of the popular movements. As we have already mentioned, the minister of justice came from the movement of the domestic workers that for more than five years had led mobilizations demanding the introduction of legislation that would safeguard labor rights in that sector. The minister of economic development and the minister of hydrocarbons, Carlos Villegas Quiroga, also had a long left-wing political trajectory and was a fierce critic of the neoliberal model (Cuba Rojas 2006, 56). The minister of water, Abel Mamani, was well known for his leadership in the Federación de Juntas Vecinales (neighborhood assemblies federation) of El Alto, while Walter Villarroel, the minister of mining, had served as executive secretary of the Federación Nacional de Cooperativas Mineras (FENCOMIN, National Federation of Mining Cooperatives). Alex Gálvez, minister of labor, is former executive secretary of the Confederación de Fabriles (Factory Workers' Confederation). Celinda Sosa, minister of development, belonged to FNMCB-BS, and David Choquehuanca has a long history in the CSUTCB. Choquehuanca did not have any previous experience in diplomatic affairs, but was considered one of the key personalities in the cabinet, thanks to his experience and contacts with European NGOs.

The first ministerial cabinet represented the rise of the popular movements, as eleven leaders from different social organizations headed ten of the sixteen ministries. Statistically speaking, the popular movements represented 68.75 percent of the cabinet compared to the 31.25 percent of the "invitees" (intellectuals/technocrats). However, nine years later it is worth asking: Have the leaders of those popular movements maintained those key positions in the administration? And most importantly, how have they utilized them?

In 2007 a major replacement of the representatives of the popular movements took place: of the sixteen ministers, only seven had a social movement background (43.75 percent, with 56.25 percent being technocrats). At the beginning of 2013, Evo Morales announced that he would retain the ministerial cabinet in its totality for the first time in seven years. However, the representation of people with a social movement background had been reduced to 15.00 percent by then.

According to Do Alto and Stefanoni (2010), the "invitees" are frequently considered as competitors by the popular sectors,[23] but they are legitimized in three ways: 1) By having assisted *campesino* organizations in their struggles in the past; 2) By simple invitation of Evo Morales, who has personally invited certain prestigious figures; and 3) By previous occupation of public positions and relevant political experience. The full ratification of the ministerial cabinet was heavily criticized by the popular movements, which perceived it as the return of the old elites to the state apparatus and maintained that the government of Evo Morales was not really representing the sectors it claims to represent. Morales has however maintained the full backing of the *cocaleros* of Chapare.

It would also be worth examining what nine years of MAS governance have meant for Bolivian society and the Bolivian poor in particular. Voices from both inside and outside the country (*La MAScarada Del Poder* 2012; Webber 2010; Webber 2014; Petras 2014) have pointed out that when it comes to issues of social inclusion, despite the government's extractivist[24] developmental logic, its radical rhetoric, and its impressive fiscal record of more than US$15 billion in foreign reserves and trade surpluses, no significant social transformation has taken place in Bolivia. The country continues to demonstrate high levels of both poverty (51.3 percent of the population below the poverty line in 2009) and extreme poverty (20 percent in 2013), and its social inequality levels[25] have not changed much since "the old political elites were defeated" in 2005 (Webber 2011). At the same time, as Webber (2010) notes, in contrast to what the initials of MAS indicate (Movement Toward Socialism), socialism has rather been "deferred to a distant future."

THE GOVERNMENT OF THE SOCIAL MOVEMENTS?

Vice president Álvaro García Linera (2006b) has argued that MAS represents a new form of government, one which is run by and for Bolivia's social movements and now in control of the state apparatus. It is also widely recognized that MAS managed to grasp state power (if not supported directly) by riding on the wave of popular protests against the privatization of public assets including water and gas that shook the country between 2000 and 2005, and demanding a more direct-democracy model of governance based on recognition of and respect for Indigenous traditions (Grisaffi 2010). However, as we have seen from the above analysis of the governmental cabinets of Evo Morales, nine years after his election the control of the state apparatus, at least at the ministerial level, is slowly yet steadily passing into the hands of technocrats and "professional politicians" instead of people with a social movement background. And in any case, as Alejandro Almaraz, ex-vice minister of lands and former national director of MAS (Almaraz, in *La MAScarada Del Poder* 2012) notes, it is not enough to have a *campesino* as a president, an Indigenous as minister or vice minister, or a *cholita* as a deputy. What matters the most is what they do when they take political power:

> Have the landowners been displaced from power? No, very partially and sec-ondarily. They don't have any ministers but it turns out that the *campesina* Minister of Agriculture does what they want. It is much more comfortable [this way].[26]

As illustrated by the examples that follow, it seems that not only are the movements and the social activists that had assisted the MAS in its quest for state power slowly abandoning it, and in some cases going against it, but also the *cocaleros* themselves—inside and outside Chapare—seem to be realizing that the political party they had created or simply supported is now imposing its decisions and policies upon them, without consultation, becoming what is known in Bolivia as a "*dictadura sindical.*"

In 2012 a number of Bolivian activists, including Oscar Olivera and Omar Fernández, the spokespersons for the Coordinadora of the Cochabamba Water War, published a manuscript called *La Mascarada del Poder* in which they criticize the government of Evo Morales and his MAS Party from a left-wing perspective. In relation to MAS's handling of the water issue, they have argued that rather disappointingly under Evo's administration, water is used as a tool of government propaganda. Through the program "Mi Agua," which is part of the initiative called "Evo Cumple," the government invested thou-sands of dollars in every municipality to supposedly improve access to pot-able water, but—they underline—*without* the direct participation of the peo-ple in either the planning or in the implementation phase of the projects. In an interview one of the authors conducted with Oscar Olivera, he further elab-orated on MAS's vertical structure, arguing that "it does not permit a demo-cratic, transparent, and wide participation [and] it is as corrupt as the govern-ments before it." In addition, Olivera contends, "the biggest crime of this government is that it did not obey those who put it in power to dismantle the state structure; it has destroyed the social fabric we had created with so much effort . . . either you are with the MAS or with the right wing. It does not leave any space to have an autonomous voice."[27]

The protagonists of the water war are not the only ones who feel betrayed. The Plataforma de Luchadores Sociales contra la Impunidad, por la Justicia y la Memoria del Pueblo Boliviano, organized by the activists who had been tortured by the country's numerous military governments, have for two years been demanding justice and the declassification of the military archives and have set up a camp outside the Ministry of Justice in La Paz, but to no avail. The government of Evo Morales, despite his own personal promises, refuses to grant access to the archives. "Who fought the water war? Us! Who fought in El Alto against 'Goni'? Us! We are anti-imperialists of actions, of facts, not of papers or discussions,"[28] argues Julio Llanos Rojas, one of those social activists who in their seventies and eighties are now fighting to get the "government of social movements" to fulfill its promises.[29]

Considering that MAS was conceived as the political instrument of the coca growers of Chapare, one would expect that at least it would be able to satisfy some of the demands of that particular social sector. However, the government of Evo Morales has found itself under international pressure to reduce the production of the coca leaf in Bolivia, a great deal of which Evo himself sometimes admits is absorbed by the drug industry (Grisaffi 2010). During fieldwork in Bolivia, one of the authors heard about a study on coca production and demand that the European Union cofunded and the government subcontracted an independent organization to conduct, but "*no les salió bien!*"—"the results were not the ones they were expecting." The government wanted to prove that the demand for coca-related products (for traditional, cultural, medical use, etc.) had risen, therefore the production should also stay at the same level.[30] But the study did not find the results the government wanted, so the government delayed its publication. Conducted by CIESS Econometrica (2013), the study began in 2009 and was concluded toward the second half of 2011 but was not published (as of November 2013). It found that Bolivia produced 46,469 tons of coca leaves (as of 2010), while the overall demand is only for 23,941tons. The question arises: If Bolivia produces double what it consumes, where is the rest of the production going? This question puts Evo and the MAS in a very delicate position, caught between the demand of their support bases (in Chapare especially) to protect coca cultivation and the pressures from the international community to reduce it. One of the responses has been to try to eradicate the *cocales* of the "non-Chapareño" *cocaleros*. As some recent attempts have shown—attempts that are supported by the Six Federations of Chapare—in 2006 the government sent troops to eradicate coca bushes in Yungas Chapare, an area to which Law 1008 attributed the status of "traditional," and in the clashes that followed two local coca producers were killed (Grisaffi 2010). Toward the end of 2013, the same story was repeated in Apolo, another traditional zone under Law 1008, again with deaths of locals and soldiers. Don Emilio, a member of the newly founded Federación de Productores de Coca Orgánica de Yungas Vandiola, believes that Evo's government is prioritizing his region and his support base in Chapare, in every possible sense, at the expense of the interests of other regions and other *cocaleros*:

They have so much development; we don't have even a street, a well. . . . We are part of the movement and we have assisted MAS; the first time Morales was running for president we put a fine of 500 Bolivianos on those who wouldn't vote for them (MAS). And ever since he came (to power) he has killed two comrades, a cousin of mine first, and another friend who was also a student at University.

They came to eradicate the *cocales* and the people resisted, there were fights and they shot them in 2006. In the first month of Evo's government. But he claims that during his mandate there's been no dead and no discrimination . . . it is worse! There are murders! And now in Apolo! And he says that we are narcotraffickers, *colombianos*, *peruanos*, *guerrilleros*, but it is not like that! [31]

Filemón Escobar, the ex-advisor to Evo Morales who conceived the MAS and spent a great deal of his time in Chapare trying to persuade the *cocaleros* to take the "electoral path," argues that given the authoritarian turn Evo and his party have taken: "Evo is becoming a small dictator." [32]

At the same time, Indigenous groups, like the ones in Isiboro Sécure National Park and Indigenous Territory (TIPNIS, Territorio Indígenas y Parque Nacional Isiboro Sécure) who resisted the construction of a highway through their area and the extractivist logic of Evo's government, were heavily repressed. The project was financed by the Brazilian Banco Nacional de Desarrollo Económico y Social and is to be executed by the Brazilian construction company OAS. The Indigenous peoples of TIPNIS point out that this action of the government violated the new Bolivian constitution that makes prior consultation with the communities in question obligatory.

In the Chapare itself, according to Thomas Grisaffi, an anthropologist who has lived there for more than two years researching the *cocalero* movement, MAS and its leader are imposing a top-down, vertical decision-making approach—contrary to the more direct-democracy, community-based one that used to be the political practice of the *cocaleros* before they "became presidents" (Grisaffi, 2013). In the past, argues Grisaffi, the *cocaleros* used to assemble and make decisions in a consensus-based manner, and leaders were accountable to the base and could be removed. Now, although they consider that the party and its leader are imposing policies on them from above, the president and the deputies cannot just be asked to step down. In these ways, the president seems to have distanced himself from the bases of his original support:

In the Chapare people are acutely aware that Morales has abandoned their political practice. Union members complain that they can no longer get close to Evo Morales when he visits the Chapare, and established leaders lament that Morales has no time to listen to their proposals. (Grisaffi 2013, 61)

Grisaffi insists though that the majority of the coca producers of Chapare keep supporting the party, mainly fearing that any other government would impose forced eradication policies on them. During our own fieldwork[33] in the Chapare, we also encountered complaints about *dirigentes* unaccountable to the grassroots, or members of the federations who were threatened with loss of their *cato*[34] when they complained about the party's or the leader's policies. Grisaffi (2013), who has worked with the community radio Radio Soberanía, also narrates how a leader involved with the radio was removed a few days after publically criticizing Evo, an incident that tells a lot about how the party is directing the movement and not the other way around, as Morales and García often claim.

CONCLUSIONS

The electoral triumph of Evo Morales in 2005 generated high expectations both in Bolivia and abroad, due to the fact that for the first time the country had an Indigenous president who did not come from the old political elites. Expectations were reinforced by the "organic relationship" of Morales's first governmental cabinet with the country's social struggles that had produced it. At the same time, the election of Evo Morales provided a rare opportunity for social movement scholars to study the relationship between a government and the movements that produced it, as well as to put the theory of "dual power"—that is becoming again increasingly popular—to the test. Can we change the world through the state? Can we have a movement-party in government? Can the condition of "dual power" be semi-permanent, as Álvaro García Linera argues, with the state apparatus being an "instrument" in the hands of the movements?

Nine years later, although the MAS has embarked on a campaign to improve its performance when it comes to meeting basic needs, extreme poverty in Bolivia remains extremely high while the wealth-poverty gap has changed little, despite the impressive foreign reserves and trade surpluses the government boasts it has achieved (Petras 2014; Webber 2011; Webber 2010). What has actually changed, as we have demonstrated in this chapter, is the participation of people with social movement background in Morales's cabinets. Even though Vice President García Linera keeps boasting that the government in which he serves is one "of the social movements," the evidence we have gathered points in the opposite direction: it is the government that has abandoned, and has in turn been abandoned by Bolivia's social movements, except for the ones that initially formed it. While the government cabinet of 2006 demonstrated a promising presence of people with an organic relationship with the social movements that brought it to power, this participation dropped steadily, as steadily as MAS's votes increased, and has been replaced by old "professional" politicians and technocrats. Furthermore, the movements that actually led the cycle of protest that brought MAS to power have slowly abandoned its cause, mainly due to its lack of correspondence between rhetoric and action when it comes to actual social change, and its repressive tactics toward those who defy it. On the other hand, some members of the Six Federations of Chapare who had envisaged the MAS as their "political instrument" have now started realizing that they have lost control over it and that the power roles have actually been reversed: there is no social control in representative democracy, however there is governmental control over its subjects, and not even the *cocaleros* of Chapare can escape it. Therefore, in Bolivia's particular "dual power condition," it is not the movements that are using the government as their "political instrument" as the country's vice president argues, but rather the other way around.

Robert Michels (1999 [1960]), in his "Iron Law of Oligarchy," famously argued that all organizations, no matter how democratically committed they may be, eventually develop a top-down, hierarchical bureaucracy that unavoidably leads to the leadership of an elite few (oligarchy). John Holloway (2002) has written that this is particularly relevant for organizations that grasp state power, while James Petras and Henry Veltmeyer (2011; 2009) have described electoral processes as a "trap for social movements," exactly because of the internal "resocialization process" that lies within the nature of capitalist representative institutions and eventually puts the movement on the same side as the ruling elites. Along the same lines, Raúl Zibechi (2012, 290), based on the experience of the Latin American "pink tide," regards leftist governments that govern from a right perspective as "the worst enemies" for social movements because they leave them "without a reference point, given that their leaders occupied those state spaces with the promise of resolving popular demands." All the above seem to be confirmed in the case of Evo Morales and his MAS Party, which was born as a political instrument of the Six Federations of Chapare and was assisted by Bolivia's popular movements, only for it to develop its own bureaucracy and elites and turn against its own creators, imposing on them its own hierarchical power logic.

NOTES

The authors would like to thank Richard Stahler-Sholk, Marc Becker, Harry Vanden, Francis Patrick O'Connor, and a reviewer of *Latin American Perspectives* for their comments on earlier drafts of this chapter. Any remaining errors and omissions are our own.

1. For an excellent discussion of the dual power situation see Rockefeller (2007).

2. Interview with Asterio Romero, conducted by Leonidas Oikonomakis and Tomás Astelarra in Cochabamba, October 10, 2013.

3. We prefer the term "colonization" instead of "settlement" in the case of Chapare because the Aymaras and Quechuas who moved to the area either in an organized or in a spontaneous manner were not Indigenous to it. The Indigenous residents of the region (the Sirionó, the Yuqui, and the Yucacaré) were displaced and marginalized with the arrival of the colonizers, at times by force (Ramos Salazar 2012).

4. The union traces its origins in the country's labor organizational units (*sindicatos mineros/fabriles*), which were especially reinforced by the 1952 revolution in an effort to incorporate the Indigenous peasants into the state structure (Dunkerley 1984, 74, cited in Hesketh and Morton 2014, 157; Postero 2010, 20). They were comprised of between 30 and 200 members (Grisaffi 2014).

5. Much later, in the 1970s, the unions would also register the *chacos* with the National Agrarian Reform Service (Servicio Nacional de Reforma Agraria) and provide its members with property titles (Spedding 2005).

6. Interview with Feliciano Mamani, conducted by Leonidas Oikonomakis and Tomás Astelarra in Villa Tunari, Chapare, October 5, 2013.

7. Interview with Filemón Escobar, conducted by Leonidas Oikonomakis in Cochabamba, October 23, 2013.

8. Interview with Fernando Mayorga, conducted by Leonidas Oikonomakis in Cochabamba, September 17, 2013.

9. In his book *The End of Poverty*, Jeffrey Sachs (2005) admits that when he was invited to come to Bolivia and "save the country's economy," he had no idea about the country, not even where it lies geographically.

10. Interview with Dario Mendoza, conducted by Leonidas Oikonomakis and Tomás Astelarra in Entre Rios, Chapare, September 29, 2013.

11. Personal interviews.

12. Personal interview.

13. It is interesting to note that Álvaro García Linera was a member of the revolutionary movement Ejército Guerillero Tupac Katari (EGTK), and was imprisoned for his participation in it; when he was released he became a prominent academic and later on the vice president of Bolivia.

14. For a detailed analysis of the Bolivian Indigenous-*campesino* movements, see Postero (2010).

15. Stronghold of Bolivian elites.

16. In the municipal elections of 1995 the ASP (under the banner of the Izquierda Unida) managed to elect ten mayors and forty-nine local councilors in Chapare, and in the national elections of 1997 it managed to obtain 16.5 percent of the vote in Cochabamba and elect four deputies, even though nationally the Izquierda Unida did not manage to obtain more than 3.7 percent of the vote. Needless to say, one of the deputies elected was Evo Morales Ayma, with 70 percent of the votes in Chapare and Carrasco, the highest percentage in that year's Congress. Felipe Quispe was still in jail for his participation in the EGTK.

17. See Gutiérrez Aguilar (2008).

18. See Dangl (2007) and Zibechi (2010) for a more detailed description of the events.

19. Oikonomakis's translation from Spanish.

20. The Katarista movement viewed the Indigenous peoples of Bolivia as exploited in two ways: in terms of class and in terms of ethnicity. It eventually took two forms of struggle as well: one that focused on trying to bring about social change within the political system, led by Victor Hugo Cárdenas, and a guerilla group led by Felipe Quispe, the EGTK. Álvaro García Linera was a member of the EGTK (Postero 2010, 21).

21. With the replacement of the old political elite, the class and ethnicity status of the governmental coalition has been modified; the linkages among the old political elites served to pursue more negotiated state transformations: similar colleges and universities of the children of the elites, shared lifestyles, family alliances, business activities, geographically similar zones of residence, which today do not exist, and that is what generates the tension between the rising and the decaying political elite (García Linera, 2010, 19–20).

22. Oikonomakis's translation from Spanish.

23. This is particularly relevant in the cases of the designation of Betty Tejada and Gabriela Montaño (as presidents of the parliament and the senate respectively), both of whom are considered as representatives of the "old political elites." Betty Tejada especially is seen as a rank-and-file member of the secessionist oligarchy of Santa Cruz, headquarters of Bolivia's right-wing economic elites. The regions of Santa Cruz, Beni, Tarija, and Pando, also known as the *media luna*, are considered to be the centers of the oligarchic separatist autonomy move-

ment that led to a political crisis in 2008. In contrast to the Andean regions that are primarily Indigenous, the citizens of the *media luna* consider themselves as mestizo or "white European."

24. The term extractivist developmental logic (or neo-extractivism) refers to the Bolivian (and not only) government's policy of basing its economy on (and making it dependent on) the extraction of natural resources such as minerals and hydrocarbons, sometimes at the cost of dislocation of Indigenous peoples who live in those areas. Those raw materials are then exported and processed abroad, exploited mostly by big multinationals of the respective sectors, with a share of the profit returning to the Bolivian state in the form of taxation or royalty rights.

25. As Webber (2010) notes, the poorest 20 percent of the Bolivian society received 1.3 percent of the national income in 1999, a figure that rose to 2 percent in 2007. The richest 20 percent of the population on the other hand received 61.2 percent of national income in 1999 and 60.9 in 2007. These figures make Bolivia one of the most unequal countries in the world.

26. Interview with Alejandro Almaraz, conducted by Leonidas Oikonomakis and Tomás Astelarra in Cochabamba, September 9, 2013.

27. Interview with Oscar Olivera, conducted by Leonidas Oikonomakis in Cochabamba, October 23, 2013.

28. Interview with Julio Llanos Rojas, conducted by Leonidas Oikonomakis in La Paz, September 9, 2013.

29. On February 8, 2014 the tent of the Plataforma was mysteriously set on fire in the middle of the night after 698 days of wake (*vigilia*). See Oikonomakis (2014).

30. The last available study on the topic was conducted in 1978 (Farthing and Kohl 2010, 205).

31. Personal focus group with the Federation of Organic Coca Producers Yungas Vandiola, conducted by Leonidas Oikonomakis in Cochabamba, November 4, 2013.

32. Interview with Filemón Escobar, conducted by Leonidas Oikonomakis in Cochabamba, October 23, 2013.

33. September–November 2013.

34. 40 x 40 meters of land in the Chapare (1600 square meters).

International Caravans for Life, Resistance, and Climate Justice, Cancún, Mexico, October 2010. (Peter Rosset)

IV

Transnational Organizing

The European invasion of the Western hemisphere in the late 1400s was only one stage in a process of globalization that has continued, most recently with the deregulation and integration of markets on a global scale. Such interactions ebb and flow, but the march toward more universal interaction moves on. Modern technology and the opening of truly global markets have not only heavily impacted the production process, they have also stimulated and intensified greater transnational human interaction, including globalization from below. As the North American Free Trade Agreement (NAFTA), the Central American Free Trade Agreement-Dominican Republic (CAFTA-DR), MercoSur, and bilateral trade agreements between Colombia and Chile and the United States facilitated the transnationalization of production and markets and finance, working people have often been hard pressed to move over national borders or engage in transnational labor and small producer organization. Yet, capitalist production in the neoliberal and post-neoliberal age has become more highly centralized and more tightly linked, even if the different productive structures are more widely spread through the world, creating an imbalance in organizing power.

We live in a world in which large privately and state-owned (in the case of China) corporations, agribusinesses, telecommunication monopolies, and mining and mineral extraction companies dominated economic production. They use and exploit natural resources, Mother Earth (the *pachamama*), minerals, and people on a global scale in their headlong rush to increase growth, production, and profits. They are not connected to or caring of communities and other human groups, and dislike any resistance to their global goals. Yet, as many of the previous chapters have shown, local resistance has sprung up throughout the hemisphere. The organization of workers on a global scale does not seem to have advanced markedly since the days of the Industrial Workers of the World (IWW, or the Wobblies), and many would argue that transnational perspectives are sorely lacking in the hemispheric labor movement. Yet a transnational movement against the massive extractive exploitation of agricultural lands and natural resource extraction through mining—the new extractivism, as Henry Veltmeyer and James Petras (2014) describe in their book by that title—is bubbling up from below throughout the Americas and in other parts of the world.

The implantation of mining in countries, communities, conservation areas, tribal lands, and tropical rain forests has done irreparable damage to environmental ecosystems and the human beings who are part of them. A transnational movement against such destructive mining is growing in the Americas (Ecuador, Bolivia, Peru and Guatemala, Nicaragua, and El Salvador among others) and in parts of Africa and the Indian subcontinent. In the chapter that follows, Rose Spalding offers a two-part analysis of the development of a successful anti-mining movement in El Salvador. The first part focuses on the construction of a broad network of organizations and activists under the Mesa Nacional Frente a la Minería, which mobilized during a critical political juncture in El Salvador to secure a moratorium on extraction. The second part analyzes a "scale shift" from the domestic to the international arena, as gold mining companies brought demands for compensation against the Salvadoran government before the World Bank's International Centre for Settlement of Investment Disputes (ICSID) in Washington, DC. The final section of the chapter offers a comparative analysis of anti-mining movements in Central America, contrasting those movements in El Salvador and Costa Rica that have been able to halt the industry's advance, with those in Guatemala, Honduras, and Nicaragua that were unable to do so. This analysis draws attention to the role of broad movement alliances with multiclass networks, major political parties, and transnational advocates as activists struggle for economic and environmental rights.

Small farmers, peasants, and agricultural workers have been suffering from the ravages of an ever-more industrialized global agribusiness that has pushed fertilizers and genetically modified organisms (GMOs) into our fields, put small Mexican corn farmers out of business, and established huge monoculture green deserts of soy in Southern Brazil, Argentina, and Paraguay. Yet in all of the Western hemisphere from Canada to Chile, in Europe, Africa, and elsewhere, the small agricultural producers have created organizations to champion rural life and fight for the rights of rural producers. Bolstered by groups like the Landless Rural Workers' Movement (MST) in Brazil, La Vía Campesina was organized in 1993 and now includes some 164 local and national organizations in 73 countries in the Americas, Africa,

Asia, and Europe. It champions peasant and small farmer production, and represents some 200 million people worldwide.

In their chapter on La Vía Campesina, María Elena Martínez and Peter Rosset argue that this transnational peasant social movement has been critically sustained and shaped by horizontalism through the encounter and *diálogo de saberes* (dialogue among different knowledges and ways of knowing) between different rural cultures (east, west, north, and south; peasant, Indigenous, farmer, pastoralist, and rural proletarian) that takes place within it. They find that this dialogue occurs in the context of the increasingly politicized confrontation with neoliberal reality and agribusiness in the most recent phase of capital expansion. As a dialogue among the "absences" left out by the dominant monoculture of ideas, it has produced important "emergences" that range from mobilizing frames for collective action—like the food sovereignty concept—to social methodologies for the spread of agroecology among peasant families. They suggest that the commitment to this form of dialogue, and the unspoken rules by which it takes place, may be key elements in the unusual longevity and continued growth of the organization.

Chapter Sixteen

El Salvador

Horizontalism and the Anti-Mining Movement

Rose J. Spalding

The twenty-first century commodities boom expanded mining activities into new territory, producing conflicts that spread across Latin America. Rapid economic growth in China created an increased demand for agricultural and mineral exports, and a spike in prices drew new investments into the extractive sector. Global recession and economic uncertainty sparked heightened interest in the value of precious metals, and gold prices rose across the decade. Latin American governments on both the right and the left tended to support rapid expansion of the extractive sector. Those state leaders who embraced a neoliberal vision emphasized global integration through foreign investment and the economic logic of exploiting a "comparative advantage" in natural resources. Leaders on the left, while highlighting the need for greater national control, focused on extractive sector expansion to finance the growing social expenditures associated with more inclusive development.

Extension of the extractive frontier into new areas triggered rising resistance and escalating conflict (Veltmeyer and Petras 2014; Bebbington and Bury 2013; Hogenboom 2012; Rasch 2012; Slack 2009; Kuecker 2008; Fulmer, Godoy, and Neff 2008). Mining struggles became persistent, particularly in Indigenous territories where the concepts of "*buen vivir*" and the "rights of nature" had shifted public discourse and been embedded in new legal frameworks. In regions where contention over land rights festered and water scarcity had become acute, movements against mining and in defense of community survival and environmental rights deepened and spread. The Observatorio de Conflictos Mineros de América Latina (OCMAL) reported 198 mining conflicts in nineteen Latin American countries in January 2014, up from 133 in fifteen countries in 2010.[1] Growing evidence of long-term damage, not simply to individuals but to whole communities, triggered the development of tenacious and recurring anti-mining mobilizations.

Threats posed by mining to the local water supply and land use placed the well-being of many communities into jeopardy.[2] Health and environmental damages, incurred as a result of both open-pit and underground mining, created spillover consequences for workers' families and neighborhoods as contaminants spread by contact, wind, and water. At a time when the weak regulatory frameworks that had been promoted during the neoliberal period provided few constraints on investors, sweeping damage accumulated quickly with little state monitoring or intervention. Heavy dependence on the mining industry for employment and tax revenues enhanced the power of mine executives, threatening democratic practices in areas where these were only weakly developed. Promised jobs and economic benefits often proved ephemeral; evidence mounted of persistent or deepening marginality inside mine-damaged communities across the region.

Growing awareness of harsh outcomes, whether directly experienced as mining advanced, recovered from documentation of earlier history, or observed in similarly situated neighboring communities, increasingly called community activists to action. These contests pitted movements against both the extractive corporations and the state, including not just neoliberal governments on the right but also left-leaning governments that had embraced a "neo-extractivist" development strategy (Veltmeyer and Petras 2014; Bebbington and Bury 2013; Becker 2013).[3]

The outcomes of these mobilizations varied widely, with many anti-mining networks losing the immediate battle. Some, however, have registered partial victories, and others have successfully derailed the mining advance, at least in the opening round. In the process, environmental and community rights claims have gained attention, providing new territory for social movement theory building and analysis. The anti-mining movement in El Salvador provides an instructive case study, demonstrating the ways in which a community-based movement grounded in horizontalist principles discussed further below, expanded outward to connect with broader networks at both the domestic and international levels. It also illustrates the ways in which democratic decision making at home can be threatened by external pressures emanating from international economic institutions and actors. The struggle to maintain local control, even as the locus of action shifted across scales, has imbued this conflict with both tensions and opportunities.

This chapter unfolds in four sections. The first provides an overview of development of the mining industry and the near-simultaneous advance of the anti-mining movement in El Salvador. The second section examines the national anti-mining coalition in greater detail, focusing on the movement's grounding in local communities that had been targeted for mine development and the connections that were forged among local groups, national organizations, and international allies. The third part identifies challenges faced by community and national-level mobilization processes when these networks face off against powerful adversaries operating through international economic institutions. This section follows the trajectory of El Salvador's anti-mining movement as it engaged the investment dispute claims filed by prospective foreign investors against the Salvadoran government. The final section concludes by highlighting the continuing challenges facing horizontalist movements as they advocate for direct democracy, local autonomy, and survival rights.

THE ANTI-MINING MOVEMENT IN EL SALVADOR

Neoliberal reform advanced rapidly in El Salvador under successive administrations led by the pro-business Nationalist Republican Alliance (ARENA) Party, which governed the country for twenty years (1989–2009). This development strategy opened El Salvador to mining investment, with a favorable Mining Act approved in 1995 and Investment Law approved in 1999. Rising gold prices and a supportive legal framework drew exploratory investments from a number of small mining companies, which quickly located commercial quantities of gold and other minerals.

As exploration advanced and the extraction permit process got under way, an opposition network began to emerge. The Mesa Nacional Frente a la Minería Metálica (National Roundtable Against Metallic Mining, henceforth, the Mesa) was founded in 2005 to connect various sectors that had begun to organize around this issue. The local community organizations on which the Mesa built emphasized grassroots activism and horizontal connections, seeking to withdraw from El Salvador's post–civil war neoliberal state project, and construct local space in which to promote autonomous development. These grassroots organizations expanded outward to connect with national-level organizations promoting human rights and the inclusionary practices associated with liberation theology, and they thickened their engagement with a growing group of environmental activists. The resulting national network expanded and consolidated over time and came to include thirteen organizations in 2008.[4] The Mesa called for a legal ban on mining in El Salvador.

This apparatus embraced a number of principles and organizational characteristics associated with horizontalism (Sitrin 2012, 3–4). These features included an emphasis on direct democracy and forms of autonomous decision making that rejected hierarchical controls; prioritization of survival and sustenance rights, with expansive implications for the concept of human rights; and close attention to the use and abuse of territory and physical space, a perspective that can lend itself to local-level activism and mobilization against environmental damage.

The Mesa's domestic struggle bore fruit, helping to split the ARENA leadership on the mining issue and bring the extraction permit process to an uneasy halt. As an informal mining moratorium went into effect, anti-mining activists joined with other citizens in 2009 to support the historic transition to new political leadership. The Farabundo Martí National Liberation Front (FMLN), established as a political party by demobilized revolutionaries following the 1992 peace process, had struggled for over fifteen years to open electoral space in the Salvadoran political system and to consolidate as a political party. Following its lopsided defeat in the 2004 presidential election with former guerrilla leader Schafik Handal as its candidate, the FMLN embraced Mauricio Funes, a center-left journalist who had not been part of the guerrilla struggle, as its standard bearer in 2009. Funes, appealing to moderates both inside and outside the party, narrowly won the election and ushered in a transition period following twenty years of ARENA dominance.

Under the Funes presidency (2009–2014), space for public debate about the impact of mining expanded. As a candidate, Funes had pledged to curtail metals mining. His inauguration was followed by a rising tally of assassinations and threats against anti-mining activists. In Cabañas communities near the proposed Pacific Rim (Canadian transnational) gold mining project, Mesa affiliates Marcelo Rivera, Ramiro Rivera, and Dora Alicia Recinos Sorto were murdered between June and December 2009. Other members of local anti-mining groups endured kidnappings, assaults, vandalism, and death threats, with little protective intervention on the part of local authorities and weak prosecutorial efforts in the aftermath.[5]

In the face of growing violence, the incoming president took several procedural steps to check the mining industry and interrogate its claims of benign or beneficial effects. Internal and external pressures, however, limited the impact of these transitions. Internally, the administration faced the challenge of governing in the face of acute polarization and ARENA resistance. Externally, concern about disrupting carefully cultivated relations with the United States and possible cutoffs in aid, investment, and remittance flows served as a further constraint. Wedged between anti-mining campaign commitments and formidable pro-mining pressures, the Funes administration eventually produced only a proposal for a mining moratorium of indefinite duration. The anti-mining movement's quest for an unambiguous mining ban remained unfulfilled, creating unresolved tensions between this network and the Funes administration.[6]

With mine development thwarted by the continuing moratorium, two foreign mining companies filed claims against the Salvadoran government before the International Centre for the Settlement of Investment Disputes (ICSID), the investment dispute settlement mechanism established by the

World Bank. These companies had been empowered by policies adopted during the period of neoliberal advancement, which included "investor-state" provisions that allowed foreign investors to bring disputes with host states before international tribunals. These companies claimed that the mining moratorium violated the terms of the recently implemented Central American Free Trade Agreement with the United States (CAFTA) and El Salvador's own 1999 investment law. They demanded that the Salvadoran government be required by the ICSID tribunal to provide them with access to the withheld extraction permits and to compensate them for revenues lost due to the moratorium.

As the anti-mining struggle was redefined by the investor challenges at the international legal level, El Salvador's anti-mining movement adapted its international alliance structure to include a widening network of allies. As the campaign expanded beyond the affected communities and incorporated new organizations and actors further removed from the primary conflict site, the struggle to maintain the principles and strategies associated with movement horizontalism intensified.

BUILDING THE DOMESTIC ANTI-MINING ALLIANCE

Local-Level Activism and Community Anchors

Local-level anti-mining activism centered on communities in an area that the mining companies labeled the "Gold Belt." This area cut across the departments of Chalatenango, Cabañas, and Morazán in northern El Salvador, where local level activists had a long history of organizing around land rights before and during the Salvadoran civil war (1980–1992). The region included several communities in which liberation theology advocates had been active in the 1970s and 1980s. Ethnographic studies of communities in this region have identified progressive catechists as "organic intellectuals" who served as agents of change, supporting popular participation and defiance of injustice (Binford 2004; see also Smith-Nonini 2010; Todd 2010; McElhinney 2004).[7] The Salvadoran military carried out intense campaigns in this zone to uproot guerrilla strongholds. Many residents, including nonpartisans, were displaced, often forced into refugee camps across the border in Honduras. This extended refugee experience, especially in Mesa Grande, the largest of the United Nations High Commissioner for Refugees (UNHCR) camps, provided a crucible in which new forms of revolutionary identity and practice were forged.

Molly Todd's (2010) ethnographic study of the Salvadoran refugee experience during the war found that repeated exposure to wartime violence and forcible relocation, combined with the intense political and social work of rebuilding community in densely packed camps, frequently stoked a sense of connection that persisted over time. The mass flight undertaken by peasant refugees of northern El Salvador to escape military invasion required adherence to discipline, sharing of resources, and mastery of secret codes that united survivors. The experience facilitated the formation of collective identity, defined by Polletta and Jasper (2001, 285) as "an individual's cognitive, moral, and emotional connection with a broader community, category, practice, or institution."

Life in the camps, which were vulnerable to assault by the Salvadoran and Honduran armed forces and were characterized by dependence on international humanitarian efforts, fostered an intense organizational effort and the expression of internal cohesion among camp residents. Some of this behavior was performative, as refugees staged a presentation of coherence to mitigate their vulnerability and improve their leverage in the complex bargaining for resources. Tensions, both political and personal, erupted as well, requiring careful management, sometimes in covert ways, to avoid dispelling the portrayal of successful self-control and unity. But wartime experiences also shaped new community identities and reinforced the push for local empowerment. The refugees' attempts at self-governance encouraged the development of organizational practices that were often genuinely inclusionary, breaking down traditional generational and gender barriers and promoting a culture of sharing and solidarity.

Summarizing her findings about wartime peasant displacement, Todd (2010, 224) concludes,

> one of the more striking aspects of this history is the campesinos' emphasis on collectivity and, more specifically the horizontal relations within their ever-shifting mobile communities. They highlighted how the organizations they established, both within and beyond their home villages, had strong foundations in the concepts of equality and justice. Members of directives and other committees, for example, were elected rather than appointed. In a similar vein, the workshops of the refugee camps gained staff and apprentices through a lottery cycle, which made the workshops accessible to all rather than a select few. Likewise, all refugees had the opportunity to attend school, receive health care, and vote in elections for (and serve as) representatives.

Salvadoran refugees, Todd argues, "came to see themselves as part of a sort of living organism, a body in which each part contributed to the survival and development of the whole" (2010, 224). Their work involved innovative strategies of self-governance and power sharing and introduced a push for an array of horizontalist principles, including local empowerment, autonomous decision-making, and direct action.

Popular education programs developed in mobile camps as dislodged populations migrated under the protection of the revolutionary army, FMLN. "*Maestros populares*" (informal teachers) introduced "*alfabetización inte-*

gral" (holistic literacy), using literacy training to re-envision Salvadoran history in order to transform it. Popular health promoters designed new health care systems in keeping with these emerging principles and practices. According to Smith-Nonini's (2010, 6) ethnographic study of health delivery in repopulated communities in Chalatenango, the popular health services developed by these autonomous revolutionary communities were distinguished from those provided by traditional government programs in two main ways: the central role of practitioners who were trained through informal apprenticeship and lived as part of their communities; and their emphasis on a participatory approach to primary health care education and service delivery, designed to improve access and collective outcomes. These distinctive practices, which emphasized lateral connections, community cohesion, local autonomy, and inclusivity, fostered a normative commitment to social solidarity and transformation.

In the late 1980s and early 1990s, sectors of this displaced population pushed to return to villages in El Salvador, even as the war continued and in the face of military opposition to resettlement. This formidable act of resistance intensified cohesion and demonstrated community capacity for autonomous decision making. The local organizations that emerged from this process became forceful representatives of these outposts of civic resistance in the postwar era.

These displaced populations often developed supportive connections with the FMLN guerrillas, who were sometimes recruited from these villages and who frequently provided protection when community members were forced to flee. FMLN militants provided health and education services and training in mobile camps and, less openly, in refugee centers. Links between displaced populations in northern El Salvador and the FMLN varied substantially, however, depending on local histories. This variation coincided with the sector of the five-part FMLN guerrilla alliance that dominated in each region. More centralized control was imposed on the refugees in Ejército Revolucionario del Pueblo–dominated Morazán, for example, than on those displaced in Cabañas and Chalatenango, where the less-directive Fuerzas Populares de Liberación Farabundo Martí and Resistencia Nacional had greater presence and reach (McElhinney 2004; Todd 2010). When the FMLN emerged as a political party after the 1992 peace accords, many of these linkages remained.

Horizontalist movements are generally differentiated from revolutionary movements, which aim for state seizure in order to secure a top-down realization of revolutionary transformation. They are also differentiated from routine forms of partisan politics in which the goal is electoral victory and the assumption of public office. In that sense, the links between progressive Salvadoran community organizations and the FMLN, as either a revolutionary military movement or a political party, may call into question the extent to which these mobilizations represent horizontalist struggles. In practice, however, the relationships between various types of movements can be quite fluid and situational. Whereas some, such as the Zapatista movement, eschewed participation in the formal political system, others had close and enduring party ties, and they moved regularly between formal institutional politics, transgressive antisystem mobilizations, and communal forms of prefigurative activism (Almeida 2006; Prevost, Campos, and Vanden 2012).

The repopulated communities in El Salvador used an array of tactics in attempting to preserve space for autonomous development. They struggled to maintain war-honed traditions of transformative popular education and local health service delivery in the postwar period. They resisted, with limited success, the replacement of their locally designed health and education programs by the bureaucratic services of the central government (Smith-Nonini 2010). They also responded to calls to mobilize in the capital in order to demonstrate their shared opposition to neoliberal reform, and they backed FMLN candidates in local and national level elections.

Revolutionary conviction and participatory practices withered, of course, in the inhospitable terrain of the postwar order. As the experience of revolutionary struggle retreated further into the past, replaced by the more individualistic and consumerist values of the consolidating neoliberal regime, even former communities in resistance were affected.[8] Visible traces of community activism and FMLN sympathy remained, however, in many repopulated communities, embedded in local history and living memory. Cultures of resistance, expressed in countless everyday practices, including nonheroic ones, can be quite enduring.[9] Although cynicism about the outcome and the value of revolutionary struggle became palpable in many quarters as ARENA consolidated national control, independent leadership structures, locally designed institutions, and interpersonal bonds persisted among many former allies in the war zone.

When mine exploration advanced in this resettled territory a decade after the peace accord, several community associations emerged as key local actors in the anti-mining movement. Chalatenango communities were represented by the Asociación de Comunidades para el Desarrollo de Chalatenango (CCR, Chalatenango Association of Communities for Development), the department-level affiliate of CRIPDES (Asociación de Comunidades Rurales para el Desarrollo de El Salvador, Rural Communities Association for Salvadoran Development), the national organization representing communities of rural people displaced by the war. Mining exploration in the department of Cabañas triggered mobilization by three additional community organizations, the Santa Marta-based Asociación de Desarrollo Económico y Social (ADES, Economic and Social Development Association), the Asociación de Amigos de San Isidro Cabañas (ASIC, Friends of San Isidro Cabañas Association), and the Comité Ambiental de Cabañas (CAC, Cabañas Environmental

Committee), all emerging in war-damaged communities located near proposed mine sites. Although tattered by outmigration and economic stress, vestiges of participatory practices sometimes remained, expressed in local assemblies, safety patrols, and community radio stations that prioritized local stories, decommercialized the news, and facilitated daily communication among activists. Building on prior traditions of engagement and struggle, these community organizations were capable of rapid action and feisty mobilization when threatened by a new round of dislocation.

Decentralization, local rootedness, agility, and spontaneity are evident in the origin stories told by anti-mining movement activists. Francisco Pineda, founder of the CAC and 2011 winner of the international Goldman Environmental Prize, describes how a sudden drop in the water flow from the San Francisco River, the principal water source for small farmers in his community, served as the catalyst for their mobilization in 2004 (Labrador and Meza 2011). Pineda, a local leader with a long history of movement activism, including collaboration with the guerrillas during the civil war and work in reforestation and soil conservation in the late 1980s, was alarmed by reports of this unprecedented water loss.[10] Tracing the riverbed upstream, his team came across heavy equipment being used to redirect the water flow. Further investigation revealed that a foreign mining company was conducting tests to determine the extent and commercial viability of nearby gold deposits. Activists learned that the cyanide-leaching gold mining process planned for the area would require massive amounts of water and raise the risk of toxic spills.

Unable to secure assistance from local authorities, who claimed there was nothing they could do, Pineda launched a community-by-community public awareness campaign. Drawing on his network of contacts and knowledge of the terrain, Pineda helped to mobilize a grassroots protest that quickly spread. As activists in other communities made similar discoveries, the protests multiplied. In November 2006, when the Canadian mining firm Pacific Rim moved in for exploratory work in Cerro Limón near Trinidad in the department of Cabañas, activists mobilized repeatedly, in ever-growing numbers, to demand eviction of the mine equipment. Telling the mine company work crew to haul the equipment away or it would be set on fire, protesters succeeded in getting the machinery dismantled and removed. Renewed rounds of protest in 2007 kept the mine work from advancing ("Comunidades se anotan 'primera victoria'" 2006; "Masiva protesta de comunidades" 2007).

As this conflict escalated, local activists moved to assume an official identity, working with an association that had been created in 2004 in response to other environmental problems. Describing the initial process of institutionalization, Pineda noted that, "We came to an agreement that no one would be president, nor would we have a formal structure, because we know that mine supporters would start to look for the leader in order to buy him or to kill him" (Labrador and Meza 2011, n.p.). Horizontalist principles of decentralization and avoidance of hierarchy were embraced, not simply as an ideological move to enhance egalitarianism, but as a survival strategy adopted in response to lethal threat.

Expanding the Network

As activists from the affected communities began to organize, they linked up with national-level organizations in the human rights and environmental activism fields. The Fundación de Estudios para la Aplicación del Derecho (FESPAD, Foundation for the Study of the Application of Law) and Unidad Ecológica Salvadoreña (UNES, Salvadoran Ecological Unity) helped the emerging network to frame collective understanding of the implications of mine development, calling attention to the broader environmental hazards and the national implications in terms of water access and quality. Concerns about the impact of gold mining in the watershed of the Lempa River, the main water source for the country, raised a national alarm. Activist-aligned research centers, such as UNES and the Centro de Investigación sobre Inversión y Comercio (CIECOM, Investment and Trade Research Center), documented El Salvador's historical experience with mining and highlighted the social, economic, and environmental dangers associated with the process (Henríquez 2008; López, Guzman, and Mira 2008; Erzinger, González, and Ibarra 2008). Religious organizations, such as the Catholic social action agency Cáritas-El Salvador and the Franciscan Justicia, Paz, y Ecología (Justice, Peace, and Ecology), added another dimension to the alliance, connecting the cause with what remained of El Salvador's once-vibrant liberation theology movement.[11]

Water was an increasingly scarce resource in El Salvador, and it faced commodification and declining quality associated with environmental deterioration and inadequate regulatory controls (Haglund 2010). As activist organizations reconfigured around the mining debate, they framed the gold mining industry as an environmental threat that jeopardized the already inadequate national water supply, raising questions about collective health and survival. This framework allowed the movement to broaden and incorporate the support of a wider array of political and social actors. Perhaps the most significant addition in 2007 was the Salvadoran Catholic bishops. Speaking with rare unity, the country's ecclesiastical leaders joined the anti-mining campaign, as had fellow bishops in Honduras and Guatemala, and declared their opposition to the introduction of metallic mining in El Salvador (Conferencia Episcopal de El Salvador 2007). The inclusion of the bishops broadened the anti-mining network beyond previously established parameters, bringing it into elite circles where Salvadoran social movements often faced a wall of silence or hostility.

As the anti-mining movement broadened domestically, it also built connections with allies from across the region. In a process of "lateral transnationalism," the Salvadoran movement constructed alliances with anti-mining activists in neighboring countries, where similarly situated activists in community and environmental organizations were doing battle with mine investors. By lateral transnationalism I mean a variant of transnational mobilization that is characterized by connections with similar and nearby networks, with whom there are few asymmetries of resources and an abundance of shared experiences (Spalding 2014). This form of transnationalism may be differentiated from "global transnationalism," a generally thinner process that connects activists across the North-South hemispheric or international divide. In the latter process, activists often struggle with predictable tensions that jeopardize authentic collaboration, including asymmetrical resources, cultural misunderstandings, and verticalist tendencies. Lateral transnationalism, in contrast, builds on connections among activists and organizations in nearby settings, who often share a similar understanding of the problems they confront and have comparable resource profiles and needs. This collaboration type, which may be of an informal and cross-border nature, can facilitate smoother information flows and mutual learning, along with innovative forms of regional strategizing and collective action.[12]

Gold mining in Honduras, which had begun several years previously, had produced population displacement and environmental contamination, including a cyanide spill. Mounting evidence of damage triggered major demonstrations, such as the protest march led by Honduran Cardinal Oscar Andrés Rodríguez in March 2002 (Slack 2009, 125–26). The hard experience of trusted counterparts in Honduras encouraged community activists in El Salvador's Gold Belt to view the advent of mining with growing alarm. Anti-mining activists in El Salvador frequently cited these collaborative consultations and on-site exchanges as a call to action. Cross-border engagement and information sharing multiplied as the number of mines in Honduras and Guatemala increased. Several of the new mines were located in close proximity to Salvadoran territory and to the headwaters of the Lempa River. Growing awareness of environmental risks associated with mining raised calls for regional action to mitigate the dangers.[13]

Engaging the State

The extent to which horizontalist movements accept or reject engagement with the state has been a matter of discussion in activist circles. Although these movements, including several described in this volume, call for the creation of spaces free from state control and question the value of conventional forms of political participation represented by partisan campaigns and elections, advocates of horizontalist action often find it necessary to engage with state actors. In spite of a preference for action "against and beyond the state" (Sitrin 2012, 4), these activists may find it critical, at the same time, to make use of established political institutions.

In the Salvadoran anti-mining case, activists generally did not retreat from engagement with the state, nor did they detach their efforts from the formal political sphere of electoral politics. Arising, as many of them did, in the context of political polarization that defined wartime and postwar life in that country, social movements in El Salvador repeatedly intersected with political parties, giving rise to what Paul Almeida (2006) calls "social movement partyism." In this model, movements on the left generally aligned with the FMLN and those to the right connected with ARENA. The debate about mining could not be resolved without state action and policy change; engagement with partisan politics and electoral processes provided one set of tools that activists could wield. Just as state policies and legal codes had encouraged mining investment to advance and protected it during the early exploratory stage, a change in state policy could now halt investment and provide relief. To achieve their objectives, anti-mining activists in El Salvador were compelled to engage in defensive mobilization, operating with and through the state.

Public protest, alliance building, and educational outreach can intersect with campaigns and elections to affect state action, particularly during critical junctures, when the durability of the dominant coalition is called into question. Electoral precariousness may even prompt market defenders to adjust their rhetoric and adapt their policies, at least temporarily. In the Salvadoran case, growing evidence of public dissatisfaction with mining led Salvadoran President Tony Saca (2004–2009) to delay the issuance of mining permits and eventually initiate an informal mining moratorium, in spite of his ARENA affiliation. His actions revealed a cleavage in the dominant party between those who endorsed ARENA's traditional enthusiasm for neoliberal reform, and those who registered the political cost of the mining initiative and sought to reduce it. In 2010 Saca led a breakaway from ARENA, the Grand Alliance for National Unity (GANA, Gran Alianza por la Unidad Nacional), a party that competed unsuccessfully in the 2014 election.

Challenging ARENA in the 2009 presidential contest, FMLN candidate Mauricio Funes embraced the anti-mining position. With support from Mesa activists, among many others, Funes won the presidency, narrowly defeating ARENA's pro-business candidate. As elsewhere in Latin America, social movement organizers generally aligned with "pink tide" candidates to challenge the advance of neoliberal reform. And as elsewhere, the subsequent relationship between activists and left-leaning leaders was not free of tension.

Proceeding cautiously and seeking international technical validation for any mining policy change, the Funes administration secured funding from the Spanish Agency for International Cooperation and Development for a "Strategic Environmental Evaluation of the Metallic Mining Sector." The resulting report, by the Spanish company Tau Consultora Ambiental (2011), identified seventeen areas in which legal and institutional reforms would be required and sixty-four actions that would be needed in order to provide an appropriate regulatory infrastructure for mining in El Salvador. This analysis emphasized the environmental vulnerability of the country and the opposition of organized civil society, citing these as factors that weighed against mine development. The report presented two scenarios: one in which the development of regulatory, monitoring, and accountability mechanisms produced an institutional infrastructure in which mining might be safely developed; and the other in which the vulnerability of the country to environmental crisis (earthquakes, hurricanes, flooding, land slides) and the improbability of successful implementation of regulatory controls led to a decision to ban the industry. Based on this analysis, the ministers of the economy and the environment presented a joint proposal to the legislature in favor of a formal moratorium on metallic mining (Labrador Aragón 2012).

The Funes administration's proposal for a formal moratorium was rejected by the Mesa's anti-mining activists, who described it as "a demagogic and false solution" (Mesa 2012). Such a step, they argued, would only postpone the decision, allowing for an easy reversal under a future pro-mining administration. Arguing that mining should be banned by law, Mesa spokespeople had worked with FMLN sympathizers in the legislative assembly to introduce a proposed mining ban in 2006. The unwillingness of the Funes administration to lend political capital to this legislative effort drove a wedge between the anti-mining activists and the administration. The willingness of FMLN legislators to introduce the measure, in contrast, reinforced the connections between the movement and the party.

Unlike many cases in Latin America, in which left-leaning presidents actively supported the expansion of the mining sector, the president in El Salvador endorsed a mining moratorium. The clash between "pink tide" presidents and anti-mining movements typically occurred when the administration prioritized the state's need for increased revenues and sectoral employment over the survival needs of the community and the costs of long-term environmental damage. In Ecuador, for example, Rafael Correa's neo-extractivist economic policy, which drew on petroleum rents to fund social programs, pitted him against social movement activists that he denounced as "infantile environmentalists" (Becker 2013, 56–57). Criticizing the accelerated extractivism in new left regimes, Veltmeyer and Petras (2014, 39) contend that it "boils down to nothing more than the state striking a better deal with global capital regarding its share of the plundered resources."

In the Salvadoran case, however, the extraction calculus was different, as was the outcome. Because the gold mining industry was not yet operative in El Salvador and was expected to be of limited duration, the projected revenues in the form of royalties and taxes were hypothetical and, in any case, likely to be short term. In addition, the country's small size, high population density, and water scarcity made the environmental risks loom large. The hinterland was not so distant; physical precariousness had a national scope. As the technical report about the prospective environmental and social costs of the industry raised a host of red flags, it was relatively easy for the Funes administration to respond to popular pressure by endorsing an official mining moratorium. He fell short of endorsing the proposed mining ban, however, in part because of mounting threats on the international front.

CHALLENGES ON THE INTERNATIONAL FRONT

In the weeks before Funes's inauguration, two foreign mining companies launched an international legal claim against the Salvadoran government. Pacific Rim Cayman filed a claim for $77 million, an amount that was subsequently raised to $315 million in 2013.[14] The U.S.-based Commerce Group followed suit, filing for $100 million in damages. Using protections provided in the 2004 CAFTA with the United States and the dispute settlement provisions in El Salvador's 1999 Investment Law, these companies claimed indirect expropriation by the Salvadoran government, based on their inability to secure extraction permits and the loss of projected future revenues.

Using investor-state provisions embedded in bilateral investment treaties, free trade agreements, and national investment laws, transnational corporations have presented a growing number of claims against host states, alleging nonfulfillment of investor guarantees and seeking compensation. The World Bank's investment dispute mechanism, ICSID, "revolutionized the relationship between foreign investors and host countries with regards to dispute settlement" (Mortimore and Stanley 2009, 9). By the end of 2013, ICSID had registered a total of 459 cases, up from 81 in 2000 (International Centre for the Settlement of Investment Disputes 2014, 7). Latin American countries (minus Mexico) were represented in 34 percent of these cases, with South America being the single most affected global region (11). Twenty-six percent of all ICSID cases involved claims in the oil, gas, and mining sector, twice as many as any other sector (12).

The use of international tribunals to pressure vulnerable states to accede to corporate demands has drawn intensified criticism in the legal, academic, and human rights communities (Orellana 2011; Fach Gómez 2011, 2012; Anderson and Pérez-Rocha 2013; McDonagh 2013; Eberhardt and Olivet

2012; Mortimore and Stanley 2009). The silent rise of international investment enforcement mechanisms has undermined the ability of states to strengthen social and environmental regulation and imposed increased financial burdens on countries where basic social services are already inadequately funded.[15] This process also challenges the principles of democratic self-government by preventing elected officials from updating laws and policies in keeping with clearly stated voter preferences and national interests.

As complaints have grown about the insular and antidemocratic nature of the dispute settlement process, its domination by a small number of Northern law firms and arbitrators and its pro-corporate bias have drawn increasing criticism. In response, modest moves toward increased transparency have been introduced. One recent reform involved the admission of amicus curiae or "friend of the court" briefs into the proceedings. These legal briefs allow groups who are not litigants in the case, but whose interests would be affected by the outcome, to present their perspective to the court. A 2006 reform in the ICSID process followed two controversial arbitrations in which community claims for an amicus curiae process were advanced. The *Aguas del Tunari, S.A. v. Bolivia* case arose from the Cochabama Water War, and the *Suez/Vivendi* case against Argentina involved the distribution of water and sewage services. In both cases, a coalition of community groups requested public access to the documents of the ICSID proceedings and asked for permission to submit an amicus brief, a petition that was denied in the first case and partially accepted in the second (Orellana 2011, 98–102; Fach Gómez 2012, 537–41).

As the number of such requests mounted and public controversy deepened over the closed nature of the process, the tribunal agreed in 2011 to accept a short amicus brief from the anti-mining network in El Salvador. With assistance from the Washington, DC-based Center for International Environmental Law (CIEL), eight Mesa organizations made their case. Their brief identified the dispute as essentially a political, not a legal one. The conflict, they argued, was between the affected communities, seeking to exercise democratic rights and protect their own well-being, and the mining company, which was attempting to evade legal requirements and make backdoor deals with discredited public officials. Actions taken by the Salvadoran government to halt the permit process, they countered, were an attempt to advance the consolidation of a democratic political system, after long years of war, conflict, and polarization, and to respond appropriately to public pressure from Salvadoran civil society (CIEL 2011).

As this case advanced at the international level, the Salvadoran anti-mining movement expanded its transnational alliance network. Mesa organizations had long received assistance from a cluster of international nongovernmental organizations (INGOs) based in the global North. Many of these INGOs had long-standing relationships with the affected communities, and several of them operated as semi-domestic actors. The Salvadoran Humanitarian Aid, Research and Education Foundation (SHARE), the Committee in Solidarity with the People of El Salvador (CISPES), and the Sister Cities project were three U.S.-based solidarity initiatives with deep roots in El Salvador dating back to the civil war. These organizations had mobilized over the severe human rights violations committed during the war and the U.S. foreign policy that, by equipping and financing the Salvadoran military, shared responsibility for this outcome.[16] Activists affiliated with these groups monitored the treatment of Salvadoran refugees in Honduras and assisted those refugees when they demanded the right of return (Todd 2010; Silber 2010; Smith-Nonini 2010).

Grounding their work in the concepts of "solidarity" and "accompaniment," these organizations established enduring ties to local communities in resistance and continued to support their development in the postwar period. These activists used their relatively privileged position as U.S. citizens to echo their partners' demands for local control and alternative forms of development, reinforcing positions in both the United States and El Salvador that had been previously articulated by their community allies. As "domesticating INGOs," they worked exclusively on El Salvador, developing a nontransferable mission strongly shaped by local frames.[17]

Other prominent international NGOs supporting the anti-mining movement included Oxfam America, which had also established a long-term presence in El Salvador and partnered with a number of domestic networks and civic organizations. With its mission-based commitment to the empowerment of local communities and demand for "free, prior and informed consent" before development plans were approved,[18] Oxfam America bolstered various community-based initiatives in Central America, including those of several communities facing off against mining investors. This organization contributed to the Mesa's anti-mining work in a variety of ways, including sharing information, financing research and publications, hosting international experts, participating in direct lobbying of key government officials, commissioning public opinion polls in the affected communities, and covering basic operating expenses for several partner organizations, including the Mesa (Spalding 2014, 173).

The Mesa's network of transnational allies expanded rapidly as the mining conflict escalated in El Salvador, and it included some with no prior experience in El Salvador. The growing numbers of assassinations and threats against Salvadoran activists, increased volume of investment disputes, growing awareness of their costs, and rising profile of the Pacific Rim case, drew the attention of international supporters. With the assistance of new international allies, the Salvadoran anti-mining movement expanded its "repertoire of contention" (Tarrow 2005), adding new tactics and strategies. An international support group calling itself "The International Allies against

Metallic Mining in El Salvador," which had begun as a small network of the long-term solidarity organizations, expanded to include twenty organizations in mid-2013, as the *Pac Rim v. El Salvador* case emerged as an international cause célèbre.[19] The Allies sponsored international delegations and informational tours; organized protests outside the Canadian embassy, mining company headquarters, and the World Bank; and launched petition drives and letter writing campaigns that called on international and Salvadoran leaders to endorse the Mesa position in favor of a mining ban (International Allies Against Mining in El Salvador 2012).

The rapid expansion of this network in the United States, Canada, and Australia worked against the emphasis on horizontality and direct local action that Salvadoran community activists had traditionally embraced. As discussed above, global transnationalism can introduce a series of distortions and open the door to replication of North-South power dynamics, even among well-intentioned northern activists. As the center of the mining conflict shifted away from El Salvador and into ICSID, however, Salvadoran activists were required to broaden their network at the international level, seeking information and resources needed to operate in global power centers. This tension calls us to theorize horizontalism across different contexts of struggle and to continue discussion of transnational movement strategies that best align with local empowerment.

As the Pac Rim case moved into the final phase of review in early 2014, the International Allies orchestrated a petition drive directed to World Bank president Jim Yong Kim. Signatories affirmed that Salvadoran communities "had been working through the democratic process to prevent a proposed cyanide-leach gold mining project, over well-founded risks that it will poison the local communities' environment as well as the country's most important river and source of water" (International Allies 2014, n.p.). Petitioners called for the World Bank to initiate an open review of ICSID, including public hearings that would incorporate community testimony, to determine if its dispute settlement process was consistent with the Bank's stated anti-poverty and sustainable development mission.[20]

CONCLUSIONS

Examination of the Salvadoran anti-mining movement allows us to trace how local communities engaged in grassroots organizing to build decentralized, horizontal networks through which to seek autonomous development. Using participatory practices and a rights-based discourse that emphasized sustenance, sustainability, and survival, this network nurtured new thinking about the practice of democracy and the meaning of development. The anti-mining coalition in El Salvador used bridging and bonding techniques to connect

ity leaders fighting the intrusion of the mines with activists in national organizations pursuing environmental sustainability and an expansive definition of human rights. Aligning their struggle with religious and moral discourse concerning protection of nature and the centrality of the collective good, Salvadoran activists opened a larger conversation about the future of their country. Engagement with formal political processes (campaigns, elections, lobbying, and bill drafting) allowed this movement to employ a significant array of tools as they looked for ways to defend the space for alternative development.

Political success in the domestic arena, however, is a limited good in an increasingly globalized market system. As the Salvadoran case demonstrates, international institutions that reinforce the neoliberal order continue to undermine local autonomy and challenge democratic practices, even in our purportedly post-neoliberal moment. Horizontalist movements that seek to open space for cultural rights, participatory deliberation, and new forms of community building have responded by mobilizing at, but also beyond, the local setting. In spite of the heft of their adversaries and the challenges associated with constructing transnational solidarity networks, Salvadoran anti-mining activists are advancing a process of change at the global level. Continuing work at the local and global scales will be required in order to develop a new institutional order that prioritizes human rights, including environmental and cultural rights; encourages decentralization, allowing fluid choices and heterogeneity based on local preferences; and introduces a fairer set of economic rules. The new horizontalism seeks to empower local and regional actors and to flatten the relations of power in a continuing effort to advance democratic inclusion and social justice.

NOTES

1. See http://basedatos.conflictosmineros.net/ocmal_db/ (accessed January 20, 2014) and http://www.olca.co/ocmal (accessed August 1, 2010). Chile and Peru registered 34 conflicts each, with parts of Mexico (29), Argentina (26) and Brazil (20) also witnessing numerous clashes. Central America (including Panama) reported 25 mining conflicts at the beginning of 2014, 6 of them in Guatemala alone.

2. These conflicts can be particularly acute in Indigenous communities, where cultural rights are precarious and community identity has been repeatedly threatened. Efforts by international organizations to affirm the rights of Indigenous peoples to participate in development planning that impacts their communities have strengthened the legal hand of mining resisters in several regions. See, for example, Rasch 2012; Fulmer, Godoy, and Neff 2008.

3. Neo-extractivism is a Latin American development policy based on resources derived from the extraction of metals (gold and silver), minerals (primarily copper, zinc, lead, tin, lithium, bauxite, coal, and iron) and fuels (oil and gas). Several left-leaning governments in the region combine neo-extractivism with resource nationalism, a development approach that emphasizes state control over "resource rents," that is, the fiscal gains from extraction acquired either through direct state ownership or through royalties and taxes paid by mining companies.

4. For a full list of Mesa members, see Henríquez (2008, 29n15).

5. For detailed discussion of the deaths and violence directed against anti-mining activists, see Steiner 2010. The local government near the Pacific Rim site was controlled by ARENA, the party whose founder Maj. Roberto D'Aubuisson had organized death squads during El Salvador's 1980–1992 civil war. Some of the assassinations of anti-mining activists bore the hallmarks of the old death squad techniques.

6. In the 2014 presidential election, victorious candidate Salvador Sánchez Cerén, a former FMLN guerrilla leader and Funes's vice-president, claimed that metal mining is "a threat to life" and pledged to prevent any mining advance (Meléndez 2014).

7. See also Wood's (2003, 234–37) work on links between liberation theology and rural mobilization, and the resulting "pleasure in agency" such action induced in insurgent cooperatives and collectives in Usulután.

8. Irina Silber (2010) describes the erosion of participatory practices and dismantling of community assemblies in Chalatenango, as emigration negatively affected that social texture. Leigh Binford (2013) documents the impact of massive outmigration on former revolutionary strongholds such as Morazán in northern El Salvador.

9. See Wickham-Crowley (1992, 130–40) on the concept of "rebellious cultures" and their contribution to guerrilla mobilizations and revolution in Latin America.

10. According to an interview with Pineda by El Salvador's digital news source *El Faro*, Pineda's father, a founder of the Unión Nacional de los Trabajadores Salvadoreños, was assassinated when his son was fourteen years old. Pineda's own political activism began with the Movimiento Estudiantil Revolucionario de Secundaria, which became a base organization for the FMLN (Labrador and Meza 2011).

11. Several of these organizations had collaborated during the 2000–2003 movement against health care privatization. Six "white marches" had mobilized over 200,000 Salvadorans, who struggled to preserve and expand public health services and avoid the further dismantling of state institutions (Almeida 2008; Smith-Nonini 2010).

12. The shared experience of civil war and dislocation in the 1980s, combined with region-wide natural disasters and environmental damage associated with hurricanes, drought, and flooding, tended to connect activists across Central America. In addition, exposure to repeated processes of neoliberal regionalism, such as the cross-regional infrastructure development project, Plan Puebla-Panamá (PPP), and the negotiation of CAFTA, Central America's free trade agreement with the United States, provided common targets for resistance mobilization across the region. See Spalding 2014 and Alicia Sword's contribution to this volume.

13. Growing concern about the cross-border consequences of mining in places like Cerro Blanco, a Guatemalan mine at the headwaters of the Lempa River, produced a call for cross-border regulation and the suspension of mining in neighboring countries (Procuraduría para la Defensa de los Derechos Humanos 2013).

14. In the ICSID process, the first round of review concerns whether a claim is significant or frivolous. Second round considers jurisdictional issues, to determine whether the ICSID tribunal is authorized to review the case. The third round focuses on the merits of claims made by the entity filing the case (typically the investor), and the rebuttal provided by the respondent (typically the government), with a more detailed arguments and documentation required. As of April 2014, the Pacific Rim case is in this third phase of review. The tribunal ruled against the company's claim to protection under CAFTA, rejecting the Canadian company's assertion of status as a U.S. business (based on a shell operation it had opened in Nevada). The case was allowed to advance, however, under El Salvador's 1999 Investment Law.

15. According to a study of the international investment arbitration process published by the Corporate Europe Observatory and the Transnational Institute, legal costs in investor-state disputes run more than US$8 million per case and may surpass US$30 million. Two cases brought by Fraport, a German airport operator, reportedly cost the Philippine government US$58 million, an amount that could have covered the annual salary of 12,500 teachers or vaccinated 3.8 million children (Eberhardt and Olivet 2012, 7).

16. For detailed discussion of the rich history of solidarity activism during the Central American civil wars, see Smith 1996; Nepstad 2004; Perla 2008.

17. Domesticating INGOs, by virtue of their long entrenchment in a country and durable commitment to local partners, come to function as quasi-national entities, engaging in cam-

paigns, lobbying, and delegation work to reinforce the positions taken by their allies. See Spalding 2014 for further discussion of this typology of INGOs and debates about their roles.

18. ILO Convention 169 and the 2007 UN Declaration on the Rights of Indigenous Peoples affirmed the right of Indigenous communities to "free, prior and informed consent" regarding development initiatives affecting their territory. The idea that community approval should be a prerequisite for development projects "is emerging more broadly as a principle of best practice for sustainable development" (Oxfam America 2013, 2).

19. http://www.stopesmining.org/j25/index.php/who-we-are2 (accessed July 26, 2013). The U.S. organizations included longtime allies SHARE, CISPES, U.S.-El Salvador Sister Cities (2008–2013), and Oxfam America, and expanded to include Institute for Policy Studies, CIEL, Friends of the Earth, Sierra Club, Maryknoll Office for Global Concerns, the Democracy Center, Voices on the Border, Jobs with Justice, the Washington Office on Latin America, Washington Ethical Society Global Connections Committee, Midwest Coalition Against Lethal Mining, National Lawyers Guild, and Miners and the Environment. The Canadian affiliates were Mining Watch Canada, Council of Canadians, and Canadians against Mining in El Salvador. Pacific Rim was acquired by the Australian mining company Oceana Gold in late 2013, sparking the expansion of the Mesa's international network into Australia.

20. The petition drive had secured 287 signatories from over 30 countries as of April 7, 2014.

Chapter Seventeen

Latin America

*Horizontal Dialogue, Agroecology,
and CLOC/Via Campesina*

María Elena Martínez-Torres and Peter M. Rosset

In this chapter we argue that the transnational peasant social movement, the Latin American Coordination of Peasant Organizations-Vía Campesina (CLOC/VC), has been critically sustained and shaped by horizontalism in the form of the encounter and *diálogo de saberes* (dialogue among different knowledges and ways of knowing) that takes place in its interior between different rural cultures.[1] These are diverse cultural expressions and experiences of peasants, Indigenous people, farmers, rural proletarians, and others. It is our contention that the horizontal processes of consensus building, decision making, and collective construction of new ideas in contemporary transnational rural social movements is done through a *diálogo de saberes* (DS). As a dialogue among the "absences" left out by the dominant monoculture of ideas and the anti-peasant policies, it has produced important "emergences." One of these emergences is the politicized and elaborated notion/practice/movement of agroecology, developed by CLOC/VC. Furthermore, the commitment to a horizontal decision-making process in this form of dialogue, and the unspoken rules by which it takes place, are key elements in the unusual longevity and continued growth of CLOC/VC.

CLOC AND VIA CAMPESINA: UNITY IN DIVERSITY

Rural social movements in Latin American began to build horizontal networks at the continental level in the 1980s. The demand for agrarian reform brought them together at the beginning of the decade, while toward the end

of the 1980s they began building popular resistance to the forthcoming celebration being planned by their governments for 1992, commemorating the
500th anniversary of the arrival of Columbus to the Americas. It seemed
strange to celebrate the colonial conquest, just when neoliberal policies were
rolling back the gains of independence and giving a new face to economic
neocolonialism on the continent. Meetings to plan continent-wide protests
brought together organizations of peasants, workers, Indigenous people, students, teachers, youth, women, academics, unions, and city slum dwellers.
Together they planned the "500 Years of Indigenous, Afro-descendant, Peasant and Popular Resistance Continental Campaign." The campaign didn't just
address the legacy of conquest but also attacked neoliberal economic policies
that, in the case of the Latin American peasantry, were eliminating—or seriously cutting back—the public-sector programs and institutions that supported peasant and family agriculture. As a result, the legitimacy of national
governments, their policies and political parties, and that of international
financial institutions, were being rapidly eroded in the eyes of rural people.
The changing nature of the state generated significant new challenges for
rural peoples, and in coping with and confronting them, peasants formed a
new generation of organizations that have moved toward the international
stage. As major policy changes that negatively impacted rural areas were
increasing imposed on states from beyond national borders, by foreign powers like the United States and the European Union, and especially by financial institutions and corporations, peasant organizations saw the need for
transnational organizing and protest that would bypass state hierarchies and
confront globalized and mobile capital (Martinez-Torrez and Rosset 2008,
2010).

   In the early 1990s, the peasant organizations that came to know each
other through the 500 Years campaign founded the Latin American Coordination of Rural Organizations (CLOC), and later were central to building the
global peasant movement La Via Campesina (Desmarais 2007; Martinez and
Rosset 2008, 2010). Nearly twenty years later they essentially merged, for-
malizing the de facto relationship in which CLOC was, and is, the Latin
American arm of La Via Campesina (LVC).[2] While it was clearly important
to have a continental expression of the peasant movement, the fact that
similar problems are found in rural areas globally helped drive recognition of
the need for unified struggle.

   A key horizontal process allowing the coalescence into CLOC, and later
LVC, was the DS that took place during the hundreds of meetings, in which
relations were built that allowed them to create horizontal decision-making
processes. Today LVC is a transnational social movement composed of national, regional, and continental movements and organizations of peasant and
family farmers, Indigenous people, landless peasants, farm workers, rural
women, and rural youth, representing some 200 million families worldwide

(Desmarais 2007, Martinez-Torres and Rosset 2008, 2010). LVC is not a single movement or organization, but rather a constellation composed of many rural movements and organizations. In this sense, LVC is a global, and horizontal, "space of encounter" among different rural and peasant cultures, different epistemologies and hermeneutics, whether East and West, North and South, landed and landless, farmer, pastoralist, and farm worker, Indigenous and non-Indigenous, women, men, elders, youth, and Hindu, Muslim, Buddhist, Animist, Mayan, Christian, and atheist (Martinez-Torres and Rosset 2010, Rosset 2013). Representatives of this immense diversity come together to exchange, dialogue, discuss, debate, analyze, strategize, build consensus around collective readings of reality, and agree on collective actions and campaigns with national, regional, continental, or global scope.

Within this diversity, there are many differences to work out, but it is remarkable that CLOC and LVC have grown and indeed become stronger over their twenty years of existence, without succumbing to internal fragmentation, as happened to many previous transnational alliances and movements (Martínez-Torres and Rosset 2010; Rosset 2013). How has this been possible? We argue that a commitment to horizontalism (Sitrin 2006), and in particular the process called *diálogo de saberes* in Spanish (Leff 2004), which roughly translates to "dialogue among different knowledges and ways of knowing," is key to the durability of the LVC constellation. It is a process in which different visions and cosmovisions are shared on a horizontal, equal-footing basis, that moves toward the decolonization of knowledge through recentering rural systems of knowledge, models of leadership, epistemologies, and understandings of the world (Hale and Stephen 2013, 17). Part of it can be thought of a rural way of solving or avoiding conflicts, because there is no single, monolithic knowledge that is imposed on others, as we shall show in the collective defining of agroecology described below.

This process of dialogue happens on multiple levels, for example *inside* each member organization, and *with* its own constellation of relationships from the local to the international level (inside and outside of CLOC/VC), and then *also* when they come together as CLOC and/or LVC. While there are differences, debates, and conflicts, the latter are typically tabled for later consideration when tensions have abated. This has repeatedly been the case with questions as diverse as relations between the peasant movement and other actors (both enemies and potential allies), conflicts between organizations that are from the same country, and issues of defining (or not) common ideological frameworks. Organizations take mutual inspiration from the experiences and visions of others. In particular, DS is how CLOC/VC grows and builds areas of internal consensus, which are often new, "emergent" proposals and ideas. As a recent LVC declaration put it, "We . . . have grown in our struggle, thanks to the exchange among cultures, to our processes, our victories and our setbacks, and to the diversity of our peoples" (La Via Campesina 2012; Rosset 2013).

DIÁLOGO DE SABERES (DS) AND HORIZONTALISM

For Marina Sitrin, "*horizontalidad* is a living word that reflects an ever-changing experience" (Sitrin 2006, 3). It is a goal as well as a tool of the new social arrangements and principles of organizations and movements that strive toward nonhierarchical ways of organizing and relating (3). However, no single word can describe the "process of continuous creation, constant growth, and the development of new relations, with ideas flowing from these changing practices" that characterize contemporary Latin American rural social movements (Sitrin 2006, 5).

In the case of CLOC/VC, we can say that relatively horizontal relations are a precondition for *diálogo de saberes* (DS). At the same time, DS is one of the most important aspects of horizontalism that have helped CLOC/LVC in the collective construction and/or further elaboration of ideas such as food sovereignty and agroecology, and to continue exist for so long without succumbing to internal splits. Among the other expressions of horizontalism in CLOC/VC that both facilitate and are strengthened by DS are: a) the collective and rotating nature of leadership; b) gender parity in all spaces of debate and decision making; c) the fact that all member organizations have autonomy, and the international network cannot intervene in national organizations; d) the depositing of the maximum authority in the International Congress, in which every organization is represented by a man, a woman, and a youth.

According to Enrique Leff (2004), DS "is a dialog with interlocutors that have been stripped of their own words and memory, traditional knowledges that have been buried by the imposition of modernity, and the dialog becomes an investigation, an exegesis, an hermeneutics of erased texts; it is a therapeutic politics to return the words and the meaning of languages whose flow has been blocked"[3] (Leff 2004, 26). It is an "opening and a call to subaltern knowledges, especially to those that sustained traditional cultures and today resignify their identities and position themselves in a dialog of resistance to the dominant culture that imposes its supreme knowledge" (26).

DS begins with the collective recognition, recovery, and valorization of autochthonous, local, and/or traditional knowledges (Leff 2011). CLOC/VC is a space where an enormous DS takes place, which puts the (re)appropriation and sharing of their knowledges (the *absences* referred to by Santos[4]) into play. This leads to emergent discourses (the *emergences* of Santos[5]) that question the dominion of mercantile and objectivizing rationality, the commodification of nature, and economization of the world. In contrast to a totalitarian and uniform dominant worldview, in the dialogue of the absences the movements and organizations are constantly creating new, emergent knowledges and collective readings of reality (Santos 2009, 2010b, Calle Collado, Soler, and Rivera 2011, Sevilla Guzmán 2013) that allow them to relate in a nonhierarchical way. These come from dialogue among the veritable "ecology of knowledges" that exist among excluded peoples, and that are closely linked to and identified with their specific territories (Santos 2009, 2010b, Cárdenas Grajales 2010). In fact we argue that CLOC/ VC itself is an emergence from the dialogue among the absences (peasant, popular, and Indigenous peoples' organizations) that took place around the 500 Years campaign in the early 1990s, and through a horizontal decision process that occurred at meetings of organizations in Managua, Mons, and Tlaxcala, as described by Martínez-Torres and Rosset (2010), Desmarais (2007) and Rosset (2013). We agree with Leff (2004, 24) in that "*meaning* in the world, is reactivated in a potent movement unleashed through the *diálogo de saberes*, which is the exact opposite of the desire to fix the meaning of concepts in dictionaries and glossaries. . . . In *diálogo de saberes*, beings and knowledges from outside the time and space of positivist knowledge relate with one another."

In this sense, and for the purpose of our discussion, we define *Diálogo de Saberes* (DS) as:

> A collective construction of emergent meaning based on dialogue between people with different historically specific experiences, cosmovisions, and ways of knowing, particularly when faced with new collective challenges in a changing world. Such dialogue is based on horizontal exchange among differences and on collective reflection, often leading to emergent recontextualization and resignification of knowledges and meanings related to histories, traditions, territorialities, experiences, processes and actions. The new collective understandings, meanings, and knowledges may form the basis for collective actions of resistance and construction of new processes.[6]

HORIZONTALISM, *DIÁLOGO DE SABERES*, AND DIVERSE VISIONS OF AGROECOLOGY

To illustrate the nonhierarchical relations and horizontal decision-making process that occurs through this DS, in this section we take the example of the collective construction of shared visions of agroecology by the organizations and movements that form CLOC/VC in Latin America. The struggles around peasant agriculture in the era of global capitalism have to do with competing visions of what kind of productive and social relations are sustainable in the long run (Chilcote 2003, Rosset and Martínez-Torres 2012), thus a questioning about models of production occurred inside many of the agrarian movements that belong to CLOC/LVC. Their exchanges of experiences and DS provoked reflection about, and called into question, the use of purchased chemicals, commercial seeds, heavy machinery, and more, on their own land. The questioning was partly because such mimicking of the model of agribusiness in peasant territories would reproduce the forces of exclusion and the destruction of nature present in the larger struggle (Rosset 2013). In their early years many organizations had called for more credit, subsidized agrochemicals, and machinery for their members, since in many cases the land gained through occupations and/or land reform from the state was poor quality land suffering from soil compaction and degradation. Through the exchanges and DS, CLOC/LVC members and leaders realized that this land could only be restored by agroecological practices to recover soil organic matter, fertility, and functional biodiversity. Thus they embarked on an internal process of recovery of traditional practices.

It has been observed that the word agroecology is variously used in the literature to refer to a *science*, a *movement,* and a *practice*[7] (Wezel et al. 2009). In this sense, from the beginning of its approach to the subject, LVC has seen agroecology as a technicism of little transcendence if divorced from food sovereignty[8] and territory, which are the larger frames that give it meaning (LVC 2013), and that is why for the LVC, "the concept of agroecology goes beyond ecological and productive principles. Other social, cultural, and political goals are incorporated into the agroecological vision" (Machín Sosa et al. 2013, 30).

With a goal of collectively constructing a shared vision of what agroecology means to LVC (the philosophical, political, and technical content and rationale that links organizations in this work), the last six years have been a period of intense DS in the form of regional and continental encounters inside Via Campesina. The members of CLOC/VC organized two "Encounters of Agroecology Trainers in the Americas"[9] held in 2009 in Barinas, Venezuela, and 2011 in Chimaltenango, Guatemala, and sent a delegation to the first Global Encounter of Peasant Seed Farmers in Bali, Indonesia, and the First Global Agroecology Encounter in Surin, Thailand in 2012; culminating with their participation in the launching of the "agroecology village" at the 2013 Sixth International Conference of LVC in Jakarta, Indonesia.

This process helped CLOC/VC itself to collectively realize the sheer quantity of ongoing experiences with agroecology and sustainable peasant agriculture that are currently underway inside member organizations at the national and regional levels. The vast majority of organizations either already have some sort of internal program to promote agroecology and peasant seeds, or they are currently discussing how to create one. At these encounters they elaborate detailed work plans to support these ongoing experiences and to link them with one another in a horizontal exchange and learning process. A key and very illustrative point during the ongoing DS over agroecology— which contributed mightily to the evolution of the concept—was the first

Continental Encounter of Agroecology Trainers of LVC in the Americas, held in 2009 on the campus of the Latin American Institute of Agroecology Paulo Freire (IALA Paulo Freire), created jointly by LVC and the government of Venezuela in Barinas, to give agroecology and political training to the daughters and sons of peasants and Indigenous people. There a debate took place, in which three emblematic rural visions that coexist within CLOC/VC confronted each other in the attempt to advance the collective construction of a peasant agroecology, a debate that became a DS, which eventually produced emergent positions and allowed for horizontal decision-making processes.

The organizations that belong to CLOC/VC can be loosely grouped into three basic and highly stylized—for the sake of argument—categories based on the mobilizing identity frame that these use in their struggles. Their positions and identities are more trends along a continuum, but we simplify here for explanatory clarity: 1) The most common are those organizations that use a *peasant* identity, thus focusing organizing efforts on people grouped by a mode of production or way of making their living. Even if such a peasant organization has mostly Indigenous peasants as its membership base, it still typically organizes around "farmer" issues, such as access to land, crop and livestock prices, subsidies, and credit.[10] 2) Organizations that use a more *Indigenous* identity typically organize around the defense of territory, autonomy, culture, community, and language.[11] 3) Organizations that use a *rural proletarian* identity typically organize the landless to occupy land and/or organize rural labors into trade union formations.[12] The latter two types tend to be more radically antisystemic than the conventional peasant organizations, while the proletarians are the most overtly ideological. They have very different ways to relate to the state and to internal decision-making processes. However in the transnational space which they are part of through CLOC/LVC, it is possible to dialogue with one another and relate horizontally.

During the encounter that took place in Venezuela, it became clear that each of these kinds of organizations perceived agroecology very differently. The Indigenous organizations saw it as a synonym for highly diversified traditional farming systems on small plots of land, with practices, like planting dates, informed by traditional calendars based on the cosmos, passed down from the ancestors over millennia. The peasant organizations emphasized the family as the basic unit of organization in rural areas, and gave many examples of the *campesino a campesino* (farmer-to-farmer) methodology (Holt-Giménez 2006) for spreading agroecology. The Indigenous organizations responded that in their world, the community is the basic unit, and that rather than farmer-to-farmer methods that abstract a single family from their community and encourage that family to make individual decisions, agroecology needs to be discussed in the community assembly. For the proletarians, on the other hand, whose basic organizing unit is the collective (of

Maria Elena Martínez-Torres and Peter M. Rosset

workers, of families, of militants), agroecology should be informed by science and knowledge transmitted in classrooms, where young people are trained as technicians to help their collectives of families transition to ecological farming, which would be practiced on large areas, possibly by collectivized families and workers. In other words, each type of organization had remarkably different utopian visions, basic units of organization, and methods of transmitting knowledge, as we show schematically in Table 17.1.

Despite sometimes intense debate and even raised voices on a few occasions, the delegates to the encounter, and thus these knowledges, were able to dialogue with each other, and also with "scientific" and "expert" opinion in form of technical staff and academic allies who were invited, creating what Guiso (2000) calls collective hermeneutics. Leff (2004, 16) concluded that "new theoretical and political discourses are invented that interweave, hybridize, mimic, and confront each other in a dialog between communities and academy, between theory and praxis, between Indigenous and scientific knowledge."

The meeting was able to come up with elements of a new vision of agroecology, including a broad range of positions to be defended by LVC within this evolving framework (i.e., "respect for the Mother Earth and Nature"), and those elements of other, more technocentric visions that were to be rejected (i.e., "the separation of human beings from Nature").[13]

Table 17.1. Peasant, Indigenous and Proletarian Organizations, and Agroecology

Identity frame	Unit of organization	Transmission of knowledge	Emblematic struggles	Source of affinity with agroecology
Indigenous	Community	Coded in cultural traditions	Defense of territory and construction of autonomy	Indigenous cosmovision and care for Mother Earth
Peasant	Family	Experiential, farmer-to-farmer	Access to land, prices, subsidies, credit	Lower production costs, self-provisioning combined with marketing
Proletarian	Collective	Classrooms and technical assistance	Land occupations, strikes, transformation of the economic model	Socialist ideology, dispute with Capital

Two issues could not be resolved, that of "agroecology as an instrument of struggle for socialism," and "the concept of scale in agroecological production" (LVC 2013, 20). The issue of scale refers to the small family plot versus large collective settlement, as different utopian visions of the Indigenous and proletarian organizations, respectively. The difficulty in achieving consensus around the idea of socialism arose because some Indigenous delegates felt that "already existing socialism" had in the past not necessarily been hospitable for Indigenous people. In the words of an Indigenous leader who participated in the encounter, responding to the words of a leader from a proletarian organization,

> Your *cosmovision* of historical materialism is an interesting one, and we could learn a lot from it. But first you must accept that it is in fact a cosmovision, one among many, and that you can also learn from our cosmovisions. If you accept that, we can have a horizontal dialogue. [14]

He went on to say:

> We might agree to the idea of socialism as a goal, but first we need a debate about what we mean by socialism. Do we mean something like the communal and cooperative traditions of Indigenous peoples? In that case, we might agree. Or do we mean certain examples of socialism in the past, where it did not go so well for us?

He then invited all the delegates to table the question of socialism in the construction of a collective vision of agroecology until the second Continental Encounter, to be held two years later in Guatemala. Everyone agreed, and the organizers of the second Encounter were tasked to organize a series of roundtable discussions between Marxist and Mayan intellectuals on historical materialism, Indigenous cosmovision, and agroecology, which effectively took place in 2011. The following is an extract from the declaration of that second encounter:

> We believe in agroecology as a tool in the construction of another way to produce and reproduce life. It is part of a socialist project, a partnership between workers and grassroots organizations, both rural and urban. It should promote the emancipation of workers, peasants, Indigenous peoples and Afro-descendents. True agroecology, however, cannot coexist in the context of the capitalist system. We affirm that agroecology is based on ancestral knowledge and practices, building knowledge through dialogue and respect for different knowledges [*diálogo de saberes*] and processes, as well as the exchange of experiences and use of appropriate technologies to produce healthy foods that meet the needs of humankind and preserves harmony with *Pachamama* (the Mother Earth). We as La Via Campesina, a multicultural network of organizations and movements, will continue to recognize and strengthen the exchange of experiences and knowledge among peasants, family farmers, Indigenous

peoples and Afro-descendents, spreading and multiplying our training and education programs "from Farmer to Farmer" ("campesino a campesino"), through both open, formal and informal education spaces as well as in community-based and territorial processes. We recognize the fact that this meeting has been held on Mayan territory, where the *campesino*-to-*campesino* movement began, based on a process that builds unity, erases borders and creates horizontal and comprehensive exchanges of experiences and knowledge. We understand that there are no standardized methods or recipes in agroecology, but rather principles that unite us, such as organization, training and mobilization. Our quest to understand our world in relation to time, to its creative energies and forces and to our historical memories (of agriculture and humanity) is complemented by a historical materialist and dialectical interpretation of reality. Together we seek to develop our political and ideological understanding through a dialog among our cosmovisions to achieve structural change in Society, thus liberating us and achieving *buen vivir* (the Indigenous concept of "living well" in harmony with the Mother Earth) for our peoples. (LVC 2013, 47–48)[15]

In other words, after a process of DS that was spread over two years and two continental encounters, a consensus was reached inside CLOC/VC in Latin America that indeed recognizes historical materialism and diverse Indigenous and other cosmovisions as equals. These are issues and differences that literally broke other movements and alliances in the past, yet the praxis of DS has allowed LVC to move forward and gradually extend the area of consensus that makes possible a horizontal decision-making process within a great diversity of visions. Here we should be clear that the area of consensus in this case, and in general from processes of DS, is consensus around emergences, and not merely a midpoint between binomials.[16] It is worth noting that this particular consensus within LVC has been possible so far only in the Americas. The declaration and new position statement produced a year later, at the Global Agroecology Encounter in Thailand contain no reference to socialism or historical materialism, though both espouse anticapitalism (LVC 2013, 54–78).

This highlights an aspect we consider to be a crucial contribution of DS to the ability of LVC to survive for so long without major splits. We might call it a peasant, Indigenous, or community way of resolving conflicts that makes possible horizontal decision-making processes. In other words, it is not a mere average or midpoint position that typically emerges from this kind of DS, but rather "notions of development, biodiversity, territory, and autonomy emerge to configure strategies that mobilize social actions that legitimize rights which reinvent identities associated with the social re-appropriation of nature" (Leff 2004, 26). These are the emergences of Santos (2009, 2010a), and many times serve as internal mobilizing frames (Benford and Snow 2000). Barkin and Rosas (2009, 40) defined it as a "new communitarian rurality," because it also includes a renewed emphasis on cooperation and strengthening rural communities. Since the founding of LVC, each time we have observed potentially divisive disputes, they have been tabled for discussion at a later time. Sometimes they are tabled for years, while they gradually work themselves out in the background, or until emotions are calmed. When they are taken up again later, the impasse is typically resolved by the emergence of something new, which extends the core area of consensus a little bit farther. With so many issues to address, no single issue can be allowed to shatter the space of dialogue. The internal culture is such that the members do not push any given contradiction to the point of rupture. The space of LVC, like all human spaces, has power rifts, but these are downplayed. Time passes, and then issues are retaken. While things are heated, no resolution is attempted. This has created a "safe space" to the point that organizations that cannot be together in the same room inside their home country, can actually participate in a civil DS beyond their national borders in LVC meetings and make decisions horizontally.

DS is a basic, though nonexplicit, underlying process in LVC, and in the case of CLOC/VC in South America, it is also an explicit methodology. In what they call *diálogo de saberes en el Encuentro de Culturas* ("DS in the Encounter between Cultures"), the Brazilian and other South American organizations in CLOC/VC are using a somewhat formal methodology based on Freire's (1984) dialogic methods for recognizing the different cultures and cosmovisions present in a given territory, and facilitating a process by which they collectively construct their understanding and positions (Tardin 2006; Toná 2009; do Nascimento 2010; Guhur 2010). The method is "capable of creating horizontal relationships between technicians and peasants, between peasants and peasants, and between them and the society as a whole, based on the philosophies, politics, techniques and methodologies that go hand in hand with emancipation and liberation" (Tardin 2006, 1–2). It is based on a horizontal dialogue between peers who have different knowledges and cosmovisions that allow participants to experience horizontal decision making. They share their life histories, and engage in collective exercises to characterize the surrounding environment and space, to collect information (data) about the reality in that space, to systematically analyze that information, and, using Freirian generative questions (Freire 1984), to move toward collective intervention to transform the reality, followed by a new sequence of reflection.

CONCLUSION

From the DS inside LVC, and between LVC and other rural peoples (Rosset 2013), as well as with intellectuals and scientists, have come a series of emergent and mobilizing new ideas and processes. These range from emergent ways to understand changes in historical contexts, new processes to collectively transform reality in material territories, and new shared interpretive frames for internal mobilization and for the battle of ideas in the larger public imagination. Agroecology illustrates this. CLOC/VC has used horizontal DS to collectively define a social-movement vision of agroecology that goes well beyond the tame versions of an alternative technological fix bandied about by many scientists, research institutions, government agencies, and think tanks, to create a rich, emergent mobilizing frame for collective action. The new vision builds upon the contributions of diverse cosmovisions. Sevilla Guzmán (2013) and Calle Collado, Soler, and Rivera (2011) have placed these new visions of agroecology among "emergences" from contemporary social movement dialogues.

NOTES

1. This chapter is partially based on Martinez-Torres and Rosset (2014).
2. For almost two decades CLOC and LVC had separate meetings and their own representatives, though CLOC always functioned like a Latin American space in LVC. In recent years CLOC voted internally to formally become the Latin American "branch" of LVC, and adopted the name CLOC/VC. This was formalized at the Continental Assembly of CLOC/VC in Managua, Nicaragua, held in October 2013.
3. This and similar quotes have been translated from Spanish by the authors.
4. Autochthonous, local and/or traditional knowledges are called "absences" by Boaventura de Sousa Santos (2009, 2010a)—absences left out by the dominant "monoculture of knowledge." The dominant monoculture of ideas is enforced by formal, instrumental, and economic "rationality," which are used as tools for domination, control, "efficiency," and economization.
5. Santos tells us that dialogues among the absences can generate "emergences," which can create totally new ideas or social and political processes.
6. Elaborated by the authors.
7. Altieri (1995) is the classic text on agroecology.
8. Food sovereignty was coined by La Via Campesina and refers to people's right to healthy and culturally appropriate food produced through ecologically sound and sustainable methods, and their right to define their own food and agriculture systems. See Nyéléni Declaration (2007).
9. All regions of LVC had their Encounter of Agroecology Trainers. The Asian region encounter took place in 2010 in Colombo, Sri Lanka; Southern, Central and Eastern Africa region in 2011 in Shashe, Masvingo, Zimbabwe; West Africa region in 2011 in Techiman, Ghana, and European region in 2012 in Durango, Basque Country.
10. Examples of this type of organization would the National Union of Autonomous Regional Peasant Organizations (UNORCA) in Mexico and National Association of Small Farmers (ANAP) of Cuba.
11. Examples of this type of organization would the National Coordination of Indigenous Peoples and Campesinos (CONIC) of Guatemala and the Bartolina Sisa National Federation of Bolivian Peasant Women (FNMCB-BS).
12. Examples of these kinds of organizations would be the Landless Workers' Movement (MST) of Brazil and the Association of Rural Workers (ATC) of Nicaragua.
13. The full list of positions to be defended or rejected can be found on pp. 19–24, LVC 2013.
14. Author's notes from the encounter.
15. For Sevilla Guzman and Woodgate (2013, 42), the declaration of the second Continental Encounter of Agroecology Trainers of La Via Campesina in 2011 is an "unequivocal statement

proclaiming the indivisibility of science, movement and practice. Today, agroecologists, whether farmers or scientists, are working together to defend rural communities and agroecological cultures against the negative impacts of capitalist industrialization."

16. Leff (2004) distinguishes DS from mediations or stakeholder processes where the goal and the outcome reflect some kind of compromise(d) solution, whose "midpoint position" reflects the geometry of power (Massey 1991). In Martínez-Torres and Rosset (2010), we describe how LVC rejects this kind of process, where they would be forced to find a midpoint with completely unacceptable positions.

Conclusion

Changing Contexts and Movement Strategies

Richard Stahler-Sholk, Harry E. Vanden, and Marc Becker

The upswing in the Latin American cycle of contentious politics since the 1980s has moved into a new phase. Social movements that were galvanized into action in part by the harsh impact of neoliberal policies now operate in the post neoliberal period in the context of declining hegemony of the old Washington Consensus. The return of formal democracy to most of the region after the eclipse of the military regimes of the 1960s–1980s proved inadequate for delivering substantive social justice to poor majorities in the world's most unequal region. Marginalized by the political class, popular sectors across the region mobilized outside conventional institutions to topple some governments and challenge others, ushering in a pink tide of left governments in the twenty-first century.

Just as the region's social movements were once faced with the dilemma of whether to return to the confines of institutional politics to avoid the breakdown of fragile new democratic regimes, today they struggle with the question of whether to continue to support self-proclaimed left governments to prevent the electoral return of the right. Many of those governments have advanced state-directed, post-neoliberal development strategies such as "neo-extractivism," arguing that nationalization of petroleum and mining industries can finance redistributive social programs. Yet the forces of global capital continue to operate, and the logics of electoral politics and state power comingle with the broad-based and participatory nature of the contentious politics that define social movements. With Bolivia's first Indigenous president negotiating a highway project with Brazilian capital through the

TIPNIS Indigenous territory, and Brazil's PT (Workers Party) avoiding agrarian reform and repressing protest in anticipation of the 2014 World Cup soccer games, the honeymoon between social movements and left governments has morphed into a more difficult and contentious relationship.

While the context for organizing has changed, so have the region's movements themselves. Decades of neoliberal globalization have undermined worker organizing, but in response social actors redefined their identities and alliance strategies, and they have shifted the locus of their efforts from making demands on the state to attempting the transformation of society. Zapatista autonomous communities in rural Chiapas, punks and graffiti artists sharing space with grandmothers on the urban barricades in Oaxaca, Brazilian MST land occupiers, Argentine workers running recovered factories, and Honduran LGBTTI activists staking out new conceptual terrain within a globalized framework of human rights, are all examples of transformations in the spatial organization of power that Zibechi (2012) has characterized as "territories in resistance." Within these reclaimed spaces, grassroots activists are not waiting for change to be structured from above, but are developing new anti-hierarchical and participatory dynamics from below in what Sitrin (2012) calls "horizontalism." The processes and practices of movement organizing are themselves transformative—a new way of viewing social and political change that Motta (2013a) calls "reinventing the lefts."

Indigenous activists in Ecuador and Bolivia have been at the forefront of broadening the agenda of struggle beyond policies, parties, and elections to propose a fundamental reexamination of values that would reconceptualize politics as the collective striving for a good life, or *buen vivir*. Five hundred years after the European invasion, grassroots activists are challenging hegemonic constructions of the nation-state from below. Beyond the notion of identity politics and the "politics of culture" (Alvarez, Dagnino, and Escobar 1998), activists are explicitly recognizing the intersectionality of their multiple dimensions of identity, and asserting their agency to define and constitute themselves as social subjects. Examples include Afro-Brazilians organizing from below on the basis of their own construction of racial identity; popular feminism in Brazil as a lens through which to view the multiple subject positions of gender, race, and class; and explicit recognition of "other ways of knowing" within the diverse transnational peasant/farmer alliance that is Vía Campesina.

The ideological legitimacy of the neoliberal paradigm is substantially frayed, but global capital remains powerful and adaptable. Mega-development projects across the region, fueled by the commodity boom of the early twenty-first century, pose a major challenge to community control across the region. Global capital has found ways to repackage these schemes (such as the Plan Puebla-Panamá, reborn as Proyecto Mesoamérica), or ducked behind shifting ownership structures and international institutions and "free trade" agreements (as in El Salvador's mining controversy). Activists responded by forging transnational social movement networks, but this strategy was in potential tension with more locally based horizontal and participatory movement dynamics. Globalization from below, involving political learning and new forms of social communication within and between regions, can be seen in the twenty-first century not only in Latin America but also in movements as diverse as Occupy in the United States, anti-austerity protests in Spain and Greece, and the "Arab Spring" uprisings.

The question of the state, and the relation between social movements and state power, will continue to be key (Webber and Carr 2012; Ellner 2014; Prevost, Oliva and Vanden 2012). The Venezuelan case suggests that mobilization from below and state-supported transformation are not necessarily dichotomous alternatives. Honduran activists, in the aftermath of authoritarian regime change and intense repression under an ostensibly "democratic" regime, struggled with the issue of whether to focus on street protests or throw their mobilized energies behind an electoral effort to regain political space. Rather than being mutually exclusive, the two strategies can build on each other, but they can also distract from and draw energy away from more effective models of building political change.

Issues such as the shape of a post-neoliberal future for Latin America, the viability and merits of horizontal organizing dynamics and radically democratic political practices, and the tradeoffs of state versus movement-directed processes of transformation, will continue to figure prominently in the landscape of the region. The contours of struggle for social justice are changing rapidly.[1] This compilation is intended to highlight these comparative themes and trends in Latin American social movements, offering contemporary cases that illustrate the dilemmas, clarify the terms of debate, and explore different models for transformative praxis. A growing sense in the region (and beyond), clearly visible and audible in the marches and voices of the grassroots (Ross and Rein 2014), is that the old politics of elites acting upon the masses needs to be reversed. New radical praxis is being forged in the struggles of these movements as they interact with, and at times struggle against, the state and the forces of global capitalism. In keeping with the original meaning of the word radical, they are indeed returning to the roots for sustenance and strength. From this base, activists will build a stronger, more effective, and more successful struggle.

NOTE

1. Some useful electronic resources for keeping abreast of contemporary movement directions (in Latin America and beyond) include: http://nacla.org; http://upsidedownworld.org; http://mobilizingideas.wordpress.com; http://www.interfacejournal.net; and http://roarmag.org.

References

Acosta, Alberto. 2008. "El sentido de la refundación constitucional en tiempos de crisis." *Tendencia: Revista de Análisis Político* 7 (March/April): 13–17.

Adital [activist in Free Turnstyle Movement in Brasilia] and Raúl Zebechi. 2013. "La lenta construción de una nueva cultura política en Brasil," July 7. Taken from "Informe Zibechi," for el Programa de las Américas. http://www.cipamericas.org/es/archives/9991 (accessed July 12, 2013).

Adriance, Madeleine Cousineau. 1996. *Terra prometida: As comunidades eclesiais de base e os conflitos rurais*. São Paulo: Paulinas.

Agathangelou, Anna M., and L. H. M. Ling. 2004. "The House of IR: From Family Power Politics to the Poisies of Worldism." *International Studies Review* 6 (4): 21–50.

Albó, Xavier. 2007. "Bolivia: avances y tropezones hacia un nuevo país plurinacional e intercultural." In *Los pueblos indígenas y política en América Latina. El reconocimiento de sus derechos y el impacto de sus demandas a inicios del siglo XXI*, edited by Salvador Martí i Puig, 335–59. Fundación CIDOB, Barcelona.

Albro, Robert. 2005. "The Indigenous in the Plural in Bolivian Oppositional Politics." *Bulletin of Latin American Research* 24 (4): 433–53.

Albuja, Verónica, and Pablo Dávalos. 2014. "Ecuador: Extractive Capital and Post-neoliberalism." In *The New Extractivism: A Post-neoliberal Development Model or Imperialism of the Twenty-first Century?* edited by Henry Veltmeyer and James Petras, 144–71. London: Zed.

Alianza Cívica, Chiapas. 2003. "Declaración final: Memoria del II encuentro Chiapaneco frente al neoliberalismo." *Poder Ciudadano*, 21.

Almeida, Lucio Flávio de, and Felix Ruiz Sanchez. 2000. "The Landless Movement and Social Struggles against Neoliberalism." *Latin American Perspectives* 27 (5): 11–32.

Almeida, Paul D. 2006. "Social Movement Unionism, Social Movement Partyism, and Policy Outcomes." In *Latin American Social Movements: Globalization, Democratization, and Transnational Networks*, edited by Hank Johnston and Paul Almeida, 57–73. Lanham, MD: Rowman & Littlefield.

———. 2008. *Waves of Protest: Popular Struggle in El Salvador, 1925–2005*. Minneapolis: University of Minnesota Press.

Almeyra, Guillermo. 2008. "La mano y el codo." *Rebelión*, January 28. http://www.rebelion.org/noticia.php?id=62482.

Alonso, Jorge. 1980. *Lucha urbana y acumulación de capital*. México: La Casa Chata.

Altieri, Miguel A. 1995. *Agroecology: The Science of Sustainable Agriculture*. Boulder, CO: Westview Press.

Alvarez, Sonia E. 1989. "Politicizing Gender and Engendering Democracy." In *Democratizing Brazil: Problems of Transition and Consolidation,* edited by Alfred Stepan, 205–51. New York: Oxford University Press.

———. 1990. *Engendering Democracy in Brazil: Women's Movements in Transition Politics.* Princeton, NJ: Princeton University Press.

Alvarez, Sonia E., Evelina Dagnino, and Arturo Escobar, eds. 1998. *Cultures of Politics, Politics of Cultures: Re-visioning Latin American Social Movements.* Boulder, CO: Westview Press.

Anderson, Sarah, and Manuel Pérez-Rocha. 2013. *Mining for Profit in International Tribunals.* (updated edition). Institute for Policy Studies. http://www.ips-dc.org/reports/mining_for_profits_update2013 (accessed July 22, 2013).

Andrews, Abigail. 2011. "How Activists 'Take Zapatismo Home': South-to-North Dynamics in Transnational Social Movements." *Latin American Perspectives* 38 (176): 138–52.

Andrews, George Reid. 1996. "Brazilian Racial Democracy, 1900–1990s: An American Counter Point," *Journal of Contemporary History* 31 (3): 483–507.

Angulo Ruiz, Luis. 2006. *Francisco Wuytack: La revolución de la conciencia.* Caracas: Ministerio de la Cultura/Fundación Editorial el Perro y la Rana.

Anria, Santiago. 2013. "Social Movements, Party Organization, and Populism: Insights from the Bolivian MAS." *Latin American Politics and Society* 55 (3): 19–46.

Anzaldúa, Gloria. 2007. *Borderlands/La Frontera: The New Mestiza.* San Francisco: Aunt Lute Books.

Anzaldúa, Gloria, and Ana Louise Keating. 2002. *The Bridge We Call Home: Radical Visions for Transformation.* London: Routledge.

Aquino Moreschi, Alejandra. 2009. "Between the Zapatista and American Dreams: Zapatista Communal Perspectives on Migration to the United States." *Migración y Desarrollo* 13 (2nd semester), 69–84. http://rimd.reduaz.mx/revista/rev13ing/rev13ing_5.pdf (accessed January 13, 2014).

———. 2013. "'No me desilusioné del movimiento, me desesperé.' Las paradojas de la militancia zapatista en tiempos de guerra." *Nueva Antropología* 26 (78): 163–89.

Arellano Chávez, Daniel. 2010. "México: A 3 años de la ocupación de Oaxaca, a 10 años de la creación de la Policía Federal Preventiva (PFP)." http://old.kaosenlared.net/noticia/mexico-3-anos-ocupacion-oaxaca-10-anos-creacion-policia-federal-preven (accessed January 19, 2013).

Arenhart, Deise. 2003. *A educação da infância no MST: O olhar das crianças sobre uma pedagogia em movimento.* Florianópolis: Universidade Federal de Santa Catarina.

Argentina Indymedia. 2002. "El MTD Lanus." http://argentina.indymedia.org/news (accessed 3 February 2014).

Ariza, Marina, and Juan Manuel Ramírez. 2005. "Urbanización, mercados de trabajo y escenarios sociales en el México finisecular." In *Ciudades latinoamericanas,* edited by Alejandro Portes, Bryan Roberts, and Alejandro Grimson, 251-302. Buenos Aires: Prometeo.

Asociación Colectivo Violeta, Asociación Kukulcan, Asociación LGTB Arco Iris de Honduras, APUVIMEH. 2012. *Movimiento LGBT en Honduras: Trayectoria histórica y desafíos actuales.* Tegucigalpa, Honduras.

Aubry, Andrés. 2003. "Autonomy in the San Andrés Accords: Expression and Fulfillment of a New Federal Pact." In *Mayan Lives, Mayan Utopias: The Indigenous Peoples of Chiapas and the Zapatista Rebellion,* edited by Jan Rus, Rosalva Aída Hernández Castillo, and Shannan L. Mattiace, 219–41. Lanham, MD: Rowman & Littlefield.

———. 2011. "Otro modo de hacer ciencia: Miseria y rebeldía de las ciencias sociales." In *Luchas "muy otras": zapatismo y autonomía en las comunidades indígenas de Chiapas,* edited by Bruno Baronnet, Mariana Mora Bayo, and Richard Stahler-Sholk, 59–78. Mexico City: UAM-Xochimilco/CIESAS/UNACH.

Azzellini, Dario. 2014. "The Communal System as Venezuela's Transition to Socialism." In *Communism in the 21st Century, Vol. 2,* edited by S. Brincat, 217–49. Westport, CT: Praeger.

———. Forthcoming. *Workers' Control and Democracy in Production: An Alternative Labour History.* London: Zed Books

Azzellini, Dario, and Oliver Ressler. 2010. *Comuna en construcción*. http://www.azzellini.net/en/films/comuna-under-construction (accessed 25 February 2010).

Bacon, David. 2006. *Communities without Borders: Images and Voices from the World of Migration*. Ithaca, NY: ILR Press.

Baierle, Sérgio Gregório. 1998. "The Explosion of Experience: The Emergence of a New Ethical-Political Principle in Popular Movements in Porto Alegre, Brazil." In *Culture of Politics, Politics of Culture: Re-Visioning Latin American Social Movements* edited by Sonia E. Alvarez, Evelina Dagnino, and Arturo Escobar, 118–38. Boulder, CO: Westview Press.

Banco de Dados Políticos das Américas. 2002. Brazil: Eleições Presidenciais de 1998. http://pdba.georgetown.edu/%20Elecdata/Brazil/pres98.html (accessed April 19, 2002).

Barahona, Marvin. 1989. *La hegemonía de los Estados Unidos en Honduras (1907–1932)*. Tegucigalpa, Honduras: Centro de Documentación de Honduras.

———. 2004. *El silencio quedó atrás: Testimonio de la huelga bananera de 1954*. Tegucigalpa, Honduras: Editorial Guaymuras.

———. 2005. *Honduras en el Siglo XX: Una sintesis histórica*. Tegucigalpa, Honduras: Editorial Guaymuras.

———. 2008. "Localidad y globalización en la dinámica migratoria hacia los Estados Unidos." *Envío Honduras* 6 (17): 22–29.

Barkin, David, and Mara Rosas. 2009. "Tradición e innovación. Aportaciones campesinas en la orientación de la innovación tecnológica para forjar sustentabilidad." *Trayectorias* 11 (29): 39–54.

Barmeyer, Niels. 2009. *Developing Zapatista Autonomy: Conflict and NGO Involvement in Rebel Chiapas*. Albuquerque: University of New Mexico Press.

Baronnet, Bruno. 2008. "Rebel Youth and Zapatista Autonomous Education." *Latin American Perspectives* 35 (4): 112–24.

———. 2012. *Autonomía y educación indígena. Las escuelas zapatistas de la Selva Lacandona de Chiapas, México*. Quito: Abya Yala.

Baronnet, Bruno, Mariana Mora Bayo, and Richard Stahler-Sholk, eds. 2011. *Luchas "muy otras": Zapatismo, autonomía, y las comunidades indígenas de Chiapas*. Mexico City: UAM-Xochimilco/CIESAS/UNACH.

Beato, Luciana Bandeira. 2004. "Inequality and Human Rights of African Descendants in Brazil," *Journal of Black Studies* 34, 766–86.

Bebbington, Anthony, and Jeffrey Bury. 2013. *Subterranean Struggles: New Dynamics of Mining, Oil, and Gas in Latin America*. Austin: University of Texas Press.

Becker, Marc. 2012. *Pachakutik: Indigenous Movements and Electoral Politics in Ecuador*. Lanham, MD: Rowman & Littlefield.

———. 2013. "The Stormy Relations between Rafael Correa and Social Movements in Ecuador." *Latin American Perspectives* 40 (3): 43–62.

Bellinghausen, Hermann. 2014. "Tzotziles interponen amparo contra la autopista San Cristóbal-Palenque." *La Jornada,* January 15, 23.

Benegas, Diego Loyo. Forthcoming. *Against Terror: Trauma and Political Action in Post Dictatorship Argentina*. Río Cuarto, Argentina: Ediciones Universidad Nacional de Río Cuarto.

Benessaieh, Afef. 2011. "Global Civil Society: Speaking in Northern Tongues?" *Latin American Perspectives* 38 (6): 69–90.

Benford, Robert D., and David A. Snow. 2000. "Framing Processes and Social Movements: An Overview and Assessment." *Annual Review of Sociology* 26: 611–39.

Benjamin, Walter. 1968. "Theses on the Philosophy of History." In *Illuminations: Essays and Reflections*, edited by H. Arendt, 253–64. New York: Schocken Books.

Berger, Susan A. 2006. *Guatemaltecas: The Women's Movement, 1986–2003*. Austin, TX: University of Texas Press.

Bermúdez, Norma Lucia. 2013. "Cali's Women in Collective Crossing through Three Worlds: Popular Education, Feminisms and Nonviolence for the Expansion of the Present, Memory and Nurturing of Life." In *Education and Social Change in Latin America*, edited by Sara

Catherine Motta and Alf Gunfeld Nilsen, 239–60. New York and London: Palgrave Macmillan.

Betto, Frei. 1994. "Teologia da libertação e espiritualidade popular." In *Mística e espiritualidade*, edited by Leonardo Boff and Frei Betto, 44–45. Rio de Janeiro: Rocco.

———. 2001a. "Valores da mística da militância política." In *Mística da militância, Encontro nacional de fé e política*. Goiás: Editora Rede.

———. 2001b (circa). *Dez conselhos para os militantes de esquerda*. São Paulo: MST.

Bhattacharjya, Manjima, Jenny Birchall, Pamela Caro, David Kelleher and Vinita Sahasranaman. 2013. "Why Gender Matters in Activism: Feminism and Social Justice Movements." *Gender & Development* 21 (2): 277-293.

Binford, Leigh. 2004. "Peasants, Catechists, Revolutionaries: Organic Intellectuals in the Salvadoran Revolution, 1980–1992." In *Landscapes of Struggle: Politics, Society and Community in El Salvador*, edited by Aldo Lauria-Santiago and Leigh Binford, 105–25. Pittsburgh: University of Pittsburgh Press.

———. 2013. "Migration, Tourism, and Post-Insurgent Individuality in Northern Morazán, El Salvador." In *Central America in the New Millennium: Living Transition and Reimagining Democracy*, edited by Jennifer L. Burrell and Ellen Moodie, 245–60. New York: Berghahn Books.

Boff, Leonardo. 1993. "Alimentar nossa mística." *Cadernos Fé e Política* 9, 7–25. Petrópolis: Movimento Fé e Política.

———. 1994a. "Que é mística?" In *Mística e espiritualidade*, edited by Leonardo Boff and Frei Betto, 33–52. Rio de Janeiro: Rocco.

———. 1994b. "Mística e cultos africanos." In *Mística e espiritualidade*, edited by Leonardo Boff and Frei Betto, 129–132. Rio de Janeiro: Rocco.

Boff, Leonardo, and Clovis Boff. 1987. *Introducing Liberation Theology*. Maryknoll, NY: Orbis.

Bogo, Ademar. 1999. *Lições da luta pela terra*. Salvador: Memorial das Letras.

———. 2002. *O vigor da mística*. São Paulo: MST.

Böhm, Steffen, Ana C. Dinerstein, and André Spicer. 2010. "(Im)possibilities of Autonomy: Social Movements in and beyond Capital, the State and Development." *Social Movement Studies* 9 (1): 17–32.

Bonafi, Hebe de. 2011. "Hebe de Bonafini's Letter to Cristina Kirchner." M24Digital.com. January 2. http://m24digital.com/en/2011/01/02/hebe-debonafinis-letter-to-cristinakirchner/ (accessed June 7, 2012).

Bonetti, Alinne de Lima. 2007. "Não basta ser mulher, tem de ter coragem: Uma etnografia sobre gênero, poder, ativismo feminino popular e o campo político feminista de Recife-PE." PhD. Diss., Universidade Estadual de Campinas—IFCH: Campinas.

Bowden, James. 2011. "The Right in 'New Left' Latin America." *Journal of Politics in Latin America* 3 (1): 99–124.

Branford, Sue, and Oriel Glock. 1985. *The Last Frontier: Fighting over Land in the Amazon*. London: Zed Books.

Breines, Wini. 1979. "Community and Organization: The New Left and Michels Iron Law." *Social Problems* 27: 496–506.

Burbach, Roger, Michael Fox, and Federico Fuentes, eds. 2013. *Latin America's Turbulent Transitions: The Future of Twenty-First Century Socialism*. London: Zed Books.

Burguete Cal y Mayor, Araceli. 2000. *Indigenous Autonomy in Mexico*. Copenhagen: International Work Group for Indigenous Affairs (IWGIA).

———. 2005. "Una década de autonomías de facto en Chiapas (1994–2004): Los límites." In *Pueblos indígenas, estado y democracia*, edited by Pablo Dávalos, 239–78. Buenos Aires: CLACSO.

Butler, Kim. 1998. "Ginga Baina: The Politics of Race, Class, Culture and Power in Bahia." In *Afro-Brazilian Culture and Politics: Bahia, 1790s to 1990s*, edited by Kraay Hendrik, 158–76. Armonk, NY: M.E. Sharpe.

Buxton, Julia. 2001. *The Failure of Political Reform in Venezuela*. Aldershot: Ashgate.

Caldart, Roseli Salete. 2000. *Pedagogia do Movimento Sem Terra*. Petrópolis: Editora Vozes.

Caldeira, Rute. 2009. "The Failed Marriage between Women and the Landless People's Movement (MST) in Brazil." *Journal of International Women's Studies* 10 (4): 237–58.

Caldeira, Teresa Pires do Rio. 1990. "Women, Daily Life, and Politics." In *Women and Social Change in Latin America*, edited by Elizabeth Jelin, 47–78. Atlantic Highlands, NJ: Zed Books.

Caldwell, Kia Lilly. 2007. *Negras in Brazil: Re-envisioning Black Women, Citizenship, and the Politics of Identity*. New Brunswick, NJ: Rutgers University Press.

———. 2010. "Advocating for Citizenship and Social Justice: Black Women Activists in Brazil." In *Women's Activism in Latin America and the Caribbean: Engendering Social Justice, Democratizing Citizenship*, edited by Elizabeth Maier and Nathalie Lebon, 175–86. New Brunswick, NJ: Rutgers University Press.

Call, Wendy. 2002. "Resisting the Plan Puebla-Panama." *Americas Program*. Silver City, NM: Interhemispheric Resource Center.

———. 2003a. "PPP Focus Moves South as Mexican Backing Loses Momentum." *PPP Spotlight #1, Americas Program* (Silver City, NM: Interhemispheric Resource Center).

———. 2003b. "Public Relations Firm to the Rescue of Plan Puebla-Panamá." *PPP Spotlight #4, Americas Program* (Silver City, NM: Interhemispheric Resource Center).

Calle Collado, Angel, Marta Soler Montiel, and Marta G. Rivera Ferré. 2011. "La democracia alimentaria: soberanía alimentaria y agroecología emergente." In *Democracia radical: Entre vínculos y utopías*, edited by Angel Calle Collado, 213–38. Barcelona: Icaria.

Campbell, Howard. 1994. *Zapotec Renaissance: Ethnic Politics and Cultural Revivalism in Southern Mexico*. Albuquerque: University of New Mexico.

Cappellin Paola Giulani. 1994. Atrás das Práticas: O Perfil das Sindicalistas. Paper presented at the GT; Trabalhadores, Sindicalismo e Política, XVIII Encontro Nacional ANPOCS, Caxambu.

———. 2000. "Os movimentos de trabalhadoras e a sociedade brasileira," In *História das mulheres no Brasil*, edited by Mary Del Priore and Carla Bassanezi, 640–67. São Paulo: Contexto/UNESP.

Cárdenas Grajales, G. I. 2010. "El conocimiento tradicional y el concepto de territorio." *Revista NERA* (Brazil) 2 (February): 1–12.

Carlsen, Laura, and Michael Collins. 2010. "The Inter-American Development Bank in Mexico: Plan Puebla-Panamá, Integration and Displacement." *CIPAmericas Program*. http://www.cipamericas.org/archives/2421

Carney, Padre Guadalupe J. 1985. *To Be a Revolutionary: The Explosive Autobiography of an American Priest, Missing in Honduras*. San Francisco: Harper and Row.

Cartilha Themis. 1998. *Direitos humanos—acesso á justiça—a experiência das promotoras legais populares*. Thêmis-Assessoria Jurídica e Estudos de Gênero, Porto Alegre. http://www.dhnet.org.br/dados/cartilhas/a_pdf_dht/cartilha_themis_promotoras_legais_pop.pdf (accessed January 20, 2014).

Castells, Manuel. 1986. *La ciudad y las masas. Sociología de los movimientos sociales urbanos*. Madrid: Alianza.

———. 2012. *Networks of Outrage and Hope: Social Movements in the Internet Age*. Cambridge and Malden, MA: Polity Press.

———. 2013. *Redes de indignação e esperança, movimentos sociais na era da Internet*. Rio de Janeiro: Jorge Zahar Editor Ltda.

Castro, Mary Garcia. 1999. "The Growth of Working-class Feminism in Brazil." *NACLA Report on the Americas* 32 (January/February): 28–31.

Ceceña, Ana Esther. 2012. "On the Complex Relation between Knowledges and Emancipations." *South Atlantic Quarterly* 111 (1): 111–32.

Ceceña, Ana Esther, et al. 2011. *Pensar las autonomías*. Mexico City: Bajo Tierra/Sísifo Ediciones.

Cedillo-Cedillo, Adela. 2012. "Análisis de la fundación del EZLN en Chiapas desde la perspectiva de la acción colectiva insurgente." *Revista Liminar* 10 (2): 15–34.

Center for International Environmental Law (CIEL). 2011. "Pac Rim Cayman LLC v. Republic of El Salvador, ICSID Case No. ARB/09/12, Submission of *Amicus Curiae* Brief." http://

www.ciel.org/Publications/PAC_RIM_Amicus_20May11_Eng.pdf (accessed February 16, 2014).

Cerda García, Alejandro. 2011. *Imaginando zapatismo: Multiculturalidad y autonomía indígena en Chiapas desde un municipio autónomo.* Mexico City: UAM-Xochimilco.

Chant, Sylvia. 2008. "The 'Feminisation of Poverty' and the 'Feminisation' of Anti-poverty Programmes: Room for Revision?" *Journal of Development Studies* 44 (2): 165–97.

Chávez, Claudia, and Adriana Terven. 2013. "Las prácticas de justicia indígena bajo el reconocimiento del estado: El caso poblano desde la experiencia organizativa de Cuetzalan." In *Justicias indígenas y Estado: Violencias contemporáneas*, edited by María Teresa Sierra, Rosalva Aída Hernández, and Rachel Sieder, 51–87. Mexico City: FLACSO/CIESAS.

Chávez Frías, Hugo. 2010. "Onwards Towards a Communal State!" *Venezuela Analysis*, February 22. Translated by Kiraz Janicke. http://venezuelanalysis.com/analysis/5160 (accessed January 28, 2014).

———. 2012. *Golpe de timón.* Caracas: Ediciones Correo del Orinoco.

Chilcote, Ronald H. (ed.), 2003. *Development in Theory and Practice: Latin American Perspectives.* Lanham, MD: Rowman & Littlefield.

Chimba Simba, Luis Fernando, and Laura Santillán. 2008. "Evaluación y revolución ciudadana: ¿Nueva forma de colonización?" *Ayni Solidaridad* 2 (June): 4.

Cholango, Humberto. 2007a. "Un estado plurinacional significa transformar el estado." *Rikcharishun* 35 (May): 3, 6.

———. 2007b. "Editorial." *Rikcharishun* 35 (August): 1.

———. 2008a. "Entrevista a Humberto Cholango." *Espacios: Aportes al Pensamiento Crítico Contemporáneo* 14 (February): 61–65.

———. 2008b. "Las razones por qué vamos a votar sí." *Rikcharishun* 36 (August–September): 2.

———. 2008c. "Confederación Kichwa del Ecuador ante el triunfo del SI." September 30. href="http:///www.ecuarunari.org/es/noticias/no_20080930.html">/

Chuji, Mónica. 2008a. "Políticas ambientales: Los límites del desarrollismo y la plurinacionalidad." *Tendencia: Revista de Análisis Político* 7 (March/April): 49–55.

———. 2008b. "El estado plurinacional." *Yachaykuna* 8 (April): 11–22.

Chukaitis, Stephen. 2009. *Imaginal Machines: Autonomy and Self-Organization in the Revolutions of Everyday Life.* London/New York: Minor Compositions/Autonomedia.

Ciccariello-Maher, George. 2013. *We Created Chávez: A People's History of the Venezuelan Revolution.* Durham, NC: Duke University Press.

CIESS Econometrica. 2013. "Productividad media de la oja de coca." Unpublished report.

Citeli, Maria Teresa. 1994. "Mulheres em Movimentos de Saúde: Desafios na luta por Cidadania Reprodutiva." Paper presented at the 18th Annual Meeting of ANPOCS, Caxambu, Brazil.

Cleaver, Harry M. 1998. "The Zapatistas and the Electronic Fabric of Struggle." In *Zapatista! Reinventing Revolution in Mexico,* edited by John Holloway and Eloína Peláez, 81–103. London: Pluto Press.

Cohen, Jeffrey H. 2004. *The Culture of Migration in Southern Mexico.* Austin: University of Texas Press.

Colectivo Situaciones. 2003. "On the Militant-Researcher." https://transform.eipcp.net/transversal/0406/colectivosituaciones (accessed March 14, 2013).

Collier, George, with Elizabeth Lowery Quaratiello. 2005. *Basta! Land and the Zapatista Rebellion in Chiapas.* 3rd ed. Oakland, CA: Food First Books.

Comisión Civil Internacional de Observación por los Derechos Humanos (CCIODH). 2008. *Informe sobre los hechos de Oaxaca:* 5ª Visita. Barcelona: Gráficas Lunas.

Comissão Pastoral da Terra. 1998. *Trabalho escravo nas fazendas, pará e amapá 1980–1997.* Belém.

Comunicación Pachakutik. 2006. "He sentido la solidaridad y la fraternidad de la gente." *Rikcharishun* 34 (September): 3.

"Comunidades se anotan 'primera victoria' contra minería metálica." 2006. *Diario Co Latino*, November 25. http://www.diariocolatino.com (accessed February 15, 2014).

CONAIE (Confederación de Nacionalidades Indígenas del Ecuador). 2007a. *La CONAIE frente a la asamblea constituyente: Propuesta de nueva constitución desde la CONAIE para la construcción de un estado plurinacional, unitario, soberano, incluyente, equitativo y laico (Documento de principios y lineamientos)*. Quito.

—. 2007b. *Constitución del estado plurinacional de la república del Ecuador: Propuesta de la Confederación de Nacionalidades Indígenas del Ecuador-CONAIE*. Quito.

—. 2008. "La CONAIE toma distancia con el gobierno." *AyniSolidaridad* 2 (June): 8.

Conçeicão, Fernando. 2010. "Power and Black Organizing in Brazil." In *Brazil: New Racial Politics,* edited by Bernd Reiter and Gladys L. Mitchell, 187–195. Boulder, CO: Lynne Rienner Press.

Conferencia Episcopal de El Salvador. 2007. "Cuidemos la casa de todos: Pronunciamiento de la Conferencia Episcopal de El Salvador sobre la explotación de minas de oro y plata." http://www.minesandcommunities.org/article.php?a=2671&l=2 (accessed February 16, 2014).

Cook, Maria Lorena. 1996. *Organizing Dissent: Unions, the State, and the Democratic Teachers' Movement in Mexico*. University Park: Pennsylvania State University Press.

Corcoran-Nantes, Yvonne. 2000. "Female Consciousness or Feminist Consciousness? Women's Consciousness-raising in Community Struggles in Brazil." In *Global Feminisms since 1945: Rewriting Histories,* edited by Bonnie G. Smith, 81–100. New York: Routledge.

CTU (Comités de Tierra Urbana). 2003. "Democratización de la ciudad y transformación urbana." Caracas.

Cuba Rojas, L. Pablo. 2006. "Bolivia: Movimientos sociales, nacionalización y asamblea constituyente." *OSAL, Observatorio Social de America Latina* 4 (19): 55–64.

Dagnino, Evelina. 1998. "Culture, Citizenship and Democracy: Changing Discourses and Practices of the Latin American Left." In *Culture of Politics, Politics of Culture: Re-Visioning Latin American Social Movements,* edited by Sonia E. Alvarez, Evelina Dagnino, and Arturo Escobar, 33–63. Boulder, CO: Westview Press.

Dangl, Benjamin. 2007. *The Price of Fire: Resource Wars and Social Movements in Bolivia*. Oakland, CA: AK Press.

—. 2010. *Dancing with Dynamite: Social Movements and States in Latin America*. Oakland, CA: AK Press.

De Angelis, Massimo. 2010. *The Beginnings of History: Value Struggles and Global Capital*. London: Pluto Press.

De Landa, Manuel. 1997. *A Thousand Years of Nonlinear History*. New York: Zone Books.

De la Peña, Guillermo. 2006. "A New Mexican Nationalism? Indigenous Rights, Constitutional Reform and the Conflicting Meanings of Multiculturalism." *Nations and Nationalism* 12 (2): 279–302.

Dellacioppa, Kara Zugman. 2009. *This Bridge Called Zapatismo: Building Alternative Political Cultures in Mexico City, Los Angeles, and Beyond*. Lanham, MD: Lexington Books.

—. 2011. "The Bridge Called Zapatismo: Transcultural and Transnational Activist Networks in Los Angeles and Beyond." *Latin American Perspectives* 38 (120): 120–37.

Dellacioppa, Kara Z., and Clare Weber. 2012. *Cultural Politics and Resistance in the 21st Century: Community Based Social Movements and Global Change in the Americas*. New York: Palgrave McMillan.

Denham, Diane, and C.A.S.A. Collective. 2008. *Teaching Rebellion: Stories from the Grassroots Mobilization in Oaxaca*. Oakland, CA: PM Press.

Denis, Roland. 2010. "Por unas comunas 'sin ley.'" *Aporrea.org*, October 19. http://www.aporrea.org/ideologia/a110539.html (accessed February 2, 2014).

—. 2014. "¿Quién está dispuesto?" *Aporrea.org*, April 17. http://www.aporrea.org/actualidad/a186428.html (accessed May 10, 2014).

Denvir, Daniel. 2008. "Wayward Allies: President Rafael Correa and the Ecuadorian Left." *UpsideDownWorld*, July 25.

Deslandes, Ann. 2009. "Giving Way at the Intersection: Anticolonial Feminist Ethics of Solidarity in the Global Justice Movement." *Australian Feminist Studies* 24 (62): 421–37.

Desmarais, Annette Aurélie. 2007. *La Via Campesina: Globalization and the Power of Peasants*. London: Pluto Press.

De Vos, Jan. 2002. *Una tierra para sembrar sueños: Historia reciente de la Selva Lacandona, 1950-2000*. Mexico City: CIESAS/Fondo de Cultura Económica.

Díaz Montes, Fausto. 2009. "Elecciones y protesta social en Oaxaca." In *La APPO: ¿Rebelión o movimiento social? (Nuevas formas de expresión ante la crisis)*, edited by V. R. Martínez Vásquez, 247–73. Oaxaca: Universidad Autónoma "Benito Juárez" de Oaxaca.

Díaz-Polanco, Héctor. 2000. "Self-Determination and Autonomy: Achievements and Uncertainty." In *Indigenous Autonomy in Mexico*, edited by Araceli Burguete Cal y Mayor, 83–96. Copenhagen: International Work Group for Indigenous Affairs.

Diez, Juan. 2011. "El zapatismo es un verbo que se escribe en gerundio. Las rearticulaciones e interacciones al interior del movimiento Zapatista." *A Contracorriente* 8 (2): 34–61. http://acontracorriente.chass.ncsu.edu/index.php/acontracorriente/article/view/413/630#. UmMFvxCFfSg (accessed October 19, 2013).

Di Marco, Graciela. 2010. "Women's Movements in Argentina: Tensions and Articulations." In *Women's Activism in Latin America and the Caribbean: Engendering Social Justice, Democratizing Citizenship*, edited by Elizabeth Maier and Nathalie Lebon, 159–74. New Brunswick, NJ: Rutgers University Press.

Dinerstein, Ana, S. Bohn, and A. Spicer. 2009. "The (im)possibilities of Autonomy." Working Paper, London School of Economics. http://opus.bath.ac.uk/18413/ (accessed May 2, 2014).

Diniz, Aldiva Sonia, and Bruce Gilbert. 2013. "Socialist Values and Cooperation in Brazil's Landless Rural Workers' Movement." *Latin America Perspectives* 40 (4): 19–34.

Do Alto, Herve, and Pablo Stefanoni. 2010. "Las ambivalencias de la democracia corporative." *Le Monde Diplomatique*, Bolivian edition (May): 4–6.

do Nascimento, L. B. 2010. "Dialogo de saberes: tratando do agroecossistema junto a uma família no município de Iporá-go." Masters thesis, Universidade Federal do Paraná, Brazil.

Dufour, Pascale, and Isabelle Giraud. 2007. "Globalization and Political Change in the Women's Movement: The Politics of Scale and Political Empowerment in the World March of Women." *Social Science Quarterly* 88 (5): 1152–73.

Dunkerley, James. 1988. *Power in the Isthmus: A Political History of Modern Central America*. New York: Verso.

Dunn, Christopher. 1992. "Afro-Bahia Carnival: A Stage for Protest." *Afro-Hispanic Review* 11 (1): 11–22.

Duque, Ana Paula, Anna Beatriz Lima, Cíntia Custódio, Luana Weyl, Lucas de Sousa, Luiza Jacobsen, and Nuni Jorgensen. 2011. "Direito e gênero: O projeto promotoras legais populares e sua orientação à emancipação feminina." *Direito e Práxis* 2 (2): 42-59.

Dussel, Enrique. 2008. *Twenty Theses on Politics: Latin America in Translation*. Translated by George Ciccariello-Maher. Durham, NC: Duke University Press.

Dzenovska, Dace, and Iván Arenas. 2012. "Don't Fence Me in: Barricade Sociality and Political Struggles in Mexico and Latvia." *Comparative Studies in Society and History* 54 (3): 644–78.

Eberhardt, Pia, and Cecilia Olivet. 2012. *Profiting from Injustice: How Law Firms, Arbitrators and Financiers Are Fuelling an Investment Arbitration Boom*. Brussels and Amsterdam: Corporate Europe Observatory and the Transnational Institute.

Eckstein, Susan Eva, and Timothy P. Wickham-Crowley, eds. 2002. *Struggles for Social Rights in Latin America*. New York: Routledge.

Ecuarunari. 2007. "Nuestra propuesta a la asamblea constituyente." *Rikcharishun* 35 (August): 4–5.

———. 2008. "Asamblea extraordinaria de la Confederación de los Pueblos de la Nacionalidad Kichwa del Ecuador." *Rikcharishun* 36 (August/September): 4.

Ecuarunari and CONAIE. 2007. *"Los Kichwas somos hijos de la Rebeldía": Propuesta para la asamblea constituyente*. Quito: CONAIE.

Edelman, Marc. 2001. "Social Movements: Changing Paradigms and Forms of Politics." *Annual Review of Anthropology* 30: 285-317.

Ellner, Steve. 1988. *Venezuela's Movimiento al Socialismo: From Guerrilla Defeat to Innovative Politics*. Durham, NC: Duke University Press.

———, ed. 2014. *Latin America's Radical Left: Challenges and Complexities of Political Power in the Twenty-first Century*. Lanham, MD: Rowman & Littlefield.

Erzinger, Florian, Luis González, and Angel M. Ibarra. 2008. *El lado oscuro del oro: Impactos de la minería metálica en El Salvador*. San Salvador: UNES and Cáritas de El Salvador.

Escobar, Arturo. 2008. *Territories of Difference: Place, Movements, Life,Redes*. Durham, NC: Duke University Press.

Esteva, Gustavo. 2003. "The Meaning and Scope of the Struggle for Autonomy." In *Mayan Lives, Mayan Utopias: The Indigenous Peoples of Chiapas and the Zapatista Rebellion*, edited by Jan Rus, Rosalva Aída Hernández Castillo, and Shannan L. Mattiace, 243–69. Lanham, MD: Rowman & Littlefield.

———. 2010. "The Oaxaca Commune and Mexico's Coming Insurrection." *Antipode* 42 (4): 978–93.

Euraque, Dario. 1998. "The Banana Enclave, Nationalism, and Mestizaje in Honduras, 1910s–1930s." In *Identity and Struggle at the Margins of the Nation State: The Laboring Peoples of Central America and the Hispanic Caribbean*, edited by Aviva Chomsky and Aldo Lauria-Santiago, 169–95. Durham, NC: Duke University Press.

———. 2003. "The Threat of Blackness to the Mestizo Nation: Race and Ethnicity in the Honduran Banana Economy, 1920s–1930s." In *Banana Wars, Power Production and History in the Americas*, edited by Steve Striffler and Mark Moberg, 229–49. Durham, NC: Duke University Press.

EZLN (Zapatista Army of National Liberation). 1993. "First Declaration of the Lacandón Jungle." http://flag.blackened.net/revolt/mexico/ezln/ezlnwa.html (accessed January 15, 2014).

———. 2003. "Chiapas: The Thirteenth Stele." July. http://flag.blackened.net/revolt/mexico/ezln/2003/marcos/resistance13.html (accessed January 25, 2014).

———. 2005. "Sixth Declaration of the Lacandón Jungle." June. http://enlacezapatista.ezln.org.mx/sdsl-en (accessed January 15, 2014).

———. 2013. *Escuelita Zapatista: Cuaderno de texto de primer grado del curso de "La Libertad según l@s Zapatistas."* Vol. 1, Gobierno autónomo I; Vol. 2, Gobierno autónomo II; Vol. 3, Resistencia autónoma; Vol. 4, Participación de las mujeres en el gobierno autónomo. Chiapas: August. http://www.narconews.com/print.php3?ArticleID=4712&lang=es (accessed October 10, 2013).

Fach Gómez, Katia. 2011. "Latin America and ICSID: David versus Goliath?" *Law and Business Review of the Americas* 17 (2): 501–49.

———. 2012. "Rethinking the Role of Amicus Curiae in International Investment Arbitration: How to Draw the Line Favorably for the Public Interest." *Fordham International Law Journal*, Vol. 25: 510–64.

Facultad Abierta. 2010. "Las empresas recuperadas en la Argentina. 2010: Informe del tercer relevamiento de empresas recuperadas por los trabajadores." http://www.recuperadasdoc.com.ar (accessed March 2, 2014).

Facultad Latinoamericana de Ciencias Sociales (FLACSO). 2007. *Dossier: Plan Puebla-Panamá*. San José, Costa Rica: FLACSO.

Faria, Nalu. 2006. "O feminismo latino-americano e caribenho: Perspectivas diante do neoliberalismo." In *Desafios do livre mercado para o feminismo*, edited by Nalu Faria and Richard Poulin, 11–39. São Paulo: Cadernos Sempreviva.

Farthing, Linda, and Benjamin Kohl. 2010. "Social Control Bolivia's New Approach to Coca Reduction." *Latin American Perspectives* 37 (4): 197–213.

———. 2013. "Mobilizing Memory: Bolivia's Enduring Social Movements." *Social Movement Studies* 12 (4): 361–76.

Fazio, Carlos. 2001. "Mexico: El Plan Puebla-Panamá y el intervencionismo de EEUU." *Rebelión*, March 24, 2001. http://www.rebelion.org/hemeroteca/sociales/fazio240301.htm.

Featherstone, David. 2008. *Resistance, Space and Political Identities: The Making of Counter-Global Networks*. Malden, MA: Wiley-Blackwell.

Fernandes, Bernardo Mançano. 1996. *MST: Formação e territorialização em São Paulo*. São Paulo: EditoraHucitec.

———. 2000. *A formação do MST no Brasil*. Petrópolis: Editora Vozes.

———. 2001. *Questão agrária, pesquisa e MST.* São Paulo: Editora Cortez.

Fominaya, Cristina Flesher. 2010. "Collective Identity in Social Movements: Central Concepts and Debates." *Sociology Compass* 4 (6): 393–404.

Fonseca, Lívia Gimenes Dias. 2012. *A luta pela Liberdade em Casa e na Rua: A Construção do direito das mulheres a partir do projeto promotoras legais populares do Distrito Federal 2012.171f. Dissertação (mestrado em direito)*. Brasília: Universidade de Brasília.

Foweraker, Joe. 1995. *Theorizing Social Movements*. London: Pluto Press.

Fox, Jonathan. 1994. "The Difficult Transition from Clientelism to Citizenship: Lessons from Mexico." *World Politics* 46 (2): 151–84.

Fox, Michael, and Silvia Leindecker. 2008. *Beyond Elections: Redefining Democracy in the Americas*. PM Press/Estreito Meios Productions.

FPFV (Frente Popular Francisco Villa). 1996. "Balance de la organización ante el Primer Congreso." mimeo.

FPFVI-UNOPII (Frente Popular Francisco Villa Independiente–Unidad Nacional de Organizaciones Populares de la Izquierda Independiente). 2006. "Ponencia para acto en la casa de Dr. Margil en Monterrey." Primer Encuentro de Comisionados UNOPII; México, November.

———. 2008a. "Primer aniversario de la comunidad Centauro del Norte." October.

———. 2008b. "Una construcción con esfuerzo colectivo." December.

———. 2009a. "Reglamento general centauro del Norte." mimeo.

———. 2009b. "XIII aniversario de la comunidad Acapatzingo." May.

———. 2009c. "Comunidad Acapatzingo, es tiempo de agracdecer." December.

Fraser, Nancy. 1997. *Justice Interruptus: Critical Reflections on the Postsocialist Condition*. New York: Routledge.

Freeman, Jo. 1973. "The Tyranny of Structurelessness." *Berkeley Journal of Sociology* 17: 151–64.

Freidberg, Jill Irene. 2007. "Un Poquito de Tanta Verdad." Mexico and U.S.: Corrugated Films.

Freire, Paulo. 1967. *A pedagogia do oprimido*. Rio de Janeiro: Paz e Terra.

———. 1984. *La educación como práctica de la libertad*. Mexico: Siglo XXI.

———. 2000. *Pedagogy of the Oppressed*. London: Bloomsbury Academic Publishing.

Fulmer, Amanda M., Angelina Snodgrass Godoy, and Philip Neff. 2008. "Indigenous Rights, Resistance and the Law: Lessons from Guatemala." *Latin American Politics and Society* 50 (4): 91–21.

Frente por el Sí y el Cambio. 2008. "Boletín de prensa." August 28.

Gabriel, Leo, and Gilberto López y Rivas, eds. 2005. *Autonomías indígenas en América Latina: Nuevas formas de convivencia política*. Mexico City: UAM-Itztapalapa.

Gadelha de Carvalho, Sandra Maria. 2006. "Educação do campo: Pronera, uma política pública em construção." Tese (Doutorado em Educação), Programa de Pós-Graduação em Educação Brasileira da Universidade Federal do Ceará (UFC). Fortaleza-Brasil.

Gadelha de Carvalho, Sandra Maria, and Ernandi Mendes. 2011. "The University and the Landless Movement in Brazil: The Experience of Collective Knowledge Construction through Educational Projects in Rural Areas." In *Social Movements in the Global South: Dispossession, Development and Resistance*, edited by Sara Catherine Motta and Alf Gunfald Nilsen, 131–49. New York/ London: Palgrave Macmillan Press.

Gamson, William A. 2003 [1973]. "Defining Movement 'Success.'" In *The Social Movements Reader: Cases and Concepts*, edited by Jeff Godwin and James M. Jasper, 350–52. Malden, MA: Blackwell Publishing.

Ganz, Marshall. 2010. "Leading Change: Leadership, Organization and Social Movements." In *Handbook of Leadership Theory and Practice: A Harvard Business School Centennial Colloquium*, edited by Rakesh Khurana Nitin Nohria, 527–61. Boston: Harvard Business School Publishing Corporation.

García Linera, Álvaro. 2006a. "State Crisis and Popular Power." *New Left Review* 37 (February): 73–85.

———. 2006b. "El evismo: Lo nacional-popular en acción." *OSAL, Observatorio Social de América Latina* 4 (19): 25-32.

———. 2010. "The State in Transition Power Bloc and Point of Bifurcation." *Latin American Perspectives* 37 (4): 34–47.

————. 2014. "Bolivia: 'No estamos pensando en socialismo sino en revolución democratiza-dora.'" Interview by Pablo Stefanoni and Franklin Ramírez. http://servindi.org/actualidad/entrevistas/495 (accessed March 31, 2014).

Gasparello, Giovanna, and Jaime Quintana Guerrero, eds. 2009. *Otras geografías: Experiencias de autonomías indígenas en México.* Mexico City: UAM-Iztapalapa.

Ghiso Cotos, Alfredo. 2013. "Formar en investigación desde la perspectiva de la educación popular." In *Entretejidos de la educación popular en Colombia*, edited by Lola Cendales, Marco Raúl Mejía, and Jairo Muñoz M., 99–130. Bogotá: Consejo de Educación Popular de América Latina y el Caribe (CEAAL).

Gibler, John. 2009. *Mexico Unconquered: Chronicles of Power and Revolt.* San Francisco: City Lights.

Gibson-Graham, J. K. 2006. *A Postcapitalist Politics.* Minneapolis: University of Minnesota Press.

Gill, Hartej, Kadi Purru, and Gloria Lin. 2012. "In the Midst of Participatory Action Research Practices: Moving towards Decolonizing and Decolonial Praxis." *Reconceptualizing Educational Research Methodology* 3 (1): 1–14.

Gilroy, Paul. 2000. *Against Race: Imagining Political Culture Beyond the Color Line.* Cambridge, MA: Harvard University Press.

Gisbert, Alan. 1997. *La ciudad Latinoamericana.* México: Siglo XXI.

Giugni, Marco. 1998. "Was It Worth the Effort? The Outcomes and Consequences of Social Movements." *Annual Review of Sociology* 98: 371–93.

Gledhill, John. 2004. "Indigenous Autonomy as a Strategy for Social Inclusion: Some Paradoxes of Social Policy in Contemporary Mexico." Social Anthropology website of the University of Manchester. Presented at ESRC Research Seminar on Social Policy, Stability and Exclusion in Latin America at the Institute of Latin American Studies, London. http://jg.socialsciences.manchester.ac.uk/ESRC_Sem_Gledhill.pdf (accessed January 11, 2014).

Goldstein, Donna 2003. *Laughter Out of Place: Race, Class, Violence and Sexuality in a Rio Shantytown.* Berkeley: University of California Press.

Gómez Bonilla, Adriana. 2011. "Visiones y sentires sobre el deterioro ambiental: Un punto de partida para el manejo sustentable y la autonomía." In *Luchas "muy otras": Zapatismo y autonomía en las comunidades indígenas de Chiapas*, edited by Bruno Baronnet, Mariana Mora Bayo, and Richard Stahler-Sholk, 489–513. Mexico City: UAM-Xochimilco/CIESAS/UNACH.

Gómez Carpinteiro, Francisco Javier. 2013. "The Subject's Tracks: The Other Campaign, Self-Knowledge, and Subjectivity in the Liberal Democratic Cycle." *Latin American Perspectives* 40 (5): 138–52.

González Casanova, Pablo. 2005. "The Zapatista "Caracoles": Networks of Resistance and Autonomy." *Socialism and Democracy* 19 (3): 79–92.

González De La Rocha, Mercedes. 2001. "From The Resources Of Poverty To The Poverty Of Resources? The Erosion Of A Survival Model." *Latin American Perspectives* 28 (4): 72-100.

González Figueroa, Gerardo Alberto. 2002. *Sociedad civil, organismos civiles y movimientos populares en los altos y la selva de Chiapas.* Posgrado en Desarrollo Rural, División de Ciencias Sociales y Humanidades, Universidad Autónoma Metropolitana, Xochimilco.

Goodale, Mark, and Nancy Postero, eds. 2013. *Neoliberalism, Interrupted: Social Change and Contested Governance in Contemporary Latin America.* Stanford, CA: Stanford University Press.

Görgen, Frei Sergio. 1997. "Religiosidade e fé na luta pela terra." In *A reforma agrária e a luta do MST*, edited by João Pedro Stedile, 279-292. Petrópolis: Editora Vozes.

Gramsci, Antonio. 1971. *Selection from Prison Notebooks.* Translated by Quintin Hoare and Geoffrey Nowell-Smith. London: Lawrence & Wishart.

Grandin, Greg. 2006. *Empire's Workshop: Latin America, the United States, and the Rise of the New Imperialism.* New York: Metropolitan Books.

Green, James A. 2010. *We Cannot Remain Silent: Opposition to the Military Dictatorship in the United States.* Durham, NC: Duke University Press.

Grisaffi, Thomas. 2010. "We Are Originarios . . . 'We Just Aren't from Here': Coca Leaf and Identity Politics in the Chapare, Bolivia." *Bulletin of Latin American Research* 29 (4): 425–39.

———. 2013. "'All of Us Are Presidents': Radical Democracy and Citizenship in the Chapare Province, Bolivia." *Critique of Anthropology* 33 (1): 47–65.

———. 2014. "Can You Get Rich From The Bolivian Cocaine Trade? Cocaine Paste Production In The Chapare." Andean Information Network Blog Archive, http://ain-bolivia.org/2014/03/can-you-get-rich-from-the-bolivian-cocaine-trade-cocaine-paste-production-in-the-chapare/ (accessed March 27, 2014).

Grossi, Miriam Pillar. 1997. "Feministas históricas e novas feministas no Brasil." *Revista Sociedade e Estado* 12 (2): 285–308.

Grugel, Jean, and Pía Riggirozzi. 2012. "Post-neoliberalism in Latin America: Rebuilding and Reclaiming the State after Crisis." *Development and Change* 43 (1): 1-21.

Gudynas, Eduardo. 2011. "Buen Vivir: Today's Tomorrow." *Development* 54 (4): 441–47.

Guhur, Dominique Michèle Perioto. 2010. "Contribuições do diálogo de saberes à educação profissional em agroecologia no MST: Desafios da educação do campo na construção do Projeto Popular." Masters thesis, Universidade Estadual de Maringá, Brazil.

Guiso, Alfredo. 2000. "Potenciando la diversidad. Diálogo de saberes, una práctica hermenéutica colectiva." *Revista Aportes* 53: 57–70.

Gunderson, Christopher. 2011. "The Making of Organic Indigenous-Campesino Intellectuals: Catechist Training in the Diocese of San Cristóbal and the Roots of the Zapatista Uprising." *Research in Social Movements, Conflicts, and Change* 31: 259–95.

Gustafson, Bret. 2013. "Amid Gas, Where Is the Revolution?" *NACLA Report on the Americas* 46 (1): 61–66.

Gutiérrez Aguilar, Raquel. 2008. *Los ritmos del pachakuti: Levantamiento y movilizacion en Bolivia (2000–2005).* Ediciones Tinta Limon.

———. 2012. "The Rhythms of the Pachakuti: Brief Reflections Regarding How We Have Come to Know Emancipatory Struggles and the Significance of the Term Social Emancipation." *South Atlantic Quarterly* 111 (1): 51–64.

Haglund, LaDawn. 2010. *Limiting Resources: Market-Led Reform and the Transformation of Public Goods.* University Park: Pennsylvania State University Press.

Hale, Charles R. 2002. "Does Multiculturalism Menace? Governance, Cultural Rights, and the Politics of Identity in Guatemala." *Journal of Latin American Studies* 34 (3): 485–524.

———. 2008 *Engaging Contradictions: Theory, Politics, and Methods of Activist Scholarship.* Berkeley: University of California Press.

Hale, Charles R., and Lynn Stephen, eds. 2013. *Otros Saberes: Collaborative Research on Indigenous and Afro-Descendent Cultural Politics.* Santa Fe, NM: School for Advanced Research, Global Indigenous Politics Series.

Hall, Thomas D., and Glen David Kuecker. 2011. "Resilience and Community in the Age of World-System Collapse." *Nature and Culture* 6 (1): 18–40.

Hamilton, Nora. 1982. *The Limits of State Autonomy: Post-Revolutionary Mexico.* Princeton, NJ: Princeton University Press.

Hanchard, Michael. 1994. *Orpheus and Power: The Movimento Negro of Rio de Janeiro and Sao Paulo, Brazil, 1945–1988.* Princeton, NJ: Princeton University Press.

Harcourt, Wendy. 2006. *The Global Women's Rights Movement: Power Politics around the United Nations and the World Social Forum.* Civil Society and Social Movements Programme. Paper 25. August. Geneva: UNRISD.

Hardt, Michael, and Antonio Negri. 2001. *Empire.* Cambridge, MA: Harvard University Press.

———. 2003. "Globalization and Democracy." In *Implicating Empire: Globalization and Resistance in the 21ˢᵗ Century World Order*, edited by Stanley Aronowitz and Heather Gautney, 109–31. New York: Basic Books.

Harnecker, Marta. 2003. *Landless People: Building a Social Movement.* São Paulo: Expressão Popular.

Harris, David, and Diego Azzi. 2006. "ALBA: Venezuela's ANSWEr to "Free Trade": The Bolivarian Alternative for the Americas." Occasional Paper 3, edited by Alec Bamford and Nicola Bullard. Bangkok: Focus on the Global South.

Harvey, David. 1997. *Justice, Nature, and the Geography of Difference.* Oxford, UK and Cambridge, MA: Wiley-Blackwell.

———. 2003. *The New Imperialism.* Oxford: Oxford University Press.

———. 2012. *Ciudades rebeldes: Del derecho a la ciudad a la revolución urbana.* Madrid: Akal.

———. 2013. "No hay nada malo en tener un huerto comunitario, pero debemos preocuparnos de los comunes a gran escala." March 15. https://www.diagonalperiodico.net/global/no-hay-nada-malo-tener-huerto-comunitario-pero-debemos-preocuparnos-comunes-gran-escala. html (accessed December 21, 2013).

Harvey, Neil. 1998. *The Chiapas Rebellion: The Struggle for Land and Democracy.* Durham, NC: Duke University Press.

———. 2004. "Disputando el desarrollo: El Plan Puebla-Panamá y los derechos indígenas." In *El estado y los indígenas en tiempos del PAN: Neoindigenismo, legalidad e identidad,* edited by Sarela Paz Rosalva, Aída Hernandez, and María Terésa Sierra, 115–36. México, D.F.: CIESAS.

———. 2005a. "Inclusion through Autonomy: Zapatistas and Dissent." *NACLA Report on the Americas* 39 (2): 12–17.

———. 2005b. "Who Needs Zapatismo? State Interventions and Local Responses in Marqués de Comillas, Chiapas." *Journal of Peasant Studies* 32 (3-4): 629–50.

———. 2006a. "El capitalismo ecológico y el Plan Puebla-Panamá: La transformación de los recursos naturales en Mesoamérica." *Comercio Exterior* 54 (4): 319–27.

———. 2006b. "La disputa por los recursos naturales en el área del Plan Puebla-Panamá." In *Geoeconomía y geopolítica en el área del Plan Puebla-Panamá,* edited by Daniel Villa-fuerte Solís and Xochitl Leyva Solano, 205–34. México: Cámara de Diputados, LIX Legis-latura.

Haugaard, Mark and Howard Lentner. 2006. *Hegemony and Power: Consensus and Coercion in Contemporary Politics.* Lanham, MD: Rowman & Littlefield.

Hellman, Judith Adler. 1992. "The Study of New Social Movements in Latin America and the Question of Autonomy." In *New Social Movements in Latin America: Identity, Strategy and Democracy,* edited by Arturo Escobar and Sonia E. Alvarez, 52–61. Boulder, CO: Westview Press.

———. 1995. "The Riddle of New Social Movements: Who They Are and What They Do." In *Capital, Power, and Inequality in Latin America,* edited by Sandor Halebsky and Richard L. Harris, 165–83. Boulder, CO: Westview Press.

———. 2008a. "The Riddle of New Social Movements: Who They Are and What They Do." In *Capital, Inequality, and Power in Latin America,* edited by Richard Harris and Jorge Nef, 133–53. Boulder, CO: Rowman & Littlefield.

———. 2008b. "Mexican Popular Movements, Clientelism, and the Process of Democratiza-tion." In *Latin American Social Movements in the Twenty-First Century: Resistance, Power and Democracy,* edited by Richard Stahler-Sholk, Harry E. Vanden, and Glen David Kueck-er, 61–76. Lanham, MD: Rowman & Littlefield.

Henriquez, Elio, and Angeles Mariscal. 2002. "Amplia oposición al área de libre comercio y al Plan Puebla-Panamá." *La Jornada,* October 13.

Henríquez, Katia. 2008. *Perspectiva de la industria minera de oro en El Salvador.* San Salva-dor, El Salvador: Ediciones CEICOM.

Hernández Castillo, Rosalva Aída. 2006. "Between Feminist Ethnocentricity and Ethnic Essen-tialism: The Zapatistas' Demands and the National Indigenous Women's Movement." In *Dissident Women: Gender and Cultural Politics in Chiapas,* edited by Shannon Speed, Rosalva Aída Hernández Castillo, and Lynn M. Stephen, 57–74. Austin: University of Texas Press.

Hérnandez Navarro, Luis. 2013. "Las mentiras sobre la reforma educativa. *La Jornada,* January 15.

Hershberg, Eric, and Fred Rosen. 2007. *Latin America after Neoliberalism: Turning the Tide in the Twenty-first Century?* New York: The New Press.

Hesketh, Chris. 2013. "The Clash of Spatializations: Geopolitics and Class Struggles in South-ern Mexico." *Latin American Perspectives* 40 (4): 70-87.

Hesketh, Chris, and Adam David Morton. 2014. "Spaces of Uneven Development and Class Struggle in Bolivia: Transformation or Trasformismo?" *Antipode* 46 (1): 149–69.

Hirtz, Natalia Vanesa and Marta Susana Giacone. 2013. "The Recovered Companies Workers' Struggle in Argentina: Between Autonomy and New Forms of Control." *Latin American Perspectives* 40 (4): 88–100.

Hobsbawm, Eric. 1995. *Historia de Siglo XX*. Barcelona: Crítica.

Hogenboom, Barbara. 2012. "Depoliticized and Repoliticized Minerals in Latin America." *Journal of Developing Societies* 28: 133–58.

Holden, Robert. 2004. *Armies without Nations: Public Violence and State Formation in Central America 1821–1960*. Oxford: Oxford University Press.

Holloway, John. 2002. *Change the World without Taking Power*. London: Pluto Press.

———. 2005. "Gleneagles: Breaking Time." In *Shut Them Down! The G8, Gleneagles 2005 and the Movement of Movements*, edited by David Harvie, Keir Milburn, Ben Trott, and David Watts, 39–42. Leeds/New York: Dissent and Autonomedia.

Holt-Giménez, Eric. 2006. *Campesino a Campesino: Voices from Latin America's Farmer to Farmer Movement for Sustainable Agriculture*. Oakland, CA: Food First Books.

hooks, bell. 1990. *Yearning: Race, Gender and Cultural Politics*. Cambridge, MA: South End Press.

Howe, Cymene. 2011. "Logics of Wind: Development Desires over Oaxaca." *Anthropology News* 52 (5): 8.

Icaza, Rosalba, and Rolando Vázquez. 2013. "Social Struggles as Epistemic Struggles." *Development and Change* 44 (3), May: 683-704.

Incite! Women of Color against Violence. 2007. *The Revolution Will Not Be Funded: Beyond the Non-Profit Industrial Complex*. Cambridge, MA: South End Press.

INREDH (Instituto Regional de Asesoría en Derechos Humanos). 2008. "Asamblea concede amnistía para los defensores de los derechos humanos." http://www.inredh.org/noticias/noticias.php?modulo=noticiasleermas&idioma=es&id=178 (accessed March 14, 2008).

Instituto Científico de Culturas Indígenas. 2008. "Plurinacionalidad, territorios y democracia: los límites del debate." *Yachaykuna* 8 (April): 5–9.

International Allies Against Mining in El Salvador. 2012. "Sign Your Organization On to Support the Mesa." October 31. http://www.stopesmining.org/j25/index.php/campaigns/2013-international-support-for-mining-ban (accessed January 22, 2014).

———. 2014. "Open Letter to the President of the World Bank in Defense of El Salvador." http://www.stopesmining.org/j25/ (accessed April 7, 2014).

International Centre for the Settlement of Investment Disputes. 2014. *ICSID Caseload-Statistics* (Issue 2014-1). https://icsid.worldbank.org/ICSID/FrontServlet?requestType=ICSIDDocRH&actionVal=CaseLoadStatistics (accessed February 10, 2014).

International Foundation for Election Surveys (IFES). 2002. http://ifes.org/eguide/turnout2002.htm (accessed March 24, 2003).

Iturriza, Reinaldo. 2013. "Desiring the Commune." *Venezuela Analysis*, August 27. Translated by Tamara Pearson (translation modified). http://venezuelanalysis.com/analysis/9974 (accessed January 29, 2014).

———. 2014a. "Comunas: Para hacer que emerja lo nuevo (Un balance de 2013)." *Saber y poder*, January 3. http://elotrosaberypoder.wordpress.com/2014/01/03/comunas-para-hacer-que-emerja-lo-nuevo-un-balance-de-2013/ (accessed January 24, 2014).

———. 2014b. "Pistas para el pueblo que vendrá." *Saber y poder*, January 29. http://elotrosaberypoder.wordpress.com/2014/01/29/pistas-para-el-pueblo-que-vendra/ (accessed January 29, 2014).

Jaua, Elías. 2013. "Chavismo." *Venezuela Analysis*, January 4. Translated by Rachael Boothroyd (translation modified). http://venezuelanalysis.com/analysis/7586 (accessed January 29, 2014).

Johnston, Hank. 1995. "A Methodology for Frame Analysis." In *Social Movements and Culture*, edited by Hank Johnston and Bert Klandermans, 217–46. Minneapolis: University of Minnesota Press.

———. 2011. *States and Social Movements*. London: Polity Press.

Johnston, Hank, and Paul Almeida, eds. 2006. *Latin American Social Movements: Globalization, Democratization, and Transnational Networks*. Lanham, MD: Rowman & Littlefield.

Johnston, Hank, and Bert Klandermans, eds. 1995. *Social Movements and Culture*. Minneapolis: University of Minnesota Press.

Jones de Almeida, Florência. 2003. "Unveiling the Mirror: Afro-Brazilian Identity and the Emergence of Community Schools." *Comparative Education Review* 47: 41–63.

Kalny, Eva. 2010. "'They Even Use Us as a Factory for their Children': Perspectives on Free Trade Agreements in Guatemala." *Social Analysis* 54 (1): 71–91.

Katsiaficas, George, and Gerardo Rénique. 2012. "A New Stage of Insurgencies: Latin American Popular Movements, the Gwangju Uprising, and the Occupy Movement." *Socialism and Democracy* 26 (3): 14–34.

Katz, Claudio. 2007. "Socialist Strategies in Latin America." *Monthly Review* 59 (September): 25–41.

Kearney, Michael. 1996. *Reconceptualizing the Peasantry: Anthropology in Global Perspective*. Boulder, Colo.: Westview Press.

Keating, Ana Louise, ed. 2009. *The Gloria Anzaldúa Reader*. Durham, NC: Duke University Press.

Keck, Margaret E., and Kathryn Sikkink. 1998. *Activists beyond Borders: Advocacy Networks in International Politics*. Ithaca, NY: Cornell University Press.

Kessels, Eelco J. A. M. 2010. *Countering Violent Extremist Narratives*. Edited by National Coordinator for Counterterrorism. The Hague, Netherlands.

Khasnabish, Alex. 2008. *Zaptismo beyond Borders: New Imaginations of Political Possibility*. Toronto: University of Toronto Press.

Kohl, Benjamin. 2003. "Democratizing Decentralization in Bolivia: The Law of Popular Participation." *Journal of Planning Education and Research* 23 (2): 153–64.

Kohn, Margaret. 2013. "Privatization and Protest: Occupy Wall Street, Occupy Toronto, and the Occupation of Public Space in a Democracy." *Perspectives on Politics* 11 (1): 99–110.

Kuecker, Glen David. 2008. "Fighting for the Forests Revisited: Grassroots Resistance to Mining in Northern Ecuador." In *Latin American Social Movements in the 21st Century*, edited by Richard Stahler-Sholk, Harry E. Vanden, and Glen David Kuecker, 97–112. Lanham, MD: Rowman & Littlefield.

Labrador Aragón, Gabriel. 2012. "No hay condiciones para el desarrollo de la minería metálica con garantías ambientales." Interview with Herman Rosa. *El Faro*, August 20. http://www.elfaro.net/es/201208/noticias-9401/?st-full_text=all&tpl=11567 (accessed February 1, 2014).

Labrador, Gabriel, and Frederick Meza. 2011. "A las amenazas de que me van a matar ni caso les hago ya." Interview with Francisco Pineda. *El Faro*, June 9. http://www.elfaro.net/es/201106/el_agora/4269/ (accessed February 1, 2014).

Laclau, Ernesto. 1977. *Politics and Ideology in Marxist Theory: Capitalism, Fascism, Populism*. London: New Left Books.

———. 2005. *On Populist Reason*. London: Verso.

Lao, Waldo, and Flavia, Anna. 2009. "El Frente Popular Francisco Villa Independiente no es solo un proyecto de organización, es un proyecto de vida." Interview with Enrique Reynoso. *Rebelión*, January 6. http://www.rebelion.org/noticia.php?id=78519 (accessed December 15, 2013).

Lara Junior, Nadir. 2005a. "A mística no cotidiano do MST: a interface entre a religiosidade popular e a política." Master's thesis, Pontifícia Universidade Católica de São Paulo.

———. 2005b. "As manifestações artísticas no processo de formação identitária do Sem Terra." *Revista Psicologia Argumento*. 423 (43): 69–79.

Lara, Katia. 2010. *Documental Quién Dijo Miedo: Honduras de un golpe*. Documentary film. Argentina-Honduras: Terco Producciones.

Latin American Studies Association (LASA). 2007. "Violaciones contra la libertad académica y de expresión en Oaxaca de Juárez." Latin American Studies Association Special Report. 1 Aug. http://www.mraroaxaca.uoregon.edu/LASAReporteDelegacionOaxaca.pdf (accessed April 23, 2014).

Latin American Weekly Report. 2007a. "Correa Should Win Slim Majority in Assembly." WR-07-36 (September 13): 11.

———. 2007b. "Correa Sweeps Constituent Assembly Elections to Consolidate Power in Ecuador." WR-07-39 (October 4): 1–2.

———. 2008. "Election Date Set for April." WR-08-46 (November 20): 8.

———. 2009. "Correa Attemptst Define Modern Socialism." WR-09-02 (January 15): 3.

———. 2013. "Brazilians Protest About More Than Just Centavos." WR-13-24 (June 20): 1

Latinobarometro. 2013. "Satisfaction with Democracy," 36. http://www.latinobarometro.org/documentos/LATBD_INFORME_LB_2013.pdf (accessed March 12, 2014).

La Via Campesina (LVC). 2012. "Bukit Tinggi Declaration on Agrarian Reform in the 21st Century." http://viacampesina.org/en/index.php/main-issues-mainmenu-27/agrarian-reform-mainmenu-36/1281-bukit-tinggi-declaration-on-agrarian-reform-in-the-21st-century.

———. 2013. "From Maputo to Jakarta: 5 Years of Agroecology in La Via Campesina." http://viacampesina.org/downloads/pdf/en/De-Maputo-a-Yakarta-EN-web.pdf.

Lavinas, Lena and Paola Cappellin. 1991. "Gênero e classe: Mulheres trabalhadoras rurais." In *Mulheres Trabalhadoras Rurais, Particiapação e Luta Sindical,* 28–41. Rio de Janeiro, DNTR/CEDI.

Lebon, Nathalie. 2013. "Taming or Unleashing the Monster of Coalition Work: Professionalization and the Consolidation of Popular Feminism in Brazil," *Feminist Studies* 39 (3): 759–89.

Lebovitz, Michael. 2006. *Build It Now: Socialism for the Twenty-first Century.* New York: Monthly Review Press.

Lefebvre, Henri. 1991. *The Production of Space.* Oxford, UK and Cambridge, MA: Blackwell.

Leff, Enrique. 2004. "Racionalidad ambiental y diálogo de saberes. Significancia y sentido en la construcción de un futuro sustentable." *Polis. Revista Latinoamericana* 7, 1–29.

———. 2011. *Aventuras de la epistemología ambiental: de la articulación de ciencias al diálogo de saberes.* Mexico: Siglo XXI.

Leiva, Fernando. 2008. *Latin American Neostructuralism: The Contradictions of Post-Neoliberal Development.* Minneapolis: University of Minnesota Press.

———. 2012. "Flexible Workers, Gender, and Contending Strategies for Confronting the Crisis of Labor in Chile." *Latin American Perspectives* 39 (4): 102–28.

Lenin, V. I. 1917. "The Dual Power." *Pravda.* April 9.

Levitsky, Steven, and Kenneth M. Roberts, eds. 2011. *The Resurgence of the Latin American Left.* Baltimore, MD: Johns Hopkins University Press.

Lewis, Tom. 2001. "Brazil: The Struggle against Neoliberalism." *International Socialist Review* 18, June–July. http://www.isreview.org/issues/18/Brazil.shtml.

Leyva Solano, Xochitl. 2003. "Regional, Communal, and Organizational Transformations in Las Cañadas." In *Mayan Lives, Mayan Utopias: The Indigenous Peoples of Chiapas and the Zapatista Rebellion,* edited by Jan Rus, Rosalva Aída Hernández Castillo, and Shannan L. Mattiace, 161–84. Lanham, MD: Rowman & Littlefield.

———. 2005. "Indigenismo, Indianismo, and 'Ethnic Citizenship' in Chiapas." *Journal of Peasant Studies* 32 (3–4): 555–83.

———. 2006. "El neo-Zapatismo: De guerrilla a social movement web." In *La guerila en las regiones de México,* edited by Verónica Oikión Solaon and Marta Eugenia García Ugarte, 725–47. México, D.F.: Siglo XX, CIESAS y El Colegio de Michoacán.

Leyva Solano, Xochitl, and Gabriel Ascencio Franco.1996. *Lacandonia al Filo del Agua.* Mexico City: Fondo de la Cultura Económica.

Linhares Pires, José Claudio. 2008. *Evaluation of IDB's Support to the Plan Puebla-Panamá Initiative.* Washington, DC: Inter-American Development Bank.

López, Dina Lario de, Herbert Guzmán, and Edgardo Mira. 2008. "Riesgos y posibles impactos de la minería metálica en El Salvador." *Revista ECA* 63, 711–12 (January–February): 77–91.

López Maya, Margarita. 2005. *Del viernes negro al referendo revocatorio.* Caracas: Alfadil.

López y Rivas, Gilberto. 2003. "Contrainsurgencia y Paramilitarismo en Chiapas en el Gobierno de Vicente Fox." *Revista Chiapas* 15. http://www.revistachiapas.org/No15/ch15lopez.html.

Lovell, Peggy A. 2000. "Gender and Race and the Struggle for Social Justice in Brazil." *Latin American Perspectives* 27: 85–102.

Löwy, Michael. 2001. "The socio-religious origins of Brazil's Landless Rural Workers Movement." *Monthly Review* 53 (2): 32–40.

———. 2004. "Le concept d'affinité élective chez Max Weber." *Archives de Sciences Sociales des Religions*, Éditions EHESS, 127 (July-Sept.): 93–103.

Lucas, Kintto. 2007. *Rafael Correa: Un extraño en Carondelet.* Quito: Planeta.

Lugones, Maria. 1987. "Playfulness, 'World'-Travelling, and Loving Perception." *Hypathia* 2 (2): 3–19.

———. 1992. "On Borderlands/La Frontera: An Interpretive Essay." *Hypathia* 7 (4): 31–37.

———. 2006. "On Complex Communications." *Hypathia* 21(3): 75–85.

———. 2010. "Toward a Decolonial Feminism." *Hypathia* 25 (4): 742–59.

Lukes, Steven. 1974. *Power: A Radical View.* New York: Palgrave Macmillan.

Lyra Filho, Roberto. 1982. *O que é direito.* São Paulo: Editora Brasiliense.

Macdonald, Theodore, Jr. 2002. "Ecuador 's Indian Movement: Pawn in a Short Game or Agent in State Reconfiguration?" In *The Politics of Ethnicity: Indigenous Peoples in Latin American States*, edited by David Maybury-Lewis, 168–98. Cambridge, MA: David Rockefeller Center for Latin American Studies, Harvard University.

Machín Sosa, Braulio, A. M. Roque Jaime, D. R. Ávila Lozano, and Peter Michael Rosset. 2013. *Agroecological Revolution: the Farmer-to-Farmer Movement of the ANAP in Cuba.* Havana and Jakarta: ANAP, and Havana: La Vía Campesina. http://viacampesina.org/downloads/pdf/en/Agroecological-revolution-ENGLISH.pdf.

Madres de Plaza de Mayo Linea Fundadora. 2006. "Carta abierta al presidente de la nación." May 26.http://www.madresfundadoras. org.ar/pagina/cartaabiertaalpresidentedelanacin/63 (accessed June 7, 2012).

Maeckelbergh, Marianne. 2009. *The Will of the Many: How the Alterglobalisation Movement is Changing the Face of Democracy.* London: Pluto Press.

———. 2011. "Doing Is Believing: Prefiguration as Strategic Practice in the Alterglobalization Movement." *Social Movement Studies* 10 (1): 1–20.

Magaña, Maurice Rafael. 2010. "Analyzing the Meshwork as an Emerging Social Movement Formation: An Ethnographic Account of the Popular Assembly of the Peoples of Oaxaca (APPO)." *Journal of Contemporary Anthropology* 1: 73–87.

Maier, Elizabeth. 2010. "Accommodating the Private into the Public Domain: Experiences and Legacies of the Past Four Decades." In *Women's Activism in Latin America and the Caribbean: Engendering Social Justice, Democratizing Citizenship*, edited by Elizabeth Maier and Nathalie Lebon, 26–43. New Brunswick: Rutgers University Press.

Maldonado Ruiz, Luis E. 2008. "El estado plurinacional desde la perspectiva de los pueblos: primera parte." *Boletín ICCI-Rimay* 10 (May).

Mariátegui, José Carlos. 1971 [1928]. *Seven Interpretive Essays on Peruvian Reality.* Translated by Marjory Urquidi. Austin: University of Texas Press.

Maricato, Ermínia. 2013. "É a questão urbano, estúpido!" In *Ciudades Rebeldes, Passe Livre e as manifestações que tomaram as ruas do Brasil,* edited by Carlos Vainer, David Harvey, and Ermínia Maricato, et al, 33–45. São Paulo: Tinta Vermelha, Boitempo Editorial.

Martinez, Jennifer Lynette. 2013. "Movement Methodologies and Transforming Urban Space." In *Education and Social Change in Latin America*, edited by Sara Catherine Motta and Mike Cole, 167–84. New York/London: Palgrave Macmillan Press.

Martinez-Torres, María Elena, and Peter M. Rosset. 2008. "La Vía Campesina: Transnationalizing Peasant Struggle and Hope." In *Latin American Social Movements in the Twenty-first Century: Resistance, Power, and Democracy*, edited by Richard Stahler-Sholk, Harry E. Vanden, and Glen David Kuecker, 307–22. Lanham, MD: Rowman & Littlefield.

———. 2010. "La Vía Campesina: The Birth and Evolution of a Transnational Social Movement." *Journal of Peasant Studies* 37 (1): 149–75.

———. 2014. "Diálogo de Saberes in La Vía Campesina: Food Sovereignty and Agroecology." *Journal of Peasant Studies* 41 (1): 1–19.

Martínez Vásquez, Victor Raul. 2007. *Autoritarismo, Movimiento Popular y Crisis Política: Oaxaca 2006.* Oaxaca: Universidad Autónoma "Benito Juárez" de Oaxaca.

Martins, José de Souza. 1997. "A questão agrária brasileira e o papel do MST." In *A reforma agrária e a luta do MST*, edited by João Pedro Stedile. Petrópolis: Editora Vozes.

Marx, Karl. 1858. "Bolívar y Ponte." *The New American Cyclopaedia*, Vol. III. http://www.marxists.org/archive/marx/works/1858/01/bolivar.htm (accessed January 28, 2014).

Marx, Karl. 1980. *Escritos sobre Rusia. II. El porvenir de la comuna rural rusa*. México: Cuadernos de Pasado y Presente 90.

La mascarada del poder. 2012. Cochabamba: Textos Rebeldes.

Mascena, Raimunda Celestina de. 2000. *Marcha das margaridas: 2000 razões para marchar contra a fome, probreza e violência sexista*. CFEMEA—Centro Feminista de Estudos e Assessoria Jornal Fêmea 20 (July). http://www.cfemea.org.br/index.php?option=com_content&view=article&id=276:marcha-das-margaridas-2000-razoes-para-marchar-contra-a-fome-probreza-e-violencia-sexista&Itemid=129.

"Masiva protesta de comunidades contra minería metálica." 2007. *Diario Co Latino*, April 24. http://www.diariocolatino.com (accessed February 15, 2014).

Mason, Paul. 2012. *Why It's Kicking Off Everywhere: The New Global Revolution*. London: Verso.

Massey, Doreen. 1991. "A Global Sense of Place." *Marxism Today*, 35 (6): 24–29.

Mattiace, Shannan L. 2003. *To See with Two Eyes: Peasant Activism and Indian Autonomy in Chiapas, Mexico*. Albuquerque: University of New Mexico Press.

Maturana, Humberto, and Varela, Francisco. 1995. *De máquinas y seres vivos*. Santiago: Editorial Universitaria.

Mayorga, Fernando. 2007. "Movimientos Sociales en El Govierno de Evo Morales." *Opiniones Y Analisis* 84.

———, ed. 2012. *Estado, ampliación de la democracia y disputa política. Bolivia 2000–2010*. Vol. 1. Cochabamba: CESU- UMSS.

McAdam, Doug, Sidney Tarrow, and Charles Tilly. 2001. *Dynamics of Contention*. Cambridge: Cambridge University Press.

McCallum, Cecilia. 2007. "Women out of Place? A Micro-historical Perspective on the Black Feminist Movement in Salvador da Bahia, Brazil." *Journal of Latin American Studies* 39: 55–80.

McCoy, Jennifer. 1999. "Chávez and the End of 'Partyarchy' in Venezuela." *Journal of Democracy* 10 (3): 64–77.

McDonagh, Thomas. 2013. *Unfair, Unsustainable, and Under the Radar: How Corporations Use Global Investment Rules to Undermine a Sustainable Future*. San Francisco: Democracy Center. http://democracyctr.org/wp/wp-content/uploads/2013/05/Under_The_Radar_English_Final.pdf (accessed Feb. 16, 2014).

McElhinney, Vincent J. 2004. "Between Clientelism and Radical Democracy: The Case of Ciudad Segundo Montes." In *Landscapes of Struggle: Politics, Society and Community in El Salvador*, edited by Aldo Lauria-Santiago and Leigh Binford, 147–65. Pittsburgh: University of Pittsburgh Press.

McElhinny, Vince, and Seth Nickinson. 2004. *Plan Puebla-Panamá: Recipe for Development or Disaster?* Washington, DC: InterAction IDB Civil Society Initiative.

Meléndez, Cristian. 2014. "Sánchez Cerén se compromete a no explotar la minería." *La Prensa Gráfica*. February 23. http://www.laprensagrafica.com (accessed March 21, 2014).

Melo Neto, João Cabral de. 2006. *Morte e vida severina e outros poemas para Vozes*. Rio de Janeiro: Nova Fronteira.

Melucci, Alberto. 1995. "The Process of Collective Identity." In *Social Movements and Culture*, edited by Hank Johnston and Bert Klandermans, 41–63. Minneapolis: University of Minnesota Press.

Mendieta, Eduardo. 2008. "Prologue: The Liberation of Politics: Alterity, Solidarity, Liberation." In *Twenty Theses on Politics: Latin America in Translation*, by Enrique Dussel; translated by George Ciccariello-Maher, vii–xiv. Durham, NC: Duke University Press.

Mendoza, Breny. 1986. *Sintiéndose mujer, pensándose feminista*. Tegucigalpa, Honduras: Editorial Guaymuras.

Mesa Nacional Frente a la Minería Metálica. 2012. Press statement, August 9. http://www.esnomineria.blogspot.com/2012/08/comunicado-de-prensa-9-de-agosto.html (accessed February 16, 2014).

Michels, Robert. 1999 [1960]. *Political Parties: A Sociological Study of the Oligarchical Tendencies of Modern Democracy*. New Brunswick, NJ: Transaction.

Mignolo, Walter. 2009. "Epistemic Disobedience, Independent Thought and De-Colonial Freedom." *Theory, Culture and Society* 26 (7–8): 1–23.

Mignolo, Walter, and Catherine Walsh. 2002. "Las geopolíticas del conocimiento y colonialidad del poder." In *Indisciplinarias las ciencias sociales. Geopolíticas del conocimiento y colonialidad del poder. Perspectivas desde lo andino*, edited by Catherine Walsh, Freya Schiwy, and Santiago Castro-Gómez, 17–34. Quito: Universidad Andina Simón Bolívar, Abya Yala.

Mijeski, Kenneth J., and Scott H. Beck. 2008. "The Electoral Fortunes of Ecuador's Pachakutik Party: The *fracaso* of the 2006 Presidential Elections." *Latin Americanist* 52 (June): 41–59.

———. 2011. *Pachakutik and the Rise and Decline of the Ecuadorian Indigenous Movement*. Athens: Ohio University Press, 2011.

Moctezuma, Pedro. 1984. "El movimiento urbano popular mexicano." Asociación Nueva Antropología, Mexico, *Nueva Antroplogía* 6 (24): 62–87.

Mogrovejo, Norma. 2010. "Itineraries of Latin American Lesbian Insubordination." In *Women's Activism in Latin America and the Caribbean: Engendering Social Justice, Democratizing Citizenship*, edited by Elizabeth Maier and Nathalie Lebon, 187–202. New Brunswick, NJ: Rutgers University Press.

Molyneux, Maxine. 1986. "Mobilization without Emancipation? Women's Interests, State and Revolution." In *Transition and Development: Problems of Third World Socialism*, edited by Richard Fagen, Carmen Diana Deere, and José Luis Coraggio, 280–302. New York: Monthly Review.

Monroy, David. 1997. *Mexican Teachers and the Struggle for Democracy*. San Francisco: Global Exchange.

Mora Bayo, Mariana. 2007. "Zapatista Anticapitalist Politics and the 'Other Campaign': Learning from the Struggle for Indigenous Rights and Autonomy." *Latin American Perspectives* 34 (2): 64–77.

———. 2008. "Decolonizing Politics: Zapatista Indigenous Autonomy in an Era of Neoliberal Governance and Low Intensity Warfare." PhD diss., Social Anthropology, University of Texas at Austin. http://repositories.lib.utexas.edu/bitstream/handle/2152/18194/moram27893.pdf?sequence=2 (accessed May 12, 2013).

———. 2011. "Producción de conocimientos en el terreno de la autonomía: La investigación como tema de debate político." In *Luchas "muy otras": Zapatismo y autonomía en las comunidades indígenas de Chiapas*, edited by Bruno Baronnet, Mariana Mora Bayo, and Richard Stahler-Sholk, 79–110. Mexico City: UAM-Xochimilco/CIESAS/UNACH.

———. 2013. "La politización de la justicia zapatista frente a la guerra de baja intensidad en Chiapas." In *Justicias indígenas y estado: Violencias contemporáneas*, edited by María Teresa Sierra, Rosalva Aída Hernández, and Rachel Sieder, 195–227. Mexico City: FLACSO/CIESAS.

Moreno, Ismael, S. J. 2005. "Miguel Facussé: Fencing Off Paradise." *Envío Nicaragua* (286).

———. 2008. "Gobierno Formal/Gobiernio Informal." *Envío Honduras* Año 6 (17), June:16–21.

Mortimore, Michael, and Leonardo Stanley. 2009. "Justice Denied: Dispute Settlement in Latin America's Trade and Investment Agreements." Working Group on Development and Environment in the Americas, Discussion Paper 27. October.

Morton, Adam David. 2011. *Revolution and State in Modern Mexico: The Political Economy of Uneven Development*. Lanham, MD: Rowman & Littlefield.

Motta, Sara C. 2009a. "New Ways of Making and Living Politics: The Movimiento de Trabajadores Desocupados de Solano and the 'Movement of Movements.'" *Bulletin of Latin American Research* 28 (1): 83–101.

———. 2009b. "Old Tools and New Movements in Latin America: Political Science as Gatekeeper or Intellectual Illuminator?" *Latin American Politics and Society* 51 (1): 31–56.

————. 2011a. "Notes towards Prefigurative Epistemologies." In *Social Movements in the Global South: Dispossession, Development and Resistance*, edited by Sara Catherine Motta and Alf Gunfald Nilsen, 178–99. London: Palgrave Macmillan Press.

————. 2011b. "Pedagogies of Resistance and Anti-capitalist Creation in Latin America." *Roundhouse Journal* 2: 64–77. http://www.scribd.com/doc/54768353/Roundhouse-Journal (accessed January 21, 2013).

————. 2012. "Reading Anarchism through Latin American Eyes." In *Companion to Contemporary Anarchism Reader*, edited by Ruth Kinna, 252–78. London: Continuum Press.

————. 2013a. "Reinventing the Lefts in Latin America: Critical Perspectives from Below." *Latin America Perspectives* 40 (4): 5–18.

————. 2013b. "'We Are the Ones We Have Been Waiting For': The Feminization of Resistance in Venezuela." *Latin American Perspectives* 40 (3): 35–54.

————. 2013c. "On the Pedagogical Turn in Latin American Social Movements." In *Education and Social Change in the Americas*, edited by Sara Catherine Motta and Mike Cole, 53–70. London/New York: Palgrave Macmillan Press.

Motta, Sara C., and Cole Mike. 2014. *Constructing 21st Century Socialism: The Role of Radical Education*. New York and London: Palgrave Macmillan Press.

Movimento Passe Livre. 2013. "Não começo em Salvador não vai terminar em São Paulo" (It Didn't Begin in Salvador and It Wouldn't End in São Paulo). In *Ciudades rebeldes, passe livre e as manifestações que tomaram as ruas do Brasil*, edited by Carlos Vainer David Harvey, and Ermínia Maricato, et al., 22-32. São Paulo: Tinta Vermelha, Boitempo Editorial.

MST (Movimento dos Trabalhadores Rurais Sem Terra). 2000. *O MST e a cultura*. Cuadernos de Formacão No. 34. São Paulo: Ademar Bogo.

————. 2001a. *O Brasil Precisa de um Projecto Popular*. São Paulo: Secretariat of Popular Consultation of the MST.

————. 2001b. "Fundamental Principles for the Social and Economic Transformation of Rural Brazil." Translated by Wilder Robles. *Journal of Peasant Studies* 28 (2): 146–52.

Nail, Thomas. 2012. *Returning to Revolution: Deleuze, Guattari and Zapatismo*. Edinburgh: Edinburgh University Press.

Nash, June. 1993. *We Eat the Mines and the Mines Eat Us: Dependency and Exploitation in Bolivian Tin Mines*. New York: Columbia University Press.

Navarro, Zander. 2002. "Mobilização sem emancipação: As lutas sociais dos Sem-Terra no Brasil." In *Produzir para viver*, edited by Boaventura de Sousa Santos, 1–28. Rio de Janeiro: Civilização Brasileira.

Negri, Antonio. 2003. *Job: La fuerza del esclavo*. Buenos Aires: Paidós.

Negri, Antonio, and Jim Flemming (eds). 1996. *Marx Beyond Marx: Lessons on the Grundrisse*. Translated by Michael Ryan, Mauricio Viano, and Harry Cleaver. Oakland, CA: AK Press.

Nepomuceno, Eric. 2013. "Es que no entiendan nada, no oyen nada, no se enteran de nada." (They Don't Understand Anything, They Don't Hear Anything, They Don't Get Any Of It.) *El Mundo*. July 11.

Nepstad, Sharon Erickson. 2004. *Convictions of the Soul: Religion, Culture, and Agency in the Central America Solidarity Movement*. New York: Oxford.

Neves, Delma Pessanha. 1997. *Assentamento rural: Reforma agrária em migalhas*. Niterói: EDUFF.

Nyéléni Declaration. 2007. http://www.nyeleni.org/spip.php?article290.

Oikomomakis, Leonidas. 2014. "We Made Morales President But We Were Misled." *ROAR Magazine* (February). http://roarmag.org/2014/02/morales-struggle-dictatorship-reparations/ (accessed May 2014).

Oleson, Thomas. 2005. *International Zapatismo*. London and New York: Zed Books.

Olivera, Mercedes. 1998. "Acteal: Los efectos de la guerra de Baja intensidad." In *La otra palabra: Mujeres y violencia en Chiapas antes y después de acteal*, edited by Rosalva Aída Hernandez Castillo, 114–24. México: CIESAS.

————. 2006. *"Violencia Femicida*: Violence against Women and Mexico's Structural Crisis." *Latin American Perspectives* 33 (2): 104–14.

Orellana, Marcos A. 2011. "The Right of Access to Information and Investment Arbitration." *ICSID Review: Foreign Investment Law Journal* 26 (2): 59–106.

Osorno, Diego. 2007. *Oaxaca Sitiada: La Primera Insurrección del Siglo XXI.* Mexico City: Random House Mondadori.

Ospina, Pablo. 2007. "Las demandas indígenas en el proceso constituyente." *Tendencia: Revista de Análisis Político* 6 (November): 102–5.

Otero, Gerardo. 2004. "Global Economy, Local Politics: Indigenous Struggles, Civil Society and Democracy." *Canadian Journal of Political Science/Revue canadienne de science politique*, 37 (2): 325–46.

Otros Mundos. 2011. *Del PPP al proyecto Mesoamérica: Eje de infraestructura y competitividad.* http://laguarura.net/wp-content/uploads/2011/09/Del-Plan-Puebla-Panam%C3%A1-al-Proyecto-Mesoam%C3%A9rica.pdf.

Oxfam America. 2013. "Free, Prior and Informed Consent in the Philippines: Regulations and Realities." *Oxfam America Briefing Paper* (September).

Padilla, Tanalís. 2008. *Rural Resistance in the Land of Zapata: The Jaramillista Movement and the Myth of the Pax Priísta, 1940–1962.* Durham, NC: Duke University Press.

Partlow, Joshua, and Stephan Küffner. 2008. "Voters in Ecuador Approve Constitution." *Washington Post,* September 29.

Pearson, Tamara. 2013. "First National Commune Conference: The Communes are the Antidote to Venezuela's Economic Problems." *Venezuela Analysis*, November 19. http://venezuelanalysis.com/analysis/10173 (accessed May 10 2014).

Peloso, Ranulfo. 1994. *A força que anima a militância.* São Paulo: MST.

Perla, Hector M. 2008. "Si Nicaragua Venció, El Salvador Vencerá: Central American Agency in the Creation of the US–Central American Peace and Solidarity Movement." *Latin American Research Review* 43 (2): 136–58.

Perry, Keisha-Kahn. 2013. *Black Women against the Land Grab: The Fight for Racial Justice in Brazil.* Minneapolis: University of Minnesota Press.

Petras, James F. 2014. "The Most Radical Conservative Regime: Bolivia under Evo Morales." *The James Petras Website.* http://petras.lahaine.org/?p=1968.

Petras, James F., and Henry Veltmeyer. 2009. *What's Left in Latin America?: Regime Change in New Times.* Farnham, UK and Burlington, VT: Ashgate.

———. 2011. *Social Movements in Latin America: Neoliberalism and Popular Resistance (Social Movements and Transformation).* New York: Palgrave Macmillan.

Philipps, Marva, and Lynn Bolles. 2006. "En solidaridad: Las mujeres en el movimiento laboral organizado en Latinoamérica y el Caribe." In *De lo privado a lo público: 30 años de lucha ciudadana de las mujeres en América Latina*, edited by Nathalie Lebon and Elizabeth Maier, 93–106. Mexico City: Siglo XXI.

Pickard, Miguel. 2003. "Grassroots Protests Force the Mexican Government to Search for a New PPP Strategy." *Americas Program*, March 1. http://www.cipamericas.org/archives/1031.

———. 2004. "Resucita el Plan Puebla-Panamá: Una mirada a su historia reciente para divisar el futuro próximo." *Americas Program.* (June 9). http://www.cipamericas.org/archives/633.

———. 2006. "The Plan Puebla-Panamá Continues as Meso-America Responds to the Empire's Plans." *Chiapas al Día,* 527. http://www.ciepac.org/bulletins (accessed Jan. 23, 2014).

Pineda, Enrique. 2013. "Acapatzingo: Construyendo comunidad urbana." *Contrapunto* 3 (November): 49–61. Centro de Formación Popular del Oeste, Montevideo, Universidad de la República.

Piñeiro Harnecker, Camila. 2007. "Workplace Democracy and Collective Consciousness: An Empirical Study of Venezuelan Cooperatives." *Monthly Review* 59 (6): 27–40.

Pinho, Patricia. 2010. *Mama Africa: Reinventing Blackness in Bahia.* Durham, NC: Duke University Press.

Pinto, Céli Regina Jardim. 2003. *Uma história do feminismo no Brasil.* São Paulo: Editora Fundação Perseu Abramo.

"'Plan Qué?' Developing Southern Mexico." 2004. *Economist* 371 (8370): 28–29.

Polletta, Francesca. 2006. *It Was Like a Fever: Storytelling in Protest and Politics.* Chicago: University of Chicago Press.

Polletta, Francesca, and James M. Jasper. 2001. "Collective Identity and Social Movements." *Annual Review of Sociology* 27: 283–305.

Portillo Villeda, Suyapa G. 2006. "Las 'cruza-fronteras': Género, sexualidad y migración (el caso de San Pedro Sula)." *Envío Honduras* 4 (special issue), December.

————. 2009. *Honduras Análise dun golpe político-militar.* Santiago de Compostela, Galicia: Terra E Tempo.

————. 2011. "Campeñas, Campeños y Compañeros: Life and Work in the Banana Fincas of the North Coast of Honduras, 1944–1957." PhD diss., History, Cornell University.

————. 2013a. *Observación internacional de elecciones Hondureñas 2013.* Claremont, CA: Institute for Global Local Action and Study, Pitzer College, May.

————. 2013b. "Pensando queer: Intersecciones entre/desde el margen de Estados Unidos y América Latina." In *Resentir lo queer en América Latina: Diálogos desde con el sur*, edited by Diego Falconí, Santiago Castellanos, and Maria Amelia Viteri. Egales: Spain.

Portillo, Suyapa, Indyra Mendoza, Gabrie Mass, and Sandra Zambrano. 2011. "Report on the State of Lesbian, Gay, Bisexual, Gay, Transgender, Transvestite and Intersex Community in Honduras." Los Angeles and Tegucigalpa, Honduras.

Postero, Nancy. 2006. *Now We Are Citizens: Indigenous Politics in Postmulticultural Bolivia.* Stanford: Stanford University Press.

Postero, Nancy. 2010. "Morales's MAS Government Building Indigenous Popular Hegemony in Bolivia." *Latin American Perspectives* 37 (3): 18–34.

Prevost, Gary, Carlos Oliva Campos, and Harry E. Vanden, eds. 2012. *Social Movements and Leftist Governments in Latin America: Confrontation or Co-Option?* London and New York: Zed Books.

Prevost, Gary, and Harry E. Vanden. 2012. "Introduction." In *Social Movements and Leftist Governments in Latin America,* edited by Gary Prevost, Carlos Oliva, and Harry E. Vanden, 1–21. London: Zed Press.

Procuraduría para la Defensa de los Derechos Humanos. 2013. *Informe especial sobre el proyecto minero "Cerro Blanco" y las potenciales vulneraciones a derechos humanos en la población Salvadoreña.* El Salvador: PDDH. http://www.ceicom.org.sv/pdf/informecerroblanco/InformeCerroBlanco.pdf (accessed July 29, 2013).

Programa Regional de Vivienda y Hábitat. 2012. *El camino posible. Producción social del hábitat en América Latina.* Montevideo: Trilce.

Quijano, Aníbal. 2005. "The Challenge of the 'Indigenous Movement' in Latin America." *Socialism and Democracy* 19 (3): 55–78.

Ramírez, Juan Manuel. 2003. "Impacto urbano de las de las organizaciones populares en México: 1980–2002." Austin, TX: Center for Study of Urbaniation and Internal Migration in Developing Countries.

Ramírez Rojas, Kléber. 2006. *Historia documental del 4 de febrero.* Caracas: El Perro y la Rana.

Ramos Salazar, Sandra. 2012. *Las federaciones del tropico de Cochabamba en el proceso de costruccion de un instrumento politico (1992–1997).* La Paz, Bolivia: Universidad Mayor de San Andres, Instituto de Investigaciones Sociologicas "Mauricio Lefebvre" IDIS.

Rasch, Elisabet Dueholm. 2012. "Transformations in Citizenship: Local Resistance against Mining Projects in Huehuetenango (Guatemala)." *Journal of Developing Societies* 28: 159–84.

Reiter, Bernd, and Gladys L. Mitchell, eds. 2010. *Brazil: New Racial Politics.* Boulder, CO: Lynne Rienner Press.

Rénique, Gerardo. 2007. "Subaltern Political Formation and the Struggle for Autonomy in Oaxaca." *Socialism and Democracy* 21: 62–73.

República del Ecuador. 2008. "Constitución de 2008." http://pdba.georgetown.edu/Constitutions/Ecuador/ecuador08.html.

Reyes, Alvaro. 2012. "Revolution in the Revolutions: A Post-counterhegemonic Moment for Latin America?" *South Atlantic Quarterly* 111 (1): 1–27.

Reyes, Alvaro, and Mara Kaufman. 2011. "Sovereignty, Indigeneity, Territory: Zapatista Autonomy and the New Practices of Decolonization." *South Atlantic Quarterly* 110 (2): 505–25.

Ribeiro, Matilde. 1995. "Mulheres negras brasileiras: De Bertioga a Beijing." *Revista Estudos Feministas* 3 (2): 446–58.

Richards, Patricia. 2004. *Pobladoras, Indígenas, and the State: Conflicts over Women's Rights in Chile.* New Brunswick, NJ: Rutgers University Press.

Riséro, Antonio. 1981. *Carnival Ijexá.* Salvador.

Robertson, Ewan. 2013. "Maduro Demands Greater Government Support for Venezuela's Communes." *Venezuela Analysis*, August 16. http://venezuelanalysis.com/news/9948 (accessed May 10, 2014).

Robinson, William I. 1996. *Promoting Polyarchy: Globalization, U.S. Intervention, and Hegemony.* Cambridge: Cambridge University Press.

———. 2008. *Latin America and Global Capitalism: A Critical Globalization Perspective.* Baltimore: Johns Hopkins University Press.

Robles, Wilber. 2001. "The Landless Rural Workers Movement (MST) in Brazil." *Journal of Peasant Studies* 28 (2): 147.

Rockefeller, Stuart Alexander. 2007. "Dual Power in Bolivia: Movement and Government Since the Election of 2005." *Urban Anthropology* 36 (3): 161–93.

Rodrigues Brandão, Carlos. 2001. *Historia do menino que lia o mundo.* Fazendo Historia No. 7. Veranópolis: ITERRA.

Rodrigues, João. 1999. "Olodum and the Black Struggle in Brazil." In *Black Brazil: Culture, Identity and Mobilization,* edited by Larry Crook and Randall Johnson, 43–51. Los Angeles: UCLA Latin American Center Publications.

Rodríguez Quevedo, Diana. 2013. "Witnessing Forced Internal Displacement in Colombia through Vallenato Music." In *Song and Social Change in Latin America*, edited by Lauren Shaw, 123–50. New York/London: Lexington Books.

Roland, Edna. 2000. "O movimiento de mulheres negras Brasileiras: Desafios e perspectivas." In *Tirando a máscara: Ensaios sobre o racismo no Brasil*, edited by Lynn Huntley and Antonio Sérgio Alfredo Guimarães, 237–56. São Paulo: Paz e Terra.

Romero, Simon. 2013a. "Protests Widen as Brazilians Chide Leaders." *New York Times*, June 19, 1.

———. 2013b. "Responding to Protests, Brazil's Leader Proposes Changes to System." *New York Times*, June 25, A7.

Rose, Fred. 1997. "Toward a Class-Cultural Theory of Social Movements: Reinterpreting New Social Movements." *Sociological Forum* 12 (1997): 468–69.

Ross, Clifton, and Marcy Rein, eds. 2014. *Until the Rulers Obey: Voices from Latin American Social Movements.* Oakland, CA: PM Press.

Rosset, Peter M. 2011. "Food Sovereignty and Alternative Paradigms to Confront Land Grabbing and the Food and Climate Crises." *Development,* 54 (1): 21–30.

———. 2013. "Re-thinking Agrarian Reform, Land and Territory in La Via Campesina." *Journal of Peasant Studies* 40 (4): 721–75.

Rosset, Peter M., and María Elena Martínez-Torres. 2012. "Rural Social Movements and Agroecology: Context, Theory, and Process." *Ecology and Society* 17 (3): 394–405.

Rohter, Larry. 2013. "Brazilian President's Attempt to Placate Protesters Backfires." *New York Times*, July 14, 9.

Rovira Kaltwasser, Cristóbal. 2011. "Toward Post-Neoliberalism in Latin America?" *Latin American Research Review* 46(2): 225–234.

Rubin, Jeffrey W. 1997. *Decentering the Regime: Ethnicity, Radicalism, and Democracy in Juchitán, Mexico.* Durham, NC: Duke University Press.

Rus, Jan. 1994. "The Comunidad Revolucionaria Institucional: The Subversion of Native Government in Highland Chiapas, 1936–1968." In *Everyday Forms of State Formation: Revolution and the Negotiation of Rule in Modern Mexico*, edited by Gilbert Joseph and Daniel Nugent, 265-300. Durham: Duke University Press.

Rus, Jan, Rosalva Aída Hernández Castillo, and Shannan L. Mattiace. 2003. *Mayan Lives, Mayan Utopias: The Indigenous Peoples of Chiapas and the Zapatista Rebellion.* Lanham, MD: Rowman & Littlefield.

Rus, Diane L., and Jan Rus. 2014. "Trapped Behind the Lines: The Impact of Undocumented Migration, Debt, and Recession on a Tsotsil Community of Chiapas, Mexico, 2002–2012." *Latin American Perspectives* 41 (3): 154–177.

Saavedra, Luis Ángel. 2006. "Leftists Split on United States." *Latinamerica Press* 38 (October 4): 1–2.

———. 2007a. "Correa's Ups and Downs." *Latinamerica Press* 39 (September 5): 5.

———. 2007b. "We've Balanced Out the Power." *Latinamerica Press* 39 (October 17): 1–2.

———. 2008. "The Good with the Bad." *Latinamerica Press* 40 (January 23): 4.

Sachs, Jeffrey. 2005. *The End of Poverty: How We Can Make It Happen in Our Lifetime.* New York: Penguin Books.

Salazar Ortuno, Fernando, Silvano Arancibia Colque, Luis Cuptiva Salva, and Delfin Olivera Vorja. 2008. *Kawsachun coca. El costo humano de las politicas de erradicacion de cultivos de coca en el tropico de Cochabamba, Bolivia 1980–2004, Vol. 1.* La Paz, Bolivia: Impresiones Sirca.

Salbuchi, Adrian. 2006. "How to Solve Argentina's Recurrent Foreign Debt Crises: Proposal for a Long-Term Solution." Center for Research on Globalization. Global Research, November 7, 2006. http://www.globalresearch.ca/index.php?context=va&aid=3750 (accessed March 12, 2014).

Sánchez, Ruth. 2003. "El Movimiento Urbano Popular a través de la Historia Oral: del Frente Popular Francisco Villa." Tesis para optar por el título de licenciado en Sociología. Facultad de Ciencias Políticas y Sociales. Universidad Autónoma Nacional de México.

Sánchez Díaz de Rivera, María Eugenia, and Eduardo Almeida Acosta. 2005. *Las veredas de la incertidumbre: Relaciones interculturales y supervivencia digna.* Puebla: Universidad Iberoamericana.

Sandoval Palacios, Juan Manuel, Raquel Álvarez de Flores, and Sara Yaneth Fernández Moreno. 2011. *Planes geoestratégicos, desplazamientos y migraciones forzadas en el área del proyecto de desarrollo e integración de Mesoamérica.* México, D.F.: Seminario Permanente de Estudios Chicanos y de Fronteras, DEAS-INAH.

Santos, Boaventura de Sousa, ed. 2007. *Democratizing Democracy: Beyond the Liberal Democratic Canon.* London and New York: Verso.

———. 2009. *Una epistemología del sur.* Mexico City: Siglo XXI.

———. 2010a. *Descolonizar el saber, reinventar el poder.* Montevideo: Ediciones Trilce.

———. 2010b. *Refundación del estado en América Latina: Perspectivas desde una epistemología del Sur.* Lima: Instituto Internacional de Derecho y Sociedad.

Saporta Sternbach, Nancy, et al. 1992. "Feminisms in Latin America: from Bogota to San Bernardo." In *The Making of Social Movements in Latin America*, edited by Arturo Escobar and Sonia E. Alvarez, 236–37. Boulder, CO: Westview Press.

Scott, James C. 1976. *The Moral Economy of the Peasant: Subsistence and Rebellion in Southeast Asia.* New Haven, CT: Yale University Press.

———. 1985. *Weapons of the Weak: Everyday Forms of Resistance.* New Haven and London: Yale University Press.

Selbin, Eric. 2010. *Revolution, Rebellion, Resistance: The Power of Story.* London/New York: Zed Books.

Sevilla Guzmán, Eduardo. 2013. "El despliegue de la sociología agraria hacia la agroecología." *Cuaderno Interdisciplinario de Desarrollo Sostenible* 10, 85–109.

Sevilla Guzmán, Eduardo, and Graham Woodgate. 2013. "Agroecology: Foundations in Agrarian Social Thought and Sociological Theory." *Agroecology and Sustainable Food Systems* 37 (1): 32–44.

Silber, Irina Carlota. 2010. *Everyday Revolutionaries: Gender, Violence, and Disillusionment in Postwar El Salvador.* New Brunswick, NJ: Rutgers University Press.

Sitrin, Marina, ed. 2006. *Horizontalism: Voices of Popular Power in Argentina.* Oakland, CA: AK Press.

————. 2012. *Everyday Revolutions: Horizontalism and Autonomy in Argentina.* London and New York: Zed Books.

————. 2014. "Defending the Earth in Argentina: From Direct Action to Autonomy: A Conversation with Emilio Spataro." *Tidal Magazine.* April 6. http://tidalmag.org/blog/everyday-revolutions/defending-the-earth-in-argentina-from-direct-action-to-autonomy/ (accessed May 2, 2014).

Sitrin, Marina, and Dario Azzelini. 2012. *Occupy Language: The Secret Rendezvous With History and the Present.* New York: Zuccotti Park Press.

————. 2014. *They Can't Represent Us! Reinventing Democracy from Greece to Occupy.* New York: Verso.

Slack, Keith. 2009. "Digging Out from Neoliberalism: Responses to Environmental (Mis)governance of the Mining Sector in Latin America." In *Beyond Neoliberalism in Latin America?*, edited by John Burdick, Philip Oxhorn, and Kenneth M. Roberts, 117–34. New York: Palgrave Macmillan.

Slater, David, ed. 1985. *New Social Movements and the State in Latin America.* Amsterdam: CEDLA.

Smilde, David, and Daniel Hellinger, eds. 2011. *Venezuela's Bolivarian Democracy: Participation, Politics, and Culture under Chávez.* Durham, NC: Duke University Press.

Smith, Christian. 1996. *Resisting Reagan: The U.S. Central America Peace Movement.* Chicago: University of Chicago Press.

Smith, Jackie, Charles Chatfield, and Ron Pagnucco, eds. 1997. *Transnational Social Movements and Global Politics: Solidarity beyond the State.* Syracuse, NY: Syracuse University Press.

Smith-Nonini, Sandy. 2010. *Healing the Body Politic: El Salvador's Popular Struggle for Health Rights—From Civil War to Neoliberal Peace.* New Brunswick, NJ: Rutgers University Press.

Snow, David A., E. Burke Rochford, Jr., Steven K. Worden, and Robert D. Benford. 1986. "Frame Alignment Processes, Micromobilization, and Movement Participation," *American Sociological Review* 51 (4) (August): 464–81.

Soares, Vera, Ana Alice Alcantara Costa, Cristina Maria Buarque, Denise Dourado Dora, and Wania Sant'anna. 1995. "Brazilian Feminism and Women's Movements: A Two-way Street." In *The Challenges of Local Feminisms: Women's Movements in Global Perspective*, edited by Amrita Basu, 302–323. Boulder, CO: Westview Press.

Souza Lobo, Elisabeth. 1991. *A classe operária tem dois sexos: Trabalho, dominação e resistência.* São Paulo: Brasiliense/Secretaria Municipal de Cultura.

Sotelo Marbén, José. 2008. *Oaxaca: Insurgencia civil y terrorismo de estado.* Mexico City: Ediciones Era.

Spalding, Rose J. 2008. "Neoliberal Regionalism and Resistance in Mesoamerica: Foro Mesoamericano Opposition to Plan Puebla-Panamá and CAFTA." In *Latin American Social Movements in the Twenty-first Century: Resistance, Power and Democracy*, edited by Richard Stahler-Sholk, Harry E. Vanden, and Glen David Kuecker, 323–36. Lanham, MD: Rowman & Littlefield.

————. 2014. *Contesting Trade in Central America: Market Reform and Resistance.* Austin: University of Texas Press.

Speed, Shannon. 2008. *Rights in Rebellion: Indigenous Struggle and Human Rights in Chiapas.* Stanford, CA: Stanford University Press.

Speed, Shannon, and Melissa Forbis. 2005. "Embodying Alternative Logics: Everday Leaders and the Diffusion of Power in Zapatista Autonomous Regions." *LASA Forum* 36 (1).

Speed, Shannon, Rosalva Aída Hernández Castillo, and Lynn M. Stephen, eds. 2006. *Dissident Women: Gender and Cultural Politics in Chiapas.* Austin: University of Texas Press.

Spedding, Alison. 2005. *Kawsachun Coca. Economia campesina cocalera en los yungas y el chapare.* La Paz, Bolivia: PIEB- Programa de Investigacion Estrategica en Bolivia.

Spronk, Susan. 2008. "Mapping Regional Tensions in Correa's Ecuador and Evo's Bolivia." *Relay* 23 (July–September): 39–43.

Stahler-Sholk, Richard. 2007. "Resisting Neoliberal Homogenization: The Zapatista Autonomy Movement." *Latin American Perspectives* 34 (2): 48–63.

————. 2008. "Resisting Neoliberal Homogenization: The Zapatista Autonomy Movement." In *Latin American Social Movements in the Twenty-First Century: Resistance, Power and Democracy,* edited by Richard Stahler-Sholk, Harry E. Vanden, and Glen David-Kuecker, 113–29. Lanham, MD: Rowman & Littlefield.

————. 2010. "The Zapatista Social Movement: Innovation and Sustainability." *Alternatives* 35 (3): 369–90.

————. 2011. "Autonomía y economía política de resistencia en Las Cañadas de Ocosingo." In *Luchas "muy otras": zapatismo y autonomía en las comunidades indígenas de Chiapas,* edited by Bruno Baronnet, Mariana Mora Bayo, and Richard Stahler-Sholk, 409–45. Mexico City: UAM-Xochimilco/CIESAS/UNACH.

Stahler-Sholk, Richard, Harry E. Vanden, and Glen David Kuecker, eds. 2008. *Latin American Social Movements in the Twenty-first Century: Resistance, Power, and Democracy.* Lanham, MD: Rowman & Littlefield.

Stam, Robert. 1988. "Carnival Politics and Brazilian Culture." *Studies in Latin American Cultures* 7: 255–63.

Starr, Amory, María Elena Martínez-Torres, and Peter Rosset. 2011. "Participatory Democracy in Action: Practices of the Zapatistas and the Movimento Sem Terra." *Latin American Perspectives* 38 (176): 102–19.

Stedile, João Pedro, and Bernardo Mançano Fernandes. 2000. *Brava gente: A trajetória do MST e a luta pela terra no Brasil.* São Paulo: Fundação Perseu Abramo.

Steiner, Richard. 2010. "El Salvador—Gold, Guns, and Choice." Report for the International Union for the Conservation of Nature (IUCN) and Commission on Environmental, Economic and Social Policy (CEESP). http://www.walkingwithelsalvador.org/Steiner%20Salvador%20Mining%20Report.pdf (accessed February 16, 2014).

Stephen, Lynn. 1997a. "Pro-Zapatista and Pro-PRI: Resolving the Contradictions of Zapatismo in Rural Oaxaca." *Latin American Research Review* 32 (2): 41–70.

————. 1997b. *Women and Social Movements in Latin America: Power from Below.* Austin: Texas University Press.

————. 2007. *Transborder Lives: Indigenous Oaxacans in Mexico, California, and Oregon.* Durham, NC: Duke University Press.

————. 2013. *We Are the Face of Oaxaca: Testimony and Social Movements.* Durham, NC: Duke University Press.

Sterling, Cheryl. 2012. *African Roots, Brazilian Rites: Cultural and National Identity in Brazil.* New York: Palgrave McMillian.

Subcomandante Insurgente Marcos. 2007. "Ni el centro ni la periferia." Intervention in Coloquio Aubry, San Cristóbal de las Casas, December 13. http://enlacezapatista.ezln.org.mx/2007/12/13/conferencia-del-dia-13-de-diciembre-a-las-900-am/ (accessed December 20, 2013).

Sutton, Alison. 1994. *Slavery in Brazil: A Link in the Chain of Modernization, the Case of Amazônia.* London: Anti-Slavery International.

Svampa, Maristela. 2008. "The End of Kirchnerism." *New Left Review* 53: 79–95.

Swords, Alicia. 2005. "The Power of Networks: Popular Political Education among Neo-Zapatista Organizations in Chiapas, Mexico." PhD Diss., Department of Development Sociology, Cornell University.

————. 2007. "Neo-Zapatista Network Politics: Transforming Democracy and Development." *Latin American Perspectives* 34 (2): 1–16.

Swords, Alicia. 2008. "Neo-zapatista Network Politics: Transforming Democracy and Development." In *Latin American Social Movements in the Twenty-first Century: Resistance, Power, and Democracy,* edited by Richard Stahler-Sholk, Harry E. Vanden, and Glen David Kuecker, 291–305. Lanham, MD: Rowman & Littlefield.

————. 2010. "Teaching against Neoliberalism in Chiapas, Mexico: Gendered Resistance via Neo-Zapatista Network Politics." In *Contesting Development: Critical Struggles for Social Change,* edited by Philip McMichael, 116–31. New York and London: Routledge.

A Tarde. 1992. October 14.

Tardin, Jose Maria. 2006. *Considerações sobre o diálogo de saberes* (mímeo). Sao Paulo: Escola Latino-Americana de Agroecologia.

Tarrow, Sidney. 2005. *The New Transnational Activism*. Cambridge: Cambridge University Press.

Tarrow, Sidney. 2005. *The New Transnational Activism*. Cambridge: Cambridge University Press.
Tau Consultora Ambiental. 2011. *Servicios de consultoría para la Evaluación Ambiental Estratégica (EAE) del sector minero metálico de El Salvador: Informe final*. Prepared for the Ministerio de Economía de El Salvador, Unidad de Cooperación Externa. http://www.marn.gob.sv/phocadownload/EAE_minero_metalico.pdf (accessed August 9, 2012).
Taylor, Verta, and Nancy Whittier. 1995. "Analytical Approaches to Social Movement Culture: The Culture of the Women's Movement." In *Social Movements and Culture*, edited by Hank Johnston and Bert Klandermans, 163–87. Minneapolis: University of Minnesota Press.
Teles dos Santos, Josélio. 1999. "A Mixed Race Nation: Afro-Brazilians and Cultural Policy in Bahia, 1970–1990." In *Afro-Brazilian Culture and Politics*, edited by Kraay Hendrik, 117–33. 1998. Armonk, NY: M.E. Sharpe.
Teles, Maria Amelia de Almeida. 1993. *Uma breve historia do feminismo no Brasil*. São Paulo: Editora Brasiliense.
———. 2012. "Quase duas décadas de promotoras legais populares no Brasil." In *Introdução crítica ao direito das mulheres*, edited by José Geraldo da Sousa Junior, Bistra Stefanova Apostolova, and Lívia Gimenes Dias da Fonseca, 47–53. Series: O Direito Achado na Rua vol. 5. Brasília: CEAD FUB.
Thayer, Millicent. 2001. "Transnational Feminism: Reading Joan Scott in the Brazilian Sertão." *Ethnography* 2 (June): 243–71.
Thompson, Becky. 2002. "Multiracial Feminism: Recasting the Chronology of Second Wave Feminism." *Feminist Studies* 28 (2): 337–60.
Thompson, Edward Palmer. 1971. "The Moral Economy of the English Crowd in the Eighteenth Century." *Past and Present* 50 (1): 76–136.
Todd, Molly. 2010. *Beyond Displacement: Campesinos, Refugees, and Collective Action in the Salvadoran Civil War*. Madison: University of Wisconsin Press.
Toná, Nilcinei. 2009. "O diálogo de saberes, na promoção da agroecologia na base dos movimentos sociais populares." *Revista Brasileira de Agroecologia* 4 (2): 3322–25.
Tonkiss, Fran. 2005. *Space, the City and Social Theory: Social Relations and Urban Forms*. Cambridge and Malden, MA: Polity.
Trotsky, Leon. 1930. "Dual Power." In *The History of the Russian Revolution, Vol. 1*. http://www.marxists.org/archive/trotsky/1930/hrr/ (accessed December 2013).
Turner, Michael J. 1985. "Brown into Black: Changing Racial Attitudes of Afro-Brazilian Students." In *Race, Class, and Power in Brazil*, edited by Pierre Michel Fontaine, 73–94. Los Angeles: The University of California.
Unión de Comunidades Indígenas de la Zona Norte del Istmo. 2006. *Plan Puebla-Panamá Exists and Mesoamerica Resists*. www.datacenter.org/reports/mesoamericaresists-eng.pdf (accessed July 26, 2012).
U.S.-El Salvador Sister Cities. 2008–2013. *Gold Mining Analysis and Resistance Series*. http://www.elsalvadorsolidarity.org/index.php/resistance-to-mining/19-sister-cities-programs/mining-resistance/178-gold-mining-analysis-and-resistance-series (accessed February 15, 2014).
Vainer, Carlos, David Harvey, Ermínia Maricato, et al. 2013. *Ciudades rebeldes, passe livre e as manifestações que tomaram as ruas do Brasil*. São Paulo: Tinta Vermelha, Boitempo Editorial.
Van Cott, Donna Lee. 2001. "Explaining Ethnic Autonomy Regimes in Latin America." *Studies in Comparative International Development*, 35 (4): 30–58.
———. 2002. "Constitutional reform in the Andes: Redefining Indigenous-State Relations." In *Multiculturalism in Latin America: Indigenous Rights, Diversity, and Democracy*, edited by Rachel Sieder, 45–73. New York: Palgrave.
———. 2003. "Andean Indigenous Movements and Constitutional Transformation: Venezuela in Comparative Perspective." *Latin American Perspectives* 30 (1): 49–69.
Vanden, Harry E. 2008. "Social Movements, Hegemony, and New Forms of Resistance." In *Latin American Social Movements in the Twenty-First Century, Resistance, Power, and Democracy*, edited by Richard Stahler-Sholk, Harry E. Vanden, and Glen Kuecker, 39–56. Lanham, MD: Rowman & Littlefield.

Vanden, Harry E., and Marc Becker. 2011. *José Carlos Mariátegui: An Anthology.* New York: Monthly Review Press.

Veltmeyer, Henry, and James Petras. 2002. "The Social Dynamics of Brazil's Rural Landless Workers' Movement: Ten Hypotheses on Successful Leadership." *Canadian Review of Sociology and Anthropology* 39 (1): 79–96.

———, eds. 2014. *The New Extractivism: A Post-neoliberal Development Model or Imperialism of the Twenty-first Century?* New York: Zed Books.

Viana, Nilton. 2013. Interview with João Pedro Stédile, "A hora das reformas." (The Time for Reforms). *Otras Palavras, Boletim de Actualização.* June 27.

Viatori, Maximilian and Gloria Ushigua. 2007. "Speaking Sovereignty: Indigenous Languages and Self-Determination." *Wicazo SaReview* 22 (Fall): 7–21.

Villars, Rina. 2001. *Para la casa más que para el mundo: Sufragismo y feminismo en la historia de Honduras.* Tegucigalpa, Honduras: Editorial Guaymuras.

Wainwright, Hilary. 2011. "Feeling our Way Forward." *Red Pepper*, August. http://www.redpepper.org.uk/feeling-ourway-forward/ (accessed December 2, 2013).

Wallerstein, Immanuel. 2013. "Levantamientos aquí y en todas partes." (Uprisings Here and All Over) *La Jornada.* July 6.

Walsh, Catherine. 2010. "Development as Buen Vivir: Institutional Arrangements and (De)colonial Entanglements." *Development* 53 (1): 15–21.

Warren, Kay B., and Jean Elizabeth Jackson. 2002. *Indigenous Movements, Self-Representation, and the State in Latin America.* Austin: University of Texas Press.

Weber, Maximilian.1990 [1962]. *Basic Concepts in Sociology.* Translated by H. Secher. New York: Citadel Press.

Webber, Jeffery R. 2010. "From Rebellion to Reform." *International Socialist Review*, September. http://isreview.org/issue/73/rebellion-reform (accessed January 19, 2014).

———. 2011. *Red October: Left-Indigenous Struggles in Modern Bolivia.* Chicago: Haymarket Books.

———. 2012. "From Left-Indigenous Insurrection to Reconstituted Neoliberalism in Bolivia: Political Economy, Indigenous Liberation, and Class Struggle, 2000–2011." In *The New Latin American Left: Cracks in the Empire*, edited by Jeffery R. Webber and Barry Carr, 149–89. Lanham, MD: Rowman & Littlefield.

———. 2014. "Managing Bolivian Capitalism."Jacobin. https://www.jacobinmag.com/2014/01/managing-bolivian-capitalism/ (accessed January 19, 2014).

Webber, Jeffery R., and Barry Carr, eds. 2012. *The New Latin American Left: Cracks in the Empire.* Lanham, MD: Rowman & Littlefield.

Weyland, Kurt. 2013. "Latin America's Authoritarian Drift: The Threat from the Populist Left." *Journal of Democracy* 24(3): 18–32.

Wezel, Alexander, Stéphane Bellon, Thierry Doré, Charles Francis, Dominique Vallod, and Christophe David. 2009. "Agroecology as a Science, a Movement and a Practice: A Review. *Agronomy for Sustainable Development* 29: 503–15.

Wickham-Crowley, Timothy P. 1992. *Guerrillas and Revolution in Latin America: A Comparative Study of Insurgents and Regimes since 1956.* Princeton, NJ: Princeton University Press.

Williamson, John. 1990. "What Washington Means by Policy Reform." Chapter 2 in John Williamson, ed., *Latin American Adjustment: How Much Has Happened?* Washington, DC: Institute for International Economics.

Wilpert, Greg. 2006. "Land for People Not for Profit in Venezuela." In *Promised Land: Competing Visions of Agrarian Reform*, edited by P. Rosset, R. Patel, and M. Courville, 249–64. New York: Food First.

Wilson, Japhy. 2008. The New Phase of the Plan Puebla-Panamá in Chiapas (Parts 1, 2, and 3). *Chiapas al Día,* 560–62. http://www.ciepac.org/bulletins (accessed Jan. 22, 2014).

Winn, Peter. 1989. *Weavers of Revolution: The Yarur Workers and Chile's Road to Socialism.* Oxford: Oxford University Press.

Wood, William Warner. 2008. *Made in Mexico: Zapotec Weavers and the Global Ethnic Art Market.* Bloomington: Indiana University Press.

Wright, Angus, and Wendy Wolford. 2003. *To Inherit the Earth: The Landless Movement and the Struggle for a New Brazil.* Oakland, CA: Food First Books.

Wright, Thomas C. 2007. *State Terrorism in Latin America: Chile, Argentina, and International Human Rights.* Lanham, MD: Rowman & Littlefield.

Yashar, Deborah J. 2005. *Contested Citizenship in Latin America: The Rise of Indigenous Movements and the Postliberal Challenge.* New York: Cambridge University Press.

Young, Kevin, and Michael Schwartz. 2012. "Can Prefigurative Politics Prevail? The Implications for Movement Strategy in John Holloway's Crack Capitalism." *Journal of Classical Sociology* 12 (2): 220–39.

Zafra, Gloria, Jorge Hernández-Díaz, and Manuel Garza Zepeda. 2002. *Organización popular y oposición empresarial: Manifestaciones de la acción colectiva en Oaxaca.* Mexico City: Plaza y Valdés.

Zamosc, Leon. 2007. "The Indian Movement and Political Democracy in Ecuador." *Latin American Politics and Society* 49 (Summer): 1–34.

Zegada, Maria Teresa. 2008. *Racismo en Bolivia: Discursos y contradiscursos.* Cochabamba, Bolivia: Centro Cuarto Intermedio.

Zibechi, Raul. 2003. *Genealogia de la revuelta: Argentina: La sociedad en movimiento.* Buenos Aires, Argentina: Letra Libre.

———. 2004. "The Impact of Zapatismo in Latin America." *Antipode* 36 (3): 392–99.

———. 2008. *Territorios en resistencia: Cartografía política de las periferias urbanas latinoamericanas.* Buenos Aires, Argentina: Lavaca.

———. 2009. Interview with Enrique Reynoso. December.

———. 2010. *Dispersing Power: Social Movements and Anti-state Forces.* Oakland, CA: AK Press.

———. 2012. *Territories in Resistance: A Cartography of Latin American Social Movements.* Translated by Ramor Ryan. Oakland, CA: AK Press.

———. 2013a. "Acapatzingo. Toda lucha empieza contra nosotros mismos." Unpublished manuscript.

———. 2013b. "Los indinados de Brasil, la revuelta de los viente centavos," (The Indignant Ones in Brazil, the Twenty Cent Revolt). *La Jornada.* June 24.

Zires, Margarita. 2009. "Estrategias de comunicación y acción política: Movimiento social de la APPO 2006." In *La APPO: ¿Rebelión o movimiento social? (Nuevas formas de expresión ante la crisis),* edited by Víctor Raúl Martínez Vásquez, 161–95. Oaxaca: Universidad Autónoma "Benito Juárez" de Oaxaca.

Zuazo, Moira. 2009. *¿Cómo nació el MAS? La ruralización de la política en Bolivia entrevistas a 85 parlamentarios del partido.* La Paz, Bolivia: Fundación Ebert.

Zunino, Mariela. 2010. "Integration for Plunder: The MesoAmerica Project, or Racheting Up the Land Grab" (Parts 1, 2 and 3). *Chiapas al Día,* 583–85. http://www.ciepac.org/bulletins (accessed Jan. 22, 2014).

Index

500 Years Campaign, 332, 335
1968 protest movement of Mexico, 50–51, 54
2009 coup d'état of Honduras: campesinos affected by, 139; chaos in aftermath, 135; female protesters, 137; FNRP formed in response, 13, 122; human rights violations, 133; Liberal Party, role in, 124, 126; media manipulation of events, 126, 144n14; ouster of Manuel Zelaya Rosales, 123–124; United States, non-recognition of, 126, 129
2013 popular protests of Brazil: corruption in government, 233, 237, 238, 246, 249; health and education system complaints, 233–234, 244, 249; stadium costs, tax money going towards, 233–234, 246, 249; transportation fee increases, 233–234, 244, 244–245, 247, 248, 249

absences and emergences in social movements, 331, 334–335, 340, 342, 342n5
Acapatzingo community of Mexico: brigades, 55, 57–58; construction of, 55–56, 63; as distinct, 49; FPFVI affiliation, 50, 60; government land loans, 55, 63; links with outside groups, 58, 59; as a safe space, 61; vigilance

commission, 55, 57, 58, 60, 63; women, role of, 64
Acosta, Alberto, 269, 271, 278
affective politics in Argentina, 30, 217, 218, 219
agroecology, 331, 334, 335–341, 338, 342
Alianza Bolivariana para los Pueblos de Nuestra América (ALBA), 125–126
Alianza Mexicana de Organizaciones Sociales (AMOS), 58–59
Alianza País (AP), 270, 271, 272, 276, 278
Alianza Republicana Nacionalista (ARENA), 313, 314, 318, 322, 329n5
Almeyra, Guillermo, 272
anti-mining movement of El Salvador: cross-border relations, 321; engagement with the state, 322, 328; extraction moratorium, 314, 314–315, 323–324; horizontalism, practicing, 312, 313, 315, 328; international alliances, 313, 315, 328; liberation theology encouragement, 320; protesters, 311–312, 319; transnational allies, 326–327
Anzaldúa, Gloria, 36, 37, 38, 39, 42n14, 42n16
Asamblea de los Pueblos (ASP), 294, 304n16
Asamblea Nacional Indígena Plural Por La Autonomía (ANIPA), 203

379

Roland, 258, 262, 286

diálogo de saberes (dialogue among different knowledges and ways of knowing, DS): agroecology and, 336–337, 339, 340; defining, 333, 334, 335; horizontalism achieved through, 16, 331, 332–333, 334, 335, 340; as a tool of CLOC/VC, 332, 333, 334, 339, 341, 342; Diniz, Aldiva Sonia, 25, 27, 29, 30

division of labor: as gendered, 64, 196; grassroots and NGO leaders, between, 117; intellectual *vs.* practical labor, 24; network politics, within, 102; politicizing of, 23, 26; dual sovereignty, 285–287, 288, 295–296, 302, 303; Dussel, Enrique, 24, 252, 263, 265n7

Economic and Social Development Association (Asociación de Desarrollo Económico y Social, ADES), 318

Ecuarunari of Ecuador, 269, 270, 273, 276, 282

Ejército Revolucionario del Pueblo (ERP), 223, 317

Ejército Zapatista de Liberación Nacional (EZLN), 55, 194, 202, 206n1, 230

ejidos (self-managed peasant communities) of Mexico, 194, 195, 196

emergences and absences in social movements, 331, 334–335, 340, 342, 342n5

Escuela Política de Mujeres Pazificas, 28, 30, 32–33, 34, 39

Esteva, Gustavo, 78, 81

everyday religiosities, 30–31

extractivism: anti-mining protestors, 311–312; as damaging, 273; extraction permits, obtaining, 324; extractivist developmental logic, 298, 301, 305n24; gold extraction in El Salvador, 324; government support, 311; neo-extractivism, 4, 6, 16, 204, 241, 281, 305n24, 323, 328n3, 345; PPP friendliness towards extractive industries, 101, 114; prior consultation with Indigenous groups, 275, 277, 281; protestors against, 280, 281; Factory Without a Boss (Fábrica Sin Patron,

FaSinPat), 214, 229–230

Facussé, Miguel, 140–141

Farabundo Martí National Liberation Front (Frente Farabundo Martí de Liberación Nacional, FMLN): alignment with the left, 322; Honduran involvement with, 128–129, 144n10; leadership of Mauricio Funes, 314, 322; local activists, backing, 318; mining ban proposal, 323; Movimiento Estudiantil Revolucionario de Secundaria as base organization for, 329n10; as a protecting agency, 316, 317

Federación Nacional de Cooperatives Mineras (FENCOMIN), 297

Federación Nacional de Mujeres Campesinas Bartolina Sisa (FNMCB-BS), 294, 297

Federación Unitaria de Trabajadores de Honduras (FUTH), 131

Federal District Housing Institute (Instituto de Vivienda del Distrito Federal, INVI), 55

Federal Preventative Police (PFP), 75, 77

Fédération Internationale de Football Associacion (FIFA), 246, 249; feminism and women's issues; Acapatzingo community, role of women in, 64; Afro-Brazilian feminism, 47, 148, 151, 154, 155, 157, 162; *econtros* (gatherings), 153, 155, 158; female protestors of Honduran coup d'état, 137; feminist autonomous organizations, 148, 153; feminist NGOs, 148, 154, 157, 160; feminized resistances, 28–29, 115–116, 136–137; gender discrimination in Bolivia, 204; historic feminists, 148–149, 151, 153, 154, 163; horizontalism, feminist groups implementing, 13, 148–149, 150–151, 159, 161, 164, 165n11; LGBTTI, absence of female participants, 135; middle class activism, 147, 148, 149, 150–151, 153–154, 154; militant motherhood, 152, 154; popular women legal advisors (Promotoras Legais Populares, PLP), 149, 157–159, 164; SempreViva Organizaçào

About the Editors and Contributors

Marc Becker is a professor of Latin American history at Truman State University. His research focuses on constructions of race, class, and gender within popular movements in the South American Andes. He is the author of *Pachakutik: Indigenous Movements and Electoral Politics in Ecuador* (2011) and *Indians and Leftists in the Making of Ecuador's Modern Indigenous Movements* (2008); coeditor with Kim Clark of *Highland Indians and the State in Modern Ecuador* (2007); and editor and translator with Harry Vanden of *José Carlos Mariátegui: An Anthology* (2011).

George Ciccariello-Maher is assistant professor of Political Science at Drexel University, having previously taught at University of California–Berkeley, San Quentin State Prison, and the Venezuelan School of Planning in Caracas. He is the author of *We Created Chávez: A People's History of the Venezuelan Revolution* (2013), as well as a number of book chapters and articles on decolonial political theory, race, and social movements in Latin America and the United States. He is currently completing two books, entitled *Decolonizing Dialectics* and *Building the Commune*.

Kwame Dixon is associate professor of African American Studies and Political Science at Syracuse University. His primary research is focused on Afro-Latin America and the Caribbean. His most recent publication is *Comparative Perspectives on Afro-Latin America* (2012).

Fran Espinoza is a political scientist with a PhD in International Studies at the University of Deusto in Bilbao, Spain. He has been a Marie Curie fellow at the Centre for Social Studies (Centro de Estudos Sociais, CES) at the University of Coimbra in Portugal. He holds a Bachelor's Degree in Political

Science and International Relations from the University Rafael Landivar in Guatemala and an International Master's Degree in Peace Studies, Conflicts, and Development from the University Jaume I in Castellon, Spain. He has been guest scholar in various universities in Brazil, Nicaragua, Bolivia, Guatemala, Spain, Belgium, and Italy, and has participated in international electoral observation missions with the Organization of American States (OAS) in Venezuela, Ecuador, Guatemala, and Bolivia.

Daniela Issa is a PhD candidate in sociology at the École des Hautes Études en Sciences Sociales (EHESS) in Paris. Her current research deals with modern slavery and human trafficking in Latin America and Brazil.

Nathalie Lebon is an anthropologist and associate professor of Women, Gender, and Sexuality Studies and Latin American Studies affiliate, Gettysburg College. She is coeditor with Elizabeth Maier of *Women's Movements in Latin America and the Caribbean: Engendering Social Justice, Democratizing Citizenship* (2010), awarded *Choice* magazine Outstanding Academic Title; and *De lo Privado a lo Público: 30 años de lucha ciudadana de las mujeres en América Latina* 2006). She has published articles in *Estudos Feministas*, *Latin American Perspectives*, *Feminist Studies and Organization*, among others, on Brazilian and Latin American women's movements. Her current project focuses on the transnational negotiation of difference in the World March of Women.

Maurice Rafael Magaña holds a PhD in Sociocultural Anthropology from the University of Oregon. His main research interests deal with understanding how youth construct themselves as political actors and how they imagine social change. His dissertation, entitled *Youth in Movement: The Cultural Politics of Autonomous Youth Activism in Southern Mexico*, examined youth organizing in the context of a broad-based social movement in Oaxaca, Mexico. As a postdoctoral researcher at the University of California–Los Angeles, he is conducting fieldwork in Los Angeles that seeks to understand how diasporic youth experienced the Oaxacan social movement. His work has been published in the *Journal of Contemporary Anthropology* and he also coauthored a chapter about Latin American immigration in Oregon.

Maria Elena Martinez-Torres is researcher and professor of Society and Environment at the Centro de Investigaciones y Estudios Superiores en Antropología Social-Unidad Sureste (CIESAS-Sureste) in Mexico, and author of *Organic Coffee: Sustainable Development by Mayan Farmers* (2006).

Sara C. Motta is a senior lecturer in politics at the University of Newcastle, NSW, Australia. Her research focus is the politics of subaltern resistance, with particular reference to Latin America and the invention of new forms of popular politics, political subjectivities, and ways of life that seek to transcend neoliberal capitalism. Recent publications include (with Ana Esteves) "Reinventing Emancipation in the 21st Century: The Pedagogical Practices of Social Movements," *Interface* (2014), and (with Mike Cole) *Constructing 21st Century Socialism: The Role of Radical Education* (2014) and *Education and Social Change in Latin America (2014)*.

Leonidas Oikonomakis is a PhD researcher in the Department of Social and Political Science at the European University Institute. His research focuses on the relationship between social movements and the state in Latin America (case studies: Zapatistas of Mexico and *Cocaleros* of Bolivia). He is a member of the hip-hop formation *Social Waste*, a coeditor of ROARMAG.org, and was an active participant in the occupation of Syntagma Square. He is also a codirector of "*Utopia on the Horizon*," a documentary on the occupation of Syntagma Square and the future of the Greek anti-austerity movement. Besides his native Greek and English, his articles have been translated into French, Urdu, Hindi, Arabic, Bahasa Indonesia, Italian, Spanish, Portuguese, Dutch, and Turkish.

Suyapa Portillo Villeda is an assistant professor in the Chicana/o Latina/o Transnational Studies Field group at Pitzer College in Claremont, California. She holds a BA from Pitzer College and a Masters and a PhD in History from Cornell University. Her research focuses on history of gender and labor in Latin America, U.S. Latino/a populations, and contemporary immigration. Her current project focuses on the 1954 strike against the United Fruit Company in Honduras, workers' roles in the banana export economy, and the formation of the labor movement. Since the coup d'état in Honduras in 2009, Portillo Villeda has documented the emerging social movements and human rights conditions they face in Honduras. In particular, she is interested in the history and human rights violations against the Honduran people in resistance. As a part of her community work, Portillo Villeda documents violence against the human rights of Lesbian, Gay, Bisexual, Transgender, Transvestite, and Intersex people in Honduras and works closely with groups to promote awareness and investigation.

Peter M. Rosset is researcher and professor in Agriculture, Society, and the Environment at El Colegio de la Frontera Sur (ECOSUR) in Mexico, and researcher at the Centro de Estudios para el Cambio en el Campo Mexicano (CECCAM). He is also cocoordinator of the Land Research Action Network (www.landaction.org).

Marina Sitrin holds a PhD in Global Sociology, a JD in International Women's Human Rights, and is a visiting scholar at the Center for Place Culture and Politics at the City University of New York Graduate Center. She is the author of *Horizontalism: Voices of Popular Power in Argentina* (2006); *Everyday Revolutions: Horizontalism and Autonomy in Argentina* (2012); and coauthor of *Occupying Language: The Secret Rendezvous with History and the Present* (2012) and *They Can't Represent US: Reinventing Democracy from Greece to Occupy* (2014). Her work focuses on social movements and justice, specifically looking at new forms of social organization, such as *autogestión, horizontalidad,* prefigurative politics, and new affective social relationships.

Rose J. Spalding is professor of political science at DePaul University. Her recent publications include *Trade Politics in Central America: Market Reform and Resistance* (2014); "Social Movements in Central America" in *Handbook of Central American Governance*, edited by Diego Sánchez-Ancochea and Salvador Martí (2014); "Los empresarios y el estado en la Nicaragua post-revolucionaria: el reordenamiento de las élites y la nueva estrategia de colaboración," in *Las élites de centroamérica,* vol. 3, edited by Eric Hershberg (2013); and "Transnational Networks and National Action: El Salvador's Anti-Mining Movement," in *Transnational Activism and National Movements in Latin America: Bridging the Divide*, edited by Eduardo Silva (2013).

Richard Stahler-Sholk is a professor of political science at Eastern Michigan University, and a visiting researcher (2013–2014) at the Centro de Estudios Superiores de México y Centroamérica/CESMECA in San Cristóbal de Las Casas, Chiapas, Mexico. He is coeditor with Harry E. Vanden and Glen David Kuecker of *Latin American Social Movements in the Twenty-First Century: Resistance, Power, and Democracy* (2008), and coeditor with Bruno Baronnet and Mariana Mora Bayo of *Luchas "muy otras": Zapatismo y autonomía en las comunidades indígenas de Chiapas* (2011). He serves on the editorial board of *Latin American Perspectives*, and on the board of directors of the Servicio Internacional para la Paz (SIPAZ).

Alicia Swords is associate professor in Sociology at Ithaca College. Her research is based on study with social movements in Mexico, Dominican Republic, Chile and the United States. Her book, *Consuming Mexican Labor: From the Bracero Program to NAFTA,* coauthored with Ron Mize, offers a hemispheric perspective on immigration and development policies. She has also published on Zapatista network politics, development, and service learning. Swords is involved with the University of the Poor, a network of grassroots leaders committed to building a movement to end poverty. In and beyond the classroom, she enjoys supporting student engagement with social change initiatives.

Harry E. Vanden is a professor at the University of South Florida, and has worked and lived in several Latin American countries. A Fulbright Scholar in Peru and later in Brazil (2007), he has published more than forty scholarly articles, numerous book chapters, and fourteen books, including *Latin America: An Introduction* (2011); *Politics of Latin America: the Power Game* (2012), coauthored with Gary Prevost; *Latin American Social Movements in the Twenty-First Century: Resistance, Power, and Democracy* (2008), coedited with Richard Stahler-Sholk and Glen Kuecker, designated a *Choice* magazine 2009 Outstanding Academic Title; *José Carlos Mariátegui: An Anthology of His Writings*, translated and edited with Marc Becker (2011); and *Social Movements and Leftist Governments in Latin America*, coedited with Gary Prevost and Carlos Oliva Campos (2012).

Raúl Zibechi is a writer and journalist. He teaches at the Multiversidad Franciscana de América Latina and is a researcher on social movements. He is the editor of the theoretical journal *Contrapunto,* published at the Servicio de Extensión Universitaria de la Universidad de la República. He is the author of *Territories in Resistance: A Cartography of Latin American Social Movements*; *Dispersing Power: Social Movements as Anti-State Forces*; and *The New Brazil: Regional Imperialism and the New Democracy*. Zibechi works with social movements in several Latin American countries.